Portraits of the Artist as a Young Woman

Portraits of the Artist as a Young Woman
Painting and the Novel in France and Britain, 1800–1860

Alexandra K. Wettlaufer

 THE OHIO STATE UNIVERSITY PRESS / COLUMBUS

Copyright © 2011 by The Ohio State University.
All rights reserved.

Library of Congress Cataloging-in-Publication Data

Wettlaufer, Alexandra.
 Portraits of the artist as a young woman : painting and the novel in France and Britain, 1800–1860 / Alexandra K. Wettlaufer.
     p. cm.
 Includes bibliographical references and index.
 ISBN 978-0-8142-1145-8 (cloth : alk. paper)—ISBN 978-0-8142-9244-0 (cd)
 1. Women artists—France—History—19th century. 2. Women artists—England—History—19th century. 3. Women authors, French—19th century. 4. Women authors, English—19th century. I. Title.

NX164.W65W48 2011
700.82'0944—dc22

                    2010044738
Paper (ISBN: 978-0-8142-5700-5)
Cover design by Juliet Williams
Text design by Juliet Williams
Type set in Adobe Garamond Pro

Dedicated with the deepest love and admiration to my mother, Gail Summerfield Ker; my grandmothers, Jessie Angus Summerfield, Virginia Penn Wettlaufer, and Emily Warren Wettlaufer; my great-grandmothers, Isobel Macdonald Angus and Irene Taylor Wettlaufer; and my great great-aunt, Margaret Macdonald Brown— women who inspired my love of art, language, literature, and travel, and without whom this book would never have been written.

Contents

List of Illustrations	ix
Acknowledgments	xiii
Introduction	1

Part I • The Studio

Chapter 1 Women in the Studio: Representing Professional Identity — 31

Chapter 2 "Why Are You No Longer My Brothers?" The *Fraternité des Arts* and the Female Artist in Marceline Desbordes-Valmore's *L'Atelier d'un peintre* — 75

Chapter 3 Sisterhood in/as the Studio: Anna Mary Howitt's *Sisters in Art* — 97

Part II • Cosmopolitan Visions: Gender, Genre, Nation

Chapter 4 Visualizing Imagined Communities: Lessons of the Female Artist in Staël, Owenson, and Lescot — 125

Chapter 5 Revolutionary Identities: Painting and Resistance in Owenson's *The Princess; or the Beguine* — 154

Chapter 6 Angélique Arnaud's *Clémence:* Art, Revolution, and Saint-Simonianism — 171

Part III • The Portrait: Romanticism and the Female Subject

Chapter 7 Margaret Gillies and the Miniature: Portraits of Radical Engagement — 195

Chapter 8 Brontë's Portraits of Romantic Resistance: *The Tenant of Wildfell Hall* — 221

Chapter 9 From Margin to Center: Sand's Portraits of Difference — 243

Conclusion 263

Notes 271
Bibliography 296
Index 313

Illustrations

Figure 1.   Richard Samuel, *The Nine Living Muses of Great Britain,* 1778. Oil on canvas, 132.1 × 154.9 cm. © National Portrait Gallery, London.   21

Figure 2.   Thomas Rowlandson, *Breaking Up of the Blue Stocking Club,* 1815. Hand-colored etching. 24.6 × 34.9 cm. The British Museum, London. © Trustees of the British Museum.   23

Figure 3.   Louis-Léopold Boilly, *Réunion d'artistes dans l'atelier d'Isabey,* 1798. Oil on canvas. 71 × 111 cm. Photo: Réunion des Musées Nationaux/Art Resource, NY.   36

Figure 4.   Jean-Henri Cless, *L'Atelier de David,* 1804. Pencil and ink wash drawing. 46.2 × 58.5 cm. Musée Carnavalet, Paris. Photo: Réunion des Musées Nationaux/Art Resource, NY.   37

Figure 5.   Adélaïde Labille-Guiard, *Self-Portrait with Two Pupils,* 1783. Oil on canvas. 210.8 × 151.1 cm. Image copyright © The Metropolitan Museum of Art/Art Resource, NY.   41

Figure 6.   Gabrielle Capet, *Madame Adélaïde Labille-Guiard peignant le portrait de Joseph-Marie Vien,* 1808. Oil on canvas. 69 × 83.5 cm. Neue Pinakothek, Munich. Photo credit: Bildarchiv Preussicher Kulturbesitz/Art Resource, NY.   44

Figure 7.   Horace Vernet, *L'Atelier du peintre,* 1820–21. Oil on canvas. 52 × 64 cm. Private collection.   47

Illustrations

Figure 8. Adrienne Grandpierre-Deverzy, *L'Atelier d'Abel de Pujol,* 1822. Oil on canvas. 96 × 129 cm. Musée Marmottan, Paris. Bridgeman Art Library International, New York, NY. 49

Figure 9. Amélie Cogniet, *Intérieur de l'Atelier de Léon Cogniet,* 1831. Oil on canvas. 330 × 402 cm. Cliché Musée des Beaux-Arts, Orléans. 51

Figure 10. Caroline Thévenin, *Atelier des jeunes filles,* 1836. Oil on canvas. 46.2 × 61 cm. Cliché Musée des Beaux-Arts, Orléans. 54

Figure 11. Rolinda Sharples, *Self-Portrait with her Mother,* c. 1820. Oil on panel. 36.8 × 29.2 cm. © Bristol's Museums, Galleries, and Archives. 59

Figure 12. Edward Rippingille, *Portrait of Edward Bird, RA,* 1817. Oil on panel. 34.1 × 26.2 cm. © Bristol's Museums, Galleries, and Archives. 61

Figure 13. Rolinda Sharples, *Trial of Colonel Brereton, After the Bristol Riots,* 1832. Oil on panel. 148.6 × 101.6 cm. © Bristol's Museums, Galleries, and Archives. 63

Figure 14. Mary Ellen Best, *Green Drawing Room at Castle Howard,* 1832. Watercolor on paper. 25.5 × 32 cm. Private collection. 66

Figure 15. Mary Ellen Best, *Painting Room in our House in York,* 1838. Watercolor on paper. 25.7 × 36 cm. Bridgeman Art Library International, New York, NY. 68

Figure 16. Mary Ellen Best, *Altpörtal, Speyer,* c. 1844. Watercolor on paper. 33 × 22.5 cm. Private collection. 70

Figure 17. Hortense Haudebourt-Lescot, *Self-Portrait,* 1825. Oil on canvas. 74 × 60 cm. Photo credit: Réunion des Musées Nationaux/Art Resource, NY. 91

Figure 18. Barbara Leigh Smith, *Ye Newe Generation,* c. 1850. Ink on paper. 11.2 × 17.3 cm. The Mistress and Fellows, Girton College, Cambridge. 105

Figure 19. Anna Mary Howitt, *Head of Lizzie Siddal,* 1854. Pencil on paper. 12.7 × 11.5 cm. Mark Samuels Lasner Collection, on loan to the University of Delaware Library. 110

Figure 20. Barbara Leigh Smith, *Head of Lizzie Siddal,* 1854. Pencil on paper. 12.5 × 9.5 cm. Mark Samuels Lasner Collection, on loan to the University of Delaware Library. 111

Figure 21. J.-A.-D. Ingres, *Portrait of Mlle Lescot,* 1814. Pencil on paper. 27.1 × 21.1 cm. Private collection. 138

Figure 22. Hortense Haudebourt-Lescot, *Le Jeu de la main chaude,* 1812. Oil on canvas. 75 × 100 cm. Copyright: Musée des Beaux-Arts de Tours. 142

Figure 23. Hortense Haudebourt-Lescot, *Le Baisement des pieds de la statue de saint Pierre dans la basilique Saint-Pierre de Rome,* 1812. Oil on canvas. 148 × 196 cm. Musée du château de Fontainebleau. Bridgeman Art Library International, New York, NY. 146

Figure 24. Hortense Haudebourt-Lescot, *Mary Queen of Scots Fainting on Being Forced to Abdicate.* Salon of 1837. Watercolor on paper. 40.7 × 31.9 cm. Private collection. Bridgeman Art Library International, New York, NY.   151

Figure 25. Honoré Daumier, *Les Femmes socialistes.* Lithograph. *Le Charivari,* 17 May 1849.   191

Figure 26. Margaret Gillies, *Portrait of Harriet Martineau,* 1833. Engraving. British Museum.   203

Figure 27. Margaret Gillies, *William and Mary Wordsworth,* 1839–40. Watercolor on ivory. 30 × 27 cm. Wordsworth Trust, Rydal Mount. Bridgeman Art Library International, New York, NY.   210

Figure 28. Margaret Gillies, *William and Mary Howitt,* 1846. Oil on ivory. 41.9 × 33 cm. Nottingham City Museums and Galleries.   212

Figure 29. Margaret Gillies, *Leigh Hunt,* 1839. Watercolor and gouache on ivory. 22.5 × 14.9 cm. © National Portrait Gallery, London.   218

Figure 30. Emily Osborn, *Nameless and Friendless,* 1857. Oil on canvas. 86.4 × 111.8 cm. Private collection. Bridgeman Art Library International, New York, NY.   231

Acknowledgments

This book is the result of the enormous generosity and support of several institutions and innumerable friends. Initial research was begun on a fellowship at the Clark Art Institute, where conversations with Tamar Garb, Elizabeth Hutchinson, Michael Ann Holly, Mark Ledbury, and the rest of the fellows and staff helped me bring the project into focus and start to wrestle with ways to deal with painting and literature in a single study. A subsequent residency at the National Humanities Center as a Florence Gould Foundation Fellow allowed me to write the bulk of the text in the most glorious and supportive setting I could ever imagine. I extend my heartfelt gratitude and affection to the NHC administration and staff for their tireless help and constant good cheer: Kent Mullikin, Geoffrey Harpham, Lois Whittington, Josiah Drewry, Eliza Robertson, Jean Houston, Karen Carroll, Josh Bond, Joel Elliott, Sarah Payne, and Marie Brubaker made my year in North Carolina as productive as it was enjoyable. My colleagues at the NHC gave new meaning to the word fellowship, and this project benefited in more ways than I can ever repay from the friendships, support, and inspiration they offered. My deepest thanks to Allison Keith, Stephen Rupp, Louise Meintjes, Maud Ellmann, John Wilkinson, Mary Ellis Gibson, Amelie Rorty, Isabel Wünsche, Judith Farquhar, Kate Flint, Beth Helsinger, Ellen Garvey, Terry Smith, Erdag Goknar, Tim Kircher, and

David Samuels. Sections of the book were presented in various forms over the years at the annual Nineteenth-Century French Studies Colloquium and the Interdisciplinary Nineteenth-Century Studies Conference, and I am grateful to my friends and interlocutors there, including Michael Garval, Larry Schehr, Jann Matlock, Nigel Harkness, Sonya Stephens, Marni Kessler, Elisabeth Ladenson, Marie Lathers, Therese Dolan, and Catherine Nesci. My students at the University of Texas at Austin have helped me formulate and refine many of the ideas here, and I am grateful, as ever, for their constant inspiration. Laura Hughes deserves a special thank-you for archival research in Paris when I could not get there. The University of Texas provided sabbatical support, and the Blunk Memorial Professorship enabled me to travel to Europe for research; the Department of French and Italian and the Program in Women's and Gender Studies generously helped underwrite the illustration permissions, without which many of these images would have remained forgotten. Sandy Crooms, Senior Editor at The Ohio State University Press, was a joy to work with, and the thoughtful comments from my two readers, Michèle Hannoosh and Antonia Losano, made this an infinitely better book.

Portions of chapters 1 and 2 appeared in different form in "Dibutades and Her Daughters: The Female Artist in Post-Revolutionary France," *Nineteenth Century Studies* 18 (2004), and are reproduced here with permission. Sections of chapter 3 were published in an earlier version as "*Sisters in Art:* Shaping Artistic Identity in Anna Mary Howitt's Fiction and Painting," *Victorian Review* 36.1 (2010). Chapter 9 includes substantially revised material from essays published as "Sand, Musset and the Empire of Genius in *Elle et lui*," in *George Sand et l'Empire des lettres*, edited by Anne McCall-Saint-Saëns (New Orleans: Presses Univérsitaires du Nouveau Monde, 2004); and "Sand's Painting Protagonists: Representing Artistic Identity from *Valentine* to *Le Chateau de Pictordu*," in *George Sand: Intertexualité et Polyphonie*, edited by Nigel Harkness and Jacinta Wright (Bern: Peter Lang, 2010). They too are reproduced here with permission of the publishers.

To my husband, Art, and my children, Walker and Isabelle, who supported me throughout, I offer my endless gratitude and love.

Introduction

In 1859, the critic and historian Elizabeth Fries Lummis Ellet published *Women Artists in All Ages and Countries* in London and New York. Addressing what she perceived as a lacuna in contemporary intellectual history, Ellet staked her claim as the first to chart women's contributions to the arts as she observed "I do not know that any work on Female Artists—either grouping them or giving a general history of their productions—has ever been published."[1] The following year, Léon Lagrange's "On the Rank of Women in the Arts" ("Du rang des femmes dans les arts") appeared in the prestigious *Gazette des Beaux-Arts* and similarly traced the history of women artists, including Marietta Robusti, Lavinia Fontana, Artemisia Gentileschi, Marguerite Van Eyck, and Angelica Kauffman, as well as a number of French painters and sculptors, from the preceding centuries to the present day. This pair of studies cites the careers and production of female visual artists for decidedly different ends: where Ellet seeks to encourage women in their pursuit of an artistic profession, Lagrange offers reassurance to his anxious male cohort that, despite the proliferation of the *femme artiste,* "male genius has nothing to fear" for "woman is content with the second rank as long as the wages for her inferior labor suffice to procure her the means to pleasure."[2] Taken together, these works by Ellet and Lagrange bear witness to the ongoing reconfiguration of the field of cultural production in nineteenth-century France and Britain, as women artists forged a new collective identity in the public sphere. By 1860, it would

1

seem the once anomalous female painter had become a recognized figure in the cultural landscape.

In *Portraits of the Artist as a Young Woman* I trace the construction of this identity from the turn of the century, when a female painter was, in Mary Sheriff's phrase, an "exceptional woman,"[3] to 1860, when the figure was established and "unexceptional" enough to merit both a history and a dismissal, reflecting female pride and male anxiety over her accomplishments. In this comparative and interdisciplinary exploration of the female visual artist in France and Britain, I focus on female painters: Gabrielle Capet, Adrienne Grandpierre-Deverzy, Marie-Amélie Cogniet, Caroline Thévenin, Rolinda Sharples, Mary Ellen Best, Anna Mary Howitt, Hortense Haudebourt-Lescot, and Margaret Gillies, and novels about female painters: Marceline Desbordes-Valmore's *L'Atelier d'un peintre* (1833), Sydney Owenson's *The Princess* (1835), Angélique Arnaud's *Clémence* (1841), Anne Brontë's *The Tenant of Wildfell Hall* (1848), Anna Mary Howitt's *Sisters in Art* (1852), and George Sand's *Elle et lui* (1858). In approaching this figure from two perspectives, I want to consider the larger questions of female artistic self-fashioning in the nineteenth century and uncover what the particular resonance of the painter may have been within the cultural contexts of Britain and France. To this end I read both paintings and novels in terms of their dialogues with each other, with contemporary male artistic production, and with the politics of gender, nation, and identity in France and Britain during the first half of the century.

My readings of these nineteenth-century women are profoundly shaped by the work of a number of twentieth-century women, who, in the spirit of Elizabeth Ellet, sought to reclaim a place for women in the history of art. Starting with Linda Nochlin's groundbreaking essay, "Why Have There Been No Great Women Artists?" (1971),[4] feminist scholars have reconfigured our understanding of the relationship between gender, power, representation, and the artistic canon—who can be trained as an artist, whose paintings will be exhibited, reviewed, purchased, considered "Art," who will be included in museums and history books—and helped us reconsider the very ideas of "great" and "artist." Following Nochlin's lead,[5] a number of feminist scholars have, in the course of the past few decades, established the explicit links between vision, art, representation, and the politics of gender in the nineteenth century. In *Vision and Difference: Femininity, Feminism, and the Histories of Art* (1988), Griselda Pollock combined feminism, Marxism, and psychoanalysis in a series of essays that reflected the theories of Foucault, Lacan, Williams, and others, asserting that "Art history itself is to be understood as a series of representational practices which actively produce definitions of sexual difference and contribute to the present configuration of sexual politics and power relations."[6] She later added (following Julia Kristeva) that "Aesthetic practices shift meaning, undo fixities and can make a difference" and asked us to "read for *inscriptions of the feminine*—which do not come from a fixed origin, this female painter, that woman artist, but from those *working* within the predicament of femininity in phallocentric cultures in their diverse formations and varying systems of representation."[7] In *Sisters of the Brush: Women's Artistic Culture in Late Nineteenth-Century Paris* (1994), Tamar Garb set out to "rewrite an old narrative from a new perspective" through the history of the *Union des Femmes Peintres et Sculpteurs* founded in Paris in 1881.[8] Chronicling the "constructions of subjectivity, sociality, and national identity" (2) in the lives and works of women artists at the *fin-de-siècle*, Garb demonstrated the role of (often utopian) collectivity and sisterhood in the professionalization of the female artist in France, closely tied to the rise of feminism and the campaigns for women's education. In a similar vein, Deborah Cherry's *Painting Women: Victorian Women Artists* (1993) traces the struggles over female professionalism in Britain, where "Women artists were located in asymmetrical and unequal relations to art education, art administration, and professional status."[9] In documenting the social conditions of female artistic production, representation, spectatorship, and signification, Cherry strove to "counter prevailing assumptions in the west that individuality as well as artistic creativity are masculine. Writing women artists into the history of art has necessitated a reformulation of the discipline since the old paradigms work to silence or marginalize women artists" (212–13). Cherry's subsequent study, *Beyond the Frame: Feminism and Visual Culture, Britain 1850–1900* (2000), maps "a visual culture in which art collided with politics, visual representation with political representation (. . .) Painting and sculpture as much as comic drawings became a battleground for intense debates about the role of women in contemporary society."[10] At the same time, Cherry notes, "women's art and feminism were inextricably intertwined: speech on one invariably incited discourse on the other" (9).

Studies of individual women painters, such as Mary Garrard's *Artemisia Gentileschi* (1989), Anne Higonnet's *Berthe Morisot's Images of Women* (1992), and Mary Sheriff's *The Exceptional Woman: Elizabeth Vigée-Lebrun and the Cultural Politics of Art* (1996), as well as those centered upon groups of women painters, including Pamela Gerrish Nunn's *Canvassing* (1986), and Nunn and Jan Marsh's *Pre-Raphaelite Women Artists* (1988), have also been influential on my own work as they locate individual female artistic production within a cultural context that reveals not only the powerful forces of ideology and the gendering of genius, but also the forms of resistance, subversion, and resilience manifested in women's art. Finally, Abigail Solomon-Godeau's *Male Trouble: A Crisis in Representation* (1997) provides a critical model of gender studies, demonstrating that "visual culture is not only gendered, but actively productive of gender ideology," and thus that "the image of ideal manhood is as much a product of fantasy, and certainly of ideology, as the more familiar icons of eroticized femininity."[11] These scholars, and numerous others quoted throughout this study, set the stage for my own intervention in the field.

By the same token, literary and cultural critics have also shaped my readings of the visual and verbal texts in *Portraits of an Artist as a Young Woman*. Most notably, Mary Poovey's work on gender, ideology, and women's professions in *Uneven Developments*, Nancy Armstrong's political history of the novel, *Desire and Domestic Fiction*, Dorothy Mermin's study of Victorian women authors in *Godiva's Ride*, and Anne K. Mellor's extensive work on Romanticism, gender, and nation contributed to my approaches to British cultural production. Margaret Waller's *The Male Malady: Fictions of Impotence in the French Romantic Novel* opened up radical new ways for us to read the Romantic hero, while Christine Planté's *La Petite Soeur de Balzac: Essai sur la femme auteur* and Naomi Schor's body of work on the nineteenth-century novel in France provided both practical and theoretical inspiration for my interpretations. Margaret Cohen's research on the sentimental, Realist, and transatlantic novels was formative in my own conceptions of these genres, while Janet Wolff's interdisciplinary work on women and culture was also influential. Pierre Bourdieu's theories of the field of cultural production and of cultural capital are fundamental to my analyses, as are Jacques Rancière's formulations of politics and aesthetics (to be discussed below). Finally, Richard Terdiman's *Discourse/Counter-Discourse* has provided a paradigmatic *point de départ* for all of my work.

By expanding the purview of my study of the figure of the woman artist to a doubly comparative praxis and examining both the *real* and the *fictitious* female painter—thus, both painting and the novel—in both France and Britain, I hope to continue to push our understandings of nineteenth-century culture, gender, and representation in new directions, much as I believe the authors and painters in *Portraits of the Artist as a Young Woman* hoped to do. As Antonia Losano asserts in *The Woman Painter in Victorian Literature* (2008), I believe that "these two media of female aesthetic production [i.e., painting and literature] are intimately connected in myriad ways."[12] Losano's fine contribution, published just as I was finishing this manuscript, shares many of the concerns of my own work, most specifically in its use of "the figure of the woman painter as a kind of Foucauldian 'dense transfer point' of power relations to engage with and intervene in the symbolic economies of gender (in particular those that underpinned the discourses of aesthetics, sexual desire, and professional identity) that were at work during the nineteenth century" (2). However, where Losano focuses exclusively on novels representing women painters and their scenes of ekphrasis in Victorian England, my study encompasses both of the sister arts in France as well as Britain; thus women's painting is not simply a theme, but an equally important area of inquiry and analysis. By pairing painting and literature in a single study, my goal is to highlight the dialogic context in which these novels and paintings were produced and consumed, and to map out aesthetic and political intersections in women's history in the arts that are too often elided by the disciplinary boundaries of study (English, French, Art History, etc.). By considering works from both France and Britain, two distinct but closely related cultures, I focus on a pair of nations engaged in ongoing artistic dialogues of rivalry and influence. France and Britain were arguably the dominant cultures of the nineteenth century in art (literary and visual), as well as in politics, and the incipient women's movement developed in multifaceted, multidirectional dialogue across the Channel. In portraying a sister in the sister art of painting, these novelists establish a collective identity for women artists that seeks to transcend the boundaries of the individual genres of expression, and in this sense these "portraits of the artist" are also self-portraits of the female writer. In order to distinguish between the collective sense of artist as artistic creator (poet, novelist, painter, sculptor, composer, etc.) and the more specific meaning of artist as painter, I will use "visual artist" to denote the painter and "artist" to signal both authors and painters together.

The very premise of this study—that we can and should examine women's painting and novels together, rather than separately—raises, of course, questions of "legitimacy" and methodological "moonlighting."[13] In my two previous books I have rehearsed many of the arguments for and against interdisciplinary inquiry, from Jean Hagstrom's "pictorialist tradition" in *The Sister Arts* (1958) and Norman Bryson's structuralist *Word and Image* (1981) to Murray Kreiger's *Ekphrasis* (1992) and James Heffernan's *Museum of Words* (1993).[14] But here, as in *Pen vs. Paintbrush,* I am less interested in formal or thematic comparisons between the two disciplines than I am in trying to "connect different aspects and dimensions of cultural experience," as W. J. T. Mitchell succinctly puts it (1994, 87). Specifically, I am interested in the *relations* between the genres, with their attendant anxieties, hierarchies, and negotiations for power, and the role played by gender in these relations. Following Mitchell, I believe that "*comparison itself is not a necessary procedure in the study of image-text relations.* The necessary subject matter is, rather, the whole ensemble of *relations* between media, and relations can be many other things besides similarity, resemblance, and analogy. Difference is just as important as similarity, antagonism as crucial as collaboration, dissonance and division of labor as interesting as harmony and blending of function" (1994, 89–90; original emphases).

Thus, during a period like the nineteenth century, when the field of cultural production was being actively reconfigured and the "sisterhood of the arts" or "*la fraternité des arts*" was a widely embraced credo in Britain and France, an interdisciplinary approach enables us to analyze both "the aesthetic norms of the period,"[15] according to Wendy Steiner, and the historical valences of the forms as they were (dialectically) constructed by authors, painters, critics, and the consuming public. As articulated by Romantic artists, the theoretical sorority between the arts allowed for shared inspiration and borrowings between the separate genres of visual, verbal, and musical expression, eliding differences in form for a commonality of content. Yet, as Mary Douglas's *Purity and Danger* indicates, this same period was also characterized by an anxious desire to classify, quantify, and purify, eschewing what Douglas terms "pollution" for clear borders and boundaries that assert and maintain difference. Indeed, as I have argued elsewhere, the relationship between the sister arts in the nineteenth century came far closer to sibling rivalry than the idealized images of *fraternité* might imply, as the separate genres struggled for domination rather than parity.[16] Of particular interest for this study is the way in which metaphors of artistic sisterhood were appropriated by women painters and authors in the nineteenth century to signal border crossings that both recognized and resisted contemporary ideologies that defined both gender and genre in terms of purity and difference. Using the trope of the "sisterhood of the arts," women crossed boundaries of gender, genre, and nation to posit new models of artistic and social identity based on equality rather than hierarchy. If male authors portrayed painting as a "feminized" form in its silent materiality, women artists in both media embraced this gendering of genre to claim a place in the field of cultural production, while at the same time destabilizing the very structures of difference.

While Ellet's *Women Artists in All Ages and Countries* may have been the first comprehensive history of women artists, between 1829 and 1860 no fewer than nine authors in Britain and France had devoted novels to the figure of the female painter.[17] Nor was Lagrange alone, for the critics of female visual artists had steadily increased in number and vehemence as well, reaching an apotheosis in Nathaniel Hawthorne's *Marble Faun* (1860), a tale positing the dangers of female sculptors in Rome—women whose very gazes are linked with death and destruction.[18] It is clear that for Ellet (who published *Women of the American Revolution* a decade earlier), as for Lagrange, Hawthorne, and indeed for all of the authors to be discussed here, the figure of the female artist was politically charged, carrying ideological resonance as a transgressive figure of difference and potential disruption. From the outset of the nineteenth century, women in Britain and France had entered the field of cultural production in small but still significant numbers and gradually begun claiming a place for themselves, however tenuous, in exhibitions, publications, and the public imagination. While their presence contributed to the reconfiguration of the artistic field, the social ramifications and symbolism of the female painter (real and fictional) reached beyond the art world to contribute to the ideological reconfiguration of women's representation and subjecthood in the nineteenth century in myriad ways. The six novels examined here appeared between 1830 and 1860, a period that coincides with the rise of French and British feminism, and both the paintings and fiction reflect contemporary ideas of female equality and the struggle for a position for women in the public sphere. At the same time, I will argue, these works of art singularly and collectively helped to shape new conceptions of female subjectivity and professionalism.

Ellet's and Lagrange's reflections on the female artist at midcentury provide useful insights into some of the complex issues surrounding this controversial figure. Ellet begins her work in a resolutely political vein, for her goal is not only to trace the careers of women artists of the past, but to shape the lives and reception of women artists of the future as well. She explains, "Should the perusal of my book inspire with courage and resolution any woman who aspires to overcome difficulties in the achievement of honorable independence, or should it lead to a higher general respect for the powers of women and their destined position in the realm of Art, my object will be accomplished" (vi). Invoking "the struggles and trials, the persevering industry and the well-earned triumphs" (vi) of women artists across temporal and national borders, Ellet crafts an image of art as a battleground and proposes a collective identity through gender that is stronger than historical or national ties. In a period of individual and national identity building, this is a significant move. But even more striking is Ellet's effort to recraft the very history of art itself, demonstrating its constructed nature (via inclusion and exclusion) and expanding the field to include both a gender and genres traditionally situated outside of the boundaries of Art.

From the opening chapter, Ellet validates ornament and craft as forms of artistic expression, thus elevating their practitioners, in a Ruskinian vein, from anonymous artisans to forgotten artists. She maintains:

> From the early days of the world, too, spinning and weaving were feminine employments, in which undying germs of art were hidden . . . The ancient sepulchres and buried palaces disclosed by modern discovery display the love of adornment prevailing among the nations of antiquity. Women rendered assistance in works upon wood and metal, as well as, more frequently, in the production of the loom. The fair Egyptians covered their webs with the most delicate patterns; and the draperies of the dead and the ornamented hangings in their dwellings attested the skills of the women of Assyria and Babylon . . .
>
> The shawls and carpets of Eastern manufacture, and other articles of luxury that furnished the palaces of European monarchs, were often the work of

delicate hands, though no tradition has preserved the names of those who excelled in such labors. (23)

In Ellet's revisionist history, the "germs of art" are found in ancient female production, while the frequently idealized art of antiquity derived its beauty from female adornment. Uncovering these "hidden" roots, buried in sepulchers and forgotten through the ages, Ellet expands the definition of art to encompass shawls, carpets, and draperies, while setting weaving, engraving, and etching on par with sculpture, architecture, and painting. Dismantling the restrictive hierarchies of genre to include what were considered artisanal crafts alongside "high art," Ellet uses the authority of the past to validate her agenda for the present, opening up ways for the attendant hierarchies of gender, which linked women to craft and men to art, also to be revised. The lengthy study also addresses historical factors for the "Barrenness" of many centuries in female artists, the lack of artistic education for women throughout the ages, and biographies of more than a hundred women painters and sculptors from the medieval Sabina von Steinbach to the contemporary American Harriet Hosmer. Pushed to the margins by history, Ellet's female artists and their production "in All Ages and Countries" are shown to be a generative or germinating force behind creation, as well as artists in their own right, and thus central to a comprehensive understanding of the art of yesterday and today. It is only, though, in reading the past with new eyes (guided by a female author) that the hidden role of female visual artists becomes once again visible.

Ellet's rhetorical and political strategies of inclusion present a subversion of what Derrida has identified as the "law of genre." As he explains, the very concept of genre itself is predicated on the notion of limits, with attendant rules and exclusions. He contends:

> As soon as the word 'genre' is sounded, as soon as it is heard, as soon as one attempts to conceive it, a limit is drawn. And when a limit is established, norms and interdictions are not far behind: "Do,' 'Do not' says 'genre,' the word 'genre,' the figure, the voice or the law of 'genre.' And this can be said of genre in all genres, be it a question of a generic or a general determination of what one calls 'nature' or *physis* (for example, a biological *genre* in the sense of *gender*, of the human *genre*, a genre of all that is general), or be it a question of a typology designated as non-natural and depending on laws or orders which were once held to be opposed to *physis* according to those values associated with *technè, thesis, nomos* (for example, an artistic, poetic, or literary genre). But the whole enigma of genre springs perhaps most closely from within this limit between the two genres of genre.[19]

These naturalized laws of human and artistic genre, where "one must respect a norm, one must not cross a line of demarcation, one must not risk impurity, anomaly, or monstrosity" (57) effectively serve to organize the world through exclusion and difference, for what is defined as "human," "male," or "art" depends on its not being "animal," "female," or "artisanal." The blurring of the boundaries of genre, and by extension gender, is thus experienced as an assault on the very identity of those on either side of the divide. Indeed, Lagrange comments on the perception that the myriad "rapins en jupons" (art students in skirts) would represent "for male artists, a veritable danger" (39) and ends his article with the hope that the existence of the *femme artiste* will ultimately "provoke among the men of our generation a return to those male virtues which their honor has so readily forsaken" (43). Just as Fredric Jameson has demonstrated that literary and artistic genres are essentially "*institutions, or social contracts*" between artist and audience,[20] Judith Butler and others have exposed the institutional and performative nature of gender.[21] For the female authors and painters in this study, the disruption of the nineteenth-century institutions of genre, from its taxonomic sense of gender to its macro level (art/not-art) and micro level (novel/poem/play and history painting/portrait/still life, etc.), entailed both social and aesthetic border crossings that sought radically to reconfigure the politics of art and identity.

Indeed, if genres "contribute to the social structuring of meaning" and "actively generate and shape knowledge of the world,"[22] by disrupting and reconfiguring artistic genres—the Romantic novel, the studio scene, the national tale, the Romantic portrait—women proposed new ways of seeing and understanding art, society, and gender, expanding the horizons of expectation for readers and viewers to include the image of a female creator. Following Todorov, Derrida, and Jameson, John Frow explains that genre is "a form of symbolic action . . . that makes things happen" (2); bound up with "the exercise of power, where power is understood as being exercised in discourse," genres "create effects of reality and truth, authority and plausibility" (2). At the same time, genres necessarily "belong to an economy," Frow tells us: "a set of interdependent positions that organize the universe of knowledge and value" (4–5), positions that are constantly changing and evolving in relation to one another. Unstable and performative, "genres exist only in relation to other genres" (Frow 4), so our understanding of the dominant genres of nineteenth-century French and British cultural production—painting and literature, Romanticism and Realism—ultimately depends on a more dialectical and dialogic reading of the noncanonical alongside the canonical and including women's voices and visions within the larger narrative of the period. Yet the questions remains, why did so many women choose to write novels about painters?

Introduction

Vision, Visuality, and Visibility in the Nineteenth Century:
ART AND POLITICS

The nineteenth century was the era of the visual and what Baudelaire dubbed "le culte des images":[23] in this age of exposition, the French and British publics negotiated their knowledge of the world through panoramas, spectacles, galleries, museums, magic lanterns, stereoscopes, and displays large and small that came to shape ways of conceptualizing self and other as well as the physical universe.[24] This "frenzy of the visible," to borrow Jean-Louis Comolli's redolent phrase,[25] was further stoked by the proliferation of illustrated books and journals, exhibitions, photographs, prints, reproductions, and paintings, all of which were circulated, reproduced, and/or displayed for unprecedented numbers of visual consumers.[26] Caricatures, physiologies, and illustrated guidebooks further asserted the power of images to categorize and contain an increasingly mystified and mystifying world. If the period from the French Revolution through the reign of Victoria was dominated by acts and metaphors of active seeing, it was equally a period of "being seen." From Balzac and Dickens to Foucault, the social imaginary was haunted by the specter of the "unseen seer" gazing upon the unconscious citizenry in anxiety-inducing iterations of panopticism.[27] As Walter Benjamin affirmed, this was a century dominated by "the activity of the eye."[28]

Yet as David Peters Corbett reminds us, "the visual is not an innocent category,"[29] for it is constructed and shaped in and by culture and history. Visuality, like ideology, reflects dominant discourses of subjectivity—who can see and who or what can be seen, invisibly reinforcing ideologies of gender, class, and power. In choosing the figure of the female painter as the focus of their novels, the authors I will examine self-consciously claimed the subject position of the viewer for women, disrupting the gendered structures of the gaze that sought to relegate women to the silent and passive role of bearer rather than maker of meaning. Laura Mulvey's influential formulation for narrative cinema holds true for the *perceived* dynamics of vision in the nineteenth century: where men were understood to embody active looking, women were understood to be "simultaneously looked at and displayed, with their appearance coded for strong visual and erotic impact so that they can be said to connote *to-be-looked-at-ness*."[30] Yet as the novels and paintings to be discussed in the following chapters will illustrate, these gendered dynamics were neither as simple nor as absolute as has been asserted. Significant numbers of women artists worked within and against these structures of the gaze to claim a (contested) subject position and the radical image of a female subject representing the world presented an unmistakable challenge to social and aesthetic ideologies with a canny nod to the power of vision. The painters in Owenson's *The Princess,* Brontë's *The Tenant of Wildfell*

Hall, and Arnaud's *Clémence,* for example, are active observers, watching and portraying men who cannot see them, constructing meaning as well as images, while passive and unseeing men are found in nearly every text. The heroine of Desbordes-Valmore's *L'Atelier d'un peintre* sees far more than her famous uncle or the male students in the studio, while Sand's Thérèse in *Elle et lui* achieves two-fold success as an artist and a mother; her lover, a Romantic genius, is doomed to failure and solitude. Anna Mary Howitt's trio of painters in *Sisters in Art* achieve perfect harmony in their collaborative creations and establish a school for future generations of female artists, anticipating Ellet's gesture to women considering a professional career.

At the same time, vision and *visibility* function on a larger metaphoric level as ways of defining the very parameters of inclusion, exclusion, and legitimacy within a culture. As Jacques Rancière explains in *The Politics of Aesthetics,* politics "revolves around what is seen and what can be said about it, around who has the ability to see and the talent to speak, around the properties of space and the possibilities of time," while aesthetics is "the system of *a priori* forms determining what presents itself to sense experience. It is a delimitation of spaces and times, of the visible and the invisible, of speech and noise, that simultaneously determines the place and the stakes of politics as a form of experience."[31] Following Rancière's formulations, art can play a political role within a social structure by creating new forms of intelligibility and rendering visible and "sayable" that which had been previously unintelligible, invisible, unsayable. The introduction of a critical mass of artworks by female artists about female artists collectively opened up new spaces in the social sphere of nineteenth-century France and Britain, reframing what could be perceived in the present.

Throughout his works, Rancière links politics and aesthetics in ways that inform my own readings of these nineteenth-century images and texts as social interventions. In particular, his theory of the "distribution of the sensible" (*le partage du sensible*) provides insights into the ways in which the "visible" functions on both a literal and metaphoric level to represent social and cultural legitimacy. Rancière explains that the "conditions of intelligibility" within a culture are determined by a "system of self-evident facts of sense perception that simultaneously discloses the existence of something in common and the delimitations that define the respective parts and positions within it" (*PA* 12). In other words, the distribution of the sensible functions as a system of laws that define what is intelligible—what can be seen, heard, understood—for a culture and what lies beyond the limits of intelligibility or perception. In keeping with the double sense of *partager,* meaning both to share and to divide, the *partage du sensible* determines social, aesthetic, and ideological legitimacy through inclusion and exclusion, establishing precisely who or what is "visible." "Police," for Rancière, is "a system of coordinates defining modes of being, doing, making, and communicating that establishes the borders between the visible and the invisible, the audible and the inaudible, the sayable and the unsayable" (*PA* 89). Where Rancière's police order functions to maintain consensus and define community through these exclusions, hierarchies, and social roles, *la politique*, or politics, emerges in the struggle for visibility on the part of those outside the boundaries of the established order. As Eric Méchoulan succinctly states, "What is visible or invisible is a matter of police. How to give visibility or audibility to someone or something invisible or inaudible—that is the stuff of politics."[32]

Politics, then, consists in the disruption of the distribution of the sensible to expand the realm of the visible within a social community. If the distribution of the sensible necessarily denies equality to some individuals or ideas in its configuration, politics is engaged in the struggle for equality (a central term for Rancière) through a mode of "subjectivization" that "transforms the aesthetic coordinates of the community by implementing the universal presupposition of politics: we are all equal" (*PA* 3). Art's role in politics is located in its engagement with perception/sense experience and its potential to modify the distribution of the sensible and thus the intelligible. Kristin Ross explains that art's function is "that of reframing, and thus expanding, what can be perceived in the present. Both art and politics reconfigure what is thinkable at a given moment."[33] Specifically, it is the relationship of painting and literature to the "regime of visibility" that endows them with political agency; for Rancière, the "aesthetic act" offers "configurations of experience that create new modes of sense perception and induce novel forms of political subjectivity" (*PA* 9).

In *Portraits of the Artist as a Young Woman*, I will trace the ways in which "aesthetic acts" by women in France and Britain individually and collectively reconfigured what was intelligible within their closely related cultures, expanding the definitions or images of what a woman could be and what an artist could be in order to render the once "invisible" woman artist "visible." In choosing to portray the figure of the female painter as heroine, these six novelists self-consciously visualize a woman in the subject position, reflecting on and representing society and the world. Through their use of images of an image-maker, these novelists open up a space within the realm of intelligibility for the professional woman artist (author, painter, poet), for visibility can reside both in words and in images. "The image is not exclusive to the visible," Rancière tells us, "There is visibility that does not amount to an image; there are images which consist wholly in words."[34] By a similar token, the women painters to be discussed portrayed women in the studio or at the writing table, highlighting their active engagement in contemporary artistic expression while frequently drawing the parallel between gender and other kinds of "otherness"—class, nation, ethnicity, genre—in order to highlight the political nature of representation and the image while foregrounding the tensions between the center and the margins. Thus, as the "police order" of 1830s France and Britain distributed roles and positions based on hierarchies and exclusions, only the male artist (author, painter) was constructed as visible within the structures of the social edifice, while women's identities were constructed primarily in terms of marriage, maternity, and domesticity. As with any theoretical or ideological framework, these structures were neither fixed nor absolute; gender is but one of the many variables that inflected these assignments of positionality. Nonetheless, they tend to evoke the prevailing or dominant ethos of a period and thus become sites of resistance as well as normativity. In the decades following 1830, while ideological resistance to the professional female artist may have continued, she gradually became visible, establishing a place, however contested, within the configuration of the sensible, as demonstrated by Ellet and Lagrange, above. Indeed, the increasing critique of the female artist in novels, criticism, and even painting from the 1850s on provides the most compelling testimony to her established visibility.

The strategies of containment constructed and enforced by Rancière's police order fix roles and positions of legitimacy and illegitimacy, determining who can speak and be heard as well as who can be seen. These borders between classes, races, and genders create radical inequalities that many of these authors and painters will address in their works in implicit and explicit ways. Much like the nineteenth-century French proletarians in Rancière's *La Nuit des prolétaires* who gathered at night to write poetry, journals, and letters, resisting their prescribed roles as manual workers for the realm of intellectual labor, the women in this study and others like them refused to be contained by the confines of what they were supposed to be.[35] Both the proletarian poets and the female artists of the 1830s-50s recognized the potential political agency of art to reconfigure the field of experience and allow them to move toward political subjecthood and "equality."[36] In keeping with this political orientation, moreover, all of the women to be discussed were engaged in some way with the early feminist movement and most participated in the parallel struggle for the recognition of workers' rights in nineteenth-century Britain and France as well.

Discourse/Counter-Discourse:
MYTHS OF THE ARTIST

The novels and paintings examined in the chapters to follow function in direct dialogue with the discourses of gender, art, power, and visibility in nineteenth-century culture, but also in a dialectical relationship with works by male painters and authors, as well as with contemporary myths of the artist—discourses and myths that contributed directly to Rancière's distribution of the sensible. Whether engaged in direct critique of the status quo (Owenson, Brontë, Sand,

Gillies, Capet, Cogniet) or a more subtle reworking of the paradigms of art and representation (Desbordes-Valmore, Howitt, Arnaud, Sharples, Best, Lescot), each of these female artists foregrounds the issue of difference, only to destabilize or deconstruct it, subverting the dominant structures of art and intelligibility with images of female subjectivity and artistic creation. In this sense, the novels and paintings, in their struggle to attain visibility within Rancière's conception of *la politique,* can also be read as counter-discourses, challenging the hegemonic systems of meaning and signification. As Richard Terdiman explains, "Counter-discourses function in their form. Their object is to represent the world *differently.* But their projection of difference goes beyond simply contradicting the dominant, beyond simply negating its assertions. The power of a dominant discourse lies in the codes by which it regulates understanding of the social world. Counter-discourses seek to detect and map such naturalized protocols and to project their subversion. At stake in this discursive struggle are the paradigms of social representation themselves."[37] Yet as Terdiman also notes, every counter-discourse is ultimately rooted inescapably in the ideologies that it seeks to subvert.

In France as in Britain, in painting as in prose, the most pervasive discourse within and against which the female artist struggled was the masculinist ideologies of Romanticism. Indeed, Desbordes-Valmore's *Atelier d'un peintre,* Gillies's portraits of Wordsworth and Leigh Hunt, Brontë's *Tenant of Wildfell Hall,* Sand's *Elle et lui,* and the rest of the works in this study can be fully understood only in terms of their dialogue with Romanticism in general and the Romantic myth of the artist in particular. Although as an artistic movement Romanticism was already being overshadowed by Realist and Victorian aesthetics by 1840, the Romantic image of woman and of the artist continued to hold sway well into the second half of the nineteenth century, and indeed, it may be argued continue to be felt today. Moreover, all of the narratives and paintings to be discussed are set in the 1820s–1830s, allowing their creators to engage more fully with Romanticism and its ideologies of gender and artistic identity. Far more than an artistic movement, Romanticism was a cultural revolution whose effects lingered long after the poetry of Wordsworth, Byron, and Lamartine had gone out of fashion.

The Romantic image of the artist—the sensitive and suffering genius, whose sensibility placed him at odds with the conventional world—was self-consciously generated by painters, poets, playwrights, and their critics in response to an increasingly bourgeois and commercial culture in Britain, France, and much of the rest of Europe.[38] Michael Wilson explains, "artists deliberately cast themselves and their fellow artists as outsiders, bohemians, dandies, visionaries, and martyrs, and in doing so, they contributed to profound shifts in attitude toward the purpose of art and its role in society."[39] This shift entailed a new conception of the artist as prophet or seer, while at the same time it erected an enduring opposition between the artist and the very world in which he lived. Essential to this constructed persona, whether conceived as a solitary individual or as a member of one of the artistic brotherhoods that proliferated during the nineteenth century, was an anxious and overdetermined insistence on the masculinity of the Romantic artist. As Abigail Solomon-Godeau reminds us, like femininity, masculinity is "a construction, an image, a fiction, a mask variously inflected by the needs, the desires, the context and the political unconscious of the moment of its making."[40] As constructed and performed by generations of Romantic artists, this image of nineteenth-century artistic manhood represented a response to the perceived "feminization" of the culture of art in the industrial age. With the ascension of the bourgeoisie and the rise of capitalism in France and Britain, masculinity became associated with labor and productivity, while art and intellectual creation were socially marginalized. Moreover, with the popular success of female novelists and an ever-growing female reading public in nineteenth-century Britain and France, male authors felt the loss of cultural capital and an unspoken competition with women for an audience, experiences that were perceived as threatening and even emasculating.[41] Eager to establish artistic production as "work," artists sought to develop forms and styles that, according to Herbert Sussman, "signified their manliness by their difference from feminized forms."[42] Male artists further defined their own activity in terms of aggressively sexual metaphors, likening the pen or paintbrush to a penis and composition to ejaculation, effectively announcing a hyper-masculine identity and distancing themselves from women and the feminine. The Romantic artist was above all a self-proclaimed man. But far from eliminating the feminine, Romanticism's anxious insistence on masculinity served only to foreground the fact that this "maleness" was a construct, hinting at a reality that was just the opposite.

One of the many paradoxes at the heart of Romanticism lies in the definition of genius, so central to the artist's identity. The qualities associated with Romantic genius—sensitivity, emotion, intuition, imagination—had long been gendered feminine, yet definitions of genius, based on a rhetoric of difference, were gendered exclusively male. Christine Battersby explains: "This rhetoric praised 'feminine' qualities in male creators . . . but claimed females could not—or should not—create. To buttress the man/animal, civilized/savage division, the category of genius had to work by a process of exclusion."[43] Thus, as male artists and critics insisted, a woman was precluded from genius (and thus from being a "real" artist) by her gender, while the exceptional woman of genius was "really" a man. As Balzac famously quipped about his friend and rival, George Sand: "She is a boy, she is an artist, she is great, generous, devoted, chaste, she has all the great characteristics of a man, ergo she is not a woman."[44] Genius was used to distinguish art from craft, male "original" production from female imitation or "reproduction," while establishing the ineffable superiority that set the Romantic artist apart. Even as the male artist increasingly turned to metaphors of pregnancy and childbirth for the creative process (employing images of conception, difficult and painful labor, ecstatic delivery, or aborted/stillborn production), women's reproductive capacities as potential mothers were central to their theoretical exclusion from the realm of artistic genius. Battersby adds, "On the one hand—even before Freud—the driving force of genius was described in terms of *male* sexual energies. On the other hand, the genius was supposed to be *like a woman:* in tune with his emotions, sensitive, inspired—guided by instinctual forces that welled up from beyond the limits of rational consciousness" (103). Thus, because Romantic artistic identity shared much with contemporary constructions of the feminine, men took great pains to assert its "truly" masculine nature. But at the same time, as the feminine was explicitly inscribed within Romanticism, these conventions inadvertently provided an opening as never before for the possibility of a female artist. Indeed the fundamental assertion that Romantic genius is supposed to be "like a woman" privileges the feminine in such a way as to implicitly suggest the very image—that of a woman artist of genius, sensitive, suffering, imaginative, and passionate—that it seeks so anxiously to resist.

Also integral to Romanticism was a renewed interest in the *fraternité des arts,* which, like the contemporaneous artistic brotherhoods (from the French *Barbus* and Samuel Palmer's "Ancients" to the Pre-Raphaelite Brotherhood and the *Nabis*), sought to establish a collective identity for male artists of every stripe. The nineteenth-century revival of intimate relations between the sister arts thus posited solidarity among painters, poets, and musicians united against a bourgeoisie deemed hostile to artistic creativity and expression. Groups like the *Jeunes-France* (Young France), led by Théophile Gautier and Petrus Borel, were said to "be born the day that painting allied itself with Romantic literature"[45] and David Scott tells us it was at precisely this moment that the French word *artiste* "acquired a new breadth of meaning, designating not only painter and sculptor but also writer and composer."[46] Consciously crossing the borders between artistic genres, poets and authors were also painters (Hugo, Gautier, D. G. Rossetti, Thackeray), painters wrote poetry, essays, and journals (Reynolds, Shee, Delacroix, Turner), and everyone wrote criticism. Novels and memoirs like Thackeray's *Paris Sketch Book* (1840), Murger's *Scènes de la vie de Bohème* (1851), Zola's *L'Oeuvre* (1886), and Du Maurier's *Trilby* (1894) present a vivid image of the Romantic bohemian life shared by a "brotherhood" of aspiring painters and poets in Paris, and it is noteworthy that here and in the majority of British *Kunstlerromane* of the nineteenth century, artistic education took place in the French capital, then considered the capital of bohemia as well.[47]

Murger's iconic tale, which originally appeared as a series of stories in *Le Corsaire-Satan* between 1845 and 1849 and then as a play (1849), a novel (1851), and an opera (Puccini's *La Bohème* of 1896), highlights "the bonds of brotherly union" (45) between Schaunard, Rodolphe, Marcel, and Colline, painters, poets, and musicians who devote their lives to art and friendship. Set in the 1830s, Murger's collection of stories paints an ironic portrait of the rebellious young artists whose iconoclastic lives are defined less by genius than by failure and poverty. While paintings and epic poems languish unfinished, the bohemians evade their creditors and romance Mimi and Musette, *grisettes* more interested in money than love. By the end of the episodic narration, the four artists have left their liminal existence at the edges of society for success and wealth, and like nearly every subsequent novel of artistic youth, the author is more interested in the struggles of his heroes than in their triumphs. Du Maurier's novel, based on his own experiences in Paris in the 1850s, follows much the same trajectory as Murger's, with the close-knit band of artistic brothers, "the three musketeers of the brush,"[48] living on the edges of respectability in bohemian Paris until the end where they too achieve success and fortune, abandoning the ways of youth in the studio for the more dignified paths of artistic manhood in London. These tales and others like them, along with broadly disseminated caricatures by Daumier, Gavarni, Gillray, and Rowlandson, reflected and shaped the popular myth of the nineteenth-century artist.[49]

The Romantic image of the bohemian artist as independent, impoverished, passionate, and irresponsible, living at the edges of society in unheated garrets and eschewing bourgeois mores, did much to shape the nineteenth-century myth of the artist but left little room for the possibility of a female painter, poet, or musician. The women populating these novels, plays, operas, and illustrations are working girls—*grisettes,* models, and washerwomen—emerging from a lower class than the artists and whose most important roles are as the artists' lovers, models, and muses.[50] Jerrold Seigel traces the close relationship between bohemia and bourgeois society, two modes of social existence that emerged side by side in the nineteenth century and served as a mutually defining Other in the construction of these modern identities. He contends that "Like positive and negative magnetic poles, bohemian and bourgeois were—and are—parts of a single field: they imply, require, and attract each other."[51] Bohemia is understood as a stage of youth from which the male artist emerges and rejoins the ranks of the middle class; the boundaries, while pronounced, remain porous between the two worlds. For a woman, crossing the boundary between bourgeois existence and bohemia could be only a one-way journey; there would be no going back. The carefree and licentious life of the mythic bohemian was yet another path closed to the middle class women in search of an artistic profession. In direct response to these discourses, the novels by Howitt, Brontë, Sand,

Owenson, et alia, propose alternate visions of artistic sisterhoods while offering new images of women in the atelier, paintbrush in hand.

At the same time that the myth of bohemia gained popularity, Thomas Carlyle's formulation of artistic manhood presented an image of the "Hero as Man of Letters," positing the artist as "Poet, Priest, Divinity" whose labors could rescue society from its modern degradation (brought about, in no small part, by the corrupting influence of French women authors like George Sand).[52] But where the bohemian artist's masculinity was established in his sexual encounters with models and *grisettes,* Carlyle formulates a myth of artistic manliness in the image of monastic celibacy in what Sussman calls "a world of chaste masculine bonding from which the female has been magically eliminated" (5). The figure of the "artist-monk," also embraced by the German Nazarene brotherhood earlier in the century, continued to relate artistic and sexual potency, simply replacing images of virility with an ideal of "productive repression" of male sexual energy. In both cases, however, artistic identity is defined in terms of male sexuality in homosocial communities.[53] Carol Christ notes, "In order to make the writer heroic, Carlyle constructs a strenuously masculine ideal." She adds, "In this world of heroic masculinity, women have almost no place."[54] Yet, I will argue, in its self-conscious expulsion of the feminine this homosocial paradigm implicitly acknowledged the power or threat of women authors, painters, and their audiences, whose presence in the field of cultural production is everywhere felt, if rarely "seen."

The Romantic myth of the artist, predicated on attendant myths of masculinity and creativity, precluded the possibility of a "real" female poet, painter, novelist, or sculptor of genius or artistry in vastly overdetermined ways. Nonetheless, the myth, with its attendant constructs and discourses, should not be confused with "reality," though it undoubtedly shaped perceptions and politics. Thus, although it remained a male-dominated movement, women participated in Romanticism in a variety of forms, and while some resisted and/or reversed the gendered paradigms, others exploited them to gain access to a subject position within dominant field of representation. Indeed, it was Mme de Staël who brought the movement to France and proposed the first and best definition of Romantic poetry in *De l'Allemagne* in 1801,[55] while Corinne and Oswald, as heroes of one of the first Romantic novels in France (*Corinne,* 1807) represent a female genius and her feminized lover in a positive, if tragic, light. Marceline Desbordes-Valmore claimed her place among the French Romantic poets, introducing themes of motherhood and familial loss to the genre, while the works of Charlotte Smith, Felicia Hemans, Leticia Landon, Mary Shelley, and Joanna Baillie are crucial to a full understanding of British Romanticism.

Romanticism undoubtedly "colonized the feminine," to quote Alan Richardson,[56] but if we read this blurring of gender boundaries, where a poet or hero could be at once male and feminine, as a way of revealing "gender itself as a fiction," following Waller (5), then a breach emerges where aspiring women artists might similarly enact both "masculine" and "feminine" identities as Romantic artists. Many of the masculinist tropes of Romanticism sought to reduce woman to a mere sign or projection of male desire, fantasy, anxiety, or inspiration. From Wordsworth and Keats to Lamartine and Chateaubriand, woman is frequently a disembodied symbol: often dead, usually silent, rarely "visible," she is an idealized and elevated figure who exists in the poet's memory and imagination, but not, it would seem, in the real world. But these poetic constructions were just that, and the fantasies of the silenced and passive female (reflecting of course, larger social and cultural mores of the period) were answered by French and British women artists who worked within and against Romantic discourses of gender and subjectivity to shape artistic forms—poetry, painting, novels—that announced "their status as agents who work on the shape of their culture even as it shapes them."[57] One of the primary themes in the novels and paintings I will analyze in the chapters below will be rendering woman visible, giving her a voice and a subject position independent of (Romantic) male desire or fantasy. These counter-discourses invoke tropes and conventions of Romanticism only to invert or deny them. While I do not argue that all, or even most, of the women artists in this study were Romantic authors or painters *per se*, I will maintain that they were writing and painting against these discourses of Romanticism, even as they lingered into the Victorian period.[58]

Gender and Art:
REPRESENTING WOMEN

If women artists were rendered "invisible" or "unintelligible" (in Rancière's terms) by the discourses of Romanticism, social discourses of gender and propriety were arguably even more powerful in their proscription of the female artist in nineteenth-century France and England. Although the gendered separation of spheres, relegating women to the private realm of domesticity, were neither as fixed nor as absolute as was previously believed (especially for women of the working classes), these ideologies nonetheless shaped what Rancière would call the "police order," making a career as a professional writer or painter difficult to conceive for women of the middle and upper classes. Post-1789, the politics of gender on both sides of the channel suffered a conservative retrenchment against feminism, linked in both France and Britain to republicanism and revolution.[59] The institution of France's Napoleonic Code in 1804 legally enshrined the subordination of women to men, reflecting the dominant ideologies of maternity and domesticity that would shape the nineteenth-century politics of gender in both nations.

Thus, where aristocratic women had enjoyed relative freedom and even admiration in the late eighteenth century as Blue-Stockings, *salonnières*, philosophers, painters, and intellectuals, the post-revolutionary period's backlash against women's rights and freedoms curtailed such possibilities for women. The original Blue-Stocking circle had included both men and women who gathered in the London homes of Elizabeth Montagu and her friends in the 1750s for intellectual conversation, debate, and "a wide range of social and philanthropic activities that promoted, in particular, women's roles as writers, thinkers, artists, and commentators."[60] Members of the circle included author and translator Elizabeth Carter, poet Hannah More, and historian Catherine Macaulay, all of whom played a significant role in the cultural landscape of the period. Richard Samuel's 1778 painting of *The Nine Living Muses of Great Britain* (figure 1) celebrates the genius of the British Blue-Stockings by portraying Carter, Montagu, More, Macaulay, the painter Angelica Kauffman, Anna Letitia Barbauld (a poet), Elizabeth Sheridan (a singer), Charlotte Lennox (a novelist), and Elizabeth Griffith (novelist and playwright) gathered in a temple of Apollo in classical garb. Their poses are serious and dignified; their demeanors reveal both beauty and intelligence. Although the use of allegorical figures in portraits of women was a popular trope, here the direct reference to the women's very real accomplishments serves to affirm and elevate their standing. The collective nature of the portrait, where the women appear to engage and inspire one another, reflects their network of learning and support and serves as an inspiration for contemporary women to follow the model of the female pantheon. The French *salonnières*, including Julie de Lespinasse, Suzanne Necker (mother of Germaine de Staël), and Marie-Thérèse Geoffrin, were similarly engaged in promoting rational exchange between men and women on contemporary literature, art, philosophy, and politics.[61]

But by 1800, Blue-Stocking and its French equivalent, *bas bleu*, had become derogatory terms designating an ambitious, unfeminine, and untalented woman whose literary or intellectual aspirations were risible, while the *salonnières* were condemned by both republicans and monarchists for the excesses of the Ancien Régime and the revolution. Thomas Rowlandson's caricature, *Breaking Up of the Blue Stocking Club* (1815) (figure 2) reflects the rapid decline of the image of the female intellectual in the early nineteenth century. The dignified grouping of Samuel's scene is replaced by a brawl, as the Blues tear each other's hair out, knocking over china and furniture in a figuration of the effect of their unseemly aspirations on domestic peace and harmony. Their burly arms and heaving breasts, threatening to pop out of their bodices, signal lower class origins and sexual license, a far cry from the aristocratic and self-consciously

Figure 1
Richard Samuel, *The Nine Living Muses of Great Britain*, 1778. Oil on canvas, 132.1 × 154.9 cm. © National Portrait Gallery, London.

virtuous Blue-Stockings of the previous century. The overturned chamber pot and the "French cream" spilled on the floor reflect the artist's views on the content of the women's discussions as well as their inspiration, for in 1815 France continued to be Britain's enemy and the (imputed) source of all revolutionary ideas. (French cream was also a cosmetic, implying again the women's immorality.) Most importantly, perhaps, is the implicit concept that women could not work together collectively, for their "catty" behavior (echoed by the bemused felines watching the fray) would eventually turn any discussion into a catfight. Shifting the focus from women's intellectual potential to their physicality, Rowlandson reasserts the traditional binaries of male/mind and female/body, denying women access to the world of ideas.

Frédéric Soulié's *Physiologie du bas-bleu* appeared in 1840 and, like Rowlandson's caricature, mocks the female intellectual for her pretensions. Closely linked to caricature, *physiologies* were small and inexpensive pamphlets that portrayed contemporary society in comically exaggerated portraits of Parisian "types" in words and images. Performing the same ideological labor as caricature, the *physiologies* frequently revealed ambient social anxieties by reducing the troubling or threatening image of the Other to a "knowable" or ridiculous figure. The popular form, meant for mass consumption, reached a peak of popularity from 1840 to 1842 and with its illustrations, descriptions, and references to physiognomy, provided ways of "reading" the visual world. Soulié offers his readers ways of recognizing the *bas-bleu* by her overly dramatic clothes and hats, rooms full of books, and above all by her ugliness and lack of elegance. Using a grammatical play on the word *genre* (denoting the gender of a word or a person), Soulié observes that while the phrase "le bas-bleu" does not "mean" anything at all he still finds it fitting, for "it denounces this feminine type with a word of the masculine genre" (i.e., *le* bas-bleu).[62] Thus, when a woman is a laundress, an actress, or a queen (*la blanchisseuse, l'actrice, la reine*), "one can write, grammatically speaking: she is pretty, she is refined, she is adroit, she is shapely, she is graceful, she is a perfect beauty. But, from the moment a woman is *bas-bleu*, one is obliged to say of her: he is dirty, he is pretentious, he is evil, he is a plague" (6). In other words, the *bas-bleu* is a woman who is not a woman, she is a man. A woman who is a "she" (*elle*) merits modifiers that privilege her grace, beauty, and physical attractiveness. A woman who is a "he" (*il*) is ugly, unpleasant, and dangerous. Violating Derrida's "law of genre" at every level, the *bas-bleu* occupies a troubling space of indeterminacy (for she never can attain "true" male status) and must be contained.

Soulié documents the many "types" of this type, in chapters devoted to the "*Bas-Bleu* aristocrat," the "*Bas-Bleu* of the Restoration," the "Married *Bas-Bleu*," the "*Bas-Bleu libéré*," the "Virgin *Bas-Bleu*," and in a final chapter, "Le Bas-Bleu artistique." While the literary *bas-bleu* had historical precedent, the artistic ver-

Figure 2 Thomas Rowlandson, *Breaking Up of the Blue Stocking Club*, 1815. Hand-colored etching. 24.6 × 34.9 cm. The British Museum, London. © Trustees of the British Museum.

sion is "a new production that has no analogue in the past" (97). These creatures are no less "pretentious" than their literary counterparts, positing opinions on art and philosophy that Soulié mercilessly mocks. One artistic Blue-Stocking shocks her listener by announcing that a gladiator is not proportionally drawn because "a man isn't made like that" (102), thus betraying an unseemly knowledge of male anatomy. Another complains that a painting of the sack of Rome isn't "modern" enough, while still others are too pious and Christian in their tastes and images. In every case, Soulié exposes the ignorance and "vulgarity" of these unwomanly women who mistakenly believe in their intellectual and aesthetic parity with men. He concludes by noting that the artistic "species of *bas-bleu* fraternizes readily with the *bas-bleu littéraire*, and they seem to understand each other" (109). Finally, he tells his reader, regardless of social rank or marital status, underneath it all the *bas-bleu* is always the same: "a creature who is cold, dry, egotistical, selfish, envious, vain, nasty, with very rare exceptions; he may or may not have talent, that is a question entirely independent of his moral qualities" (109–10). Leigh Hunt's "Blue-Stocking Revels" (1837) takes a more humorous but no less pointed look at the British Blue-Stockings who are too often, he complains, "masculine, vain, and absurd."[63] Margaret Gillies's painted response in her portrait of the Romantic poet and publisher (discussed in chapter 7) emblematizes one of the many forms of resistance by women artists of the period as they were summarily dismissed both as women and as artists. From Amélie Cogniet to Sand and Brontë, the women artists in this study respond to these caricatural images with a series of counter-discursive visions of the female painter (and by extension the female author) that highlight her existence as a *both* a woman and an artist, viable and even successful in both identities. In passages of sweet revenge, the characters who doubt the heroine's artistic capacities or femininity are in their turn mocked as "masculine, vain, and absurd."

France and Britain:
NATIONAL AND CULTURAL IDENTITIES

The relationship between France and Britain has been historically fraught: from the Norman Conquest, through the Hundred Years War and the Napoleonic Era, the two nations engaged in a seemingly endless battle for dominance. The economic and political rivalries between them were echoed in the constructions of their national identities in which France served as Britain's Other and vice versa; to be French was to be "not British," and to be British was to be "not French."[64] From food to fashion, religion to royalty, the dueling cultures engaged in dialectical self-definition throughout the centuries and these oppositions became reified in ways that overshadow or even obscure the fertile cultural exchange between France and Britain that peaked from 1814 (following the end of the Napoleonic Wars) through 1830, but continued well into the Victorian period. Indeed, as Margaret Cohen and Carolyn Dever establish, the modern novel "did not develop along two separate, nationally distinct trajectories; it developed through intersections and interactions among texts, readers, writers, and publishing and critical institutions that linked together Britain and France."[65]

Pierre Daniel Huet, the genre's first theoretician, identified the novel's transnational origins and practices as early as 1670, and from the seventeenth century onward, Margaret Doody confirms, "novels rapidly crossed national and other boundaries,"[66] most notably between France and Britain. Joan DeJean adds, "During its formative period the modern novel was most often the result of massive shifts of influence back and forth across the English Channel—from 1660 to 1750, the prose fiction created both in England and in France was massively 'French'; from 1750 on, it became increasingly English."[67] In "Eloge de Richardson" (1762), Diderot advised, "Painters, poets, people of taste, people of integrity, read Richardson; read him continuously,"[68] while a century later, Walter Kendrick notes, "In mid-Victorian fiction, a sure sign of sophistication, and of questionable morals, is the presence of a 'French novel' on one's bedside table."[69] Mary Helen McMurran explains, "Many translators were novelists themselves—from Aphra Behn, Penelope Aubin, Eliza Haywood, Tobias Smollett, Oliver Goldsmith, Frances Brooke, and Elizabeth Griffith to Alain-René Le Sage, Denis Diderot, Marie-Jeanne Riccoboni, and abbé Prévost, among others—and they were often conscious of blending the two processes."[70] Thus, translations of eighteenth-century novels were "marked by the permeability of the two languages and cultures," according to McMurran, and "the contact between France and Britain cannot be properly described as the simple intersection of two distinct others but was a more fluid interaction based on a history of cultural intimacy" (51). In the nineteenth century, political hostilities and the ever-increasing links between the novel and national identity construction did little to diminish intellectual and cultural exchange. Cohen and Dever explain:

> The Napoleonic Wars did not prevent writers and readers on either side of the Channel from enjoying or reworking each other's fiction; indeed [. . .] the historical novel, perhaps the form most closely associated with imagining the origins of the modern nation, was facilitated by the generic fertilization catalyzed by trans-Channel exchange during this time. And even as Victorian disciplinary society was bolstered through invective against French immorality, G. H. Lewes went off to his bookseller after finishing *Jane Eyre* only to find 'the new volumes of unfinished novels by Alexandre Dumas, enough to have

tasked the energies of the British Museum to catalogue,' along with 'volumes by Théophile Gautier, Michel Masson, Madame Reybaud, Jules Sandeau, Badon, Feuillet, Roger de Beauvoir, d'Arlincourt, de Gondrecourt,' to say nothing of new books by Sand, Balzac, and Hugo. The transnational culture of the Channel zone differs from postmodern transnationalism not only in predating the nation-state and helping to shape its emergence but also by its position squarely at the center of national cultural formations, overdetermined and ambivalent as this position might be. (12–13)

In *Crossing the Channel: British and French Painting in the Age of Romanticism*, Patrick Noon also establishes "the extraordinary network of cultural exchange that developed between Britain and France in the three or so decades following the end, in 1815, of their long war."[71] Specifically, a "profound engagement" arose between Romantic painters on both sides of the Channel, and despite political differences Stephen Bann documents "a convergence between British and French visual cultures that was developing from 1800 onwards."[72] Although it is important not to ignore the fundamental differences between nineteenth-century French and British art and fiction, their intersections bear further exploration, especially in terms of women's contributions to the various fields of cultural production. Outside of the mainstream, female authors and painters from both sides of the Channel looked to their sisters in art, frequently finding far more in common with a foreign female writer than with a male author from the same nation. In their efforts to forge new paradigms of artistic identity, women crossed the borders of gender, genre, and nation, while actively embracing horizontal models of inclusion rather than hierarchies of distinction.

The works of art (both verbal and visual) at the center of *Portraits of the Artist as a Young Woman* represent this trans-Channel exchange in deliberate as well as less obvious ways. All privilege travel, foreignness, and difference as a source of inspiration, education, and sister- or brotherhood rather than a reason for animosity, competition, or antagonism. There is evidence that many, if not all, had read or seen each other's works, and both British and French intertexts and references abound in the novels and paintings from both nations. Whether depicting Scott's heroines (Lescot and Gillies) or reworking Balzac (Desbordes-Valmore, Arnaud, Howitt, and Sand), the shared desire to represent the active role of the female subject in art, politics, and history transcends the limits of national discourses for these female artists. The complex network of influence, friendship, admiration, and inspiration among and between these authors and artists crosses the boundaries of genre and nation: Anna Mary Howitt studied painting with Margaret Gillies, who was a close friend of her parents; Gillies studied painting in Paris in the studio of Ary Scheffer, where she undoubtedly read Sand's novels and saw works by the recently deceased Hortense Haudebourt-Lescot.[73]

Marceline Desbordes-Valmore includes frequent reference to Lescot in *L'Atelier d'un peintre,* and her daughter would later study in the painter's atelier. Sydney Owenson travelled frequently to Paris, where she was often compared to Mme de Staël (a figure who influenced all of the authors here), and described her visit to Lescot's studio in *France in 1829–30.* Angélique Arnaud, a committed Saint-Simonian and feminist, actively pursued a meeting with Sand and records her great pride at receiving words of encouragement from the *Bonne Dame de Nohant.* Sand herself was painted in the early 1830s by Haudebourt-Lescot, and her novels, translated into English almost immediately upon publication, appear to have influenced or inspired nearly every woman in this study, including Anne Brontë. Yet ultimately, personal connections are less important than the larger picture of resistance and assertion that arises from these works and others like them, as women actively shaped a new image of the female artist and female subjectivity in nineteenth-century France and Britain.

Portraits of the Artist as a Young Woman

The study is divided into three thematic sections corresponding to three central artistic subjects: "The Studio"; "Cosmopolitan Visions: Gender, Genre, Nation"; and "The Portrait." Each section considers a number of paintings by a female artist or artists and a pair of novels—one French, one British—in order to analyze the ways in which each reflects on a key series of themes. In chapter 1 of "The Studio," I examine the figure of the woman in the atelier in paintings by Adélaïde Labille-Guiard, Gabrielle Capet, Adrienne Grandpierre-Deverzy, Amélie Cogniet, Caroline Thévenin, Rolinda Sharples, and Mary Ellen Best, focusing on the issues of artistic education, professionalism, and space (real and metaphoric) for women painters in the nineteenth century. In chapters 2 and 3, I continue discussion of these themes in Marceline Desbordes-Valmore's *L'Atelier d'un peintre* (1833) and Anna Mary Howitt's *Sisters in Art* (1852), locating these novels in the context of their own dialogues with Balzac and the Pre-Raphaelite Brotherhood. The second section, "Cosmopolitan Visions: Gender, Genre, Nation," begins with Mme de Staël's *Corinne* (1807) and Sydney Owenson's *The Wild Irish Girl* (1806) and their images of gender and nation, before turning to the work of Hortense Haudebourt-Lescot, an influential painter of the 1810s–1840s credited with inventing the Italian genre scene. Just as Lescot's images both romanticized and radicalized the representation of nation, class, gender, and otherness, Owenson's *The Princess* (1835) and Angélique Arnaud's *Clémence* (1841) take the anodyne and popular genre of the sentimental novel and use it to liberal and feminist ends, enlisting the figure of a female painter to interrogate the naturalized structures of alterity at the heart of ideologies of gender and nation. Singly and collectively, these paintings and novels reflect links between the female artist and the Other (foreign, political, social) and propose revisions of the hierarchies of subjecthood. The last section is devoted to "The Portrait: Romanticism and the Female Subject." In chapter 7, "Portraits of Radical Engagement," I consider Margaret Gillies's use of the genre in her famous images of Harriet Martineau, William and Mary Wordsworth, William and Mary Howitt, and Leigh Hunt to highlight the role played by women in culture and to critique Romantic masculinity. Finally, chapters 8 and 9 examine the portrait in Anne Brontë's *The Tenant of Wildfell Hall* (1848) and George Sand's *Elle et lui* (1858), tracing the ways in which the painted and literary likeness also serves as a way of revealing difference, exposing the distance between the Romantic male gaze and the realities of female existence. Gillies's paintings, along with Brontë's and Sand's novels, reflect on the gendered politics of representation in Romantic art while presenting alternative images of women as subjects, rather than objects of the constitutive gaze. Finally, in a brief conclusion, I examine the "visibility" of the female artist in the decades following 1860 in France and Britain and the ongoing construction of women's artistic identity in the field of cultural production.

Part I

The Studio

Women in the Studio

Representing Professional Identity

Artistic Education:
WOMAN AS AMATEUR

> No one can be really esteemed accomplished, who does not greatly surpass what is usually met with. A woman must have a thorough knowledge of music, singing, drawing, dancing and the modern languages, to deserve the word.
>
> —Jane Austen, *Pride and Prejudice*[1]

As women sought to establish professional artistic status in nineteenth-century France and Britain, they confronted myriad obstacles, both practical and ideological. In nineteenth-century culture, dominant discourses of art and gender figured forth woman as amateur, practicing drawing or painting for personal rather than public ends. Although middle and upper class women were expected to be "accomplished" in the art of drawing, these skills in the *arts d'agrément* were closely aligned with the marriage market. The "lady amateur" practiced art "to display her taste and skill, to strengthen the domestic bonds of love and duty, to serve the community, and to improve her taste and that of the nation," Ann Bermingham tells us, reflecting above all "women's commodity status."[2] As Jane Austen sardonically illustrates in the conversation between Miss Bingley and Mr Darcy cited above, the "accomplished woman" was a catachresis of sorts: Elizabeth Bennet remarks to Darcy "I am no longer surprised at your knowing *only* six accomplished women. I rather wonder now at your knowing any" (39). Recognized as a work of art herself, the accomplished woman necessarily remained outside of the circuits of real artistic accomplishment or genius. Trained at home or at boarding school in drawing and painting by governesses or private tutors, women of the gentry practiced their skills within the domestic sphere for personal or familial entertainment or decoration; their subject matter, execution, and consumption marked the drawings and paintings of the accomplished woman as "feminine" and necessarily amateur productions.

Moreover, Deborah Cherry explains, within the languages and institutions of nineteenth-century art, "femininity was positioned as the very antithesis of the professional artist . . . As a category of value amateur is mobilized against women's art to secure masculine definitions of the artist and the professional."[3] Even as Female Design Schools and the *Ecole Gratuite de dessin pour les jeunes filles* opened in London and Paris in the early decades of the century, these institutes for working-class girls, providing practical training in industrial or commercial design, served only to increase the distance between contemporary constructions of "woman" and "artist," while at the same time intensifying the resistance of male visual artists to female incursions into the realm of professionalism. As in previous centuries, many female visual artists who achieved professional status from 1800–1860 were the daughters, sisters, or wives of male painters and thus able to acquire the studio training generally inaccessible to women.[4] Both the French *Académie Royale de peinture et de sculpture* (established in 1648) and the British Royal Academy (est. 1768) continued to serve as arbiters of professional artistic legitimacy during the period; although a handful of women had been granted conditional membership in the eighteenth century, none were counted among the members of either institution in the nineteenth century.[5] Artistic training at the Academy schools was barred to women in England until 1860 and in France until 1897, thus preventing aspiring female painters from receiving the official artistic formation deemed necessary for a professional career, not the least of which was the life class, in which the students drew from the nude model. History painting, the most elevated of all the genres within the hierarchies of art, was theoretically predicated on an artist's ability to depict the human form in action, which was in turn dependent on learning to draw from the live model. "To be deprived of this ultimate stage of training," Linda Nochlin observes, "meant, in effect, to be deprived of the possibility of creating major art works"[6] and women were *de facto* relegated to the "minor" genres of portraiture, landscape, still life, and genre painting. While women's artistic productions were ultimately included in Salons[7] and RA expositions, they generally constituted a small percentage of the work exhibited.

Despite these and other obstacles, however, professional female artists did emerge in nineteenth-century France and Britain in ever-increasing numbers, gaining access to training and exhibition both within and beyond the traditional structures of power in ways to be discussed in the chapters to follow. Like the male visual artist of the period, the female painter sought to construct her professional identity within the public sphere in direct and implicit dialogue with contemporary discourses of art, gender, and professionalism. Although women were principally associated with amateur art, a handful of female painters in France and England did achieve artistic renown in the course of the centuries, but these predecessors were by and large figured forth as "exceptional women" whose existences were, by definition, inimitable. Eighteenth-century painters Elizabeth Vigée-Lebrun and Angelica Kauffman, the most notable of these "exceptional women," had fashioned their self-portraits (and public images) in such a way as to emphasize their beauty and uniqueness, while at the same time aligning themselves with their aristocratic subjects in ways that obscured the commercial nature of their enterprise. Exempted from the social laws applied to her sex, the exceptional woman is "a traditional figure of masculinist discourse," Mary Sheriff tells us, who is "tolerated, even admired in her originality,"[8] for her exceptional status serves to affirm rather than subvert the very laws she transcends. Thus Vigée-Lebrun and Kauffman, whose artistic talents elevated them above the female fray, were constructed as *sui generis* in France and Britain, eschewing pupils and doing little to make the idea of women *artists,* rather than a singular woman artist, conceivable. As Sheriff explains, "exceptional women trouble the public order only to reinforce its rules. Thus defined, the exceptional woman can only be a problematic role model, for aspiring to her position implies collusion with the general subjugation of women. Separation from other women is the price a woman pays for her exceptionalness" (2).

The women painters in this study, interested in collective as well as individual visibility, turned away from the model of exceptionality for a more communal image of women artists while constructing her subject position as one that could be shared by all women. Rejecting the distancing forms of classical myths and allegorical representations embraced by Vigée-Lebrun and Kauffman, these nineteenth-century female visual artists sought to portray themselves in spaces and places that were recognizably real (though ultimately, perhaps, no less mythologized), suggesting their irrefutable presence in the field of cultural production and in the social order, on equal footing with men. One of the most popular settings for scenes of professional self-fashioning was the atelier, and paintings by women of women artists in the studio presented the public with alternative visions of gender and artistic creation. In France, these images were staged in the studio in direct dialogue with contemporary images of male painters in the atelier, while in Britain, where studio culture did not exist as it did in Paris, women artists transformed domestic and public settings into surrogate studios, self-consciously constructing the image of the female painter as a professional. In all cases, these paintings of women in the atelier, depicting them as working subjects rather than objects of the representing gaze, are political interventions, in Rancière's sense of the word, as they seek to render visible and intelligible the figure of the professional woman artist.

Portraits of the Artist in the Studio:
GENDERED NEGOTIATIONS OF IDENTITIES IN FRANCE

The image of the male artist in the studio had been a popular theme since the Renaissance and served over the centuries as a scene of self-fashioning where the painter could perform a social and aesthetic identity for an audience. From Pliny's account of Apelles and Alexander in the studio to the various interpretations of Pygmalion, Zeuxis, and St. Luke, the topos has staged the artist's negotiations for power, status, and cultural capital within the artistic and social spheres, while at the same time offering up new mythologies of art.[9] In "L'Atelier comme autoportrait" (The atelier as self-portrait), Philippe Junod remarks that beginning in the nineteenth century, the studio increasingly functioned as a "social theatre" as well as a "mirror of the artist"; doubling as a social space and a private one, the atelier may be read as an artistic "program or manifesto" while at the same time presenting an "allegorical tenor."[10] As a working space, the studio represents the locus of artistic creation and production, complete with a vocabulary of standard signifiers: plaster casts and models of ancient sculpture to indicate classical training; musical instruments and tobacco pipes pointing to inspiration; cast-off drapery to suggest the nude model; and palette, brushes, easel, and maulsticks as the tools of professional artistry.

The complement to this solitary site of creativity is the studio as social nexus where students are trained by an artistic master and friends gather to confer. These images reflect a different side of the myth and reality of the nineteenth-century artist, emphasizing the collective identity and shared experience of brotherhoods discussed above. As Thomas Crow, Carol Ockman, and Abigail Solomon-Godeau have shown, the artist's studio in post-revolutionary France was the scene of homosocial bonding and erotics where artistic identity was formulated in response to changing conceptions of masculinity.[11] Constructed as a sphere of masculine production and exchange, the studio was closely tied to the institutional structure of the Academic system that established aesthetic and social hierarchies through inclusion and exclusion. Official training at the *Ecole des Beaux-Arts* in Paris produced the painters and sculptors who dominated the Salons, receiving both commissions and cultural capital. Women and indeed all painters who were excluded from classes at the *Ecole des Beaux-Arts* were thus denied access to the theoretical and practical training that came to distinguish artist from artisan, and high art from commercial production.

Boilly's *Gathering of Artists in Isabey's Studio* (1798) and Cless's *L'Atelier de David* (1804) serve as paradigmatic announcements of the ethos of masculinity and homosocial camaraderie of the post-revolutionary atelier in France, as they highlight the collective and collaborative nature of identity formation in the space of the studio. Boilly's ambitious and successful *Gathering of Artists* (figure 3) announced a new vision of the artist for the new century. The thirty-one artists are elegantly dressed and intellectually engaged, while the atelier is striking in its equally elegant modern décor. History painters, miniaturists, landscape, genre, and still life painters are portrayed together without obvious distinction, as Boilly collapses academic hierarchies of the past to elevate painters, as a unified group, to a higher social and artistic status. Susan Siegfried contends, Boilly "presented the contemporary artist as a new kind of cultural hero."[12] Even more radical is his use of the word "artiste" to include architects, engravers, a musical composer, actors, a singer, and "un homme de lettres" in the gathering, and this new collective definition served to expand generic limitations while positing a more generalized image of the artist not as painter, sculptor, etc, but as Artist, a man of the world and member of a prestigious assembly of creators. Boilly's constructed image of artists in the studio sought to establish the elevated status of the artist as cultivated professional for a new consuming audience, while at the same time emphasizing his individuality.

Cless's scene from 1804 (figure 4) portrays David's studio at the Louvre, where students of the master would sketch from live and plaster models as they prepared for careers executing the noble history paintings David's studio was famous for. By 1804 the first generation of Davidian students—Girodet, Gérard, Gros—had become the leading painters of the Napoleonic regime, but they, like the *rapins* (art students) depicted here, were actively engaged in negotiating artistic identity in post-revolutionary France. Once again, the homosocial dynamic of the all-male studio is evident in this energetic depiction, where students observe the nude model, drawings of the model, and one another, while the naked male form is echoed in the classical statues and oil paintings hanging above the scene. The repetition of virtually the same image on multiple easels attests to a shared or common vision; as David, still in his top hat, corrects a student's sketch at the front of the room, his engagement in the formation of this generation of painters is evident. The conflation of artistic training and masculine intimacy is illustrated on the left side of the scene, where one student, pointing to his fellow student's canvas and to the model, wraps his friend from behind in a suggestive embrace. The painter's right foot is placed between those of his friend, his brush is held over his gesturing

Figure 3
Louis-Léopold Boilly, *Réunion d'artistes dans l'atelier d'Isabey*, 1798. Oil on canvas. 71 × 111 cm. Photo: Réunion des Musées Nationaux/Art Resource, NY.

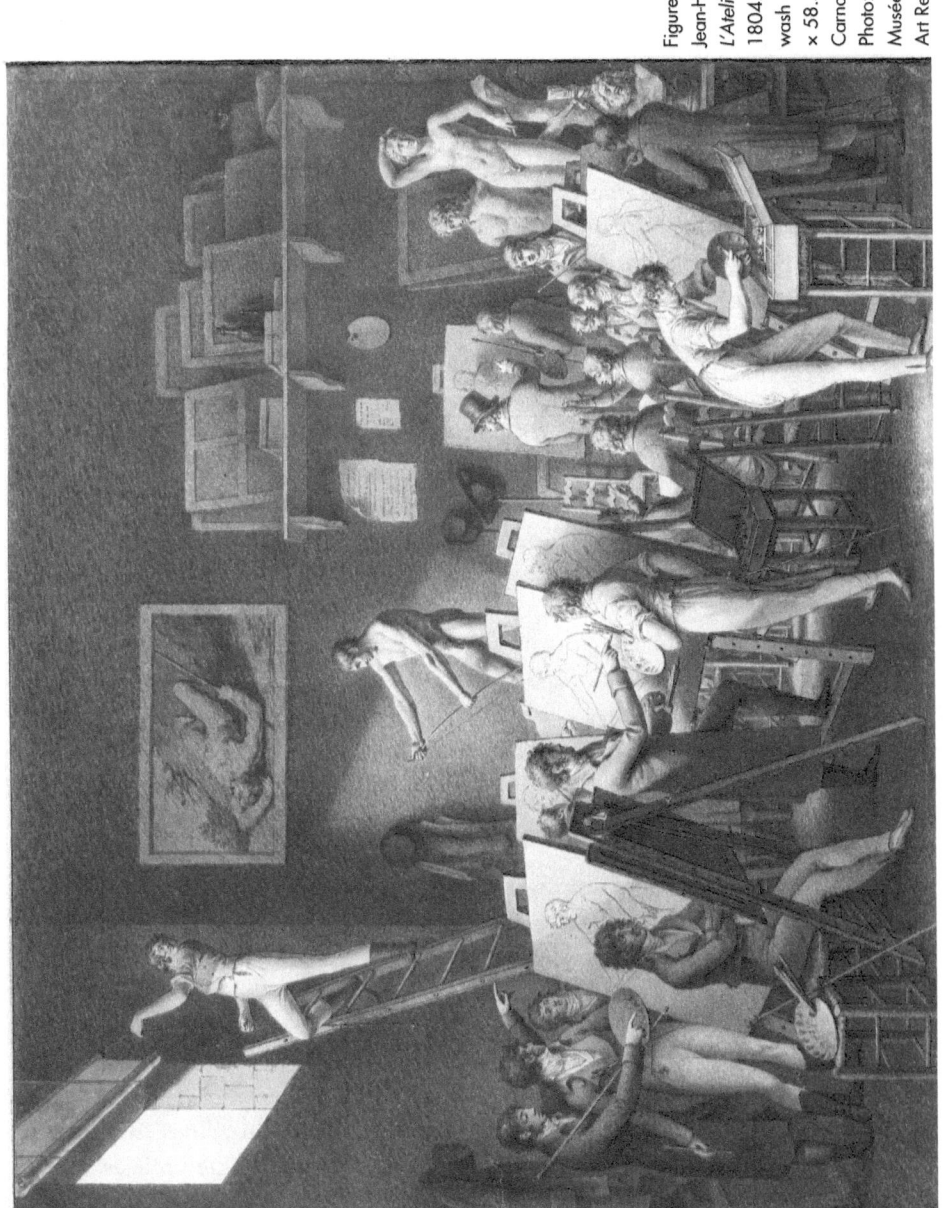

Figure 4
Jean-Henri Cless, L'Atelier de David, 1804. Pencil and ink wash drawing. 46.2 × 58.5 cm. Musée Carnavalet, Paris. Photo: Réunion des Musées Nationaux/ Art Resource, NY.

colleague's midsection, and his maulstick juts out behind him to rest on his fellow student's shoulder. On the surface level, this crowded and chaotic drawing illustrates the working life of the atelier with busy students sketching and painting among canvases, easels, models, and stretchers, giving a slice of life of the exotic milieu of the studio. As a "self-portrait," the scene reveals Cless's own identification with the homosocial group, his own sense of being an artist tied in to his place within this larger configuration of men.

Yet this image and others like it elide the fact that during this period women were in fact included in David's studio. Indeed, although they continued to be excluded from institutional training, some women in France did gain access to professional instruction post-1789. In the wake of the Revolution and the destabilization of the art market, many academically trained painters, including Greuze, Regnault, Vien, and Girodet, as well as David, began to take on female students outside of the Academy to support themselves. David, whose influence on male painters of the period is legend, also trained at least thirteen women, including Constance Charpentier, Marie-Guillemine Laville de Benoist, Césairine Mirvault Davin, Angélique Mongez, and Aimée Duvivier. Regnault and his wife taught Sophie Guillemard, Pauline Auzou, Claire Robineau, and Adèle Romany, while Greuze's pupils included Constance Mayer, Jeanne Philiberte Ledoux, and Mme Elie.[13] Like the myriad paintings, contemporary memoirs of life in the studio by Delécluze and Coupin also rendered the women there invisible by excluding them from their accounts;[14] as Solomon-Godeau notes, the women in David's studio are "effectively conjured away, banished from historical memory, and for the most part banished from modern art as well."[15] Although admitted to some lessons, women were, in general, excluded from the life class, and the fact that Cless (and Cochereau, Massé, Delécluze, Coupin, etc.) chose to focus on precisely the scenes where women could *not* participate in the life of the atelier highlights both their marginalization and perhaps even more significantly, the male artists' investment in asserting the masculinity of their vocation.

Training in a male studio was not the only option for French women in the post-revolutionary period: a number of female painters also opened studios for women in the early decades of the nineteenth century. Marie Guillemine Benoist, who studied with David, opened an atelier for women in 1804[16] and Mme Regnault, wife of the Academician, also trained students alongside her husband. The history painter, Pauline Auzou, ran a studio for women for more than twenty years and was known to have studied from the male and female nude.[17] Although categorically excluded from the Commune des Arts and the Institut National, in an important reversal of Ancien Régime policies women were allowed to exhibit in unlimited numbers at the open Salons, beginning in 1791. In 1800, critic Bruun Neergaard lamented the fact that so many unskilled artists "who barely know how to hold a pencil" had taken up portraiture, but when lauding those whose portraits he admired, Neergaard included Adélaïde Labille-Guiard, Jeanne-Elisabeth Chaudet, and Madame Laville Leroulx (Marie-Guillemine Benoist) alongside Girodet and Gérard.[18] By 1801, the press was commenting on the "swarms" of *femmes artistes* included in the Salons,[19] and while hyperbolic, the comment reflects dramatic shifts in exhibition demographics. Margaret Oppenheimer documents the increase of women artists at the Salon from three in 1789 to "22 in 1791, 32 in 1801, 50 in 1806, 76 in 1810, and 84 in 1819." Moreover, she adds, women "became eligible to receive grace-and-favor lodgings at the Louvre or other residences for artists, *encouragements* (monetary prizes given to works of particular merit exhibited at the Salons), and government commissions for paintings and sculptures" (7). Undeniably, many critics remained skeptical, but some supported the influx of female painters at the Salons and in 1812, R. J. Durdent remarked "there is no country, in any previous period, which could boast of having witnessed the birth at a single time of so many women cultivating painting with such decided success."[20]

As women gained access, however unequal, to artistic training and exhibition in France, they began actively to construct their own artistic identity in both discursive and counter-discursive ways, while the hyper-masculinity of contemporary male images of the atelier reflects a response not only to cultural constructions of gender during the period but also to the undeniable presence of women in the artistic field. Adélaïde Labille-Guiard and her student, Gabrielle Capet, who was featured in her mentor's Salon painting of 1785, represent a pair of early voices in the effort to render the female visual artist visible in nineteenth-century France.

Labille-Guiard, admitted to the Academy on the same day as Elisabeth Vigée-Lebrun, was a committed teacher, liberal, and proto-feminist whom Laura Auricchio identifies as a "non-conformist" who should be recognized for "her innovations as a portraitist, her prominence as a teacher in the 1780s and her notoriety as a politically active woman in a revolution that, despite claims to liberty and equality, paradoxically silenced female voices."[21] Until recently, Labille-Guiard has been read almost exclusively in terms of a contrastive relationship to the more successful Vigée-Lebrun, whose affiliation with the French royal family led her into exile during the revolution, while Labille-Guiard remained in Paris and actively supported the Jacobin cause. Mary Sheriff has analyzed the gendered opposition constructed by eighteenth-century critics between Vigée-Lebrun's "feminine" painting, with its "soft" (*molle*) touch, brilliant colors, and obvious artifice, and Labille-Guiard's "virile" and "masculine" painting with its "strong and vigorous" brushwork and fidelity to "nature and truth."[22] But of particular interest in this study is Labille-Guiard's role as mentor to the next generation of female artists.[23]

Labille-Guiard opened her studio to young women "sans fortune,"[24] and by teaching painting as a profession to the poor, rather than an *art d'agrément* to the wealthy, played a role in establishing a new collective identity of professional *femmes artistes* that following generations of women would develop. Upon gaining entry into the Academy in 1783, she began to campaign—unsuccessfully—to increase the number of women admitted. Failing to change the status quo, she submitted a portrait to the Salon of 1785 (figure 5) that included her students, Gabrielle Capet and Mlle de Rosemond, thus effectively subverting the Academy's limit of four female painters at the Salon by including two more. In contrast to the "exceptional" status embraced by Vigée-Lebrun, Labille-Guiard forged a public identity as a woman among women with whom she shared a common talent and presumably a common goal: to succeed as artists.

The title listed in the 1785 *livret*, *Full-Length Painting Representing a Woman Painting and Two Pupils Watching Her*, emphasizes the fact that the two young women are more than mere spectators, and the tension between the unseen canvas before her and the vivid image of the girls behind reveals Labille-Guiard's desire to foreground the next generation of female artists as her subject matter and creation. The strong vertical line of the easel and stretcher delineates the left side of the composition with a gesture that further highlights the constructed nature of what we are looking at: the ragged edge of the canvas and rough wood create a contrast with the polished surfaces of skin and gowns while implicitly acknowledging their existence as two sides of a single (painted) coin. Borrowing this trope of the back of the painting from Velazquez and Rembrandt, Labille-Guiard enters into a dialogue with her male predecessors, playing with the structures of revelation and refusal while showing her spectators both painting and what Victor Stoichita has called "antipainting," that is, "an image whose central theme is the inaccessibility of the image."[25] Through this confident invocation of her skills as a painter and her fluency in the languages of art and its history, Labille-Guiard lays claim to her own place within the field of cultural production. On a more immediate level, she implicates the viewer with her confident, appraising gaze, echoed by the more reserved look of Mlle Rosemond behind her, in a way that requires engagement with the scene. For if Labille-Guiard is at once subject and object of her own painting, a split authorial self, the spectator occupies a similarly unstable position as the painter's subject or mirror.

Much like the studio portraits of an earlier age, Labille-Guiard's image seeks not to reflect "reality" but rather to forge an identity in contested terrain. Just as Vasari and his followers strove to elevate their social status as painters by portraying themselves as liberal humanists, Labille-Guiard seeks to establish herself as a "legitimate" female painter, a real, rather than allegorical figure wielding a paintbrush and palette. For if Painting had been iconographically represented by men as a woman,[26] here a woman represents herself as a *painter*

Figure 5
Adélaïde Labille-Guiard, *Self-Portrait with Two Pupils*, 1783. Oil on canvas. 210.8 × 151.1 cm.
Image copyright © The Metropolitan Museum of Art/Art Resource, NY.

surrounded by all the accoutrements of the atelier—palette, paintbrushes, maulstick, *portecrayon,* canvas, acolytes—while at the same time engaged in the act of artistic production, thus a concrete rather than symbolic embodiment of art. The elegance of the setting (indicated by the intricate parquet floor and Louis XV furniture) and of her dress partake of a long tradition of artistic self-representation that nonetheless takes on slightly different implications when the painter is a woman. Labille-Guiard's magnificent gown and elaborate hat, her effort to portray her own beauty and relative youth, celebrate both her skills as an artist and her gender, reinforced by the beautiful and beautifully painted figures of the girls standing over her. Having made her reputation creating delicate pastels of her male contemporaries at the *Académie,* Labille-Guiard answers the modest earlier images with a large-scale Salon painting in oil, thus portraying the female artists in a more elevated medium, form, and setting. Even the scope of the scene, as a group portrait–cum–genre scene, places this painting above the portraits of the *Académiciens* while nonetheless evoking them as important intertexts.

As the three women occupy the center of the canvas in a tightly executed pyramid, the background presents a second level of meaning. Visible in the shadows is a sculpted bust gazing blindly at the warmly lit *femmes artistes.* The image of Labille-Guiard's own father, Claude-Edme Labille, sculpted by Pajou and also exhibited at the Salon de 1785, may be interpreted as a *clin d'oeil* to her friend and fellow artist, announcing her membership in the intimate world of artistic brotherhood, and an offering of filial devotion. But perhaps more complexly, the marble bust evokes a dialogue with Labille-Guiard's own work and with the mythology of artistic creation. In 1783 Labille-Guiard's *morceau de reception* for the *Académie* had been her portrait of Pajou modeling the painter LeMoyne: a studio painting of a male artist creating the image of another male artist, painted by an (invisible) female artist. Two years later, a member of the *Académie* in her own right, Labille-Guiard now looks to the future of art in her studio painting, foregrounding the *femmes artistes* in all their glory and temporarily relegating earlier representations of the patriarchy to obscurity. By subordinating the representation of the only male figure in the image to a marble bust, at once fragmentary and frozen, the painter reverses the gendered structures of art where men are the active subjects and women the passive objects of artistic representation. In a reversal of the Pygmalion paradigm, she removes art from the economies of heterosexual desire and fetishization with an image of women as conscious, engaged, and productive. Finally, the vestal virgin behind the sculpted bust and even further in shadow represents both what Labille-Guiard consciously gives up and what she aspires to. As chaste goddess of hearth, home, and family, the vestal virgin invokes the socially constructed female identity that Labille-Guiard eschewed. Separated from her first husband not long after their marriage, the painter lived with her students and her lover for several decades, devoting herself to her work rather than domesticity.[27] But if the vestal virgins represented home and hearth, they also worked *collectively* to maintain the flame, passing it from one woman to the next without ever letting it expire, an image far more in keeping with Labille-Guiard's construction of the identity of the *femme artiste*.

Gabrielle Capet (1761–1818) was Labille-Guiard's favorite student and carried the torch for her mentor. Well known in artistic circles and highly praised by the critics, Capet was frequently compared to Isabey, known today as the most important miniaturist of the era. Like her teacher, Capet focused primarily on portraits and frequently pastels, and her reputation was similarly enhanced by her images of contemporary male artists, including Suvée, Meynier, Vandoeuvre, Houdon, and Vincent. At the Salon of 1808, five years after Labille-Guiard's death, Capet exhibited her most ambitious canvas to widespread acclaim: a large-scale image of a female artist in the studio (figure 6), which earned for her the designation of "peintre d'histoire" in the *livret*.

Capet's posthumous portrait represents a scene that took place twenty-five years earlier, as Labille-Guiard campaigned for her place in the *Académie*, and offers another interpretation of the female artist at work that reflects a post-revolutionary sensibility. In this alternative view of her mentor, the intimate female trio of 1785 has been transformed into a resolutely social scene, where Labille-Guiard and Capet are inserted into a predominantly male world. The tight focus and somber palette of the earlier image have been broadened and brightened, as Capet indicates that women painters belong to the larger sphere of cultural production, on equal footing with men. Labille-Guiard, no longer burdened by her elegant gown and coquettish hat, is portrayed as a serious artist absorbed in her work, while her student has moved from passive observation to the active role of preparing the palette, now an artist in her own right.

In Capet's composition, Labille-Guiard paints the portrait of Joseph-Marie Vien, while his pupil and her teacher (and later husband), André Vincent, looks on. The elderly Vien is surrounded by his son and daughter-in-law (behind him) and by his student, Vincent's, students, including Pajou, Jean Alaux, Etienne Pallière, Léon Pallière, Jean-Joseph Ansiaux, Jean-François Mérimée, Charles Thévenin, Charles Meynier, and François Picot. These young men of 1783 (when the scene is set) were, in 1808 (when it was executed and exhibited), some of the leading academic and Troubadour painters of the post-revolutionary period. By including Pajou, Meynier, Picot, *et alia* in her composition, Capet creates a genealogy of teachers and students, from Vien to Vincent to Labille-Guiard to herself and the other young artists in the room, placing male and female artists side by side in a group portrait and implicitly locating her own work in the same tradition as that of Vien, Vincent, and her male contempo-

Figure 6
Gabrielle Capet, *Madame Adélaïde Labille-Guiard peignant le portrait de Joseph-Marie Vien*, 1808. Oil on canvas. 69 × 83.5 cm. Neue Pinakothek, Munich. Photo credit: Bildarchiv Preussicher Kulturbesitz/Art Resource, NY.

raries. By moving the scene into a more public and populated setting, Capet thus opens up the scope and ambitions of the female artist in an image that reflects as much on the politics of art in 1808 as it does on its purported subject of 1783.

In a significant reversal of time-honored roles, it is the men who are the object of the female gaze, as Labille-Guiard paints the Academician and Capet paints the scene. The simple clothes of the pair of female artists attest to their status as artistic producers, while the men are adorned in luxuriously embroidered silks, satins, and lace. Mulvey's formulation of the gendered gaze is effectively subverted here, as the male becomes the passive object of an active female gaze, while his showy finery emphasizes the very "to-be-looked-at-ness" that has traditionally been coded female.[28] Yet unlike the homoerotic canvases produced in and/or inspired by David's studio (i.e., Figure 4), this male figure is neither nude nor beautiful: he is old, frail, and fully dressed. With an idle brush hanging in his limp hand, Vien's representation depends on the power of the active female artists—that is, both Labille-Guiard within the scene and Capet, who has painted the image of female painting and here gazes knowingly at her audience. The chaotic, often sexually charged representations of studio life as presented by Cless and myriad others are replaced here by a calm scene of dignified professionalism.

Boilly's *Réunion d'artistes dans l'atelier d'Isabey* also serves as an intertext for Capet's scene. Borrowing both compositional and narrative elements from this early announcement of the new culture of the post-revolutionary artist's studio, Capet's invocation of Boilly's image recasts the scene in significant ways. Where Isabey's studio is notable for the absence of artist elders—David, Vien, Regnault and other masters are conspicuously missing—Capet stresses continuity with the immediate past and solidarity between artistic generations. Indeed, where male post-revolutionary painters struggled to establish an identity outside the broad shadow of their fathers, female artists like Capet sought artistic identity by connecting with the legitimating traces of these predecessors. If each delineates an important sense of artistic collectivity, gender is central to both. In Boilly's, the homosocial dynamic of the all male studio is translated into a broader context (including architects, actors, singers, etc), but remains unquestionably masculine in its orientation. In Capet's, on the other hand, the collective artistic identity for the new age remains tied to successful painters and sculptors, but expands to include women in the ranks of its past and future. A third woman in the scene (Vien's daughter-in-law), gesturing to the drawings on the table and listened to attentively by three of the men surrounding her, suggests women's active presence in society as well. Faced with the possibilities and uncertainties of a new social order and a new century, Boilly and Capet represent two visions of the construction of the nineteenth-century Artist. The first—Boilly's—would be embraced and developed in the decades to come, contributing to the construction of the Romantic artist and hero; the second—Capet's—would also contribute to Romanticism, but in an oppositional sense, as a threatening discourse to be countered, suppressed, and denied.

Under the Restoration women continued to seek professional artistic training, but as they began to establish a foothold in the artistic marketplace of the conservative regime, more determined resistance began to be felt in the escalating insistence on the *masculine* nature of artistic identity in the works of painters, authors, and critics. The proliferation of male-authored atelier scenes reflected the instabilities of artistic identity in modern France, and like the growing number of artistic brotherhoods, further evidenced the anxieties of gender that accompanied these changes. As Laura Morowitz and William Vaughan explain, "If the very notion of masculinity depended upon negotiation of the marketplace and the earning of income, the financially strapped artist faced a constant challenge to his manhood,"[29] a challenge only exacerbated by the presence of women producing art—and images of themselves producing art.

Restoration scenes of male artists such as Jean Alaux's *L'Atelier d'Ingres à Rome* (1818), Horace Vernet's *L'Atelier du peintre* (c. 1820), and Auguste-Xavier Leprince's *Artist's Studio* (1826) reasserted the studio as an exclusively male enclave. Vernet's *L'Atelier* (figure 7) is emblematic in its self-conscious escalation of the gendered signifiers of artistic masculinity. Like earlier images by Boilly and Cless, Vernet's scene is crowded with men drawing, painting, and conferring upon art. The atelier itself is full of traditional markers of artistry and inspiration—canvases and easels, palettes and paint boxes; men puff on pipes, while a violin hangs on the wall. Yet the plaster casts and classicized models of old are replaced here by a large white horse, a dog, a deer, and a monkey, and in a significant departure Vernet introduces a new register to the old topos: the atelier as battleground. Nina Athanassoglou-Kallmyer has read the painting in terms of Vernet's radical militarism as a committed liberal Bonapartist under the conservative Restoration regime,[30] but extending the polyvalent metaphor to the politics of art and identity, *L'Atelier* may also be understood as an announcement of the painter's embattled persona and his desire to assert a masculinity more closely tied to the animality of war than the elevated salon culture Boilly proposed for the artist.

Vernet's artistic manifesto defines art as a battle between generations where the master (Vernet himself) fences with his student at the center of the scene, épée in one hand, palette in the other. Meanwhile, a pair of bare-chested students in boxing gloves looks on, alongside yet another young man leaning against a chair with a rifle by his side, indicating that they too are engaged in a struggle for a place within this artistic combat zone. Saddles, drums, and trumpets, tricorne hats and military attire, coupled with the unexpected animals in

Figure 7
Horace Vernet, L'Atelier du peintre, 1820–21. Oil on canvas. 52 × 64 cm. Private collection.

this eclectic interior scene establish an atmosphere that is at once bellicose and bohemian, at odds with bourgeois values and aggressively anti-establishment. If the Bloomian battle with the next generation of artists is foregrounded, Vernet's own battles are also inscribed here, as he includes at the back of the atelier a bust of his grandfather, the eighteenth-century landscape painter Joseph Vernet, and a painting by his father, Carle Vernet. Simultaneously signaling his artistic provenance and his independence from the patriarchal structures of the past, Vernet's Romantic artist is at once more certain of his difference from the dominant social order and perhaps, in his overdetermined insistence on his phallic manhood, less certain of his masculinity.

These male group portraits were answered by Adrienne Grandpierre-Deverzy (1798–1865) in her 1822 canvas of *L'Atelier d'Abel de Pujol* (figure 8). In contradistinction to the nonconformist chaos in Vernet's studio, the artists here are well-dressed and dignified, as women artists took great pains to avoid the associations of bohemianism that would undermine their legitimacy. The studio is clean and well-lit, while bearing the now familiar markers of artistic training and practice (easels, models, canvases, casts), and a general air of camaraderie reigns. This scene of bourgeois propriety and productivity includes a lone man (Pujol, later Grandpierre-Deverzy's husband) surrounded by more than a dozen women sketching, painting, and conferring on their art. In a departure from the images produced by Labille-Guiard and Capet, Grandpierre-Deverzy locates her scene in a realistic milieu that reflects more upon what is than upon what might be. Thus, although the studio is devoted to training women, a man remains at its center both literally and symbolically, as indicated in the title of the composition. Pujol (1787–1861), an established academic painter who ran separate studios for both men and women, occupies the dominant position on the canvas and is shown in a slightly larger scale as he critiques a young artist's sketch, while the three oil paintings hanging on the walls are his own. None of the women's own works is visible, save the drawing that Pujol holds in his lap and thus under his sway.

Grandpierre-Deverzy displays the full range of training available to women at the time, as her *femmes artistes* are seen painting and drawing after master paintings, plaster casts, and human models. In contrast to Cless's iconic image of the male studio, the model here is a fully dressed woman rather than a naked man, at once an indication of the gentility of this atelier and a tacit acknowledgment of its limitations as well. On the shelf above the women painters' heads, the cast of a nude male torso is pointedly, if playfully, turned to the wall. Yet answering the proscription implicit in the positioning of the plaster cast at the far left of the canvas, at the right two young women likewise turn away from the scene, momentarily rejecting the hermetic world of the studio for the "real" world outside. If the principal narrative of the painting highlights a harmonious world of women absorbed in artistic practice, and if that world is kept in check by the signs of limitations on that practice, the group behind Pujol's back represents an alternative vision of the purview of the female artist. As Pujol addresses the presumed author of the sketch, and her companion looks directly at the viewer of the painting, a third student occupies two positions within the visual narrative. With her arm around the woman whose work is being critiqued, she is physically attached to the group surrounding the master, but she is psychologically removed from the trio, as she joins another young woman in contemplating a different framed scene: the view of the street from the atelier's window. Turning their backs on the master, this pair of errant pupils pulls back the curtain to the world outside in a move that signals the transfer of the female gaze and its corollary subjecthood to the larger and more threatening realm of the public sphere. Refusing the spatial and intellectual limitations of the studio, these female painters lay claim to seeing and representing forbidden realms and spaces.

The atelier, a liminal space between the domestic interior and the public arena of social labor, here functions as a switching point for the gradual transition of women from the home to the workplace, from amateur to professional status and from the isolation of the *foyer* to a new collective identity with other

Figure 8 Adrienne Grandpierre-Deverzy, L'Atelier d'Abel de Pujol, 1822. Oil on canvas. 96 × 129 cm. Musée Marmottan, Paris. Bridgeman Art Library International, New York, NY.

women laboring outside of the home. Grandpierre-Deverzy, who would later run Pujol's atelier for women, exhibited at the Salon for nearly thirty years and was best known for her portraits and genre scenes of female subjects from history and literature, including images from the life of Queen Christina and *La Princesse de Clèves*.[31] *L'Atelier d'Abel de Pujol*, much like her own career, stands as testimony to the increased presence of women in the field of artistic production in France during the 1820s and 1830s, in studios, at the Salon, and in the marketplace. While their work would remain secondary in terms of both critical reception and aesthetic influence, the very fact that this painting was purchased by Giovanni Sommariva, the most important patron and collector of the period, indicates that the subject was of interest to connoisseurs and *amateurs*.[32] Sommariva's vast collection, including works by David, Girodet, Prud'hon, Guérin, Gérard, and Canova, was displayed in galleries in his homes in Paris and Lake Como, both of which were open to the public and frequented by artists, guaranteeing that Grandpierre-Deverzy's canvas of women in the atelier continued to be viewed alongside some of the most important artists of the early nineteenth century. In this sense, the female painter in France became visible to both artists and cognoscenti, as both the subject and the object of this confident image by a woman artist of women artists at work.

By the 1830s, the artist's studio had become a popular theme in French literature and music as well as painting, and Marc Gotlieb contends that "from the imaginary ateliers detailed in fiction and illustration to backdrops prepared for opera and the theatre, the studio served as a public stage in the guise of a private arena."[33] In a pair of paintings from two women associated with the studio of Léon Cogniet (1794–1880), some of the escalating tensions of gender and artistic identity under the July Monarchy become apparent. Cogniet, a friend of Géricault and Delacroix who remained more academically oriented than his Romantic colleagues, was best known for his portraits and history paintings that celebrated the *juste milieu*. In 1830 he founded a studio for male students and one for female students, directed by his sister Marie-Amélie Cogniet (1798–1869), and the following year, her portrait of her brother and herself in their shared atelier was exhibited at the Salon de 1831.

Amélie Cogniet's *Intérieur de l'atelier de Léon Cogniet* (1831) (figure 9) portrays a polarized artistic arena: Cogniet stands at the far left of the canvas and his sister sits at the far right, with the expanse of the entire studio between them.[34] As he stands back to assess the canvas they appear to be working on together, she looks back at him from her position in front of the painting-in-progress with an expression that seems at once wary and challenging. This iteration of the male and female painter in the atelier shares elements of Grandpierre-Deverzy's version, while at the same time introducing new aspects that reflect the changing dynamics of the contemporary field of cultural production. Amélie Cogniet

Figure 9
Amélie Cogniet, *Intérieur de l'Atelier de Léon Cogniet*, 1831. Oil on canvas. 330 x 402 cm. Cliché Musée des Beaux-Arts, Orléans.

portrays a single female artist in front of the canvas wielding her brush while looking back at her male counterpart who gazes at their shared artwork. The large history painting they are collaborating upon is *L'Expédition d'Egypte sous les orders de Bonaparte*, a *grande machine* commissioned for the ceiling of the Louvre. Despite the discarded clothes strewn upon the chair at center, there is no model evident for this composition, and the only woman present is a painter who is clearly contributing to this canvas. The eroticized structure of male subject/female object central to so many atelier scenes is thus replaced by the male/female dyad of brother and sister painters as Léon and Amélie face one another across the studio. Léon Cogniet's easy pose upon a platform, with an arm slung over one rung of a ladder and a foot upon another, intimates ambition and confidence as he towers over his sister and the scene. Amélie's more contorted position, hunched uncomfortably before the canvas, bespeaks the subordination also implied in Grandpierre-Deverzy's painting while suggesting social and political hierarchies as well. The large canvas looming behind her and the equally substantial gilded frame jutting into the pictoral space from the right seem to contain and oppress her in an almost claustrophobic fashion. As Susan Sidlauskas has shown us, the painted interior in the nineteenth century "became a deeply contested terrain where the very nature and limits of identity were debated rather than resolved."[35] She explains, "when spectators viewed painted figures stranded on opposite reaches of a gaping space, pressed into a corner or subsumed into the furniture around them, they were cued to experience a visceral response, a bodily empathy, for the discomfort of the protagonists. The visual provocation to unease and disorientation were thus translated into an imagined experience of another's psychological state" (3). Cogniet's composition uses space in precisely this fashion, communicating a psychological as well as a physical discomfort that the audience would recognize and even share. While she is present in the studio and actively working as a painter, the female artist in this composition remains dominated by the male artist and his production.

Yet in reading the space of this atelier in terms of the metaphorics proposed by Junod above, we find that Amélie Cogniet does not entirely cede the space of creation to her brother. The studio is divided down the center by a stove and its chimney pipe running up the back wall: on the left of the scene, where Léon holds sway, are another large canvas of a classicized male nude (his own *Caïn et Abel*), numerous plaster casts, and the corner of his epic *Briséis pleurant Patrocle* (1815). On the right, presided over by the Venus de' Medici and Amélie, the wall is covered with small oil sketches from nature, while another painter is absorbed in a portrait head. A desk behind him is covered with sheets of paper, painted canvases, and a figurine of a white horse, while a full portfolio leans up against it. Falling under the sign of the masculine, the left side of the canvas is associated with the past, stasis, and death (via Abel and Patrocles) in its collection of ancient themes, models, and styles. The right side, associated with the feminine, signifies a more modern, Romantic aesthetic, with its suggestive, sketchy landscapes and portraits speaking to the contemporary mode of painting. Where all is completed and framed on the left, process and productivity are emphasized on the right. The clock in the middle of the wall, surrounded by the small canvases, further implies the theme of contemporaneity. Amélie's facture in her execution of the figures is equally loose and creamy, in keeping with a Romantic suggestiveness, and even her psychological distress is in a sense a Romantic trope, as she struggles to escape the oppressive forces of tradition.[36] As the naked Hercules looks back at the male painter, who gazes upon his unfinished canvas, Venus looks forward to the future and the female artist who is poised to return to the act of painting. The blank canvases on the floor at her feet further suggest future works for the female artist. Amélie Cogniet, who ran her brother's atelier for women and exhibited at the Salons in 1831, 1833–36, and 1842–43, articulates an artistic identity in direct, if uncomfortable dialogue with her more successful sibling. No longer merely a student and not quite a full peer, the woman in the atelier was engaged nonetheless in the production of art and ultimately the next generation of artists.

A second painting (figure 10), by Caroline Thévenin (1813–92), represents the distaff side of Cogniet's atelier some five years later, in 1836. Thévenin, who shares a name with several Parisian painters of the period, was born in Lyon and joined Cogniet's studio in Paris in the early 1830s, as did her sister Rosalie a few years later.[37] She exhibited regularly at the Salons from 1835 to 1843 and in 1848, 1852, and 1853. In 1865 Caroline married Cogniet at the age of 52; he was 69. From the wedding registry, it appears to be Thévenin's first marriage, pointing to the likelihood that she continued work as a painter for most of her adult life, perhaps assisting Amélie in Cogniet's atelier as well. This scene, which shares much with Grandpierre-Deverzy's 1822 canvas, is notable in the absence of the master, for unlike *L'Atelier d'Abel de Pujol,* Thévenin's atelier does not include Léon Cogniet. Although both women would go on to marry their painting teachers, here the position at center is held by a woman helping a younger student prepare her palette. The power differential is shaped by age, rather than gender, and a spirit of mentoring rather than critique prevails. While the woman who has just entered the atelier and is warming her hands on the ceramic stove bears a strong resemblance to several of Cogniet's portraits of Amélie, it is not clear in this composition that she is indeed the *institutrice,* but the self-sufficiency of the group of female painters here is indisputable. Where contemporary Romantic portraits of the artist portrayed a melancholy and solitary figure (Géricault, Girodet, Delacroix, etc.), Thévenin's insistence on the group establishes the professional nature of the training, as well as the solidarity among these well-dressed and serious women. Again, the chaos and

Figure 10
Caroline Thévenin, *Atelier des jeunes filles*, 1836. Oil on canvas. 46.2 × 61 cm. Cliché Musée des Beaux-Arts, Orléans.

promiscuity of bohemia are replaced by an image of gentility and organized study. Vernet's battling *rapins,* with their guns, sabres, and boxing gloves, are answered in peaceful pairs of women working harmoniously together.

Unlike Cogniet's own studio, the women's space is relatively empty, except for a few plaster casts on a shelf. Without the massive history paintings dominating the room, the focus falls on the women themselves, who nonetheless copy from Cogniet's *oeuvre.* The most clearly visible painting, on the easel just to the left of center and opposite the door, appears to be a classical nude female figure and is in fact a copy of Cogniet's oil sketch of Helen of Troy for his Prix de Rome painting from 1817. Helen, the most beautiful woman in the world, was the subject of Zeuxis's legendary painting and one of Angelica Kauffman's self-portraits, and this multilayered intertext is repeated in the portfolio on the right.[38] As the two girls seated on the floor gaze on yet another copy of Helen in the open portfolio, women are at once subjects and objects of art at every level of the scene. On the wall to the far right of the room, the women's somber cloaks and bonnets hang neatly in a row, while a more fashionable green hat sits atop an easel, a piece of complicated finery suggesting the beauty and desirability of these women as well, temporarily set aside but never entirely absent. The woman painting Helen at center is echoed in a second woman with her back to the viewers on the far right. Where one is absorbed in painting, the other adjusts her turban in the mirror, and the visual parallel implies similarities between canvas and mirror. Indeed, Thévenin seems to tell us, in a highly Romantic vein, that the subject of art is always the artist herself and the framed representation, whether painting or mirrored reflection, reveals its creator. By extension, then, this atelier scene reveals Thévenin's identity as part of a community of women artists working within the discourses of the artistic tradition but outside of the direct sway of the male painter.

Surrogate Studios:
REPRESENTING PROFESSIONAL SPACES IN BRITAIN

Studio culture never achieved the same kind of currency or influence in Britain that it did in France, and British painters eager for studio experience routinely trained in Paris, Rome, or Munich well into the final decades of the nineteenth century.[39] Reynolds's emphasis on "industry," "restraint," and "individualism" in his Discourses (delivered from 1769–90 and setting forth the RA's academic doctrine), was inherently at odds with the group ethos and revolutionary orientation of David's studio during the period, and the collective, bohemian experience of students and masters so intimately tied to French Romantic art remained at odds with British artistic training.[40] Indeed, as the "British School" developed in the nineteenth century, it privileged "notions of genius equated with originality and grounded in a Protestant tradition of individuality and freedom of control"[41] that were predicated in opposition to conceptions of French, Catholic "conformity," while the idea of British "liberty" had long been conceived in opposition to French "absolutism," linking artistic and monarchical principles. Holger Hoock explains that "the constitution of 'national culture' was seen to be bound up with the development of a nation's visual culture" (109), and the British artist's solitary nature emblematized national difference from France. Similarly, British artistic culture was more diffuse. While London and the Royal Academy were indeed central, they did not hold the monopoly on artistic training and exhibition that Paris did; numerous provincial art centers—Bristol, Leeds, Manchester, Liverpool—maintained their own viable academies and exhibitions, allowing more decentralized artistic cultures to emerge.

The limited studio training available to French women was nearly nonexistent in England, though small groups of young women did band together to work, study, and draw after hired models in studio spaces most frequently within their family homes. The most ambitious female artists (or those with the greatest means) traveled abroad for their professional training, joining studios in Paris, Germany, or Italy. Statistics compiled by Charlotte Yeldham confirm that French women exhibited far more self-portraits and studio scenes from 1800–1860 than British women did, reflecting the differences in female artistic culture at the time. Yeldham documents twenty-seven self-portraits by women at the French Salon from 1800–1830, and thirty over the course of the following three decades, for a total of fifty-seven female self-portraits from 1800–1860. French women exhibited eighteen paintings of women painting, eleven studio scenes, and eleven portraits of women artists from 1800–1860, while in Britain the numbers are substantially lower. From 1800–1869, there were only twenty-two self-portraits of British women artists shown at major exhibitions and a handful of female authored portraits of women artists.[42] Yet despite the significant disparity in images of female painters at public exhibitions, British women were also actively engaged in forging artistic identity in the public sphere. Thus, although there are few paintings that correspond precisely to the French atelier scene, British women visual artists portrayed women at work in a variety of settings that sought to shape discourses of professionalism and reflected the politics of art, labor, domesticity, and the public sphere in the first half of the nineteenth century.

The life and works of Rolinda Sharples (1793–1838) emblematize some of the ways in which family and domestic imagery shaped the discourses of professionalism for British women artists in the early nineteenth century. The daughter of professional painters, Sharples was born in Bath and spent much of her youth in America, where her father and mother built a modest fortune traveling through the new nation executing small-scale pastel portraits. James Sharples trained with Romney, exhibited at the Royal Academy, and produced well-known images of George Washington, John Adams, Jefferson, Hamilton, and Burr; his wife Ellen was also a talented painter (James had been her instructor at an art class in Bath) who produced both original commissioned portraits (exhibited at the RA in 1807) and copies of her husband's works. As Ellen noted in her diary, her versions of James's portraits "were thought equal to the originals, price the same" and these reproductions were sold both in the United States and in Britain, allowing the family to live "in good style associating in the first society."[43] Raised in a Quaker family, Ellen Wallace Sharples embraced a progressive educational philosophy: all three children (two sons and a daughter) were exposed to music, literature, art, and philosophy from an early age, and Rolinda enjoyed the same artistic training as her brothers. Ellen proudly announced that by her thirteenth birthday, Rolinda had decided on becoming a "professional artist" with the full support and encouragement of her family (Knox 21). For Ellen Sharples, painting represented a means to self-sufficiency: as she began miniature painting in 1803, she mused in her diary, "Should I excel in this style of drawing it will be a great satisfaction to me. I shall then consider myself independent of the smiles or frowns of fortune."[44] In the same vein, Ellen later reflects in her diary that Rolinda's artistic training would allow her daughter to enjoy financial independence and "have resources within herself should a diminution, or loss of fortune, ever be experienced. I had frequently thought that every well educated female, particularly those who had only small fortunes, should at least have the power, if they did not exercise it, by the cultivation of some available talent, of obtaining the conveniences, and some of the elegances of life."[45]

Following James Sharples's death in 1811, Ellen and Rolinda settled in Bristol, where the focus shifted to Rolinda's professional practice. Although primarily taught by her parents, Rolinda did study in London on two separate occasions with Philip Reinagle, and supplemented her practical training through constant study at museums, private collections, and exhibitions in London and throughout Britain. During the period, Bristol supported a lively and coherent school of artists (now referred to as the Bristol School), including Francis Danby, Edward Bird, Edward Rippingille, Samuel Jackson, and James Baker Pyne.[46] As a portraitist, Rolinda established her professional ambitions in the size and format of her paintings; shifting from the small scale head and shoulders pastels produced by her parents, she painted larger full-front oils and complex narrative scenes of contemporary events (influenced by Rippingale's realist canvases) that she exhibited at the Royal Academy in 1820, 1822, and 1824. She was invited to become an honorary member of the Society of British Artists in 1827, and exhibited with them frequently until her death. Rolinda

Sharples's works were also included in expositions in Liverpool, Bristol, Dublin, Leeds, Birmingham, and Southampton, as well as the Carlisle Academy.[47]

In *Self-Portrait with her Mother* (c. 1820) (figure 11), Rolinda Sharples announces her status as an artist. This oil on panel portrait shows the artist at work on a genre scene in a gallery/studio in her home surrounded by ornately framed portraits, landscapes, and history paintings. By placing herself in this context, Sharples describes a life in art; like many of her French female predecessors (whose work she would have seen in circulating prints), the British painter makes visible a woman's artistic formation, portraying herself in the very act of making art. Without the studio training available in France, as portrayed by Grandpierre-Deverzy and Thévenin, British women's art education was generally limited to private tutors and independent efforts at copying from Old Masters in museums and private collections like the one pictured here. Lacking the supervision of a male teacher/master and the company of other students, the female artist takes her place within the field as a solitary figure, in direct dialogue with the art of the past. Yet as Sharples has composed the scene, there is an intimate link between the artist and the art around her: far from being at odds with her surroundings (as seen in Amélie Cogniet's menacing image), the space here embraces and reflects the female artist. A large unfinished canvas leans against the wall to the far left, indicating that this is a working space, its size implying a more professional ambition than her dainty dress and domestic setting might otherwise denote. Similarly, her steady and confident gaze, communicating concentration and perfect ease in her performance of painting, is utterly devoid of the coquetry or diffidence of a lady amateur. Directly behind her upper back, the trees in a partially obscured landscape follow the contours of her body, almost pushing her toward her easel. On the other side of her torso, a second landscape illuminates her face from below with an unseen sunrise over distant mountains while a tower points toward her eyes. Above her head, a portrait of a mother and child mirrors the mother/daughter dyad in Sharples's own composition and in the painting within the painting, the mother leans in toward her child with a tender gesture that is echoed in Ellen Sharples's own body. The two juxtaposed images figure forth past and present: in the framed image on the wall (which seems to invoke a portrait by Romney, James Sharples's master), the child appears to be on its mother's lap, while in Rolinda's image, the adult child occupies her own seat, yet maintains the physical intimacy with her progenitrix. The fact that each head in the principal pair is now framed by its own gilt *cadre* indicates intellectual independence as well as emotional interdependence. Ellen's presence behind the easel metaphorically suggests her support of Rolinda's painting.

Most importantly, this double portrait of mother and daughter portrays two professional artists, as Sharples, like Labille-Guiard and Capet, delineates

Figure 11
Rolinda Sharples, *Self-Portrait with her Mother*, c. 1820. Oil on panel. 36.8 × 29.2 cm. © Bristol's Museums, Galleries, and Archives.

a female artistic genealogy to the Bristol viewers who knew them. If Labille-Guiard's magisterial image focused on the three women in the studio, refusing the viewer access to the painting itself (see figure 5), Sharples creates a relationship focused around the canvas with mother, daughter, and artwork in a tight triangulation. As Rolinda looks off for inspiration, her mother gazes upon her daughter's production, while the audience gazes upon the two women whose relationship is mediated through painting. In this relay of regards, the poised and self-assured younger artist looks outward, her eyes focusing beyond the spectator upon her subject—the canvas she is copying and/or a mirror reflecting the scene that we are beholding, in a painterly mise-en-abyme. Her more diffident mother, whose hands and posture denote her reserve,[48] concentrates on her daughter's production, the metaphoric offspring of her child. In this intimate double portrait, Ellen Sharples is an active and engaged party, her body leaning in toward Rolinda's in such a way as to communicate her interest and intelligent evaluation of the image. Rolinda's fashionable white gown contrasts with her mother's more conservative black dress, while her dark curls are answered by her mother's white cap in an image of opposing complements united by the delicate lace decorating both. Similar yet different, the two female painters represent continuity and confidence, a mastery reinforced by the brushes and maulstick jutting forth from Rolinda's lap to rest upon the canvas.

In comparing Sharples's double portrait with Rippingille's *Portrait of Edward Bird, RA* (1817) (figure 12), painted at virtually the same moment in Bristol, her distinctive perspective on the atelier scene becomes even more apparent. While both reflect on the relationship between two painters, their means and import are decidedly different. The highly Romantic image of Bird at his easel, painted by his friend and pupil Rippingille, shows a solitary artist entirely absorbed in his work in a disordered studio. While the author of the scene remains invisible, his admiration for the master is expressed in the halo of light around Bird's head and pencil that signals the illumination of genius. Artistic creation is here, as in the majority of British studio scenes in the nineteenth century, denoted as an individual endeavor while inspiration emerges from the artist's imagination. With the shade covering the window, the interior scene points to the inner world of the painter. The younger, provincial artist gains cultural capital from his relationship to the Academician who would die two years after the portrait was finished, while a lineage is established in the chain of painters implied in Rippingille's painting of Bird painting. On the other hand, a female painter in early nineteenth-century Britain eager to project professional rather than amateur status needed to establish connection to the world of art rather than isolation, and the visual signifiers of Romantic genius are replaced with more concrete symbols of artistic prowess and production. Sharples, like Bird, is portrayed in front of the canvas with paintbrush in hand, but here the studio

Figure 12
Edward Rippingille, *Portrait of Edward Bird, RA*, 1817. Oil on panel. 34.1 × 26.2cm. © Bristol's Museums, Galleries, and Archives.

is a shared space and her mother—at once parent, teacher, and inspiration—embodies and renders visible a collective female artistic identity.

Sharples expanded the purview of the portrait and the female visual artist in a series of narrative paintings begun around 1817. In these complex images of the social spaces of provincial life—*Cloakroom, the Clifton Assembly Rooms* (1817–18), *A Market* (c. 1819), *Rownham Ferry* (1820–22), *St James Fair* (1825), *The Clifton Racecourse* (1830)—Sharples included precise portraits of large numbers of local figures in group scenes that reflected the often unseen position of women (in general) and the female painter (in particular) within the public sphere. The artist worked directly from life, sketching on site and gathering details to give her scenes a documentary verisimilitude that drew crowds of admirers at London's Royal Academy, where she exhibited *A Market* in 1820, *Rownham Ferry* in 1822, and *A Mouse* in 1824. The paintings were favorably reviewed in the London and in the local press and attracted buyers and new commissions.[49]

Rolinda Sharples's most ambitious composition was *The Trial of Colonel Brereton* (1832–34) (figure 13), a large-scale (40 x 58.5 in.) representation of the aftermath of the Bristol Riots of 1831, triggered by the defeat of the second Reform Bill. In the autumn of 1831, the House of Lords rejected the bill that would have provided more representation in the House of Commons for rapidly growing industrial towns like Bristol, leading to widespread protests in towns across Britain. The eruption of the angry mob in Bristol raged on for three days, with violence, looting, and arson, until the dragoons quelled the riots with a charge through Queen's Square. The leader of the troops, Colonel Thomas Brereton, was subsequently court-martialed for his leniency; sympathizing with the cause, he initially tried to use persuasion rather than force to disperse the crowds and refused to open fire on the rioters. Accused of neglect of duty, Brereton shot himself only days after the trial began. In Sharples's sympathetic portrait, more than 100 people crowd the courtroom in what has been called a "social almanac of who's who in Bristol at the time" (Metz 9). It has been noted that the painter used considerable artistic license in her portrayal, moving the scene to a different set of rooms, including her mother, Ellen Sharples, who did not attend, and rendering Colonel Brereton significantly younger than his fifty years. These alterations reveal Sharples's identification with the accused, and in her own journal she reflected her sympathy for "the poor and much pitied Col. Brereton: he sat . . . with a countenance of hopeless abstraction . . . In my small book I had taken pencil sketches of poor Brereton, whose earthly tribunal was so dreadfully terminated."[50] While Rolinda requested sittings with many of the Bristol citizenry included here, most striking of all is her inclusion of a self-portrait with her sketchbook at the trial. By portraying herself at work in the courtroom (seated toward the front on the far left side of the canvas), Rolinda Sharples establishes her role as a chronicler of current events, claim-

Figure 13
Rolinda Sharples, *Trial of Colonel Brereton, After the Bristol Riots*, 1832. Oil on panel. 148.6 × 101.6 cm. © Bristol's Museums, Galleries, and Archives.

ing a place within the public realm for the female artist. In choosing to paint herself documenting Brereton's trial (given that he was only briefly present before his suicide), Sharples aligns her politics with those of the liberal Colonel, thus advocating both clemency and also representation for the disenfranchised. Although Sharples has been accused of "meticulous literalism" in producing work "devoid of social comment or satire,"[51] her staging of this scene, which she labored over for nearly two years, reflects implicit comment and even critique of the very society that condemned Brereton and the rioters who sought a political voice. The self-reflexive inclusion of the figure of the female artist at work in this politically charged context hints at Sharples's own bid for women's social and political representation within the public sphere.

The work of Mary Ellen Best, a provincial painter from York, reflects another iteration of female professionalism and the domestic scene, while at the same time documenting the integral role of travel and study on the Continent for many female painters of the 1830s and 1840s. While Best's work does not rise to the level of some of the other artists in this study, she represents an important component of the larger thrust of the aesthetics and politics of nineteenth-century women's art—the widespread desire to render viable and visible women's labor in the public sphere. While not every female painter attempting to support herself as a professional fine artist was prodigiously gifted (or even adequately trained), the majority of these women working in France and Britain from 1800–1860 did predicate their representations in terms that sought to reconfigure the *partage du sensible* in greater or lesser ways.

Mary Ellen Best (1809–91) came from a wealthy and progressive family who supported her ambitions from childhood on. Following her father's death in 1817, Ellen and her sister Rosamond were raised in Yorkshire in a predominantly female household by their mother, unmarried aunts, and grandmother who lived nearby; bequests from their father gave both daughters a small income that assured them a level of independence throughout their lives. Like most girls of her class, Ellen received her artistic training at boarding school, but unlike most she had an excellent drawing master in the person of George Haugh, a successful painter who exhibited regularly at the RA and was well connected in London.[52] Soon after leaving school, Ellen established herself as a "semi-professional" artist in York; although she did not have to paint in order to support herself, Best did sell her work as portrait commissions to private patrons and to London dealers until her marriage in 1840 when she was 31. Eager to distinguish herself from a lady amateur, Best "called herself an artist and strove for recognition" (Davidson 9). Bent on improvement, she painted every day, studied and copied Old Masters in country homes, and sketched outdoors, ever in pursuit of more and better training. In 1834, she set off for the Continent for an extended tour with her mother, spending over a year in

Germany studying art. Although it does not appear that she joined a painter's studio during her time there (as Anna Mary Howitt and Jane Benham would do a decade later), Best dedicated herself to the study of Old Masters and contemporary German art, while befriending several women painters there. After her mother's death in 1837, Best returned to Holland and Germany, where the culture was more hospitable to a female visual artist. Although she had happily embraced an unmarried life devoted to art (after 1835, she was independently wealthy and did not need to marry to survive), Best met Anton Sarg, a German schoolteacher and amateur musician, during her sojourn and married him in 1840. The couple had three children and spent the rest of their lives on the Continent.

Working primarily in watercolors, Best executed portraits of friends and of commissioned subjects, as well as still lifes that sold to collectors and to London dealers, including Ackermann's. Most compelling for this study, however, were her domestic genre scenes of daily life at home (in York) and abroad (in Germany and Holland), in which she reflected on the integration of women's lives, work, and art. As Lynne Walker has argued, "For many women artists, designers, and architects based in Britain in the nineteenth century, the studio was located in the domestic space of the home. Whether in new or refurbished buildings, creative middle-class women devised, altered, and/or subverted private space, redefining the home to advance social, political, and artistic projects and to promote social change."[53] With an exacting eye to detail, Best focused on domestic interiors in compositions that highlight the metaphoric or narrative nature of space, allowing furniture and pottery, carpets and teakettles to recount the quotidian life of British and German women. Her scenes of kitchens and drawing rooms reflect an entire worldview through their clutter or cleanliness and render visible what would generally be hidden from public view. These spaces are occupied by women, children, servants, but in nearly every scene the room and its décor dominate and when human figures are absent, the presence of things (most often paintings) take on a life of their own that runs the gamut from mundane to menacing.

In a series of watercolors from the 1830s, Best portrayed picture galleries in Britain and Germany. These rooms in private country estates and public exhibition spaces were the only real "academies" open to women like Best in search of the advanced artistic training available in a studio. In the absence of any public art galleries in Yorkshire, Best had obtained permission to study and copy the collection at Castle Howard, and in *Green Drawing Room at Castle Howard* (1832) (figure 14) Best represents one of the rooms where she worked, copying paintings by Reynolds, Caracci, Bellini, Domenichino, Van Dyck, Bassano, and Tintoretto.[54] What is particularly striking in Best's rendition is the juxtaposition of high art and domesticity, where the furniture in the drawing room with its

Part I: The Studio

Figure 14
Mary Ellen Best, *Green Drawing Room at Castle Howard*, 1832. Watercolor on paper. 25.5 × 32 cm. Private collection.

baggy slipcovers coexists with the Old Masters to the extent that one framed image is perched on a settee. While this odd positioning probably signals that the image had been taken off the wall to enable a visitor to copy or study it with greater ease, the framed painting of what appears to be a statue occupies a spot on the couch much as a person might, leaning back and surveying the room. To the left of center is a smiling housekeeper, keys in hand. Best thus depicts, as she would repeatedly do, the coexistence of women and art within the private or domestic sphere. Although this chatelaine does not own the paintings that surround her, for she belongs as much to the Castle Howard as they do, the Old Masters nonetheless fall into her domain, as signaled by the keys. Her rose-colored dress complements the green of the walls and echoes the red robes of the painted figures above and behind her. It is she who opens the doors to cede visitors access to images, and like Best herself, the housekeeper is in fact responsible for exposing these hidden treasures to viewers from outside the Castle walls. Here, as in a large number of her interiors, Best composes her image in such a way that the framed view through an open door to a brightly

66

illuminated window provides a counterpoint to the paintings on the wall and suggests both parallels and departures. Looking beyond the enclosed space of the drawing room with its gold-encased portraits and landscapes lies another world, another framed view, and for Best, the path to this world is traversed through the mastery of the Old Masters.

In Best's most intriguing self-portrait, the artist depicts herself in an 1838 representation of her *Painting Room in our House in York* (figure 15). Seated at a table by a window at the extreme right of the scene, Best dips a brush into blue pigment as she works on an unseen image on her easel. Pushed to the edges of this interior, the artist and her work are self-contained: a finished watercolor lies drying on the table between the easel and a closed portfolio, while her tools—box of colors, water, and palette—are neatly arrayed on the table. Surrounding the artist, even engulfing her, are all the signs of bourgeois domesticity that occupy the majority of the image. A dog sits obediently at the glowing hearth, the mantel is crowded with pastoral porcelain figurines, and numerous framed images decorate the walls. Portraits of Best's parents and family, silhouettes, a landscape, and a still life that might be by Best herself all struggle to be seen against the busy green wallpaper whose green vines, leaves, and tendrils undulate across the wall in an almost dream-like animation. The matching curtains bulge into the window frame behind the painter, threatening to consume the artist in her solemn black dress. A table at the center of the composition is also covered in a green patterned cloth, adding to the overwhelming, almost menacing feeling that the inanimate objects and materials in this room will bury its occupant in exuberant excess. In this claustrophobic interior, surface ornament encroaches on the artistic subject in such a way as to suggest the oppressive weight of domesticity and its all-consuming busyness.

From her chosen position at the margins, Best looks straight ahead with a steady and serious gaze. Her left hand holding onto the easel and her feet planted firmly on the floor cloth covering up the patterned rug, Best asserts her place within this space while at the same time asserting her difference from her environment. The straight lines of the table, box, and easel stand in stark contrast to the voluptuous curves of the wallpaper and curtains, and the black, brown, and gray of the wood and her gown provide a somber counterpoint to the greens and creams that dominate the rest of the interior. The three empty chairs poised at various angles testify to other occupants of this sitting room, only temporarily displaced and present even in their absence. There is a psychological intensity to this scene that anticipates some of Edouard Vuillard's interiors at the end of the century, as Best uses space and pattern to signal a subjective state of being. The female artist has carved out a place for herself within the bourgeois parlor; her working space, like her existence as an artist, occupies a liminal area at the edges of the arena, yet she is solidly ensconced.

Figure 15
Mary Ellen Best, *Painting Room in our House in York*, 1838. Watercolor on paper. 25.7 × 36 cm. Bridgeman Art Library International, New York, NY.

With her back to the hearth, Best's illumination comes from the sunny exterior world, and she holds a double position as a woman and an artist, part of both worlds yet at the margins of both as well. Like Amélie Cogniet, Best exploits the dynamics of the working space to portray the challenges facing the female visual artist. As Walker explains, "spatiality participates in the structuring and production of subjectivities and identities; as well as playing a crucial role as the site of contestation of meanings that in part determines ideas and feelings about social relations between genders, sexualities, age groups, and classes" (122).

Mary Ellen Best's scenes of Germany, Holland, and Belgium include both private and public interiors—homes and hotels, schools, orphanages, and a nunnery—which give her viewers an intimate portrait of domestic and quotidian lives across the Channel. Her focus on kitchens, bedrooms, and parlors, often populated by children and the detritus of family life, is notable in its privileging of a world at once foreign and entirely familiar. Outdoor scenes of marketplaces and street processions similarly highlight daily life and culture, much as Anna Mary Howitt's narrative, *An Art Student in Munich,* would do in 1853. In an image painted in the mid-1840s, Best portrays herself as an artist at work in the public sphere in a gesture that recalls Rolinda Sharples's self-portrait in the courtroom. *The Altpörtel, Speyer* (c. 1844) (figure 16) depicts, at center, the clock tower, which serves as the main gateway to the city, while in the foreground we see the female visual artist sketching the scene before her. With her back to the viewer, Best is absorbed in her work, but even in Germany the female artist is a source of curiosity for the crowd surrounding her. Melding local color, architecture, and self-portraiture, Best portrays herself in typical English garb, with a heavy dark shawl, lace collar, and straw bonnet, while the children before and around her, in much smaller scale than the British artist, wear the colorful skirts and tunics of the Rhineland region. Even as a pair of boys climbs upon the water pump to see her, Best towers over the group, mirroring perhaps the solidity of the building she paints. Once again at the edges of the scene, the female visual artist nonetheless remains confident and committed to her task, part of the landscape but always other.

A final, representative image of British women in the studio is found not on the canvas but on the page, in Anna Mary Howitt's *An Art Student in Munich*. A painter and writer (to be discussed in chapter 3), Howitt was actively committed to a professional career as an artist and like so many female painters of the period (including Best and Margaret Gillies), turned to the Continent to acquire the advanced artistic training not available to women in Britain. Along with friend and fellow painter, Jane Benham, Howitt traveled to Germany in 1850 to study with the history painter Wilhelm von Kaulbach. Anna Mary and Jane lived together (without parents or chaperone) and painted under Kaulbach's tutelage, pursuing art with a quasi-religious passion while also study-

Figure 16
Mary Ellen Best, *Altpörtal, Speyer*, c. 1844. Watercolor on paper. 33 × 22.5 cm. Private collection.

ing German language and culture. Before they left Britain, both women were commissioned to send back articles describing their experiences for a variety of periodicals: Benham for the *Literary Gazette* and *Art Journal,* Howitt for *Athenaeum, Household Words,* and Henry Chorley's *Ladies' Companion.*[55] In this sense, Anna Mary and Jane were ambassadors for the cause of the female artist abroad, and their widely circulated reflections on artistic life in Germany provided inspirational images for their readers. At the encouragement of her mother and Mrs Gaskell, Anna Mary compiled *An Art Student in Munich* from her letters and articles, publishing it in 1853 (with a second edition in 1880) to much popular acclaim.[56]

From the very first page, Howitt establishes her identity as "a woman studying Art,"[57] and the intimate address of the transcribed letters (presented with dates but without addressee) gives her readers a sense of immediacy and inclusion in the experiences of the "Art Student." The pursuit of art and artistic training, frequently described as a quasi-divine calling, is inextricably tied to space and place throughout the narrative. Denied admission as women to the Academy in Munich, the painters approach Kaulbach as "acolytes" in the hopes of being able to work in his studio. Addressing the master with "a reverence, a faith in him unspeakable," Howitt tells Kaulbach "how we longed *really to study;* how we had long loved and revered his works" (*Munich* 4), and the master's response—"Come and draw here; this room is entirely at your disposal . . . Every day, and as early as you like, and stay as long as there is daylight" (*Munich* 4)—is related in terms that elevate him to a god-like status. Howitt reflects, "As I left the studio, I could have fallen upon my knees, and returned fervent thanks to God, so mysterious was the fulfillment of my long-cherished poetical dream" (*Munich* 6). Once they have gained admittance on a daily basis, the students refer to the studio as "our art-temple" and Kaulbach becomes "the high priest" (*Munich* 40). If the studio in contemporary fiction took on aspects of a temple or sanctum for the male artist as a Romantic, deified figure, Howitt plays on these associations with the women's initiation into the consecrated space.

Indeed, access to the studio and the "rooms of their own" at their lodgings in Munich become integral to the narrative construction of the women's artistic identity. Howitt's description of the contents and decoration of their rooms transforms the domestic space into one that signifies their professional aspirations: "Last night we busily unpacked all our paintboxes, looked up, with delighted eagerness, porte-crayons, chalks, everything; chose out such anatomical drawings, and drawings from the antique, as we thought most worthy; we laid out our twin-copies of Wilson's *Vade-Mecum,*—even scraped our chalks, and thus had everything ready for starting" (*Munich* 9). Transforming their "pretty little sister bed-rooms" into expressions of their own artistic visions, the painters remove the prints and paintings hung by the owners and replace them with their own. The narrator "Anna" explains, "I fastened up my Raphael prints and my studies of color from the National Gallery, with one of Justina's lovely water-color landscapes . . . Clare's little bed-room presents pretty much the same appearance when the door is open, only that instead of my Raphael she has a clever copy of a Rembrandt, and a Christus Consolator instead of my Highland landscape" (*Munich* 16). Significantly, Howitt includes her own work and that of her "art-sisters" Justina (a thinly disguised Barbara Leigh Smith, to be discussed in chapter 3) and Clare (Jane Benham) alongside Old Master prints, positing not only their position in the artistic field but also the collective nature of their endeavor. From start to finish, this artistic education and identity is a shared, collaborative experience.

Where painted studio scenes used physical signifiers—canvases, easels, brushes, models—to denote professional identity, written narratives such as Howitt's focused equally on the inner life of the artist in the atelier. Anna's and Clare's experiences in Kaulbach's studio teach them new ways of seeing, feeling, and understanding the world and its representations; thus the exhaustively detailed descriptions of the studio and ekphrases of the paintings there are filtered through the artist narrator's developing consciousness and imagination in terms that resonate with Romantic and Ruskinian overtones. Where "your Englishman" would find the untamed landscape surrounding the studio "very untidy" and disparage "Kaulbach's wild field" and his equally tumultuous canvases (*Munich* 21), Howitt's narrator makes manifest her artistic identity by translating the German aesthetic for her non-artist English readers. She explains that Kaulbach's paintings, too often dismissed in "hasty judgment" by the English and French, must be understood as "*poems,* and new subjects treated in an original manner," reflecting and addressing "that dreamy imagination which invests all nature with a tender poetry, which gives an individual life to every bud and leaf,—that imagination which . . . has raised up an immortal band of musicians, philosophers, and artists!" (*Munich* 22). Her apprenticeship in the master's studio grants Howitt's "Anna" membership in this "immortal band," allowing her to perform the role of Virgil to her unenlightened audience and locating difference not in gender, but in artistic identity. In keeping with Carlyle and Ruskin, Howitt elevates the artist to the position of a "*Seer*" whose work manifests a power "with such a vividness of truth that your very soul is thrilled" (*Munich* 22) and the artist is "ennobled through his art, ennobling humanity" (*Munich* 37). The remainder of the lengthy text is in many ways a verbal transcription of these "ways of seeing," and if Howitt does not claim the status of a "Seer" for herself, she becomes a conduit for the artist's vision; an artist herself, she helps others to "see" and joins the ranks of those "ennobling humanity."

In contrast to painted studio scenes, Howitt's *Art Student in Munich* rarely depicts the women in the act of painting; instead, the narrative portrays German culture, landscape, and people through the eyes of the British female artist, while transforming the text into a visual experience for her readers as Germany itself becomes an atelier of sorts and the letters her canvas. Nonetheless, when "Justina" (Leigh Smith) comes to visit her "dear art sisters" the most important moment comes when her friends show her their studio in a scene that emphasizes both the journey and the space of artistic creation: "I was obliged to hold Justina's hand in mine, else nothing could have persuaded me that this was not one of my many dreams. We passed through the bushes; we stood under the vine, we opened the heavy grey door: we were in the little room. The clock ticked as loudly as usual; there stood the two sister easels, and a sister painting-blouse hung on each: the casts, the books, the green jug with flowers, all looked so familiar, that to set to work at once and fancy that I had only dreamed of Justina, seemed the most natural thing" (*Munich* 92). The passage highlights both gender and collectivity through the repetition of "sister easels, and a sister painting-blouse," affirming that they are women who indeed have a place in the studio, where they both live and, importantly, labor. Like the implied readers of her epistolary text, Howitt's Justina, "having now seen what we were beginning, and having taken into her memory all the features of the beloved little room" would later be able to "picture our lives when she should have again vanished" (*Munich* 92). Thus, the central (implied) image to be taken away from the art students in Munich is that of the pair of female students in the studio.

Finally, although Howitt confessed in her preface to donning rose-colored glasses in her memoir,[58] a conversation with a male painter hints at the darker side of the experience. When Howitt's Anna waxes rhapsodic on her love of Munich to a local artist, he immediately responds with a litany of all she *cannot* experience of artistic life. "There is one feature in Munich life from which you, unfortunately, as a woman, have been cut off," he explains, "the jovial, poetical, quaint life of the artists among themselves" (*Munich* 241), and goes on to elaborate the many traditions, festivals, and "odd usages," the "meetings at their Kneips," and "their masked balls, where all is deliciously artistic and poetic" (*Munich* 241) that were accessible only to the fraternity of male artists. At once part of the master's atelier and always other, Howitt's Anna and Clare construct an artistic identity together as "Sisters in Art" that will be fully elaborated in Howitt's novella of that name upon her return to England (and examined in chapter 3). Acknowledging difference, Howitt concludes *An Art Student in Munich* with a meditation on art, gender, and forms of equality:

> I cannot but believe that all in life that is truly noble, truly good, truly desirable, God bestows upon us women in as unsparing measure as upon men. He

only desires us, in His great benevolence, to stretch forth our hands and to gather for ourselves the rich joys of intellect, of nature, of study, of action, of love, and of usefulness, which He has poured forth around us. Let us only cast aside the false, silly veils of prejudice and fashion, which ignorance has bound about our eyes; let us lay bare our souls to God's sunshine of truth and love; let us exercise the intelligence which He has bestowed on us upon worthy and noble objects, and this intelligence may become keen as that of men; and the paltry high heels and whalebone supports of mere drawing-room conventionality and young ladyhood withering up, we shall stand in humility before God, but proudly and rejoicingly at the side of man! Different always, but not less noble, less richly endowed! (*Munich* 454)

Howitt's optimistic vision of women's ability to transcend social oppression through "earnestness and fixedness of purpose" reflects an idealism shared by many at mid-century, while at the same time proposing a role for the female artist not within the male brotherhood, but parallel to it, equally noble but always different.

For the British female painter—Sharples, Best, Howitt, Benham, and myriad others—aspiring to a career as a professional visual artist presented even more complex challenges than those faced by their French counterparts, most notably in the dearth of academies and studios in which to acquire training and, by extension, professional artistic identity. Notwithstanding these limitations, nineteenth-century British women gradually forged a place for themselves in the field of artistic cultural production: turning to private collections, private and group tutorials, and above all travel and study abroad, they attained artistic education. Exhibiting and selling their work in the public sphere, they claimed a place in the public imagination, and like their contemporaries in France (albeit in more limited numbers), they deliberately crafted an image of female artistic identity through self-portraits of the artist at work. This ideological labor—the political act of rendering visible the incomprehensible or unimaginable figure of the professional woman artist—took a variety of forms in Britain as in France, in novels and narratives as well as in paintings and drawings. Most notably, where French women frequently represented an integrated studio, with male and female painters sharing the working space in varying degrees of harmony, from Capet's idyllic scene to Cogniet's anxious one, British women reflected Howitt's formulation of "separate but equal," privileging rather than effacing gender difference. Singly and collectively, however, these images by women of women representing the world contributed to incontrovertible shifts in the structures and constructions of art, gender, and professionalism.

"Why Are You No Longer My Brothers?"

The *Fraternité des Arts* and the Female Artist in
Marceline Desbordes-Valmore's *L'Atelier d'un peintre*

The figure of the female artist was as anomalous in fiction as she was in the visual arts at the turn of the century, and remained largely "invisible" in Rancière's sense of the term until the onset of the July Monarchy.[1] By the early 1830s, the painter's atelier had become a popular setting for French fiction and served as a stage for male novelists to rehearse their own artistic vision either through the voice of the painter (in Nodier's *Le Peintre de Salzbourg*) or more commonly, in contradistinction to the painter, as in the cases of Balzac, the Goncourts, and Zola, among myriad others in the decades to follow.[2] As I have discussed elsewhere, male authors entered into an unspoken rivalry with the visual arts in the nineteenth century, and the failure of every fictional painter from Balzac's Frenhofer in 1831 to Zola's Claude Lantier in 1886 stands as testimony to the revival of Leonardo's *paragone* and the struggle for representational dominance in the bourgeois marketplace.[3] As will become clear in the chapters to follow, while female authors embraced the topos of the painter in the studio, they eschewed the rivalry between the sister arts for a close identification with the visual artist, employing tropes of similarity and solidarity to resist the dominant discourses of difference in the contemporary *Kunstlerroman*.

Part I: The Studio

Writing from the Margins:
THE FEMALE ROMANTIC POET

For Marceline Desbordes-Valmore (1786–1859), the most acclaimed female poet of the French Romantic era, artistic identity and difference were inextricably linked as gender was foregrounded in both her production and her reception. Although many women composed and even published Romantic poetry, Desbordes-Valmore was exceptionally successful, achieving a unique status in the ranks of the male Romantics. The only woman included among Verlaine's *poètes maudits* (1884), Desbordes-Valmore was celebrated during her lifetime by Hugo, Vigny, Béranger, Sainte-Beuve, Baudelaire, and Barbey d'Aurevilly, albeit in terms that consistently referred to her gender. Desbordes-Valmore's first book of poems, *Elégies, Marie et romances* (1819) appeared a year before Lamartine's *Méditations poétiques* (1820) and, argues Barbara Johnson, "could well be considered the starting point of a new style of French lyric poetry. With its personal and emotional tones and its renewal of the elegiac tradition, *Elégies, Marie et romances* presents many of the characteristics that have come to be associated with Romanticism."[4] Although Lamartine has since been credited with "fathering" Romantic poetry in France, Johnson posits "It is even possible that readers in 1820 turned to Lamartine as a way of marginalizing Marceline Desbordes-Valmore," reflecting "a certain ambivalence toward female power" (628).

This ambivalence was most often manifested in a gendered language of tempered praise that allowed Desbordes-Valmore to be an exceptional *woman* poet but never an equal to her male *confrères*. Martin Danahy argues that "in the formation of the literary canon, it is the authors themselves, the canonized, before and perhaps more than the future generations of critics, the canonizers, who divided up the literary genres according to gender roles. The literary canon was thus doubly 'en-gendered'; its formation results from an aesthetic code predetermined for each genre, but each genre is embodied in a gendered and gendering model that helps to situate its author in the canon."[5] If the novel had long been "feminized," poetry remained the most elevated and "masculine" of the literary genres. "A superior female poet," explains Danahy, "undermined the masculinization of the genre, for she created an anomaly in the categories of power and virility" (388). Thus, Desbordes-Valmore and her work were bracketed by her male peers and categorically considered in terms of their gendered identity: for Vigny she was "the greatest feminine mind of our time";[6] for Barbey d'Aurevilly, "the ultimate woman of talent" ("la femme la plus femme de talent"),[7] while Hugo allegorized her as "la femme même" and "la poésie même" ("woman herself" and "poetry itself").[8] Sainte-Beuve, the critic's critic of the nineteenth century and a long-time friend of Desbordes-Valmore, reflected in his preface to *Poésies de Madame Desbordes-Valmore* (1842): "she sang with no other science than the emotion of her heart, by no other means than the natural note."[9] Later in his *Memoirs of Madame Desbordes-Valmore* (1869), Sainte-Beuve stressed the female poet's life of suffering which was expressed in "the heart-rending but always humble and submissive moan of her whom I do not hesitate to call the Mater Dolorosa of poetry" (116). And in *Réflexions sur quelques-uns de mes contemporains* (1869), Baudelaire's carefully chosen words epitomize the position of the *fraternité des poètes* vis-à-vis Desbordes-Valmore: "Mme Desbordes-Valmore was a woman, was always a woman and was only, absolutely a woman; but she was to an extraordinary degree the poetic expression of all of the beauties natural to woman."[10]

By extensively lauding the "natural" and "feminine" aspects of her poetry and attributing the "artless" verse to "instinct" and "spontaneity," rather than skill or genius, Baudelaire, Sainte-Beuve, and the Romantic cohort refuse the female poet the status of a true artist, as if the work were excreted rather than crafted by the author. For even as these qualities of natural expression and spontaneous emotion were validated within the Romantic aesthetic (if not entirely by Baudelaire), they were tropes and techniques, vehicles for virtuoso performances more than invitations for real feeling. But perhaps most importantly, by identifying "femininity" with the female poet, the male Romantics could establish difference within the genre, distancing themselves from the feminine while at the same time "colonizing" as Alan Richardson argues, "the conventionally feminine domain of sensibility."[11] In this sense, Desbordes-Valmore served as Other to the Romantic poets, embodying difference (and implicitly inferiority) and allowing them to establish the masculine nature of their own production. Thus, while Desbordes-Valmore was acknowledged as a Romantic, she was nonetheless relegated to the margins of the artistic field. It was, however, from this (arguably Romantic) position at the margins that the female poet asserted her own identity as an artist, reclaiming the feminine for a Romantic aesthetic that could encompass female subjects and poets on equal footing with their male counterparts.

One of the many distinguishing features of Desbordes-Valmore's poetry is its dialogic nature. Having begun her artistic life as a highly successful actress, she brought a dramatic sensibility to her poems, vividly engaging with interlocutors and introducing musical, conversational rhythms to her verse.[12] Frequently we find woman speaking to woman—a mother, a daughter, a sister, a friend—though the lover, or absent lover, is also a frequent addressee. Moreover, through her titles, dedications, apostrophes, and allusions, Desbordes-Valmore invoked contemporary authors, including many of what Aimée Boutin has called the "sorority of poets"—Sophie Gay, Amable Tastu, and Elisa Mercoeur, among others.[13] Less often examined, however, and perhaps less obvious, is her dialogue with male poets and authors, in which she responds to their limitations and interdictions in an ironic and often playful but also pointed way. In 1831, following the publication of her three-volume *Poésies complètes de Mme Desbordes-Valmore,* Lamartine penned a 105-line poem, "To Madame Desbordes-Valmore," in which he distinguished between male and female poetry.[14] Returning to his metaphor of the poet as a boat (made famous in "Le Lac"), he develops a phallic image of the firm mast of the male vessel "vigorously" withstanding the wind and waves of the tempest, for "the vast sea is his empire, / His horizon has nothing but smiles / And the universe lies before him." Conversely, the female poet is a humble skiff, battered by the waves, its sails shredded by the gales. Lamartine proclaims: "This poor boat, oh Valmore / Is the image of your destiny."[15] In the guise of a sympathetic tribute to the hardships of her life, Lamartine employs a series of violent images that portray the metaphoric female poet lost at sea, her realm a "foyer flottant" (a floating household), her verses "broken like a glass . . . beneath the feet of fate."

Desbordes-Valmore's response appeared in *Les Pleurs* in 1833, the same year she published *L'Atelier d'un peintre,* and in "To M. Alphonse de Lamartine" she masterfully reworks his images so that the storm is not "destin," but a human construct, for she is "unknown" and "forgotten" ("tout m'ignore ou m'oublie") and suffering in a polyvalent obscurity that reflects a poetic ("my name is dead before me") as well as emotional state. Unseen and unheard, the poetic narrator is saved by the "angel" Lamartine whose words bring illumination: "from the heights of his sublime flight / Lamartine threw my name, / As from an invisible peak, / To the boat, on the edge of the abyss, / The heavens, touched, threw a beam of light."[16] Skating a fine line between the sincere and the potentially sardonic,[17] Desbordes-Valmore intones:

> I am a feeble woman;
> I have known only how to love and to suffer;
> My poor lyre is my soul,
> And you alone uncover the flame
> Of a lamp that is going to expire.
>
> Before your hymns of a poet,
> At once the words of an angel, alas! and a man,
> This uncultivated, incomplete lyre,
> Long set aside and silent,
> Barely dares to take a voice.
>
> I am the indigent gleaner
> Who, from a few forgotten kernels

Has adorned her thorny sheaf,
When your luminous charity
Pours some pure wheat at my feet.

The obvious tension between this disclaimer and her poetry, between the persona of "faible femme," silent and meek, and the woman who had already published six volumes in the preceding decade, reveals Desbordes-Valmore's own strategy of resistance. Implicitly acknowledging the power of the male voice, she also implicitly gestures to his role, as a god-like force ("voix puissante . . . voix d'en haut . . . comme si Dieu m'eût répondu"), in shaping her own reception. In the third stanza above, Desbordes-Valmore's trope of the female poet as gleaner (*glaneuse*) who takes the discarded "épis" (ears of wheat) and turns them into a "thorny sheaf" (*gerbe épineuse*) plays precisely on the movement from *épi* to *épineuse*, that is the double sense (in both French and English) of thorny as literally and figuratively prickly, troubling, and barbed. By portraying her poetry (the sheaf of wheat suggesting a sheaf of poems) as vexed and vexing, she recognizes the problematic nature of her creation for poets like Lamartine and his Romantic brethren who seek to delimit her position within the field of cultural production to a prescribed place at the margins.[18]

Conceding the power of the male poet, Desbordes-Valmore nonetheless refuses his construction of her artistic identity. Recrafting Lamartine's image of the female poet as a broken vessel smashed upon the shore by the storms of fate, she proposes a poetic persona whose fate is shaped by human and social forces but who can claim a voice ("prendre une voix") alongside the "Poète" himself. In the final stanza, she addresses Lamartine directly, questioning the very idea of difference so central to his own poem dedicated to her. "But you," she begins, "whose glory is complete / Beneath its beautiful aegis of flowers, / Poet! Tell the truth, has your powerful light / Stopped many of the tears gathered in your eyes?" Desbordes-Valmore suggests that male or female, in the light of glory or the darkness of obscurity, the nature of the poet is inescapably tied to suffering. Despite his power and her lack thereof, she proposes they are more similar than different, thus claiming her own identity as Poet alongside Lamartine. Including his poem *after* hers in *Les Pleurs,* Desbordes-Valmore ensures that they be read as a dialogue, while at the same time subordinating Lamartine's stanzas to her own.

A similar thematic informs *L'Atelier d'un peintre,* in which the author recounts the life and death of a female painter in the male studio. This early novel is most often read as a *roman à clef* based on Desbordes-Valmore's experiences in her uncle Constant Desbordes's studio, where she lived and studied with the successful painter on and off between 1819 and 1822.[19] Yet, on a more complex level the novel also presents an allegorical portrait of the female

Romantic artist, highlighting the poet's vision of gender, identity, and difference in the male dominated field of cultural production. While the grounding in real experience is significant, for the accuracy of Desbordes-Valmore's image of the atelier and its inhabitants only adds to its legitimacy, *L'Atelier d'un peintre* is most fruitfully read in dialogue with the already mythic construction of the Romantic artist and the studio found in paintings, novels, and criticism of the period. Her novel challenges some of the most fundamental assumptions of the genre of the contemporary *Kunstlerroman* while at the same presenting an alternative portrait of the Romantic artist as a woman.

Balzac and the Female Artist:
LA VENDETTA

In poetry, Lamartine served as Desbordes-Valmore's primary male interlocutor, but in this novel of 1833 it is Balzac, with whom she had recently become acquainted,[20] that the poet engages in direct and indirect ways. In the early 1830s, as Balzac began to develop his Realist aesthetic, the painter became the author's dark Other, manifesting his anxieties of failure in art, life, and love. Three of his early novels—*La Maison du chat qui pelote* (1829), *Sarrasine* (1830), and *Le Chef-d'oeuvre inconnu* (1831)—reprise the *paragone* in their competitive portraits of painters who are blind to the world around them and whose *oeuvres* are ultimately obliterated in violent scenes of destruction, as the written word rises triumphant.[21] Balzac, ever a barometer of ambient social anxiety, reflected rivalries of gender in his fiction as well. By the end of the Restoration, women's activism in the social, political, and artistic arenas, coupled with the ideas of sexual freedom and female equality proposed in the Saint-Simonian and Fourierist movements, began to exert pressure on conceptions of gender roles and social structures in France that led in turn to efforts by some to reassert traditional hierarchies. These struggles for power were both reflected and negotiated in contemporary fiction and art: Balzac's novels manifest the author's desire to "put women back in their place"[22] by punishing his "unfeminine" women of learning or ambition with mockery, misery, and even death. Richard Bolster notes that "class war was joined by a war between the sexes" in the French novel after 1830.[23]

This artistic "war between the sexes" was exacerbated by the increasing influence of female authors and female readers in the literary marketplace. The author of *La Comédie humaine* remarked, "A *woman's novel* is a much better speculation on fame than a manly work,"[24] while his contemporary, Stendhal, concurred, noting: "All the women in France read novels . . . There is scarcely a woman in the provinces who does not read five to six volumes a month, and many read fifteen or twenty."[25] This avid female audience frequently turned to female authors publishing novels, serialized fiction, and poetry in ever-increasing numbers during the July Monarchy, and the popularity of women writers presented an unheralded challenge to the male author in his own quest for readership, profit, and prestige. Male authors thus entered into an unspoken rivalry with the growing ranks of female authors, while at the same time working concertedly toward the "masculinization" of what had long been considered a "feminine" genre.[26]

Indeed, as women established their positions in the *champ littéraire* of nineteenth-century France, disrupting ideologies of art and gender, male authors, like male painters, struggled to assert or reclaim their previous positions of cultural dominance by establishing the masculinity of their genre while demonstrating the incompatibility of women, as reproducers, with artistic creation. Both tales of female painters to which I now turn—Balzac's *La Vendetta* (1830) and Desbordes-Valmore's *L'Atelier d'un peintre: Scènes de la vie privée* (1833)—highlight the fictional atelier as an overdetermined setting for negotiations of authorial identity as well as painterly, while questions of gender, genre, subject position, and creation are foregrounded in these stories of women, art, and power.

Balzac locates his morality tale of the dangers of female artists within the realm of the resolutely political. The story begins in 1800 with a brief scene depicting the arrival of a Corsican family at the Tuileries, then the entrance to the Louvre. The home to royal painters and the *Académie* since the seventeenth century, the Louvre was also a royal palace and the residence of Napoleon, with whom the Corsicans seek an audience. Recognizing his countrymen, the First Consul offers Bartoloméo di Piombo, his wife, and daughter support and protection in France. This seemingly tangential episode, preceding the action of the story by fifteen years, sets up the affiliation between the émigrés and Napoleon, establishing both their outsider status and the theme of usurpation, for Balzac was a passionate royalist. By opening in the courtyard of the Louvre, the author subtly evokes the Academy and the studios of the "dix-neuf Illustres," the nineteen artists chosen by the king to inhabit the apartments at the royal palace, their officially sanctioned legitimacy standing in proleptic contrast to the female atelier that will be central to the rest of the narrative. Moreover, this literal juxtaposition of art and politics within the buildings of the Louvre suggests metaphoric connections between the realms of representation and power that will be developed in Balzac's tale.

The rest of the story unfolds in 1815 in the studio of Servin, a distinguished painter who supports himself by giving lessons to rich young ladies of only the best families but who refuses to teach "young girls who wanted to become artists."[27] By insisting on girls without ambition, Servin assures his popularity with aristocratic mothers who seek *arts d'agrément* for their marriageable daughters, and his students are trained "to judge paintings at the museum, make a striking portrait, copy an ancient master, and compose a genre scene" (1040). With the fall of Napoleon and the restoration of the Bourbon monarchy, the studio has been divided between the aristocratic monarchists and the bourgeois Bonapartists. The girls segregate into warring camps within the atelier, in an image of rivalry and discord that contrasts with the scene of amicable harmony in Grandpierre-Deverzy's Restoration studio (figure 8). Physically staking out different sections of the atelier, the aristocratic Amélie moves the easel of Ginevra di Piombo to a distant corner, ostracizing the beautiful and talented arriviste for her fidelity to the fallen Napoleon who had bestowed wealth, power, and a title upon her father. Ginevra, the most gifted painter in the studio, has aroused the animosity of her classmates both for her politics and for her talents, which set her apart from other women in literal as well as metaphoric ways. Compounding her otherness, the foreign-born *Bonapartiste* has furthermore refused marriage, for "her taste for painting had replaced the passions that ordinarily excite women" (1047). Balzac's female painter is, from the outset, distanced from other women both physically and temperamentally.

From her position at the back of the atelier, Ginevra's curiosity is aroused by mysterious sounds emanating from a closet, and, like the wayward students peering out the window of Pujol's studio, she becomes a voyeur, reversing the gendered structures of vision. Climbing up on a chair, she peeks through a crack in the partition and discovers a sleeping soldier, and thus an active female gaze is directed upon a passive and unknowing male body. Recognizing the imperial eagle on the soldier's uniform, she realizes that he is a political refugee (*un proscrit*) and the fleeting image that Ginevra retains is "as graceful as that of the Endymion, that she had copied several days earlier" (1051–52). Girodet's *Le Sommeil d'Endymion* (1791), which Balzac uses as a central image in *Sarrasine* as well, was a revolutionary representation of ephebic heroism. The image of Endymion's passive androgyny posed a fleeting ideal of masculine beauty that had come, by the onset of the July Monarchy, to signal for Balzac the impotent Romantic rhetoric of the failed Republic and Empire. The painting's inversion of gender hierarchies, in the boy ravished by the implied gaze of Diana, is echoed by the Realist author in this tale of female art, vision, and ultimately destruction.[28]

For the conservative and territorial author, the female artist further represented the traversal of boundaries that can bring social and artistic disaster. When Ginevra meets her soldier, sheltered by the liberal Servin, she assures him that *she* can take care of *him*—she is rich, he is poor; she is strong, he is weak, and love blossoms between the clandestine Bonapartists. In an obvious reference to the Napoleonic soldier's emasculation, on his forearm is a "long, wide wound made by the blade of a sabre." When Ginevra sees it unwrapped, "she shivered" and "let forth a moan" while her lover "began to smile" (1058). The young painter returns home to her aging parents (now a baron and a baroness), and announces her decision to marry the penniless soldier. In a continuation of the unhealthy hierarchical inversions of this tale, her adoring and powerful father has been dominated by this brilliant and beautiful daughter. His love for Ginevra has resulted in "a very great ill: Ginevra lived with her father and mother on the basis of an equality that is always fatal" (1068–69). Thus, although her father forbids the union, the female painter ignores his edict, and when it is discovered that her lover is none other than Luigi Porta, the sole survivor of a vendetta carried out by Piombo some fifteen years earlier, Ginevra's love is redoubled. Rejecting her family for her family's enemy, in an ironic Romeo and Juliet redux, Ginevra braves her father's attack with a dagger and marries Luigi. Disowned by her parents, Ginevra and her husband both go to work: she copies paintings, while he copies out manuscripts, his only marketable skill being his elegant handwriting, and for a brief while, their derivative arts prove profitable. But soon the market changes, and both Luigi and Ginevra confront artistic rivals even poorer than they, who will produce copies for even less, leaving the young couple penniless. The final blow comes when the artist gives birth to a son. Entering the more "natural" world of motherhood, her artistic reproductions are replaced by biological reproduction, but it is too late for the impoverished couple. By the end of the tale, the entire family has succumbed, destroyed by the imprudent inversions of familial, artistic, and gender hierarchies.

Balzac presents the female painter only to destroy her, asserting the dominance of male creation. Indeed, the very idea of revenge or retribution found in the title, *La Vendetta,* linked to feuding families and retaliatory destruction, points to a deep violence motivating the structure of this tale. On a literal level, if Bartoloméo di Piombo's vendetta on the Porta family ultimately failed to destroy the last son, the Porta family's own vendetta is indirectly carried out upon the Piombi through the errant daughter who destroys both families equally. On a metaphoric level, Balzac's own vendetta on his artistic rivals—women and painters—ends with his destruction of the ambitious, transgressive Ginevra who embodies the dangerous, feminizing influence of women's artistic and literary endeavors. Thus, *La Vendetta* takes its place alongside *La Maison du chat-qui-pelote, Sarrasine,* and *Le Chef-d'oeuvre inconnu* as a concomitant announcement of the young author's nascent aesthetic and bid for a position within the field of cultural production in post-revolutionary France. With the collapse of political and artistic hierarchies, Balzac's anxieties are intensified by the perceived collapse of gender hierarchies as well. The theme of the competition between the sister arts is intensified when the sister artist is female, and here the female painter further stands as a thinly veiled substitute for the disruptive presence of the female author in the *champ littéraire*. Ginevra's ambitious move into the male world of art, representation, and power brings on her demise in a cathartic move for the author who felt the threat of the "unnatural" female authors who were similarly claiming a voice and an audience in post-revolutionary France. In this double-edged attack on his competition, Balzac conflates women and painters in a single image of failure and destruction. Through tropes of imitation, tracery, reproduction, and childbirth, Balzac highlights the differences of gender and genre that render the female painter a failure while the male author rises triumphant.

Desbordes-Valmore and the Female Artist:
L'ATELIER D'UN PEINTRE

By titling her novel *L'Atelier d'un peintre: Scènes de la vie privée*, Desbordes-Valmore makes direct reference to Balzac's own collection of stories, *Scènes de la vie privée* of 1830, a publication that included both *La Maison du chat-qui-pelote* and *La Vendetta*. At the same time, her title juxtaposes the world of art with the private sphere, not only promising a tale of the inner workings of the studio and the interior life of the artist but also perhaps hinting at her shift of focus from the public sphere, traditionally gendered male, to the domestic or private sphere, generally associated with the feminine. In her Preface, Desbordes-Valmore announces her strategies for establishing the legitimacy of the female artist in the Romantic atelier, using this paratextual space as what Gérard Genette has called a zone of "transaction" between author and reader. As Genette explains, the preface (like other paratextual matter) serves as "a privileged place of pragmatics and a strategy" allowing the author to shape "a better reception for the text and a more pertinent reading of it."[29] For Desbordes-Valmore, who writes under her own name and signs the preface as such, these opening pages before the body of text become the site of subtle assertion where the female author claims both authority and her own artistic identity. In marked contrast to Sand and many other contemporary women who wrote under male pseudonyms, disguising themselves in the paratext, Desbordes-Valmore establishes the connection between the fictitious female painter and the real female author from the first sentence, grounding the narrative to follow in first-hand experience. Opening the Preface with the phrase "Ces souvenirs chers" (these precious memories), she enters into a direct dialogue with her reader, and this "transaction," to use Genette's phrase, lays the groundwork for an implied reading that locates the source of the "fiction" in the "real," inviting the audience to interpret her tale in ways that reflect on Desbordes-Valmore's own career, and those of her fellow female creators. Significantly, the Preface is further couched in terms that highlight a distinctly Romantic aesthetic and, by extension, a Romantic identity for the female author, whose "souvenirs" are evoked in melancholy terms as "faded flowers" that will elicit "warm tears."

Thus, where Balzac is at great pains to demonstrate the *unnatural* status of the female artist in *La Vendetta*, Desbordes-Valmore continues her Preface to *L'Atelier d'un peintre* by insisting on the natural parallels between women and artists. Mapping the home and the atelier as similar realms of private suffering, she avows "The woman who is born, lives, and dies close to home, the artist who spends his days in solitude [. . .] each have both their despairs and their celestial joys."[30] With an emphasis on literal and figurative interiority, Desbordes-Valmore's comparison signals the metaphoric importance of space in the narrative to follow, while at the same time underlining the fundamental commonalities between women and artists and foregrounding the very imbrications that male artists sought so anxiously to deny. The "feminine" nature of the Romantic artist—isolated, sensitive, suffering—is naturalized in the female painter from the outset of her novel, much as it is in her poetry. Desbordes-Valmore's opening salvo thus highlights what was habitually obscured or repressed, disrupting the fixed categories of gender and artistic genius by directly identifying the feminine *as embodied in the female* with the Romantic artist who can be, within her formulation, just as easily a woman as a man. Turning from lyric poetry to the novel and to the painter's atelier, Desbordes-Valmore makes the case for a Romantic artistic identity that transcends the differences of gender and genre. Yet difference remains central to *L'Atelier d'un peintre*, as Desbordes-Valmore reflects the position of the female artist in the nineteenth century.

Situating her story within the discourses of the atelier past and present, Desbordes-Valmore's Preface exploits the vocabulary of mystical initiation and arcana so common to the fictional and historical accounts of artists' lives published during the July Monarchy.[31] Eschewing the distance of a neutral narrator, however, her Preface identifies the work to follow as the "precious memories" of "a woman who found herself initiated into such mysteries . . . of this little known life" (7–8), establishing both the author's and, by extension, her protagonist's membership in the artistic elite. Desbordes-Valmore thus indicates that it will be a woman who will translate and interpret for the reader the secret life of the atelier and, like Howitt to follow, claims the role of a female Virgil. Otherness, an existence apart requiring explanation and illumination, is located not necessarily in gender but rather in artistic identity.

She concludes the Preface by continuing to consolidate not only the author and her character, but also their respective arts. In a traditional disclaimer of authority that asserts precisely what it purports to deny, Desbordes-Valmore professes: "Unskilled in the art of the novelist, she can only present, in a frame that will emphasize them, the touching riches of the subject that she wants to paint" (9). This parallel between writing and painting, and between the female author and her fictional female painter, reveals a sympathy for and identification with the sister art of painting not found in Balzac's agonistic narratives in his *Scènes de la vie privée,* nor indeed in many male-authored tales of visual artists published during the period. Desbordes-Valmore thus signals to the reader, who may expect an opposition between the positions of the author and the fictitious painter, that her story will reflect a kinship, rather than a rivalry, between the sister arts and sister artists. Here, the difficulties facing the female painter will reflect the author's own struggles for legitimacy and expression in the masculinist world of Romantic poetry, while her more idealistic vision of cooperation rather than competition between genders and genres reveals the poet's hopes for all creators. As she shifts from the engaged first-person voice of the Preface to the more neutral third-person of the body of the narrative, these themes of female artistic identity, Romanticism, and collectivity will be developed in ways that allow the reader, thus primed by the Preface, to recognize Desbordes-Valmore's challenge to the mythos of Romantic masculinity.

The story begins in the painter's studio with the young artist, Ondine, who lives and studies with her uncle Léonard. In the opening lines of the tale, the master addresses his niece, "Du talent, mademoiselle, du talent!" (13), linking the ideas of women, art, and talent from the outset. In this predominantly masculine milieu, Ondine is immediately identified as a member of the artistic community; in keeping with the construction of Romantic identity, she is continually lost in "éternelles rêveries" (10). In contrast to the political and hierarchical rivalries that marked Balzac's exclusive, all-female studio, Léonard's inclusive studio is open to rich and poor alike, and Desbordes-Valmore creates an artistic world of male and female painters where "a spirit of concord and equality reigned." The very concept of equality, at the core of the crisis in *La Vendetta,* will conversely be posited as an ideal in this tale of a female artist. By extension, there is equality rather than hierarchy established between words and images. Ondine is a writer as well as a painter who composes letters to her sister throughout the tale, both for herself and for her uncle. In an early exchange, he says to his niece, "Read me this draft; I wouldn't mind seeing once again (*revoir*) what I was thinking then; every year our ideas change as much as our faces do. A letter is the portrait of the soul that paints itself there the day it is written" (17). Once again linking her own craft and that of her character, Desbordes-Valmore asks us to see the poet as painter and the painter as poet, rendering concrete the Romantic *fraternité des arts* as she constructs a collective identity that includes women and men, painters and poets under the title of Artist.

The metaphor of family is central to the narrative, but in ways that again offer a contrast to Balzac's image of the riven relations of *La Vendetta.*

Desbordes-Valmore extends the intimacy of Ondine and her uncle to artists in general. Members of a race apart, "a nation distinct from all others" (23), artists have their own language, gestures, and group identity; when two painters meet on the street, even as strangers they will recognize each other as "their family, their sublime, their humble family" (24). Significantly, Desbordes-Valmore chooses the inclusive term, *famille,* over the restrictive *fraternité,* subtly shifting the metaphor of artistic relations from an exclusively male cohort to one that embraces male and female alike. While Ondine's presence in the atelier as the niece of the master reflects the reality of many women's training, the studio itself functions as a family (rather than a brotherhood) in which the female painter is, at least initially, included. In the larger senses of the words, *fraternité* and *egalité,* linked to revolutionary ideals within the French collective consciousness, are privileged here as values that pertain not simply to male *citoyens* but to all.

Léonard's atelier is located in the ruins of a convent, a powerful reminder of revolution that invokes the popular Romantic image of art as a religion as well.[32] At the same time, the combination of two powerfully symbolic spaces—the convent gesturing to female spirituality and retreat, the studio denoting male artistic creation—creates a hybrid realm of inspiration shared by male and female acolytes. Desbordes-Valmore's description of the atelier, located in the upper reaches of the crumbling building and reached only by ladder, functions on both a literal and a symbolic level, in keeping with the conventions of the genre. Revealing the identity of its inhabitants, the crowded studio is full of sketches, plaster casts, and easels, its damp walls decorated with two sacred images: a portrait of Raphael and one of M. Léonard's mother, a painting which resembles Ondine, thus foregrounding her own potential as both artistic and maternal creator. Surrounding the paintings of the two progenitors of the artist are "casts of hands, Mercury's winged feet, the arms of a child molded from life, a skull, and a frame with butterflies" (24). These hands and feet reflect the nature of an art based on both direct observation of the real ("les mains modèles") and the mythic ("les pieds ailés du Mercure"), while the child and the skull summon forth the birth and deaths that will take place in the atelier in the course of the story. "Le cadre aux papillons" is an image of ephemeral beauty captured in art, yet at the same time reflecting curtailed freedom and death. It is worth noting that these images also render concrete central themes in Desbordes-Valmore's own poetry, which focused on birth, death, fragmentation, the body, and nature.

In the first of many references to real painters of the post-revolutionary period, Léonard's upstairs neighbor and artistic hero is the proto-Romantic Girodet, who also haunts Balzac's artistic novels of the period. In Desbordes-Valmore's tale (as in Balzac's), Girodet is an absent presence, but if he is evoked in almost entirely negative ways *chez* Balzac as a model of fetishistic failure, he serves as a more benign, if mystified, force here.[33] In a striking early conversation between Ondine and her uncle, they discuss Girodet's *Scène de Déluge* of 1806. An epic image which won the Prix Décennie in 1810 (defeating David's *Rape of the Sabine Women*), the *Scene of a Deluge* portrays a man burdened by the weight of the generations. With his father clinging to his back, the central figure grasps his wife's outstretched arm as she teeters on the brink of the precipice below him, children clutching her from both sides. The vertical composition emphasizes the taut energy of the straining muscles of husband and wife, while the latter seems fated to plunge into the roiling waves below. While Léonard praises its brilliance, Ondine offers up a critique not of the aesthetics but of the narrative that simultaneously elides the importance of the female figure and her emotion. The young painter objects to the composition that privileges the father over the spouse, who is sacrificed by a husband who "is no longer worried about his wife." Symbolically, Girodet's composition, as it is evoked here, reflects the patriarchal orientation of both art and society, fixated on the past while the future, embodied by the mother and her children, slip from the hero's grasp into the void. The contorted female figure, whose expression is echoed by another woman floating in the water below, is rendered strange by Ondine, who observes that she "doesn't show a single sign of emotion or suffering . . . the calm of this mother surprises me." Her uncle's response: "It is that she is first of all a mother, my dear" (32–33), reveals the ideologies of art, culture, and gender of the period that posited female identity in a naturalized maternal stoicism and sacrifice. While Desbordes-Valmore's poetry frequently focuses on the themes of motherhood, suffering, and loss, both her verse and her novel offer forth a female subjectivity entirely absent not only from Girodet's canvas but also from Romantic art and literature in general. Ondine's objection to the great painter's subordination of the woman's emotion to her husband's draws the reader's attention to the shaping force of gendered subject position in both the production and consumption of art. As both a mother and an artist, Desbordes-Valmore seeks to reverse the structure of the allegorical sacrifice and embrace a future freed of the burden of the patriarchal past.

Aesthetically, Ondine prefers the more contemporary Prud'hon (closely linked to Constance Mayer, a leading female painter of the day) because "his paintings delight my eyes and it seems to me there is something sad that speaks from their depths" (29). But even more than in the images of these revered painters and their manufactured emotion, she finds beauty in "a smooth pebble on the water's edge, a festoon of lilac escaping the walls of the boulevard, a sheep walking down the road" (34). Ondine's aesthetic preference of nature over great men and their creations delineates a Romantic taste available equally to both genders. Embracing the direct experience and observation of nature over a more mediated appreciation of history, myth, and human drama, Ondine and Desbordes-Valmore privilege an art that can also be made by women and the uninitiated. Unlike history painting, dependent on academic training and extensive knowledge of privileged discourses, Romantic scenes of natural beauty are accessible to anyone with talent, imagination, and feeling. Again, Desbordes-Valmore closely links the female artist to a Romantic aesthetic, but in contradistinction to her critics, who saw in the woman poet a different (and inferior) sensibility, here Ondine's "natural" predilections are those of a more generalized, "masculine" Romanticism.

The only female member of a male atelier, Ondine shares little with the vicious female dilettantes of *La Vendetta* who were deliberately screened for professional ambition, and here the heroine secretly dreams of glory and "future recognition" (38). Although she hides her hopes from her uncle and fellow students, Desbordes-Valmore's heroine identifies her real-life role model as the enormously successful Hortense Lescot. The female painter, whose name "is on everyone's lips" at the Salon and whose tableaux were attracting "the eyes and souls of the swirling crowds" brings both hope and pride to the young artist, for Lescot "had just inscribed a woman's name among the prize winners of the French school" (39–40). One of the best-known women artists of her time, Hortense Haudebourt-Lescot (1784–1845) exhibited more than 100 paintings to great acclaim at the Salon from 1810–40, and was awarded a first-class medal in 1828 (see chapter 4). Like Desbordes-Valmore, who began her artistic career as an actress, Haudebourt-Lescot started out as a dancer, and each attracted the praise and support of the famous composer, André Grétry; both married relatively late and hyphenated their names to reflect their own *noms de famille* as well as their husband's patronyms; and each carved a place for herself in a male dominated field of artistic expression.[34] For Ondine, Lescot serves as inspiration and role model, creating a virtual community while at the same time counterbalancing Girodet and Raphael in the story's own structure of artistic genealogies, much in the spirit of Capet's 1808 portrait of Labille-Guiard at work. When Ondine is alone in her corner of the studio, the memory of the female artist's triumph at the Salon encourages and inspires her "as she searches the past for some counsel to support her vague hopes for the future" (40).

It is emblematic of Desbordes-Valmore's desire to highlight the viability of a woman's success in the art world that Lescot's name is frequently mentioned throughout her tale. But beyond her renown, Lescot serves as an important referent in Desbordes-Valmore's novel at a number of other levels. For indeed, if we may consider *L'Atelier d'un peintre* a verbal self-portrait, Haudebourt-Lescot's groundbreaking *Self-Portrait* of 1825 (figure 17) stands as a visual intertext for both Desbordes-Valmore's own project and that of her female painter,

Ondine. Although women artists like Vigée-Lebrun and Kauffman frequently incorporated reference to the Old Masters in their *autoportraits,* they usually alluded to female subjects of the past, taking care to highlight their own beauty as well as accomplishment. In her 1825 painting, Lescot turns to the Old Masters as well, but in a radical departure from her foremothers, crafts her own portrait of the artist as a middle-aged woman directly after the male model. Thus, where Vigée-Lebrun's alluring *Self-Portrait in a Straw Hat* (c. 1763) playfully alludes to Rubens's painting of Susanna Luden, the *Chapeau de Paille* (1620–25), Lescot chooses Raphael's image of Baldassare Castiglione of 1515 as her inspiration, a painting that was also copied by Rembrandt for his own self-portrait. She opens up a dialogue with the present and the past by necessitating a comparison between the female painter and the male artist, rather than his female subject. Moreover, the very question of the copy, and of originality, is at once foregrounded and obviated, for by placing herself within a long tradition of artistic quotations and intertexts, Lescot posits herself as a modern-day Dibutades tracing the images of her male predecessors, who traced those before them.[35] This subdued but confident portrait echoes Raphael's muted palette and the solemn gaze of Castiglione, while highlighting Lescot's intellectual and artistic status rather than her beauty. In choosing the author of *The Courtier* (1528) as her primary visual referent, Lescot invokes a book that gives voice to women as well as men,[36] while also alluding to her own unprecedented success in Italy (see chapter 4).

The most successful female painter of her generation, she was awarded government commissions, was widely reproduced in prints and engravings, and was the sole female artist to be included in François-Joseph Heim's *Charles X Distributing Prizes to Artists at the Salon of 1824.* Yet despite her success, Lescot was not unaware of her contested position within the male-dominated field, and she encodes her own assertion of professional status in this *autoportrait.* Eschewing the fashionable finery of an earlier generation of women painters, she wears the artist's beret, like Rembrandt before her, and even more audaciously includes a gold chain around her neck, the mark of artistic favor conferred by a monarch, traditionally dated back to Titian. Though Lescot had not earned the right to the chain, neither had Rembrandt, and she engages in a self-conscious creation of artistic identity that plays off of female accoutrements—hats and jewelry—recrafting them into symbols of her position in the male *champ artistique.*

Desbordes-Valmore was engaged in similar negotiations for recognition in the male dominated field of literature, and Haudebourt-Lescot's successful reworking of the male model is echoed in the author's dialogue with Balzac's contemporary fiction and Romantic poetry in general. While *La Vendetta* is the most obvious intertext, it is not incidental that she chose a female painter whose name homophonously echoes that of the courtesan-model, Catherine

Figure 17
Hortense Haudebourt-Lescot, *Self-Portrait*, 1825. Oil on canvas. 74 × 60 cm. Photo credit: Réunion des Musées Nationaux/Art Resource, NY.

Lescault, from his *Chef-d'oeuvre inconnu*. In this influential story of 1831, the response to the anxieties aroused by female artists in the marketplace takes on an even more aggressive/repressive form. If Balzac's Ginevra is condemned to death in *La Vendetta* after she has entered the public sphere as a painter, she has nonetheless enjoyed some small success as an artist before her undoing. In the *Chef-d'oeuvre inconnu*, the female painter is erased entirely, as the gifted Lescot is transformed into the absent Lescault, reduced to the passive subject of an impossible painting, rather than the active agent of art. Hortense Lescot, the most significant woman artist of the July Monarchy, is metamorphosed in Balzac's Pygmalion redux into a naked courtesan destroyed by the male painter, Frenhofer, who buries her form beneath a wall of paint and later burns the canvas. Catherine Lescault is a woman who is not a woman, but an illegible representation; she is a woman in the atelier who is given neither voice nor ultimately form, metaphorically negating the representational power of her corporeal artistic counterpart.

For Desbordes-Valmore, well aware of Balzac's attitudes toward women artists of every genre, *L'Atelier d'un artiste* serves as a corrective counter-discourse to these misogynistic fantasies. By providing a narrative that validates the lives and productions of female painters, both real and fictitious, while simultaneously demonstrating the talents of a female author, she works within and against the dominant structures. Much like Haudebourt-Lescot, Desbordes-Valmore provides readers and viewers new ways of seeing the female artist. By the same token, Desbordes-Valmore gives life to the model in her uncle's atelier in a way that deliberately counterbalances the one-dimensional Gillette and the non-dimensional Catherine Lescault in *Le Chef-d'oeuvre inconnu*. In *L'Atelier d'un peintre*, the model's body is real, rather than ideal, and in a self-conscious subversion of the dominant tropes of art and creation, in a chapter entitled "Le modèle," it is the model who is pregnant and gives birth to an illegitimate child after she is abandoned by her artist lover. The childbirth metaphor for the production of art, although popular with the Romantics, may be traced back to Plato's *Symposium* and turns on the image of the mind as womb. Gaining currency in the early modern period with Shakespeare and Sydney (who represents the poet as "great with child to speake"),[37] the trope of intellectual generation as a form of male procreation became a dominant metaphor for creation by the end of the eighteenth century as genius was increasingly associated with virility and male sexual energies. Significantly, the metaphor establishes a distinction between creation and reproduction that imagines an exclusively male form of production and reflects, in Susan Stanford Friedman's formulation, the "fundamental binary oppositions of patriarchal ideology between word and flesh, creativity and procreativity, mind and body."[38] Thus, paradoxically, the trope of childbirth carried the negative associations of "base" reproduction when linked with women, yet carried positive valences of genius for Romantic male creators when talking or theorizing about their own (male) artistic production. For Desbordes-Valmore, who frequently wrote of motherhood and maternity in her poetry, the image was understood in its most literal terms as confessional or autobiographical, while also suggesting metaphoric resonances of artistic creation. As Friedman notes, for a female author, the childbirth metaphor can constitute a self-conscious challenge to male authors, demonstrating "not only a 'marked' discourse distinct from phallogocentric male use of the same metaphor but also a subversive inscription of woman's (pro)creativity" (74).

In *L'Atelier d'un peintre*, Desbordes-Valmore reclaims the trope and its reality for women, who are equally capable of giving birth to art as inspiration (the model), making art (the artist, Ondine), and giving birth to children (the model and Ondine's sister). Negating the reductive essentialism of woman as imitator/man as creator, Desbordes-Valmore asserts woman's multiple capacities of creation and procreation while placing them on a plane of equal value. Upon discovering that her sister is pregnant, Ondine muses "the steady soul hatches masterpieces. My sister! Where will I paint mine?" (95). Desbordes-Valmore's desire to demonstrate that a woman could be an artist *and* a mother, as well as an artist *or* a mother, was by no means unique, and it is not coincidental that the author's own daughter was named Ondine, thus conflating the novel, as artistic creation, with her maternal creation.[39] Countering the popularity of male interpretations of Dibutades and the co-opting of maternity into a masculine trope, painters such as Vigée-Lebrun and Constance Mayer celebrated motherhood in their own artistic creations, reflecting what Griselda Pollock has called "the desire for some way to acknowledge and speak of the maternal in all its ambivalence and structural centrality to the dramas of the subject [and] the narratives of culture."[40] Here, the poet renowned for her maternal themes and imagery answers the dominant artistic discourses with literal and figurative sisters giving birth to children and paintings without hierarchical distinction and providing a counter-discourse to the dominant ideologies where, as Friedman notes "maternity and creativity have appeared to be mutually exclusive to women writers" (75).

Like *La Vendetta*, *L'Atelier d'un peintre* is also a love story, or perhaps a series of love stories. Ondine falls in love with Yorick, a German student introduced to her uncle's studio by Abel, a young painter based on Abel de Pujol (who would come to direct the female studio portrayed in Grandpierre-Deverzy's scene (figure 8).[41] Abel has returned from Rome for love, while his friend Yorick's perpetual Romantic melancholy owes much to Goethe's Werther as well as of course to Hamlet. Ondine's love for Yorick is ultimately evident to everyone but the German artist himself, who pines for Camille, and her uncle, whose ancient and unrequited love for Marianne is the source of his own blinding sorrow. In keeping with the thematic of collectivity, each of these passions is ill-fated: none of the central characters will find happiness in love, and the mirrored suffering and misunderstanding functions to mutually reinforce their shared status as Romantic artists, male and female alike, condemned to perpetual grief and solitude. Nearly a third of the novel is devoted to Léonard's story of love and loss, and interpolated within his narrative are those of a *curé* and a *comédien* during the Revolution. Desbordes-Valmore gives voice to figures at the margins of society, victims of fate and society outside of the structures of power. As Chantal Bertrand-Jennings notes, this thematic is found in all of Desbordes-Valmore's fiction, which portrays "children, the elderly, the poor, beggars, the sick, in short the victims, the weak, the humble whom she systematically defends," anticipating Hugo's socially engaged Romanticism and Flora Tristan's pariahs.[42] But here, as in her later novel, *Domenica* (1843), Desbordes-Valmore focuses on the marginal position of artists who, like women, are voiceless and powerless in the face of social and political hierarchies.

Yorick, as a German, and Ondine, from Flanders, are outsiders in Paris, doubly marginalized by their status as artists and foreigners, and the atelier serves as their home and family. In one of the most critical scenes, Yorick and Ondine, alone in the studio, discuss their work. Where Ginevra's paintings were never evoked, and she was ultimately condemned to copying the works of others before dying in poverty, Desbordes-Valmore takes great care to give substance and legitimacy to the female painter's original production, and her tableau of a group of children is the subject of serious consideration and praise from her male counterpart. When her uncle joins them, the three artists in the atelier gathered around a painting recall the highly charged triangulations of Poussin, Porbus, and Frenhofer in the *Chef-d'oeuvre inconnu*. Yet, while the artistic vocabulary echoes Balzac's earlier insistence on color, light, and life, there is a spirit of cooperation and admiration here that stands in stark contrast to the simmering rivalry between the male painters, while the female is the author, not the subject, of the canvas.

Love in the atelier, an anathema to Balzac, proves no more successful for Desbordes-Valmore's Ondine. However, in contradistinction to her male counterparts, love is deemed positive and even necessary for Desbordes-Valmore's female artist, who dies not because love destroys her genius, but rather because without love and fellowship, she cannot create and cannot live. When the other students in her uncle's studio notice her passion for Yorick they ostracize her. Love introduces difference, and "the dear companions of her studies who treated her as a sister" now see her "with other eyes" and Ondine becomes "the object of the attention and envy of all" (398). Where there was once companionship, there is now jealousy and competition, fragmenting the family of the atelier and ultimately destroying the female painter. Before Yorick's arrival, "not one [of the other students] dreamed that she was of a different nature than he himself" (402). But when the students who used to be "her young brothers, careless and confiding," recognize her passion for the German artist, they abandon her and she "no longer has a single friend among them" (402). With the introduction of love, Ondine becomes embodied as a woman for her fellow *rapins,* and thus no longer a painter and a friend. The *recognition* of sexual or gender difference entails exclusion for the female artist, but importantly, reflects neither on her talent nor on her skills, but rather on the perceptions and jealousies of her male cohort. A woman can be a painter and a member of the atelier only as long as gender difference is less important than artistic similarity; once difference is foregrounded, the female artist is excluded from the brotherhood.

Although she feels pushed out of the atelier, she perseveres, for she *needs* to keep painting as much as she needs to love. When she can take it no more she cries out "I am still your sister . . . But why are you no longer my brothers?" (420). Denied fraternity and ultimately love, Ondine dies a highly Romantic death, a victim not of over-reaching and the dangers of inverting hierarchies, but of an artistic social structure that ultimately isolates and rejects woman-qua-woman once difference is established. The metaphor of the atelier, serving as a synecdoche for the more general field of artistic production, serves to illustrate in spatial terms the marginalization of the female artist—painter, poet, author—in nineteenth-century France and the destructive power of this denial. In a letter written on her deathbed, Ondine invokes her sister, an absent presence throughout the novel, lamenting "My sister! I am searching for you . . . I am alone, alone in myself" (437). Although she has lived and died in an all-male milieu, the female artist calls out for sisters to take the place of the brothers that have abandoned her. The exceptional woman artist, Desbordes-Valmore suggests, dies alone and only when she is joined by her metaphoric sisters in art will the atelier/artistic field become a place she can survive and thrive.

Taken to the church for her humble funeral by her heartbroken uncle and Yorick, Ondine's casket is placed by her lover on "le trône funèbre" elevated for the expiation mass to be celebrated the following day—21 January—on the anniversary of the death of Louis XVI. Only too late, Yorick had recognized Ondine's love for him and his for her; his letter asking for her hand reaches Léonard after her death. Overcome with remorse, he lights every candle in the chapel of the virgin and prays for "expiation." Finally, in a Werther redux, the German artist pulls out a gun and shoots himself in the head at her burial, falling into the grave upon her casket. Ondine's apotheosis, where she is elevated to the level of the martyred king, signals her sacrificial status—she is sinned against by society, unlike Ginevra who, in the eyes of her author, has sinned against society. Desbordes-Valmore's dialogue with Balzac, Lamartine, and the

Romantic *fraternité* of male artists resists the gendered construction of artistic identity that excluded women, demonstrating its pernicious toll on male as well as female artists. Yorick's suicide, evoking along with Ondine's death the suicide of Constance Mayer, the talented painter and partner of Prud'hon, demonstrates that not only women will suffer from the repressive ideologies of a phallocentric society.

Sisterhood in/as the Studio

Anna Mary Howitt's *Sisters in Art*

The collective identity sought by Desbordes-Valmore's Ondine in her uncle's studio becomes central in the work of Anna Mary Howitt, a painter and writer whose fiction reflects on women's artistic education and their construction of professional artistic identity. Faced with limited venues for training in Britain, Howitt turned to real and metaphoric sisterhoods as a virtual studio for women's artistic formation. In her life as in her fiction, Howitt sought artistic instruction in London and abroad, but it was through the increasingly politicized idea of sisterhood that she envisioned women's true collective education and their achievement of visibility (and thus legitimacy) in the public sphere. For Howitt and her British cohort, art became emblematic of larger possibilities of women's work and was closely tied to the burgeoning women's rights movement; as Deborah Cherry has established, by 1850 "women's art and feminism were inextricably intertwined" in Britain.[1]

Anna Mary Howitt's concept of sisterhood in the arts was shaped in no small part by her close relationship with her progressive family and feminist friends (most notably Barbara Leigh Smith Bodichon), but also reflects a response to contemporary artistic brotherhoods as well. These artistic fraternities emerged in Europe during the post-revolutionary period and as Laura Morowitz and William Vaughan observe, "must be seen as both a response to, and a reflection of, the particular economic, social, and political crises of the nineteenth century."² In a more general sense, the brotherhoods provided community and familial structure in a fragmented, urbanized modernity. These elite confraternities were predominantly formed as a mode of opposition to the dominant hierarchies of the Academy, yet at the same time were characterized by their secret, selective nature: open only to the chosen few (male) artists, nineteenth-century artistic brotherhoods paradoxically replicated the very institutions they sought to resist in their exclusionary, patriarchal configurations. Indeed, like the fraternal associations of the period (trade guilds, *compagnonnages,* Masonic orders, *Gesellenverbande*), the artistic brotherhood was "defined by masculinity" in a "type of association 'between and among men,'" Mary Ann Clawson tells us, "that was as much a part of the social relations of male dominance as the more recognized complex of male-female interchange."³ Much like bohemia, the artistic brotherhood served as a stage in the career of the nineteenth-century male painter: a stage defined in no small part through the exclusion of women. For Howitt, Leigh Smith, and their sisters in art, these artistic fraternities (the Pre-Raphaelite Brotherhood in particular) provided models of inspiration but also sites of resistance, and the artistic sisterhood proposed in Howitt's fiction reflects a feminist counter-discourse to the masculinist politics of art, and by extension work, independence, and subjecthood in nineteenth-century Britain.

The most famous of the artistic fraternities, the Pre-Raphaelite Brotherhood, was, in Jason Rosenfeld's terms, "an insistently patriarchal construction" of seven young men banded together in 1848 against the artistic establishment; by 1852 the group had devolved into "otherhood," as their focus shifted to individual interpretations of the Pre-Raphaelite vision.⁴ Led by Dante Gabriel Rossetti, John Everett Millais, and William Holman Hunt, the group also included William Michael Rossetti, Thomas Woolner, James Collinson, and Frederic George Stephens. Hoping to reform what they saw as the modern corruption of art, the Brotherhood turned to medieval and early Renaissance art and culture for a model of truthfulness and spirituality. Embracing a painstaking Truth to Nature in minutely detailed compositions, the Pre-Raphaelites manifested a Romantic nostalgia for an idealized artisanal past. Similarly, their image of the artist as a monastic figure, a social outsider linked only by the bonds of male friendship, self-consciously echoed the relationships between Shelley and Byron, Wordsworth and Coleridge and, observes Herbert Sussman, replicated "the Romantic model of artistic manhood."⁵ Yet unlike the Romantics, the PRB associated creation with hard work and self-determination rather than abstract inspiration, while during its initial phase, Elizabeth Prettejohn argues, "the collaborative working practices of the group produced an output that was even more important than the individual inputs of its members."⁶ Through unremitting labor and close observation, the Brotherhood sought collectively to establish a manly English art of social as well as economic value.

For Anna Mary Howitt and her sisters in art, the Pre-Raphaelite Brotherhood served as both an inspiration and yet another symbol of exclusion. Loosely affiliated with the group as both a painter and a writer, Howitt sustained a long-term friendship with D. G. Rossetti, who visited and corresponded with the Howitts frequently. Yet despite their participation in some of the group's activities (such as the Portfolio Club and publication in *The Germ*),[7] women were never considered members of the fraternity.[8] And if critics labeled her work "of the Pre-Raphaelite school," Howitt was emphatically not one of the Brotherhood.[9] Indeed, Howitt, Barbara Leigh Smith, Jane Benham, Joanna Boyce, Christina Rossetti, and the other female painters and poets who worked alongside the PRB are conspicuously absent from the memoirs of the Brotherhood,[10] just as women also disappeared from the accounts of the French ateliers discussed above. Yet the spiritual impetus, the desire for a socially engaged art, the belief in the strong connection between work and identity, and a commitment to collaboration were all ideas that Howitt and her friends embraced in the early 1850s, while thematically and stylistically their paintings and poems reflect a Pre-Raphaelite aesthetic. Like the Rossettis, Howitt was both an author and a painter; like the PRB, she and her sisters in art saw their productions as a means to challenge the artistic and social status quo; and like the Brotherhood, they formed an artistic identity through labor, community, and collectivity. Although images of female friendship and close, even intimate, relations between women were staples of nineteenth-century culture and literature,[11] Howitt's construction of an artistic sisterhood goes beyond these models to manifest a direct engagement with the politics of gender, art, and society as represented by the PRB. Anna Mary Howitt's novella, *The Sisters in Art*, thus makes its claim for a place for the female artist in the public sphere not only through the narrative plot but also through reference to and implicit revision of the masculinist models of artistic brotherhood in nineteenth-century Britain.

Anna Mary Howitt:
ART, LABOR, AND THE COLLABORATIVE PARADIGM

Anna Mary Howitt (1824–84) herself embodied the metaphoric sisterhood of the arts as an accomplished author, painter, and illustrator flourishing from the late 1840s through the 1850s.[12] Howitt's books included memoirs, fiction, poetry, and biography, while her writings on art and culture appeared in the *Athenaeum*, in Dickens's *Household Words*, and in the Pre-Raphaelite literary magazine *The Crayon*. After working as an illustrator for books and journals as a teenager, Howitt trained at Sass's Academy, one of the very few places a woman could receive professional training,[13] and her paintings were displayed at the National Exhibition at the Portland Gallery and at the Royal Academy. During the brief period she actively exhibited, Howitt's work received positive reviews in *Art-Journal, Athenaeum, Saturday Review, The Spectator, The Critic: London Literary Journal, The Crayon,* and *Illustrated London News.*

Howitt's family and friends played no small part in her development of the idea of a more concrete sisterhood of collaborative labor. Her parents, William and Mary Howitt, were lifelong collaborators in prose, poetry, and publishing, working together on *Howitt's Journal* among other liberal and reformist enterprises. William and Mary published a joint collection of poems in 1823, shortly after their marriage, a venture that was echoed by Anna Mary and her husband, Alfred Watts, in their 1875 *Aurora: A Medley of Verse.* More striking, however, was the translation of their political beliefs into the domestic and familial realm. Actively engaged in improving the lives of the working classes, the Howitts believed, in Mary's words, that "the remedy for the wrongs of labor to be the adoption of the cooperative principle, or the combination of work, skill, and capital by the operatives themselves."[14] These "cooperative principles" were applied to their own literary productions, where each member of the family—children, sisters, cousins—contributed to a series of books and chronicles and all were expected to participate in some way in the family enterprise. Linda Peterson explains that from their first collaborative venture, *The Children's Year,* in 1847 to Mary's posthumously published *Autobiography* (1889), "the Howitts' life writing expressed . . . their ideology of work, including the work of collaborative writing to which they as a family were professionally committed."[15]

The *Autobiography,* edited by her younger daughter Margaret and illustrated by Anna Mary, is substantially compiled from letters written to Mary's sister, Anna, who is present as an implied reader throughout, while letters from another sister, Emma, were transformed into a volume entitled *Our Cousins in Ohio* (1849), again illustrated by Anna Mary.[16] From an early age, Mary Howitt encouraged her daughter to write and paint professionally, for, as she observed to her sister Anna, "Girls must be made independent. I am bent on A.M. making £300 next year by translating; experience shows me that 9/10ths of the troubles and discomforts of families in this country come from lack of money. When I think of some, how wretched and hopeless does the lot of woman seem!"[17] As this 1844 letter makes clear, work for women was seen as both a financial and a social necessity, tied to improving women's positions at every level. Although Anna Mary ultimately chose painting over translation, she conceived of her vocation in her mother's terms of financial and feminist independence.[18] Refusing offers of marriage until she completed her artistic training,[19] Anna Mary was also conscious of her family's dependence on her income. In 1854, she regretfully declined an invitation to Rome because "those pictures I have already begun—and which are a little fund of money for us, upon which we have been calculating—would remain unfinished."[20]

The Howitts were connected to the leading poets and thinkers of period, among them Wordsworth, Tennyson, Browning, and Dickens. Internationalists, they promoted the works of Continental authors (most notably George Sand) in the pages of their journal, while Mary translated Hans Christian Andersen, Fredrika Bremer, and several other Scandinavian writers for the English reading public. Their circle of friends in the 1840s included Thomas Southwood Smith, Mary and Margaret Gillies, Leigh Hunt, R. H. Horne, and W. J. Fox, a group that shared an interest in literature, the arts, and political liberalism (see chapter 7). Carl Woodring notes, "All opposed the Corn Laws. Each sought municipal reforms, popular education, factory acts, further rights for women."[21] Recognized as a poet in her own right, Mary was in frequent correspondence with the most influential women writers of the day—among them Felicia Hemans, Geraldine and Maria Jewsbury, Joanna Baillie, Letitia Landon, Anna Jameson, and Mrs Gaskell—and she often passed their words on to her daughter Anna Mary. Emerging from this intellectually and politically engaged milieu, Anna Mary conceived an artistic identity in terms of collectivity and professionalism.

Her own idea of nonfamilial sisterhood of painters and poets further developed out of a long-term friendship devoted to communal study, artistic training, and women's rights with Barbara Leigh Smith, Bessie Rayner Parkes, and Jane Benham. Together, the women conceived an image of female (artistic) identity closely tied to labor, social engagement, female independence, and collectivity, and the significance of Howitt's *Sisters in Art* (1852) becomes all the more resonant when read in relation to her friends' and fellow artists' subsequent interventions in the public sphere. Leigh Smith (later Barbara Bodichon) was a landscape painter and feminist reformer better known today for her politics than her art. Independently wealthy, Leigh Smith spearheaded the Married Women's Property Bill in 1856, formed the first Women's Suffrage Committee in 1866, and co-founded, with Emily Davies, Girton College for women at Cambridge (opened in 1873), one of the first of its kind.[22] Bessie Parkes was a poet who was equally committed to women's education and work: along with Leigh Smith, Parkes established the *English Woman's Journal* in 1858 to promote "the present industrial employments of women, both manual and intellectual, the best mode of judiciously extending the sphere of such employments, and the laws affecting the property and conditions of the sex."[23] The author of a collection of *Poems* (1852) dedicated to Barbara, with "The World of Art" inscribed to "A.M.H. and all true Artists," Parkes also published *Essays on Women's Work* (1865) and was instrumental in launching the Victoria Press in 1860.[24] Jane Benham (later Jane Benham Hay) exhibited successfully at the Royal Academy, Liverpool, the Society of Female Artists, and the French Gallery up to 1887. Also a distinguished illustrator (known best for her pencil drawings for Longfellow's works), Benham was more engaged with the cause of Italian independence than British politics and moved to Florence by 1857.

Thus, central to the group's ethos from the late 1840s onward was a commitment to working for women's education and women's labor in public and collective ways, and their political engagement is reflected and refracted in Howitt's fiction, which serves as an early announcement of the group's conception of art as *productive work* for women, a model profession, and a path to independence. Following Leigh Smith's publication of *A Brief Summary, in Plain English, of the Most Important Laws of England concerning Women* in 1854, she organized a committee to gather support for the Married Woman's Property Bill, both of which were closely linked to issues of women's labor and compensation.[25] Anna Mary Howitt and Bessie Parkes, along with countless others, helped collect over 26,000 signatures for the petition, including those of Elizabeth Barrett Browning, Harriet Martineau, Elizabeth Gaskell, Anna Jameson, Mary Ann Evans, Mary Howitt, and Geraldine Jewsbury. As founders of *The English Woman's Journal,* Leigh Smith and Parkes used the pages of the periodical to advance women's causes, including the right to work and the necessity for improved education, while at the same time, the journal's offices in Langham Place became the administrative center of the Society for Promoting the Employment of Women. In her pamphlet, *Women and Work* (1857), Leigh Smith gave voice to the group's beliefs when she announced "Women want professions." She continued, "One great corresponding cry rises from a suffering multitude of women, saying, 'We want work.' Women are God's children equally with men. . . . To do God's work in the world is the duty of all, rich and poor, of all nations of both sexes. No human being has a right to be idle."[26] In another section, she indicated "Professions want women" and voiced her group of friends' fervent belief that society would benefit as much as individual women would from women's labor.

The mid-century crusade for women's professions reflected the developing Victorian conception of identity in general—and professional identity in particular—not simply in terms of "being," but also in terms of "doing." As Regenia Gagnier explains, the nineteenth century was characterized by "the pursuit of material well-being, scientific knowledge, and political emancipation," while identity in "market society" became closely tied to labor, production, and consumption.[27] For early feminists like Leigh Smith, Parkes, and Howitt, this intimate connection between economics, emancipation, and identity was reflected not only in women's quest for professions, but also in their need for improved education, which would prepare them for occupations that would enable them to become independent and self-defining. For if, following Gagnier's formulations, we are what we do or make, women increasingly sought ways to forge identities as producers, rather than simply consumers, economic subjects in their own right, rather than aesthetic objects. Indeed, as Jane Rendall notes (quoting Bessie Parkes), "education alone could offer a degree of financial independence, and do away with 'the taint diffused through the female character *by the consciousness of dependence on marriage for the means of existence.*'"[28] For Parkes, Howitt, and their cohort, education was understood in both a general and a vocational sense, encompassing the needs of women from the full spectrum of social classes and further tied to a spiritual as well as an economic identity. By mid-century, work had become associated with "a meaningful life," "self-development," "self-reliance," and a contribution to the greater good of society not only for men, but for women as well, at least within the feminist formulations of progressives.[29] Well before Leigh Smith embarked upon her crusade to found a women's college at Cambridge, Parkes published numerous articles and papers arguing, as she did in "What Can Educated Women Do?" that "our social institutions stand in the utmost need of the introduction of educated women in almost every department, working with and working under men."[30]

Even before this cohort of young women became collectively engaged in public strategies of political engagement, through pamphlets, petitions, and publication of articles in journals and newspapers, they recognized the power of art (painting, fiction, poetry) to promote the cause of female education and the image of the female professional. At the same time, art *as profession* and the woman artist (author, painter) *as professional* served as a model of female independence and social engagement. Thus, Anna Mary Howitt's contribution to the discourse took its most notable form in her novella, *The Sisters in Art*. As Jennifer Ruth has shown us, the Victorian novel "attempted to 'theorize' the professional," and to "make mental labor visible as productive labor."[31] Myriad novels of the period, explains Ruth, struggled to resolve the paradox of the professional—"neither in the capitalist nor the laborer's camp and yet both a (mental) capitalist and an (intellectual) laborer" (4), while at the same time the author sought to claim a place "as part of the professional class s/he was helping to usher forth" (10). Central to these formulations was the idea of the "value" to society of the ideas put forth by the professional and by extension, the artist; if male authors were conscious of "the precarious gendering of masculine intellectual labor," for female authors this effort to bestow value and professional status on their fiction "as productive work rather than leisured play" (35) was similarly tied to the desire to escape the associations of "feminized" amateurism. In *Sisters in Art,* Howitt employs the image of the female painter and her construction of a collective professional identity to the same ends as Leigh Smith's later campaigns and Parkes's essays: to present a compelling argument for the social and ethical importance of women's education and professions. Just as Leigh Smith and Parkes embraced collective female action not only through their friendship, but also through their petitions, *The English Woman's Journal*, and activities at Langham Place, Howitt foregrounded the idea of sisterhood in art announced in *An Art Student in Munich* as a political means of advancing the visibility and viability of women in the fields of economic and cultural production. For all the women in the group, as well as their wider circle of friends and feminists, art was seen as integral to the shifting discourse of work, professionalism, and female identity.

Thus, as discussed in chapter 1, this politically engaged group of proto-feminists painted and wrote together, traveled through Europe, and strove to establish a new model of the artist as woman. As Leigh Smith's ink drawing, "Ye Newe Generation" (c. 1850) (figure 18) playfully illustrates, from the very outset of their careers the young women saw themselves as a united front, warriors taking on the world together, in a sisterhood that was central to their formation as artists and modern women. Portrayed against the backdrop of the mountains, suggesting at once the heights they will scale and most probably their time together in Germany, Leigh Smith, Parkes, Benham, and Howitt wield their artistic tools like weapons in comic gestures of bravado. Palette, brushes, and maulsticks doubling as alpenstocks are brandished at the bull by the three painters (Barbara, Jane, and Anna Mary) while poet Bessie waves her notebook in the air. In an image of solidarity and forward movement, the bodies of the artists merge together clad in the loose skirts, jackets, and boots they preferred; outfits made for comfort and ease of movement rather than fashion or flattery.[32] At the same time, their unconventional garb signals their difference from more conservative women and their membership in an artistic sisterhood. Mirroring artistic brotherhoods who announced their association with flowing beards and robes (the *Primitifs* and the Nazarenes) or outrageous vests, capes, and accoutrements (*Les Jeunes France* and bohemians), Howitt and her friends use the language of clothes to establish their collective identity as women for whom mobility, labor, and art are more important than elegance and bourgeois propriety.

Their gesturing arms and open but unified stride denote an almost celebratory energy, full of freedom and lack of restraint that is striking in a group portrait of mid-Victorian women. Their adversary, the bull, stands as a symbol of aggressive masculinity as well as stubborn stupidity, while implicitly invoking Britain (John Bull) itself. Leigh Smith represents their antagonist through his horns, head, and tail, eliding the body and thus the threat he poses, reducing the bull to a glowering caricature of disapproval. Behind them, a woman covers her face in horror or in tears, though it is unclear whether it is the sight of the bull or the "Newe Generation" that has traumatized her. Leigh Smith's mock

Figure 18
Barbara Leigh Smith,
Ye Newe Generation,
c. 1850. Ink on paper.
11.2 × 17.3 cm. The
Mistress and Fellows,
Girton College,
Cambridge.

Old English orthography signals the women's self-conscious dialogue with their medievalist brethren in art, while emphasizing their own interest in the future rather than the past.

The image portrays the four women at the height of their optimistic youth, most probably during the fall of 1850 when they met in Munich, where Howitt and Benham were studying art (see chapter 1). In a letter from Munich dated 25 October 1850, Anna Mary first used the term "the sisters"[33] (in quotation marks) to refer to herself and Jane in their artistic endeavor and later, in *An Art Student in Munich,* as Howitt recounts a visit from her friend Justina (Leigh Smith), she rhapsodizes, "What schemes of life have not been worked out whilst we have been together! As though this, our meeting here, were to be the germ of a beautiful sisterhood in Art, of which we have all dreamed long and by which association we might be enabled to do noble things" (*Munich* 95). In this early formulation, art and sisterhood are tied not only to doing "noble things," but also to models of collective labor and solidarity for women. Moving from the idea of Associated Homes for working class families (an idea frequently discussed in *Howitt's Journal* and elsewhere in the 1840s), Justina proposes a single-sex Associated Home "at some future day, for such 'sisters' as had no home of their own" (*Munich* 95).[34] She goes on to elaborate an "Outer and Inner Sisterhood." Howitt's Justina explains:

> The Inner, to consist of the Art-sisters bound together by their one object, and which she fears may never number many in their band; the Outer Sisterhood to consist of women, all workers and all striving after a pure moral life, but belonging to any profession, any pursuit. All should be bound to help each other in such ways as were most accordant with their natures and characters. (*Munich* 95)

The "Art-sisters" thus serve as a model or inspiration for larger and more far-reaching cooperative societies, centered on the idea of noble and ennobling labor, the professionalization of women leading to their spiritual elevation. Here, as in *The Sisters in Art,* collective space for women's collaboration, education, and inspiration is central to the ideal of art, labor, and sisterhood.

The Sisters in Art

It is emblematic of the social as well as artistic aims of this sisterhood, that Anna Mary Howitt presented its most elaborate articulation in *The Sisters in Art,* a novella about female painters that proposes a feminist politics of education, representation, and labor. The story, published in serial form in *The Illustrated*

Exhibitor and Magazine of Art, recounts the artistic education of Alice Law and her two "sisters in art" in a collective *Kunstlerroman* that self-consciously evokes the contemporary genre of the novel of development through the filter of gender, while at the same time engaging with current ideologies of artistic brotherhoods and women's work. Here, as in Desbordes-Valmore's *L'Atelier d'un peintre,* space plays a significant role in concrete and symbolic ways. With echoes of Dickens and Balzac, Howitt's tale opens in the overdetermined setting of a curiosity shop, and the first scene presents a vivid portrait of the Silvers, the main character Alice's wealthy aunt and uncle, through a reading of the chaotic commercial space in which they live and work. This conflation of spheres, where the domestic, artistic, and entrepreneurial intermingle is, as Matthew Rowlinson points out, "rarely a happy conjuncture, and often touches on the uncanny."[35] Indeed, just as Master Humphrey, framing narrator of *The Old Curiosity Shop,* confessed "I have all of my life been attached to the inanimate objects that people my chamber . . . I have come to look upon them rather in the light of old and constant friends,"[36] so too does William Silver value objects above human relations, and money above love.

Thus, when a stranger arrives at the shop to report the death of Mrs. Silver's sister, Anne, and the existence of an orphaned niece, Alice, Silver's response is one of suspicion and fear that the girl will seek out his financial support. *Sisters in Art* is equally focused on mothers in art, and Alice's dead mother, Anne, is the intermediary between the young artist and the shopkeepers, who were Anne's sister and brother-in-law. The family has been fractured by the commodification of art, and after twenty years, Silver remains infuriated with his sister-in-law Anne for not marrying a Dutch art dealer "though he had sixty thousand pounds—and two Rubens' that were worth five more. Ah! Those Rubens; I never made such a miss before; for if the girl would but have married the old man, I should have got 'em for a hundred or so apiece" (*Sisters* 215). Fleeing London to escape the unwanted marriage (here clearly understood as an exchange of woman for painting),[37] Alice's mother Anne took a post as a female companion in Yorkshire. In the first of many familial substitutions, Anne's employer, the kindly Mrs Fountains, becomes a mother figure to the runaway living under the assumed name of "Miss Gray." This nod to Anne Brontë, via Yorkshire and "Miss Gray" also alludes to the more apposite *Tenant of Wildfell Hall* published four years earlier, a novel of a female painter resisting the bonds of marriage by leaving her husband and assuming a false name (see chapter 8). Thus, in the first pages of her story, Howitt establishes female artistic lineage in the sister arts of literature, between herself and Brontë, and painting, between the fictitious Alice and *The Tenant*'s Helen Graham. The themes of marriage, labor, money, and independence are also announced, establishing difference between the generations of women.

Tackling the social and artistic constructions of woman, Howitt opposes Silver, who sees both women and art in terms of commodities, and Alice, who will represent an active female subjecthood engaged with the aesthetic and ethical values of art as social labor. Although Silver worries that his niece will request his financial support, Wood explains that Alice has an income of £50 a year and seeks only shelter and protection as she continues her study of art in London. Silver agrees to house the sixteen-year-old, but again sees the girl in terms of her value to his business. In a passage that directly recalls Balzac's *Pierre Grassou* (1840), Howitt reflects, "the old uncle, who never could be perfectly disinterested in word, act, or thought, began to consider that it was even politic to be kind, as she would be able to retouch a picture, hide with fresh tints any woeful fracture in a precious jar, or even paint some Holy Family or Italian landscape that, with a little baking, smoke drying, and varnish, would pass for a Correggio or a Claude" (*Sisters* 240). These derivative and dishonest forms of art represent a view of the female artist as "unoriginal" or purely artisanal, which Alice resists as she shapes her own identity as an active creator. Alice carves her own space within the curiosity shop, filling the "small studio" with greenery she has brought from Yorkshire and transforming this corner of the commercial venture into a Romantic haven, with "its old china, its growing plants, its sketches of seaward coast and moorland height, and old quaint shapes in statuary" (*Sisters* 287). The objects filling her studio, reflecting an interest in craft and design as well as nature and the antique, will later be central to the education she and her sisters will offer the next generation of female artists. Moreover, this image of an aesthetic oasis, shaped by the conscious will of its occupant, stands in stark contrast to the popular images of little Nell, dwarfed and dominated by the accumulated objects in her grandfather's curiosity shop, and signals Howitt's determination that Alice will be neither a passive child nor a doomed victim, overwhelmed by the forces around her.[38]

Nonetheless, at home with the Silvers and even at the master's academy, Alice feels "a want of recognition and sympathy" (*Sisters* 240) that resonates with Ondine's isolation in *L'Atelier d'un peintre* and the psychological alienation evident in Amélie Cogniet's studio scene. With the Silvers, "If they talked of art—and both the curiosity dealer and his wife professed to know much about it in all its forms—it was the age and price of a picture or a vase, by whom last purchased, or when and where. But not a thought had they about the painter or the potter, not a word about shape or grace or grandeur—nothing but the length of years and amount of money price" (*Sisters* 240). In the atelier where she is training, "gossip and commonplace talk was the rule without exception, and the only word about the picture on the easel or the sketch from life, was as to when it would be finished, or whether it was better than Miss So-and-so's" (*Sisters* 240), echoing the petty world of Servin's Parisian studio in *La Vendetta*.

As in so many *Bildungsromane* of the period, the hero here is at odds with her environment, a Romantic soul struggling in a bourgeois world, while the institutions of learning fail to provide the education she seeks. Unlike Wilhelm, Pip, Julien Sorel, and their myriad brothers, however, Alice's formation will take place without any amorous attachment and without direct conflict with society itself. Instead, Alice's education will only truly begin when she reaches out to others like her, overcoming the initial alienation alluded to above. It is only in creating and sharing her own artistic space, first as a studio and later as a school, that she will become an artist. At the same time, her vision of art as disinterested labor rather than commercial enterprise delineates her professionalism.

If the specters of Dickens, Balzac, and Brontë are raised in the opening of *Sisters in Art,* subsequent installments of the text engage the questions of female artistic identity in terms that address contemporary formulations of artistic brotherhood, challenging the masculinist conception of the Artist as (Male) Hero with counter-discursive images of women's collective artistic labor and spiritual social engagement. Howitt's tale thus centers on Alice's artistic education as a collaborative endeavor, while her Ruskinian vision of art places painting, drawing, and design on equal footing. Opposed by her uncle, Alice is supported by a variety of older women who recognize her talent and goodness, "mothers in art" who support her endeavor in a variety of ways. The female network of metaphorical mothers includes Mrs Fountains, Anne's employer and Alice's namesake who was herself an accomplished painter; Mrs Cohen, a wealthy elderly Jewish woman who offers both financial and aesthetic encouragement; and Alice's aunt, Susan Silver, who defies her husband in order to help her niece in her artistic aspirations. By extension Alice reaches out to other young women, forming her collaborative sisterhood early in the story with Lizzy Wilson and Esther Beaumont. Importantly, the group is neither secret nor exclusive, and each girl represents a different artistic strength that complements those of the other two.

The orphaned Alice chooses Lizzy, the daughter of a poor tailor, as her friend and fellow art student, because she demonstrates a talent in and passion for design. Directly addressing the question of class, Alice tells her snobbish aunt "I don't believe that because people are poor, or in a humble class of life, they are vulgar" and insists that friends may come from any class when they are "those whom nature has made noble and good" (*Sisters* 240). The working class artist's name and demeanor echo that of Lizzie Siddal, the Pre-Raphaelite model and muse who was also an aspiring artist and friend of Howitt, Leigh Smith, and Parkes. Anna Mary and Barbara spent time with Lizzie at Scalands, the Leigh Smiths' Sussex retreat where the "art sisters" frequently gathered to paint and write. In a letter from Hastings to his brother, William, Dante Gabriel

Part I: The Studio

Figure 19
Anna Mary Howitt, *Head of Lizzie Siddal,* 1854. Pencil on paper. 12.7 × 11.5 cm. Mark Samuels Lasner Collection, on loan to the University of Delaware Library.

Rossetti recounted: "Everyone adores and reveres Lizzy. Barbara Smith, Miss Howitt, and I, made sketches of her dear head with iris stuck in her dear hair the other day, and we all wrote up our monograms on the panel of the window, in memorial of the very pleasant day we had spent at the farm" (figures 19 and 20).[39] But where the real Lizzie, a sickly young woman best known as Millais's *Ophelia* (1851) and Rossetti's mistress, saw her own efforts at creation subordinated to those of the Pre-Raphaelite Brotherhood and died of a laudanum overdose, Howitt's Lizzy is an active representing subject rather than a represented object—an artist rather than a model—who thrives under the encouragement

Chapter 3: Sisterhood in/as the Studio

Figure 20
Barbara Leigh Smith, *Head of Lizzie Siddal*, 1854. Pencil on paper. 12.5 × 9.5 cm.
Mark Samuels Lasner Collection, on loan to the University of Delaware Library.

and nurturing of her sisters in art.[40] This solidarity is extended to Esther as well, whose wealth and education further complement the attributes of the other two.

The metaphor of space is developed within the Silvers' lodgings in the forbidden apartment rented to Dr Falkland, an occasional tenant whose rooms contain anatomical models. When the girls transgress the forbidden boundary, in search of a modeled hand to draw for an indigent artist friend, they are caught sketching in the darkened chambers by Alice's avaricious uncle. The violation of the male sanctum, associated with the body and its representation

111

and thus with the studio and the nude, generates both "rage and fear" (*Sisters* 318) in Uncle Silver, who declares: "I'll hate you henceforth, as I once hated your mother" (318). This overdetermined fury and his determination that the girls are "ruining me, ruining me—robbing me of my yearly rent" (318) points to larger fears of incursions across boundaries of gender and profession. The female trespass into forbidden male terrain—the workplace, the field of cultural production, politics, and enfranchisement—precipitates fear, rage, and revenge, as the male subject feels his identity and livelihood threatened. Accordingly, Silver explodes a second time at his niece, who determines to leave immediately to establish her own home and studio where she, Esther, and Lizzy can live and labor together "with one interest as sisters in art" (319).

Driven from the curiosity shop by uncle Silver, the three women establish a studio together in Fitz-Roy Square, a well-known artistic quarter, and five years' time allows them to draw into "a holier and truer communion of sympathy, taste, and pursuit, and to evolve from the unity of separate talents, a result of which singly they were not capable" (*Sisters* 319). This cooperative art brings together "three truths rarely found so united in design—the natural, the scientific, and the artistic" (*Sisters* 334). Together they win a design competition for a Belgian firm and Alice explains to the owner how the three women created a single work of art: "The larger outlines you so much admire are mine; the geometrical curves, running from point to point, so beautiful in themselves, are Miss Beaumont's; whilst the filling up in detail, the stray flower, the rounded boss, the delicate touches, so small in themselves, so much as a whole, are those of our young friend here" (*Sisters* 334). Beyond the concrete, the description suggests metaphoric meanings as well, for far from highlighting their individual insufficiencies, Howitt demonstrates the strength of their collective endeavor achieved through education, empathy, and shared labor.

Much of the novella concerns the practical and theoretical parameters of the artistic education of women, as Alice, Lizzy, and Esther undertake their own training, studying art and literature, history and geometry, languages and anatomy, crossing the borders of gender and genre in their formation. Antonia Losano has noted that Howitt's emphasis on the "low arts" of illustration and design rather than more elevated genres for her art sisters represents an effort "to effect a reevaluation and recuperation of these art forms" while at the same time "question[ing] the Victorian artistic hierarchies" (120). Importantly, there are no male masters or students in this feminocentric world, in sharp contrast to Desbordes-Valmore's all-male atelier. But like her French counterpart, Howitt also engages in a dialogue with contemporary fiction, challenging male-authored portrayals of female ambition and subjecthood. In *Sisters in Art*, Tennyson's *The Princess* (1847), a poetic "medley" dedicated to a female university, serves as intertext in both concrete and theoretical ways. Like *L'Atelier d'un peintre,* Howitt's British novella generates meaning as a counter-discourse, interrogating and subverting dominant ideologies of gender, genre, and art. However, where Desbordes-Valmore sought to claim a position for the woman artist (poet, painter, or actress) within the extant structures of Romanticism, questioning the very gendering of art and genre and denying difference, Howitt proposes an altogether new structure, in an equality achieved in parallel systems that are indeed based in difference, where women learn, create, and support one another without the participation of men.

When the Howitts moved to Lower Clapton in 1844, Tennyson had become a frequent visitor, reciting his poems and conversing into the night, and his grandson, Charles Tennyson, claimed that *The Princess* had been shaped by the Howitts' views on women's rights and education.[41] In December 1847, Anna Mary's letters to Barbara are full of Tennyson's *Princess,* proclaiming "we are delighted with it . . . It is a poem on woman's education, woman's rights, woman's true being—and according to our notions noble and true."[42] Howitt confesses to Leigh Smith that Princess Ida "strangely reminded me of you throughout" and urges her to read the poem, only to worry in a letter a week later than her friend won't like it after all.[43] In fact, Bessie Parkes had given Barbara a copy of *The Princess* for Christmas, and all three equally admired Tennyson's "medley."

Both Lilia's desire to be "some mighty poetess" in the contemporary framing narrative, and Ida's ferocious feminism in the medieval fairy tale within, would have resonated for the young artists in their longing to escape the "convention" that "beats them down," in the belief that "The woman were an equal to the man" and "Better not be at all / Than not be noble."[44] But Tennyson's mock serious verse privileges the voices of the seven young men who recount the tale over those of Ida and her fellow students, and if the Prince and his friends Cyril and Florian demonstrate the intimacy of a brotherhood (also mirrored in the alternating male narrators, "seven and yet one" [Prologue, 221]), the women within the fortress devolve into conflict ("division smolders hidden" [III, 63]) and Ida's brother Arac notes "the woman is hard / Upon the woman" (VI, 205–6). Female independence, privileging head over heart, cannot be sustained in Tennyson's verse and the maternal ultimately triumphs when Ida takes pity on the wounded Walter. The harmonious ending, where the rebellious Princess cedes to love and to the Prince, comes at the cost of her idealistic female sanctuary, which collapses once men penetrate its walls. As Sir Walter proclaims, "seeing either sex alone / Is half itself" (VII, 283–84), Ida and her cohort are subsumed into the marriage plot; admitting "she had fail'd" (VII, 213), Princess Ida abandons her feminist project to claim her position as complement to man.[45]

In William Howitt's review of the poem in 1848, the author and critic praised Tennyson's treatment "of the great question which has been agitated of late years . . . with increasing zeal,—the question of the rights and true social position of woman."⁴⁶ Reflecting an essentialist vision, Howitt applauds Tennyson's effort "to place woman in her true position as the mother of the race and the companion of man," adding "But to do that, we must not attempt to make her what she never was intended to be—a she-man" (*HJ* 29). In a passage that reveals a deep ambivalence toward contemporary feminists, the noted progressive reformer expostulates:

> Men must be taught that women are their equals, not their slaves, and love and enlightened intellect must establish the equal footing, and equal property of the wife; but every attempt to turn woman into a hard, bold, public and prating she-man, as is opposed to the evident laws and institutions of nature, instead of advancing the cause of woman, which the poet truly says is the cause of man too, injures and retards it. The she-philosophers and politicians who would be in Parliament instead of the domestic circle, who smoke cigars or hookahs; who do coarse men's work in coarse mannish attire, are neither the persons to win the crown of true womanhood for themselves or for the sex in general. (*HJ* 29)

While supporting woman's right to legal equality, Howitt maintains that it is man's right and duty to "give" it to her, while "true womanhood" holds fast to the traditional, gendered roles of nurturing wife and mother. But if William Howitt agreed with Tennyson's views, Mary, who encouraged her daughter's independence at every turn, may have been less convinced by his parodic vision of learned women and conservative conclusion. Indeed, Tennyson himself wrote "I don't believe you'll like it" when he sent her a copy of *The Princess* in exchange for her new collection of ballads.⁴⁷ In their early twenties, Anna Mary and her friends shared her father's enthusiasm for *The Princess* upon its publication; a few years later, however, they came to see female solidarity as integral, rather than antithetical, to "true womanhood," while moving steadily away from the domestic ideal embraced by Tennyson and William Howitt, toward a more progressive model of female labor and education.

In the intervening period, between late 1847, when Anna Mary Howitt was just beginning her professional artistic training at Sass's and developing her friendship with Barbara Leigh Smith, and 1852, when she published *The Sisters in Art*, the painter and her friends had become, if not radicalized, then increasingly aware of the social and institutional limitations imposed on women in Victorian England, limitations that they would battle in the course of the decade. In 1850, after attending a lecture at the Royal Academy, Howitt reflected despairingly on women's exclusion from the studio classes there, and implicitly from the realms of power and legitimacy. She observed to Leigh Smith:

Oh, how terribly did I long to be a man so as to paint there. When I saw in the first room all the students' easels standing about—lots of canvasses and easels against the walls, and here and there a grand 'old master' standing around, a perfect atmosphere of inspiration, then passed on into a second room hung round with the Academicians' inaugural pictures, one seemed stepping into a freer, larger, and more earnest artistic world—a world, alas! which one's womanhood debars one from enjoying. Oh I felt quite sick at heart—all one's attempts and struggle seemed so pitiful and vain—for the moment—it seemed as though after all the Royal Academy were greater and more to be desired than the Academy of Nature.[48]

During her sojourn in Munich a year later, Anna Mary conceptualized "a set of Art-lectures I should like to deliver if the Female Academy is established . . . I can see some *very* beautiful lectures especially addressed to *woman* artists—their Art must be of so different a character, of such a more *spiritual* character than ordinary Art."[49] This spiritual nature would come to dominate Howitt's vision after 1856, but at the beginning of the decade she saw it as deeply connected to the unique and important qualities of female artistic production.

Thus, by 1852, in her own tale of a woman's art college, Tennyson's ironic and conservative interpretation is subverted in an image of successful and supportive women working and learning together in harmony. Unlike *The Princess*, Howitt's tale cedes neither voice nor her heroines' futures to men. If Princess Ida's separatist world is quickly infiltrated by the Prince and his friends in disguise, while marriage, rather than female improvement is the ultimate end point, the Sisters in Art retain their independence throughout the narrative, refusing offers of marriage to complete their women's College of Art. Built on the site of the former curiosity shop, with the fortune left to Alice by her repentant Uncle Silver, the women's school represents the triumph of Alice's vision over Silver's, in a space dedicated to intellectual and artistic development rather than economic profit. Where Princess Ida's university was a physically and intellectually isolated citadel, the Sisters in Art construct a public institution in the middle of London with the support and admiration of men and women alike.[50] Moving from the individual to the universal, Alice and her friends want to extend their opportunities to all women, and they envision the school as "a grand, noble life of duty, usefulness, and ministry to the true advance of art, in connection with woman's mind and woman's labor" (*Sisters* 347).

In a final stage of their own education, the Sisters in Art spend three years studying in Rome while the school is being built and, while there, embark on a search for the great-granddaughter of an elderly Italian sculptor they had befriended in London. Giuseppe, who had rejected his own daughter decades earlier when she became an artist's model, has spent his life mourning her loss and cherishing all that remains of the girl he had loved: a sculpture he had made of her as a child. Once again, the female author gives new significance to the artist's model, whose role in the studio is transformed from mere object of art to a generative matrix of meaning. The daughter and her own daughter had died in poverty, but Alice, Lizzy, and Esther find and rescue the fallen model's granddaughter, educating and nurturing her until, when they return to Britain with the girl they are able to exchange "flesh for marble—life for what has no life," giving Giuseppe "the richest blessing which this world holds for you," the girl "over whose childhood I and my dear Art-Sisters have watched with holy care" (*Sisters* 364). In a subtle play on the Pygmalion paradigm so popular with male artists throughout the ages, Howitt's Galatea come to life is not a beautiful female nude, but a perfect female child. Exchanging fetishistic fantasy for an image of creation-as-motherhood, Howitt's female artists bring marble to life through love and generosity, rather than sexual desire. The child, like their artwork, is the product of the collaborative, loving labor of the Sisters in Art and further embodies the generations of women artists they will form in their own image at the Art College. In naming the child Angelica, Howitt ends with an evocation of a final artist mother, Angelica Kauffman, who represents here both the past and future of British art. Refusing the male artistic myth of autogenesis, Howitt's sisters in art recognize connection and continuity, while transforming the offspring of the artist's model into a potential artist herself.

In stark contrast to the individual impetus that had overtaken the Pre-Raphaelite Brotherhood, Anna Mary Howitt's artistic sisterhood embodied collectivity and collaboration in their art as well as their lives and undertakings, while refusing the secretive and exclusionary nature of their association for a social and artistic engagement that embraces all, or at least all women. Where the Romantic quest for inclusion in the male sphere of creation in Desbordes-Valmore's novel was met with abject failure and death, Howitt's utopic fictional sisterhood succeeds as the women create a separate or parallel structure for female painters that simultaneously mirrors and revises the male sphere—here figured as artistic brotherhood—in female terms. Ironically, where Desbordes-Valmore did succeed in finding a place as a poet, however marginal, in the Romantic field of cultural production, the more optimistic Howitt, who confessed to adopting "rose colored glasses," ultimately failed in the long term to realize her dreams of artistic sisterhood. But if her own career as an artist ended abruptly (as will be discussed below), her political image of female solidarity and a working sisterhood became critical in the feminist movement of the decades to follow.

Howitt's Heroism:
BARBARA AND BOADICEA

Four years after the publication of *Sisters in Art,* Anna Mary Howitt displayed her first large scale history painting, the most prestigious of the genres and one typically inaccessible to women due to lack of training in representing the human form.[51] In choosing *Boadicea Brooding over her Wrongs* as the subject of her ambitious canvas, Howitt continued the challenge to the contemporary institutions of art and representation that she enunciated in her earlier novella, while again positing the benefits of female intervention to both art and society. While the painting is lost, reviews in the *Athenaeum* of 7 June 1856 indicate that the scene was executed in the Pre-Raphaelite style, and thus engaged in direct dialogue with the Brotherhood. In keeping with the resolutely British orientation of the PRB, Howitt turns to English history for her subject matter, choosing the warrior queen famous for leading an uprising against the Romans. Thus, where Millais portrayed *Elgiva seized by order of Odo, Archbishop of Canterbury* (1846) showing the humiliation and banishment of the Anglo-Saxon queen,[52] Howitt's choice of Boadicea reflects a vision of active female agency and engagement in the face of injustice. Avenging her own abuse and the rape of her daughters, Boadicea led the Iceni people against their oppressors and her speech, as recorded by Tacitus, proclaimed "heaven is on the side of a righteous vengeance."[53] Howitt's model for the warrior queen was none other than Barbara Leigh Smith, the most vocal and recognizable feminist campaigner of the day. In portraying her friend and sister in art, a painter and feminist who led the struggle for equal rights for women in both the social and artistic spheres, in the guise of the ancient crusader, Howitt makes a parallel between past and present rebellions that few would have missed. Furthermore, in keeping with the idealist leaning of her prose, Howitt proposes the regeneration of British art and society through the intervention of female artists.

Boadicea was the last major painting Anna Mary Howitt ever exhibited.[54] In a decidedly mixed review in *The Athenaeum,* the critic identified *Boadicea* as "the most promising new picture" in the north wing of the gallery, only to compare it unfavorably to her "*Gretchen*" of 1854.[55] Where the earlier painting is lauded for "so beautifully elaborating the pathos of Goethe's peasant girl," the same emotion ("a variation of Gretchen's") is less palatable in "the face of the agonized and revengeful mother," considered an "unhappy" subject not suited to the artist's "genius."[56] The critic concedes that "Miss Howitt's painting has grown firmer and fuller in tone. The mind expended on the picture is visible in every touch," yet in turning her attention from woman as victim

(Gretchen) to woman as avenger (Boadicea) she is condemned as "pretentious and affected." Focusing on the Pre-Raphaelite detail in her treatment of the forest, the reviewer denounces "the wearisome green salad of the background—the mincemeat of raw leaves" which he fatuously concludes is "Botany, not Art." But ultimately it is clear that it is neither the composition nor the facture of Howitt's scene, but rather her choice of subject that provokes the reviewer's overdetermined censure. The final observation, "What is this but an angry woman, whose wrongs we only know by the Catalogue?" reveals the gendered politics of criticism at play in the reception of Howitt's warrior queen.

Although notably sensitive, Howitt could probably have withstood such scorn, as it was in keeping with critical attitudes toward women painters and Pre-Raphaelites in general. Identifying herself in an 1855 letter as a "pioneer" and her work as "pioneering," Howitt acknowledged the difficulties she anticipated for her work. Continuing in her missive to Leigh Smith she averred, "I mean however to struggle on manfully—or rather *womanfully*—through all fogs—even through the *fogs of bad criticism* which I have an expectation will close around my pictures this year" (original emphases).[57] It was instead the attack of John Ruskin, the defender of the PRB and the most influential art critical voice of the century, which effectively ended Howitt's career. For Howitt, who appended an epigraph from Ruskin to *An Art Student in Munich*, the author of *Modern Painters* stood as a moral authority as well as an aesthetic one, for his commitment to "the Beautiful and the True" was one shared by Anna Mary and her friends. As a friend and patron of the Pre-Raphaelites, it was to be expected that Ruskin would understand and appreciate her approach in ways that other critics might not. As a friend and admirer of the Howitts (Ruskin directed his readers to William Howitt's *Rural Life* as "very suggestive and helpful" in an appendix to the third volume of *Modern Painters*), it was to be hoped that he would respect and appreciate her own commitment to artistic labor. Yet, when Anna Mary asked him directly for his thoughts on what she considered her masterpiece, he wrote to her "What do *you* know about Boadicea? Leave such subjects alone and paint me a pheasant's wing,"[58] dismissing her aspirations out of hand. A cousin recounts Howitt's response on receipt of the note:

> Annie snatched and tore open the letter. Then came a cry of grief and anger as from a wounded creature—one could never forget it nor how she read out—almost screamed the words, "What do *you* know about Boadicea? Leave such subjects alone and paint me a pheasant's wing." Waving the letter she rushed into the house crying, "A pheasant's wing—I'll paint him a pheasant's wing," and then as the family gathered round, sank down in a passion of hopeless grief.[59]

Ruskin's famously conflicted views of/on women—oscillating between idealization, paternalism, and dismissal—were no less evident in his responses to contemporary women artists, and like the author of the *Athenaeum* review, he found Howitt's subject particularly objectionable. While Ruskin sporadically supported a handful of female painters, they were most frequently women he perceived to have limited ambition or professional aspiration. The same year that he condemned Howitt's *Boadicea* in private, he publicly praised Annie and Martha Mutrie in the following equivocal terms: "I cannot say more of the work of the two Misses Mutrie than I have already said. It is nearly as good as simple flower-painting can be; the only bettering it is capable of would be by more able composition, or by the selection, for its subject, of flowers growing naturally."[60] And while rejecting the work of a female painter loosely associated with Pre-Raphaelitism, the author of *Modern Painters* embraced the production of the quintessential Pre-Raphaelite model when he purchased all of Lizzie Siddal's drawings in 1855 and offered her £150 a year for all of her subsequent work. As Pamela Gerrish Nunn notes, this arrangement effectively removed Siddal from the artistic marketplace,[61] keeping her doubly dependent on the interventions of her "teacher" (her lover, Rossetti) and her patron (Ruskin), precluding the economic and aesthetic independence Howitt, Leigh Smith, and their cohort actively pursued. Ruskin's financial support of Siddal reflected, moreover, a mediated desire to help Rossetti by assuaging his worries about an indigent mistress,[62] in a complex triangulation as redolent of homosocial as of artistic motivation. Lizzie, waifish and other-worldly, frequently ill and utterly reliant on her lover, became Ruskin's "Ida," a nickname he began using in 1855 in clear reference to Tennyson's *Princess*. Siddal herself turned frequently to Tennyson for her artistic subjects, including "The Lady of Shallott" and "The Lady Clare," but in choosing Ida for her soubriquet, Ruskin focuses on a failed rebellion and a woman who ultimately abandoned her ambitions for love, trading independence for domesticity. In May 1855 he wrote to Siddal, addressing her as "My dear Ida," and admitted "My principal theory about you is that you want to be kept quiet and idle,"[63] paradoxically containing the "genius" he purports to promote and directly refusing her a role as productive worker.

Anna Mary Howitt's initial outrage at Ruskin's words and her desire for vengeance ("A pheasant's wing—I'll paint him a pheasant's wing") resonate with Boadicea's own response to the "Wrongs" visited upon her. But for the nineteenth-century painter, it was quickly followed by despair. In refusing the legitimacy of her efforts at entering into the discourses of art, history, politics, and heroism, Ruskin denied Howitt the right to signification. Counseling her instead to paint a pheasant's wing, he returns the female artist to the realm of the copy and the still life, reproduction rather than creation in a literal *nature morte*. The dead pheasant was in fact a favorite motif of Ruskin's: Turner's watercolor *Dead Pheasant* (c. 1815) was a treasured part of his art collection and he turned his own hand to the subject several times. But in urging Howitt to focus on "a pheasant's wing"—a fragment of the whole—he cruelly directs her toward an image of curtailed mobility and freedom, severed from its corporal totality. Dead, dissected, and disconnected, the pheasant's wing figures forth Ruskin's own desire to keep women artists in check, relegating their production to *membra disjecta* without coherence or meaning.

Howitt's devastation, and her ensuing nervous breakdown, led her to destroy most of her paintings and the remainder of her life was devoted to spiritualism. Producing "automatic" drawings and writings guided by the spirit world, Anna Mary shifted the onus of responsibility for her artistic production to another realm, while moving away from oil painting to pencils, pastels, and sketches deemed by Margaret Oliphant to be "wonderful scribble-scrabbles."[64] For Anna Mary's friends and fellow painters, her movement toward the spirit world signaled the loss of their sister in art. William Michael Rossetti lamented "If only the spirits had left her alone she would have drawn and painted very much better than she ever did under their inspiration,"[65] a belief held by many. And even Anna Mary herself confessed in 1859, "Oh my most dear Barbara, if you could ever comprehend how, for three years or more, I have hung bleeding upon a cross of artistic martyrdom, you would comprehend what it was to lie as I am now lying in a sepulchre buried to the world, but alive to God."[66]

Recent critics, however, have taken a less pessimistic view of Howitt's late work and legacy. As Linda Peterson suggests, spirit drawing may be seen as yet another form of collaboration,[67] and Marlene Tromp contends that, in the crossing of boundaries between the material and spiritual worlds, "Spiritualism undermined the very social structures that defined a narrow circuit of behavior for women, and . . . granted women a new kind of self-determination."[68] If painting in the public sphere was contested territory, spiritualism, argues Alex Owen, "validated the female authoritative voice and permitted women an active professional and spiritual role largely denied them elsewhere."[69] Indeed, Howitt continued to write both prose and poetry until her death, and her voice in her 1883 publication *The Pioneers of the Spiritual Reformation* ("Biographical Sketches" of Justinus Kerner and William Howitt) is at once confident and authoritative, making the case for the "moral or intellectual truth" of spirit writing and drawing, while tracing these forms of expression back to the Old Testament.[70] Far from being a lost soul, Howitt became a committed advocate for spiritualism while continuing her commitment to women's causes. Rachel Oberter argues that Howitt's spirit drawings, many of which were focused on a female Christ, as well as "majestic" symbolic women, offered "a version of divine femininity" that ultimately "ushered in a strand of theological feminism" at the end of the century.[71] Her efforts to integrate a female element into the holy Trinity and her understanding of God in terms of male and female aspects shared much with the socialist utopian thought of the Fourierists and Saint-Simonians who would influence Angélique Arnaud and (to a lesser extent) George Sand.

Finally, although Howitt's *Boadicea* may have been destroyed, her legacy lived on in Thomas Thornycroft's monumental statue of the warrior queen erected on the Westminster Bridge, near the Houses of Parliament.[72] Commissioned in 1856 by Prince Albert, the bronze *Boadicea* was dedicated in 1902, just as Emmeline Pankhurst organized the Women's Social and Political Union in the final, militant push for women's suffrage. The triumphant representation of the ancient queen in her chariot was a tribute to Victoria and a celebration of British imperial rule, yet the inscription at its base from William Cowper's "Boadicea" (1782), "Regions Caesar never knew / Thy posterity shall sway," might also pertain to Howitt's own legacy. For despite the virtual end of her professional artistic career after her daring representation of her sister artist and feminist as the warrior queen, Anna Mary Howitt's early novel and lost painting remain a powerful, if poignant, testimony to the utopic vision of social and aesthetic sisterhood shared by many in Britain and beyond, as women slowly but surely achieved visibility and even legitimacy as artists and heroes in British history and culture.

Part II

Cosmopolitan Visions
Gender, Genre, Nation

Visualizing Imagined Communities

Lessons of the Female Artist in Staël, Owenson, and Lescot

> The relations of the arts are like those of countries, of clans, of neighbors, of members of the same family. They are thus related by sister- and brotherhood, maternity and paternity, marriage, incest, and adultery; thus subject to versions of the laws, taboos, and rituals that regulate social forms of life.
>
> —W. J. T. Mitchell[1]

The construction of female artistic identity in nineteenth-century France and Britain was inarguably a transgressive act, as women crossed social and artistic boundaries, defying the accepted limitations of art and of gender. As Mitchell notes above, the constructed laws of artistic genre, with their reified borders and interdictions, closely resemble other socially constituted laws, including those that regulate family and nation, and he adds: "The adulteration of the arts, of the genres, is an incitement to the adulteration of every other domestic, political, and natural distinction" (109). The political nature of these distinctions, based on inclusion and exclusion, reflected the dominant ideologies of the hegemonic cultures and Rancière's police order; it was precisely these boundaries of distinction, defining or legislating the hierarchies of legitimacy and visibility, which the female artists in this study sought to overturn. The very tropes of artistic borders, boundaries, and transgression invoke the contemporary discourses of nation and Romantic nationalism which located identity in

125

a dialectic of difference.[2] Thus, as women artists disrupted the hierarchical relations of gender and artistic genre, some turned to the political distinctions of nation as well, demonstrating the constructed nature of these boundaries while claiming a place for women as subjects in the larger public sphere.

If we understand politics in Rancière's sense as the "organization of dissent,"[3] the novels and canvases to be considered in the following chapters take part in political resistance to discourses of nationalist, colonialist, and class domination. The authors and painters below propose alternative visions of nation and gender based on cosmopolitan or social utopian ideals—imagined communities that refuse the hierarchies of difference for structures of national, class, and gender harmony and equality. In keeping with Kwame Anthony Appiah's definition of cosmopolitanism, these novels and paintings reflect "a receptiveness to art and literature from other places, and a wider interest in lives elsewhere," as well as "the recognition that human beings are different and that we can learn from each other's differences,"[4] both of which stand in marked contrast to the discourses of nationalism and imperialism in nineteenth-century Britain and France. Although they remain, for the most part, potential or projected rather than concrete and real, these imagined communities, based on border crossings and hybrid cultures, demonstrate the potential advantages of difference and pluralism for the nation. Where Anne K. Mellor has identified an "embodied cosmopolitanism" in British Romantic women writers' narratives of "cultural harmony through romance,"[5] Hortense Lescot, following in the footsteps of Staël and Owenson, similarly thematizes a "transnational boundary crossing that constructs a new form of subjectivity" (297) through the embodied lessons of the female artist. As avatars of difference, these women artists traverse the borders of gender, genre, and nation to propose new ways of seeing the world that bring with them the possibility of cross-cultural connection and renewal.

Corinne and *The Wild Irish Girl:*
MASTER NARRATIVES OF GENDER, NATION, IDENTITY

The questions of art, national identity, gender, and difference played a central role in the works of Germaine de Staël (1766–1827) and Sydney Owenson, Lady Morgan (1776?–1859),[6] whose novels, critical texts, and travel accounts proposed a counter-discourse to the dominant narratives of nation and empire. Owenson's *The Wild Irish Girl: A National Tale* (1806) and Staël's *Corinne, ou l'Italie* (1807) challenged the hegemony of British colonial rule and French imperialism in a pair of tales that highlight a more cosmopolitan vision of the dominated cultures of Ireland and Italy while at the same time establishing the political engagement of the female author. Both novels were enormously popular throughout Europe, serving as master narratives that inspired imitations and acolytes while demonstrating the powerful role women could play in art and in the nation.

Born ten years apart, the Swiss Staël and Irish Owenson belonged to nations linked by language, geography, and empire to the dominant cultures of France and Britain, but distinctly at the peripheries of power. Eschewing the domestic roles and topics consigned to women and their art, Owenson and Staël directly addressed the ethics of empire, challenging the structures of British and French hegemony over the cultures of Ireland and Italy, and as a result they were among the most controversial women of the day.

Indeed, each considered the novel a political forum: John Isbell tells us that "art *equals* politics" in Staël's oeuvre,[7] while Lisa L. Moore acknowledges the "overt political agenda" of Owenson's work.[8] Moreover, their political engagement went beyond nation to reflect on sexual politics as well, as their fiction reflected "a metaphorical system in which the social construction of sexual difference and the social construction of cultural difference stand in for each other."[9] Thus, as they deconstruct hierarchies of cultural difference, making a claim for the equal value of multiple cultures, the female authors also deconstruct the hierarchies of gender, claiming equal value for women's aesthetic and political interventions. The popularity of their novels only added to their perceived (and real) threat to the status quo: *The Wild Irish Girl* was an immediate success upon its publication in 1806, appearing in nine editions in England and the United States in two years' time, and translated into French by 1813. *Corinne,* one of the most widely read books of the period, was translated into English in 1807 and Italian in 1808, circulating throughout Europe and the United States in forty editions between 1807 and 1872.

In keeping with their political orientations, both Owenson and Staël occupied a visible place in the public sphere that reflected the impact of their literary creations as well as their polemical writings. In a conflation of woman and nation, Glorvina, Owenson's wild Irish girl, was understood to embody Irish culture, while Corinne, in keeping with the title of Staël's novel, personified her adopted homeland of Italy. By extension, Owenson herself was frequently referred to as Glorvina[10] and represented as such in portraits and frontispieces of her playing the harp. Mme de Staël was painted as Corinne by Vigée-Lebrun and Gérard and similarly took on the persona of the ill-fated woman of genius, responding to the public "I am not Corinne, but if you like, I shall be."[11] In what Patrick Vincent has called "A Continent of Corinnes," Staël's followers (including Letitia Landon, Felicia Hemans, Delphine Gay, Elizabeth Barrett Browning, and Margaret Fuller, the "Yankee Corinna") celebrated the persona of the female poet, but also the topoi of Italy and exile.[12] Although *The Wild Irish Girl* preceded *Corinne* by a year, Owenson was soon called the

"Irish Corinne" and early in her career she cultivated the comparisons, speaking frequently of her admiration for Staël.[13] If *The Wild Irish Girl* entered Staël's consciousness as she was writing *Corinne* in 1806, *De la littérature* and *De l'Allemagne* most certainly shaped Owenson's later writings, including her two works on France (1817 and 1829), *Italy* (1821), and *The Life and Times of Salvator Rosa* (1824).

Glorvina and Corinne represented the colonized cultures of Ireland and Italy in complex and frequently unexpected ways; while the parallels between the subordinated, dependent status of women and of colonies were obvious, this pair of female figures resisted stereotypes of passive and willing subalterns, appearing instead as active agents of culture and subjectivity. Moreover, Glorvina and Corinne stood in stark contrast to the allegorical images of nation generated post-1789, where women embodied Liberty, Equality, France, or Britannia in abstract or entirely iconic ways.[14] Indeed, the fact that these authors so quickly became conflated with their creations in widely circulated paintings and prints suggests the intimate connections forged between women authors and alternative representations of national identity in the nineteenth century, while highlighting the central importance of the visual image in these constructions. Within each narrative, visual experience is tied directly to transnational sympathy and understanding, and the male protagonists learn to "see" the foreign culture only through the lessons of a female artist. The ways in which *The Wild Irish Girl* and *Corinne* stage difference and the cultural encounter are in turn reflected in the paintings of Hortense Haudebourt-Lescot, whose scenes of Italian peasants similarly present new models for seeing and conceiving the foreign Other and new kinds of imagined communities.

In both novels, the politics and poetics of national difference are foregrounded as Owenson and Staël reconfigure Rancière's "distribution of the sensible," giving voice and visibility to the invisible and incomprehensible Other of the colonized nation. In each of these master narratives, an Englishman moves from the British center to the colonized periphery (Ireland and Italy), where he meets a beautiful woman who introduces him, through travel and direct experience, to the aesthetic and ethical value of the foreign culture. In the process of his education, he falls in love with the foreign Other, who embodies difference both as a woman and as an avatar of her nation, and this attraction allows the hero to recognize the constructed nature of his previous conceptions of superiority and inferiority. Questioning the legitimacy of empire and hegemony, Owenson and Staël refuse the imperial model of domination and submission for what Susan Tenenbaum has called a "pluralistic nationalism,"[15] that embraces a diversity of equally valid, mutually beneficial cultures. In *Corinne,* and to a lesser extent in *The Wild Irish Girl,* women—both as characters in the novel and as authors thereof—are active agents of culture who, in crossing the boundaries between the private and public spheres, play a critical role in historical progress. Finally, Owenson and Staël expand the boundaries of the novel as genre in both form and content, introducing a textual hybrid of political theory, history, travelogue, and romance in their tales.

Both novels are focalized through the melancholy gaze of a noble British protagonist who is exiled from his fatherland, and importantly, from his father. Oswald, Lord Nelvil, is mourning the death of his parent at the outset of *Corinne* as he travels from Scotland to Italy to forget his sorrows. "Disenchanted with life,"[16] Oswald is a Romantic figure whose lassitude renders him indifferent to everything around him. Filled with a sense of bitter loss, Oswald blames his illicit love affair in France for his father's demise and is consumed by remorse and self-pity. At the opening of *The Wild Irish Girl*, Horatio M— is in prison for his debauchery and subsequently banished to Ireland by his father. Like Oswald, this son of an English lord is a "mortal disappointment"[17] to his parent, and his life of dissipation, like Oswald's, has alienated him from paternal approval. Horatio is an equally Romantic figure who is at once restless, sorrowful, and bored. Both are in a state of emotional paralysis that is emblematic of the Romantic *mal du siècle* and ennui that haunted so many of their fictional counterparts to follow. In a significant departure, however, from the more typical trajectory in contemporary Romantic narratives, Oswald and Horatio are awakened from their existential torpors by the experience of a culture foreign to their own. As they journey through the landscape, confronting language, ruins, art, literature, religion, and folkways entirely at odds with those of England and Scotland, this pair of melancholy and mournful heroes discover a renewed passion for life.

The education of the heroes in these quasi-*Bildungsromane* takes place as they learn to move from a focus on the perceived inferiority of the foreign culture to an appreciation and even admiration of it. In turn, the concept of "difference" shifts from a negative to a positive valence: where Horatio and Oswald initially conceive the Otherness of Irish and Italian culture in terms of its absolute inferiority to their own, at the end they come to recognize difference as both necessary and desirable, finding value in pluralism rather than hegemonic purity. This transition is central to both levels of the narratives—the romantic plot and the implicit political allegory—and is charted through metaphors of blindness, sight, and insight. Owenson and Staël demonstrate that intellectually constructed national prejudice can be deconstructed most effectively through visual experience. While language, based in difference, may in fact reify otherness, here vision becomes a means of bridging the divides between cultures to arrive at mutual understanding. Thus seeing and visual representation are privileged in *The Wild Irish Girl* and *Corinne* both thematically and stylistically, for as the British protagonist learns about Irish or Italian culture as he observes the landscape, art, and folk culture, so too does the reader.

Glorvina and Corinne are central figures who represent the cultural peripheries: in their beauty and brilliance they outshine the male protagonist while demonstrating knowledge and artistry that lie beyond the limits of the dominant discourses yet are given value both by the author and by the hero. Despite the distance between Ireland and Italy, there is substantial overlap between the characters of Glorvina and Corinne, as well as important differences. Both Glorvina and Corinne are beautiful and talented; but where Corinne is a wealthy orphan living independently, Glorvina is closely tied to her ancient, impoverished father. Each invokes the classical tradition in her clothes and coiffure, and their erudition includes the antiquity of their respective nations, which they teach to their foreign lovers. However, where Glorvina is a pure embodiment of Irish history and culture, Corinne represents Staël's ideas of productive hybridity.[18] The daughter of a British noble and an Italian mother, Corinne combines elements of both cultures, and her choice of a life in Italy over England is a telling political statement.

Glorvina's and Corinne's artistic expression in poetry, music, and dance (for each is also a gifted performer of her national dance), do much to reveal to Horatio and Oswald the beauties of Irish and Italian culture. But it is in their roles as tour guides, providing the histories of the nation and its rituals, religion, and artifacts, that each plays the most influential role in shaping the impression of the colonized culture for the foreign visitor and by extension for the French and English readers. It is here that the voices of Owenson and Staël come closest to those of their characters, as they narrate the landscape and ruins in a series of verbal tableaux that interpolate the form of a travelogue into the novel, privileging visual experience as a means to understanding.

The conflation of Corinne and Italy, signaled by the title, clearly links the subordinated nation with the feminine, and as noted above, the entire novel metaphorically evokes gender as well as national politics.[19] Even before Staël's novel, the trope of "Italy as a woman" had become a commonplace, as the "backward" country, associated with passion, superstition, and beauty was feminized in the hegemonic cultural imagination. Similarly, observes J. Th. Leerssen, *"The Wild Irish Girl* fits into a longstanding tradition which had personified Ireland as a female and had represented her colonial relationship with England as one of sexual exploitation or oppression."[20] Yet in their respective novels, Stael and Owenson seek to escape the hierarchical circuits of power and subjectivity that would construct or constitute the female Other and the feminized nation exclusively through the dominant male gaze. Instead, through images of pluralism, hybridity, and the potential subversion of the traditional marriage plot, the authors posit a conscious resistance to the ideologies of subordination (national, gender) which nonetheless includes a final recognition of its own limitations. In both, the union between the British protagonist and the female, foreign Other is prevented by a paternal interdiction that posits the power of the patriarchy to uphold the hierarchies of difference. In *The Wild Irish Girl*, Glorvina is ultimately bestowed upon Horatio by the Prince and the Earl (their respective fathers), and the troubled rivalry between generations and nations is ostensibly resolved through the final exchange of the woman between the three men. In the most famous proclamation of the novel, Horatio's father writes: "let the names of Inismore and M— be inseparably blended, and the distinctions of English and Irish, of protestant and catholic, forever buried. And, while you look forward with hope to this family alliance being prophetically typical of a national unity of interests and affections between those who may be factiously severe, but who are naturally allied, lend your *own individual efforts* towards the consummation of an event so devoutly to be wished by every liberal mind, by every benevolent heart" (250).

Yet the proposed union of England and Ireland is not consummated in the pages of *The Wild Irish Girl*, and both Horatio and Glorvina are silenced. The idealistic marriage of cultures is deferred to a future moment beyond the trajectory of the narrative, and the call for "national unity" is put forth by the same patriarch who saw in marriage the opportunity for a husband "to give soul to beauty, and intelligence to simplicity, to watch the ripening progress of your grateful efforts, and finally clasp to your heart that perfection *you have yourself created*" (227; my emphasis). For Owenson, Glorvina is no more Horatio's "creation" than he is hers; nor should Ireland be England's "creation" in any kind of union. Although Owenson is frequently criticized for her apparent support of the union of England and Ireland here, careful examination of the text leaves her meaning far more ambiguous. For in the disappearance of Glorvina and Horatio at the end of the narrative, both silenced and invisible, the patriarchal pronouncement rings less hopeful. Horatio's father, the voice of English authority and benevolent superiority, proposes the elimination of difference where the two cultures would be "inseparably blended," an image that points to the absorption of Ireland into England, just as his image of marriage absorbs the wife's identity into the desires and values of her husband. This model of subordination rather than equality, clearly enunciated in all of the father's utterances on marriage in the novel, runs counter to what Owenson figures forth in the relationship between Glorvina and Horatio. Moreover, Owenson's own paratextual presence in *The Wild Irish Girl*, in the form of extensive footnotes that account for more than half of the text, also disappears in the conclusion. Owenson's footnote annotations, providing detailed references to first-hand experience, previous scholarship on Celtic culture, and historical context, operate on a parallel plane to the plot and establish the clear, if (visually, physically) subordinated intervention of the voice of the female Irish artist alongside that of the first-person (male) British traveler, supplementing his subjective impressions of the nation with her "objective" facts and scholarship. As the heteroglossic narrative gives way to the hegemonic discourse of patriarchal authority, women's voices disappear, as does the representation of Ireland as an independent and valuable culture. In the end, of course, Owenson's voice is heard in the publication of the novel itself, inspiring future generations of authors and patriots. Her vision of culture and women's role in history emerges from the space between the text and the paratext, the interstices between fiction and history, and the tension between the idealized, utopic vision of gender and national equality and the reality of hegemonic domination.

The ending of *Corinne* demonstrates similar ambiguities between what Kari Lokke has dubbed "utopian hope and a melancholy defeatism."[21] As was the case in *The Wild Irish Girl*, the fathers play a definitive role in disrupting the union of the British protagonist and the colonized Other. Here, Oswald bows to his father's wishes and renounces his love for Corinne in order to marry her British half-sister, the passive and childlike embodiment of "English womanhood." Oswald's betrayal, abandoning Italian Corinne for English Lucile, moves the novel to a melancholy and somber close. Yet despite the triumph of the patriarchal law, liminalizing and ultimately destroying the woman of genius, *Corinne* ends with some degree of hope for the future, if not the present. The unhappiness of Oswald's marriage to Lucile signals the danger or even creative sterility of national purity. Staël's ideal of cultural hybridity, announced early in the narrative, is presented in a discussion of literature but is echoed throughout the novel as a transnational ideal for the political as well as the personal. As Nelvil, d'Erfeuil, and Corinne argue the merits of the different genres of poetry, drama, and prose in relation to the language, politics, and national culture of Italy, France, and England, Staël's own connections between these themes (artistic genre, politics, and nation) become apparent. As Oswald asserts the superiority of English poetry, Corinne counters with examples of Italian verse, conceding that while British poetry excels in expressing "cette mélancolie profonde" of the human heart (174), the Italians triumph in giving voice to the imagination. Importantly, she criticizes as well as praises her native literature. Highlighting both its strengths and its weaknesses, Corinne attributes the flaws in Italian prose to the country's current lack of independence and the negative effect of its unhappy political state. By contrast, the parodic figure of d'Erfeuil can see nothing but perfection in anything French and believes all nations should follow the Gallic model. Voicing Staël's own critique of French *belles lettres*, Corinne replies that the nation's "literary orthodoxy" which opposes any innovation, ultimately renders its literature "très stérile" (176–77). Thus Staël, via Corinne, advocates a plurality of voices and styles expressing the spirit of all the nations and their peoples, rather than a single and universally privileged aesthetic.

As the conversation draws to a close, the Prince Castel-Forte, Corinne's friend and Staël's frequent mouthpiece, expounds the importance of mutual influence, intoning "I think we all need one another" (177). This plea for reciprocal understanding and influence in both the political and the literary realms proposes a model of productive hybridity, where difference is recognized and appreciated for its ability to stimulate new ideas and new ways of seeing things. Staël's ideal, as it is posited here, is one of accretion, where each nation (or individual) would add to its/his/her strengths without abandoning what makes it uniquely itself. This utopic vision of common influence and cooperation is implicitly applicable to gender difference as well, for both men and women, within Staël's paradigm, could learn from one another while maintaining the qualities that distinguish them. Indeed, as Castel-Forte indicates, the Other may be seen as a complement to lack rather than a threat to totality.

If Oswald is ultimately unable to internalize what he has learned from Italy and from Corinne, the image of hybridity or cross-fertilization nonetheless manifests a vision of hope at the end of the novel. Juliette, the daughter of Oswald and Lucile, resembles neither her father nor her mother, but rather Corinne. Demonstrating a belated solidarity with her foreign sister, Lucile embraces the lessons learned by her dark daughter from Corinne, who passes her talents onto the child, teaching her to play the harp and sing the native songs of both Scotland and Italy. Thus, though on her deathbed, Corinne becomes a metaphoric mother of the next generation, and even the offspring of the British couple can carry forth her transcultural artistic aesthetic. As Corinne expires, she plans one final performance, where again, through a substitute or surrogate, her words can reach an audience. Unable to perform, Corinne is reduced to being a spectator of her own "swan song," and she sits in the shadows, covered by a veil in order "to see Oswald, without being seen" (581). A young girl in white, who represents both Corinne and perhaps Juliette, gives voice to the woman who can no longer occupy the stage and embodies the future, where the female artist's creations will continue to give her life.

Corinne and *The Wild Irish Girl*, a pair of early and influential novels reflecting on gender and national identity in the nineteenth century, served as master narratives for future generations in their depiction of the political roles that art and women could potentially play in the public realm. Each posited a counter-discourse to the dominant images of colonial power and superiority with a narrative that reflected the value of the oppressed culture in ways that also reflected on contemporary constructions of gender and oppression. In these transnational romances, sympathy between the main characters vies with cultural difference: in Owenson's tale, love triumphs over difference, while in

Staël's difference ultimately prevails, at least within the confines of the story itself. But for both narratives, what April Alliston has called "transnational sympathies" between the male representative of the colonizing culture and the female representative of the "colonized" create idealized communities outside of the constructed borders of nation. Alliston notes that French and British authors used "the code of sympathy to imagine utopian alternatives to the nation-state in part by legibly mapping out its fragmentation both from within and from without, and also by representing alternatives to the family at its heart, the private sphere that anchors and images the public nation."[22] For Owenson and Staël, as for their followers, these sympathetic communities could be created only within or beyond the boundaries of the nation-state once the dominant culture, class, or gender could "see" in literal and figurative ways the dominated, who too often occupied a position of invisibility and by extension, silence. In the paintings of Hortense Lescot, as in the later novels of Owenson and of Angélique Arnaud, these conceptions of nation, gender, and identity as formulated in *Corinne* and *The Wild Irish Girl,* would be developed in ways that sought to transform the "conditions of intelligibility" (Rancière, *PA* 12) in French and British culture by making visible not only the female artist but also the social and national Others outside of the structures of political and cultural hegemony.

Hortense Haudebourt-Lescot:
PAINTING ITALY

Antoinette-Cécile-Hortense Viel Lescot (1784–1845), universally acknowledged as one of the most important female painters in France from the Empire through the July Monarchy, played a similar role to that of Staël and Owenson in rendering the Other of the colonized culture (in this case, Italy) "visible" in France, while also demonstrating the role played by women (artists) in culture. Like Owenson and Staël, Lescot was socially and politically engaged in contemporary events, actively committed to her career as an independent female artist, and no stranger to controversy. Echoing her sister artists, Lescot turned to a foreign culture to reflect on art, gender, and national identity, and like the Irish and Swiss authors, she expanded the limits of form and genre to give voice to new ways of seeing and representing the world. The intersections between Lescot and Corinne are striking: both lived an exceptional life in Rome as an independent female artist, both were renowned for their skills as dancers as well as a poet/painter, and both played a role in representing Italian culture to a French audience. Like the fictitious Corinne, Lescot was crowned with a laurel wreath on the steps of the Capitol[23] in a ceremony that may well have been a tribute to her resemblance to Staël's heroine. Elected to the Academy of Saint Luke in 1812, Lescot achieved recognition and status abroad that were not possible for a female artist in France and frequented an international community of artists gathered in Rome during this period of French occupation. Upon her return to Paris, she would become an influential teacher to the next generation of female artists, but perhaps even more significantly, Lescot, like Staël and Owenson, sought through her art to reconfigure the hierarchies of national and artistic discourses, and render visible, and thus intelligible, the "invisible" cultures of the colonized. While not entirely immune to the fetishizing impulses of an idealized ethnography, Lescot nonetheless constructed a female artistic identity that proposed an imagined community privileging commonality over difference while destabilizing the division between the gendered realms of the public and the private spheres.

Though almost entirely forgotten today, during the course of the nineteenth century Lescot (later Haudebourt-Lescot, following her marriage in 1820) was the subject of critical praise, governmental commissions, and popular acclaim. From her first Salon submission in 1810, critics admired her scenes of Italian peasants: C. P. Landon (never a fan of female artists) wrote of her *Prédication dans l'église de St Laurent, hors des murs, à Rome* (1810), "Composition, design, character, costumes, architecture, accessories of many kinds, everything here is treated with intelligence and ease."[24] One of the most influential art critics of the period, Landon would go on to devote several pages of most of his subsequent *salons* to Lescot's paintings, accompanied by engravings of her work, and later credited her with the invention of the Italian genre scene.[25] In 1827, at the mid-point of her career, Antony Béraud observed: "The reputation of Mme Haudebourt-Lescot has long been established; we do not know of one more legitimately acquired; no jealous voice has dared to contest her success. The public praise that intoxicates our women artists is often rescinded in private; the likeable author of so many charming paintings, all of which have obtained the most brilliant success, must be an exception to this common rule; and as Mme Haudebourt owes these triumphs to no one but herself, from afar as in her presence, it is to her alone that a unanimous homage is addressed."[26] Charles Blanc, France's first official art historian, added an appendix devoted to Haudebourt-Lescot to the final *Ecole française* volume of his influential *Histoire des Peintres* in 1863, a source book for following generations of artists. In it he maintains that in her early Italian scenes, "which are her best, there is a certain pictorial strength, *vis pictoria,* that impels us to include her in the ranks of the family of painters."[27] And in 1887, some forty years after her death, Antony Valabrègue consecrated a lengthy article to her life and work, in which he pays tribute to her talent and "brilliant celebrity" which enabled her to "take her place among the illustrious women of her day."[28] Haudebourt-Lescot rightfully figures "in the company of all the best known masters of the period," Valabrègue tells us, including "Gros, Gérard, Hersent, Lethière, Granet, and Drölling" (104). Finally, in Walter Sparrow's *Women Painters of the World* of 1905, Lescot is lauded as "the creator of the type of exotic subjects borrowed from Italy, to which numerous artists in France devoted themselves" and an influence on the Romantic school of local color.[29]

If the critics frequently celebrated Haudebourt-Lescot's art and inventiveness, they just as frequently made reference to the exceptional nature of her life and her training. Born Mlle Viel, she was first renowned not as a painter but as a dancer during the *Directoire,* becoming "une femme à la mode" who "shone at the salons" and was "admired, acclaimed" at the "brilliant soirées" of the period.[30] Hortense Viel, as she was then known, first entered the public eye at fourteen or fifteen as what Valabrègue called a "mondaine" (103), reflecting a connection to the decadent social world of the Directory and Consulat that also hints at less savory associations. In Auguste Jal's *Critique sur le Salon de 1819,* as well as all of her obituaries, Lescot's past as a denizen of the post-revolutionary salons and her initial renown for her dancing rather than painting are highlighted. Jal, and later Valabrègue and Blanc, linked her name to the "famous quadrilles of Tréniz, Violette, and Dupaty" (Valabrègue 103, Blanc 47), making the explicit connection with famous male dancers (Tréniz) and politicians (Dupaty) that further tied Viel/Lescot to the decadent world of the *merveilleuses*. When she took on her stepfather's name (Lescot) and left for Rome to pursue her painting career, the composer André-Ernest Grétry was quoted as saying, "My dear friend, you have done well to transfer to your hands the talent that you had in your feet."[31]

With their emphasis, overt or implied, on Lescot's body, public reputation, and sexuality, these articles draw the reader's attention to her gender rather than her talent, to the transgressive nature of her career(s), to the performative nature of her identity, and to her reinvention as a painter. What they fail to mention (but certainly attempt to evoke) is the very real scandal that emerged when Lescot followed her teacher, Guillaume Guillon Lethière (1760–1832), to Rome after he became Director of the French Academy in 1807. Lescot demonstrated an early gift for painting and drawing and began art lessons with Lethière at the age of seven. It was he who introduced her into the social whirl of the *Directoire,* whether as a lover or as a protégée, and it was through his connections with Lucien Bonaparte that Lethière procured his appointment at the Villa Médici. The rules at the French Academy in Rome prohibited women (including wives) from living at the Villa and from taking classes there, so Lescot's decision to join her teacher there in 1808 was unprecedented. It is more than likely that there was indeed a liaison between teacher and pupil: the widespread rumors are substantiated by Ingres's dedication of an intricate pencil portrait of Lethière "à Mlle Lescot" and by a lengthy letter from Lethière (who was married, with children) defending himself from the accusations of "concubinage." Protesting a bit too vehemently, he refers to the twenty-four year old Lescot (who had been dancing in public for a decade) as an "enfant" and "une jeune fille," claiming paternal solicitude for the daughter of his friends, while at the same time claiming he "took appropriate precautions not to feed the rumors" and "always avoided being seen in public with her. She only came to the Academy of France to study there and make use of the right of all foreigners to draw the antique statues in the gallery."[32] It is, however, also clear that Lescot pursued her painting career in Rome with unusual determination, gaining access to training and connections unavailable to a woman artist in Paris. Thus, although she could not join in the official classes at the Academy offered to the Prix de Rome winners, she was able to study the art and architecture of the classical and modern masters in Italy, both *in situ* and in the public galleries at the Academy.

During her sojourn in Rome, from 1808–16 Lescot also took the opportunity to turn her gaze from antiquity to the present, and unlike her male peers, whose training was focused on copies and themes of the classical past, she began to paint contemporary scenes of Italian peasants engaged in daily activities. As noted above, Lescot was widely credited with inventing this type of genre scene and was lauded for her originality. The author of *Lettres à David sur le Salon de 1819* wrote to the exiled master of Lescot's "paintings sent from Rome" which "offered us a new and piquant genre."[33] Landon maintained that "Madame Haudebourt is the first French artist to establish a reputation through the simple representation of scenes of popular customs of Italy" (*Salon de 1831* 139–40), and Valabrègue numbered her among "the group of innovators" in the pre-Romantic period (103). Although Haudebourt-Lescot was ultimately eclipsed in history by the male painters of Italian folk life who followed her, including Léopold Robert, Jean-Victor Schnetz, and Achille-Etna Michallon and is barely mentioned in recent studies of the topoi of peasants and local color, in the nineteenth century she was considered the originator of the Italian genre scene.[34]

When Lethière arrived in Rome to assume his position at the French Academy, Ingres was beginning his second year there. The artists forged a long-term friendship witnessed by a series of pencil portraits by Ingres of Lethière, his wife, and children dating from 1808–1818, as well as a striking portrait of Hortense Lescot (figure 21) executed in 1814.[35] In the portrait, Lescot is wearing the costume of a woman of the Italian countryside, thus identifying herself with her painted subjects. While Ingres executed a great number of these portraits in 1814–15, his images of expatriates in Italy portrayed them in their native attire and Lescot is the only sitter depicted *à l'Italienne*. Whether at

137

Part II: Cosmopolitan Visions

Figure 21
J.-A.-D. Ingres, *Portrait of Mlle Lescot,* 1814. Pencil on paper. 27.1 × 21.1 cm. Private collection.

Ingres's suggestion or more probably her own initiative, this elaborate costume with the embroidered apron and lace headdress of the Frascati region refers directly to the garb of the women in her popular paintings, exhibited both in Rome and in Paris at the Salons of 1810 and 1812. By posing not as "herself," that is, a French woman or a French woman painter, but as a woman in the costume of the Italian countryside, Lescot foregrounds the questions of identity and nation: like Owenson and Staël in their willingness to perform Glorvina and Corinne, she self-consciously collapses the difference between herself and her painted subjects. She inhabits the clothes with ease and grace, neither uncomfortable nor overwhelmed by their foreign splendor. Her face, an exquisitely executed *jolie laide,* communicates the intelligence and self-possession of the thirty-year-old female artist at the height of her career in Rome, while her hands, in typical Ingres fashion, express both grace and awkwardness, reflecting perhaps her difficult position within her chosen profession. Her necklace and earrings form an energetic frame for her face, the tight circles of the beads echoing her curls peeking out from beneath the lace. A pin in the shape of a hand emerges from her scarf in a gesture that directs us beyond the frame, counterbalancing the gentle tilt of her head. Just as Corinne's and Glorvina's dress set them apart, establishing their connection with Italian and Irish culture, so too does Lescot's self-fashioning here announce her identification with her sisters of the Roman countryside. Ten years later, Haudebourt-Lescot's self-portrait (figure 17, discussed in chapter 2) would similarly use the language of clothes and accessories to reflect on the politics of female artistic identity.

Lescot's innovative genre scenes reflect the "ethnographic impulse" that emerged at the end of the eighteenth century, when, as Melissa Calaresu explains, travelers exploring Italy "became increasingly interested in the customs and traditions of the popular classes—what Peter Burke describes as the 'discovery of the people.'"[36] By the onset of the nineteenth century, the Grand Tour had come to encompass visits not only to ancient sites, but also to "popular fairs and festivities," including street music, story-tellers, and puppet plays, Calaresu tells us, as guidebooks encouraged travelers "to observe the customs of different societies and hopefully reflect on their own" (201). Italian *vedutisti* such as Bartolomeo Pinelli (1781–1835) translated peasant life into bucolic scenes for touristic consumption, highlighting costume and custom in drawings, prints, and watercolors that appealed in both their simplicity and their humor but remained closer to illustration than to Salon painting.

Lescot's scenes, at once innovative and influential, sought to move beyond the documentary and anecdotal for a more complex vision of what Michel de Certeau has called "the network of social practices" that constituted Italian culture.[37] In her portrayal of popular traditions, street and market scenes, domestic interiors, and religious ceremonies, Lescot privileges the practices of everyday life over history, the quotidian over the epic. At the same time, by virtue of the act of representation, the ordinary is validated and even transfigured into something both timeless and emblematic. For Lescot and indeed all of the French artists portraying the Italian peasantry from 1810 onward, finding a suitable visual discourse for this "low" subject matter was central to the new genre, and in many cases these canvases represented a break with traditional theories of thematic propriety. Indeed, Neil McWilliam identifies "a sense of crisis over the languages available to art—and the repertoire of moral values they were capable of articulating—which persisted through much of the century and provided one of the fundamental discursive boundaries structuring debate over popular subject matter."[38] Many of Lescot's male contemporaries, trained in the studios of David and Girodet, treated the popular subjects in an idealizing Neo-Classical style, ennobling the peasants in such a way as to draw implicit parallels between the contemporary Italian *paysans* and their ancient Roman ancestors. This blurring of the hierarchies of subject matter, as emblematized by Léopold Robert's oeuvre, prompted conservative critic E.-J. Delécluze to complain of Robert's *Improvisateur napolitain* (1824): "Je le redemande encore, est-ce un tableau de genre? est-ce un tableau d'histoire?" [I ask again, is it a genre painting or is it a history painting?]. Robert, whose subject matter closely followed Lescot's own, sought ways to depict the Italian peasantry "conflating history and genre, moral elevation and anecdotal immediacy" and to "infuse his subjects 'with this character of nobility and truth, of taste and naivety'" (McWilliam 79). Representing the figures with an historicizing elevation that "denied contemporaneity to their humble subjects" (Brettell 14), Robert hoped to imbue the Italian genre scene with the aesthetic and moral value of history painting; with overt references to ancient Roman culture, Raphael, Leonardo, and Poussin, "Robert linked classical civilization, Renaissance Italy, and France in the Golden Age with the naïve gestures and costumes of the Italian peasantry" (Brettell 16).

While Robert and the male French cohort who followed Lescot turned to a classical past and the intertexts of high art, they also retained an exoticizing emphasis on distance and difference in their portrayals of the Italian popular classes, most notably in images of swarthy brigands and fortune-tellers. Thus, even as they "translated" the foreign culture into the familiar visual discourses of high culture, these French painters of Italian scenes highlighted costumes, traditions, and mores unfamiliar to Salon audiences, locating the Southerners in an indeterminate space and time outside of the parameters of modernity. Just as frequently, these narratives of folk culture and peasant life conflated peasants and the landscape into a totalizing "picturesque," constructing the Italian *contadini* as quaint, even primitive Others, while keeping the realities of national and class distinctions at a comfortable distance.

Although Lescot is credited with originating the Italian genre scene, her approach to portraying the Italian peasantry differed in significant ways from that of those who followed her. Lescot also sought ways to "translate" the Italian peasantry into a visual language accessible to her Parisian audiences, but if her male contemporaries (Robert, Schnetz, Michallon) emphasized national distance and difference from their subjects, Lescot sought to underscore a sense of intimacy and commonality between cultures. To this end, the female artist turned not to history painting or Davidian Neo-Classicism for her model, but rather to the traditions of French and Dutch genre painting of the seventeenth and eighteenth centuries. In her genre scenes of peasant life, often centering on women, children, and the elderly, Lescot depicts the homely and familiar in scenes of public and private rituals that encode the social and political values of the contemporary nation. But in an important departure from traditional genre painters (Metsu, Steen, Chardin, Greuze, etc.), Lescot turns her gaze to a foreign culture rather than her own, thus defamiliarizing the form of the genre scene, transforming it from a self-reflexive medium to one that reflects on both the differences and similarities of the cultural Other.[39] In shifting the focus to the domestic and private realm of Italian peasants, Lescot simultaneously foregrounds gender, class, and nation in a gesture that renders the modern Italian *contadini* active subjects representing a culture that is at once distant from that of the French audience and fundamentally familiar in its everyday practices. The fact that nearly all of Lescot's images were displayed first in Rome before being sent back to Paris and the Salon testifies to her engagement in both worlds. Like Staël and Owenson, Lescot proposes a transnational or cosmopolitan lesson in ways of seeing the foreign Other.

Among the numerous paintings Lescot conceived and/or executed in Rome, including *The Fair at Grottaferrata, The Notary Public, The Piferari Playing before the Madonna, The Relic Seller, The First Steps,* and *The Old Man and the Children,* two in particular epitomize Lescot's politically and socially oriented genre scenes. In the *Jeu de la main chaude* (1812) (figure 22), she depicts a game being played by Italians with an almost ethnographic precision that nonetheless renders the minutely detailed scene familiar as well. In this traditional guessing game, someone hides his eyes and extends a hand behind his back; another player slaps his hand and he tries to read the faces of the other players to see who has done it. Played in France and Holland as well as Italy, this game of "hot hand" was the subject of genre paintings by Janssens, Rembrandt, Fragonard, Greuze, and Boilly, and these visual and cultural intertexts establish Lescot's claim to a position within a larger tradition of portraying folkways. Yet Lescot's scene, painted by a woman living and working in a country recently annexed to France, carried different valences than those of her male predecessors as she renders visible the shared traditions of the foreign Other, while at the same time foregrounding the act of "reading" the world.

The tightly knit group of women surrounding a young man is presided over by a paternal figure in a chair and a priest, whose very presence establishes the innocence of the activity, removing the game from the erotic context found in Fragonard and Boilly. Yet, in keeping with the phrase "la chaleur de la main

Figure 22 Hortense Haudebourt-Lescot, *Le Jeu de la main chaude*, 1812. Oil on canvas. 75 × 100 cm. Copyright: Musée des Beaux-Arts de Tours.

égale à la chaleur du coeur" (the warmth of the hand equals the warmth of the heart), the scene clearly hints at a courtship ritual between the young woman on her knees and the young man behind her, whose face is illuminated by the sun. The structure and lighting of the canvas recall Greuze's sentimental genre scenes (most notably *L'Accordée du village*), but here the players are defamiliarized both by their costume and by the setting in a covered courtyard, which opens onto a Roman garden. The women's dresses and scarves mark their difference from their contemporary French counterparts, as does the architecture, while the emotion and even the activity are universalized. The inclusion of multiple generations, from the elderly woman next to the priest, to the father figure in the chair, the mother at far right holding a naked baby, and the young people playing the game all offer Lescot's audience a view of Italian culture and mores, the intertwining bodies and game shared among all ages reflecting an idealized vision of joyous solidarity that again points back to Greuze's sentimental canvases. As Emma Barker explains, sentimentalism was frequently linked to reform through the "experience of common humanity."[40] Greuze's scenes (like Lescot's to follow) "offered a utopian vision of an enlightened social order" (105) achieved through the viewer's identification with the painted drama: "in thus drawing the viewer or reader to identify with fellow human beings and share their emotions, the tableau works toward merging discrete individuals into a community of feeling, thereby undermining the distinction between self and other. In other words, these aesthetic effects are directed toward a moral project of social solidarity" (111). In Greuze's genre paintings, the "community of feeling" was understood in terms of breaking down barriers between classes; in Lescot's scenes, this utopic idea of community is extended to nations as well. In both cases, the idealizing impulse runs the risk, of course, of eliding distinctions in pursuit of bourgeois sympathy. If the moralizing genre scene frequently homogenized the French peasant or working class family, when it is translated into a foreign setting this moralizing genre painting can alternately domesticate the cultural Other or exoticize that otherness through an ethnographic lens. Lescot's work falls somewhere in the middle, showing both difference and sameness, and by focusing on love and flirtation, family and maternity, timeless games and daily life, she brings Italian culture and local color into a familiar register in search of a "common humanity."

In "Objects of Ethnography," Barbara Kirshenblatt-Gimblett argues that the ethnographic representation of culture runs the risk of aestheticizing difference in dangerous ways. She contends, "By aestheticizing folklore—no matter what is gained by the all inclusive definition of folklore as the arts of everyday life—we are in danger of depoliticizing what we present by valorizing an aesthetics of marginalization."[41] In Lescot's work, both here and in her myriad representations of Italian folk culture, the risk of reifying the colonized Other of the Roman *campagna,* of romanticizing and aestheticizing the "simple ways" of the peasants is very real, and there are inarguably images in which this depoliticization of their existence at the margins for the hegemonic center occurs. But just as frequently, Lescot, in recognizing her own position at the margins and identifying with the dominated culture rather than the dominating one, foregrounds these tensions, refusing the hierarchies of center/periphery, self/other for a more troubled depiction of identities.

In this early composition, the intimacy of the interior stands in vivid contrast to the scene beyond the arched portals. There we see a vivid blue sky, clouds, trees, bushes, and flowers illuminated by the bright sunlight that also streaks across the interior scene, but highlights only some of the figures, leaving others in obscurity. If the interior is the realm of the present and the feminine, the exterior world appears to lie under the sway of four classical statues that face away from the game players toward the sun-dappled landscape. The inclusion of these clear classical references in the architecture and ancient sculptures towering over the domestic scene invokes both Italy's rich historic past and the equally rich tradition of French painters' portrayals of Italy in the seventeenth and eighteenth centuries: representations that privileged ruins and the remnants of antiquity, visualizing the contemporary landscape through the lens of its history in what Richard Wrigley has called a "well-recognized mode of apprehending Italy as a historical and cultural continuum" (251). Lescot subordinates the past to the present by placing these signifiers of antiquity in the background, behind the plane of dramatic action, yet their position above and beyond the domestic scene nonetheless signals a powerful presence.

Beyond these abstract references, the sculptures themselves carry specific narrative import. Véronique Moreau identifies the pair of statues on the left as "a bearded toga wearer" and "perhaps a philosopher, an allegory of abundance, or a muse"; the nude figure at center is the Borghese *Discophore* and that on the far right a Dacian Prisoner.[42] By including these copies of classical antiquity, Lescot refers to the models and subject matter her male counterparts at the Academy were limited to, contrasting their focus on the distant past with her portrayal of the immediate present. Like the nude male torso in Grandpierre-Deverzy's atelier painting of 1824, the statues face away from the viewer and the female painter, alluding perhaps to the forbidden or inaccessible realms of artistic training. But this choice of figures (for this is an imagined locale) brings together allusion to classical culture that can be read against the contemporary political situation in Rome. The *togatus* or toga wearer was understood as Roman citizen as well as a symbol of peace, as distinguished from the *sagum*-wearing soldier, while the Dacian prisoner evokes war and occupation, in implicit reference to the French occupation and annexation of Italy and the collapse of the Roman Republic. Between these two figures stand the obscured image of philosophy or art and the athletic form of the discus thrower. One of the most famous effigies from the Borghese collection, the *Discophore* would have been recognizable as one of statues being shipped from Rome to Paris for Napoleon's ever expanding national collection. This symbol of empire and conquest (a Roman copy of a Greek original, now being transferred to the ownership of another imperial power) stands in contrast to the internal and quotidian image of shared humanity that Lescot foregrounds in the most literal sense.

In *Le Baisement des pieds de la statue de saint Pierre dans la basilique Saint-Pierre de Rome* (1812) (figure 23), Lescot moves to the public space of St Peter's and transforms the church into what Mary Louise Pratt has called a "contact zone," that is "the space of colonial encounters, the space in which peoples geographically and historically separated come into contact with each other" (6). Here, an entourage of French citizens visits the Roman basilica; as they observe both the architecture and the celebration of a religious festival, they occupy the margins of the scene. While a wide variety of Romans are absorbed in worship—monks, pilgrims, penitents, a beggar, ecclesiastics, and women and children from the Roman countryside—the French are absorbed in one another, and not a single gaze within the group is directed at the church or its occupants.[43] The visiting entourage includes recognizable images of Lethière, Pierre-Adrien Pâris, an architect linked to the French acquisition of Roman antiquities, and Antonio Canova, the leading sculptor of the day.[44]

These representatives of France and the international artistic elite (Canova was Venetian) are strangers within the context of Lescot's scene: at the margins of the image, they are the objects of interest and scrutiny for the Roman women and beggars who are at home in the milieu. In this sense, they stand in for her viewers as aesthetic tourists witnessing the rites of a foreign culture. This shift in power, or the leveling of hierarchies, is reflected in the scale of the image where, in the tradition of ecclesiastic architecture, the human figures are equally dwarfed by the magnitude of the pillars, statues, and vaults. The piety of the various groups of women, children, and religious figures, who kneel or incline toward the altar, stands in marked distinction to the more worldly orientation of the tourists. The foreign visitors are set off not only by their upright posture (echoed only by that of the Swiss Guard), but also by their clothes and in this populous scene, costume is a marker of identity and difference. Somberly clad in dark jackets, tight breeches, and white jabots, the tailored elegance of Canova and company presents a stark contrast to the shapeless hooded habits of the penitents on the opposite side of the canvas. The simple and modern Empire dresses of the two (presumably) French women standing to the far right of the canvas similarly distinguish them from the *contadine* in their traditional embroidered gowns. A tonsured priest prostrates himself on the floor at center in his Franciscan robes, while an altar boy and a celebrant in white proceed

Figure 23 Hortense Haudebourt-Lescot, *Le Baisement des pieds de la statue de saint Pierre dans la basilique Saint-Pierre de Rome*, 1812. Oil on canvas. 148 × 196 cm. Musée du château de Fontainebleau. Bridgeman Art Library International, New York, NY.

toward the statue of St. Peter. Arrayed in splendid sacerdotal vestments and jeweled crown, the statue of the apostle further signals the semiotic nature of dress, for his crimson robes mark this as the Feast of the Chair of Saint Peter.[45] Within the church calendar, the celebration of the Chair (or *Cathedra*) recognizes the literal as well as metonymic "seat" of the Catholic Church in Rome. But historically, the feast marks the day when St Peter came to Rome from Antioch to combat paganism and convert "the throne of the Caesars" to "the throne of the heads of the church of Jesus Christ."[46] This celebration of "the taking possession of Rome" by St Peter of course invokes the more recent "possession taking" of Rome by Napoleon, the self-styled Caesar of the nineteenth century. Thus the tensions between religion and empire, between traditional Roman culture and the hegemonic secular culture of imperial France, are enacted in this scene that depicts two distinct world views in the contact zone of the basilica. An image of neither military triumph nor oppressed subjugation, Lescot's painting portrays the peaceful, if somewhat disjunctive, coexistence of the two cultures. A dove representing the Holy Spirit, but also peace and redemption with an olive branch in its beak, is figured on the wall behind the French women, hinting at Lescot's political position.

While assorted groups of women and children in the dress of the Roman *campagna* look on, a child kisses the toe of St Peter in an act of worship that also speaks of ancient traditions of faith potentially exotic to the French viewer. Yet compositionally, these heterogeneous worshippers, denoted by their various costumes, are privileged over the more homogenous visitors whose position at the margins is repeated in another tiny group looking down from the balcony. A mendicant appeals for charity, but it is not clear that he will be heard by the artists and colonists. Beyond the pious assembly in the foreground, Lescot includes the statue of Saint Helen, mother of Constantine (yet another emperor), who converted to Christianity and performed great acts of charity. Holding the True Cross, she presides over the crowd, a female complement to Saint Peter. Vertically divided into thirds, the painting balances the swath of orangey red encompassing the bronze statue of the apostle with the brilliant gilt splendor of Bernini's monument to the Chair of Saint Peter. The Baroque reliquary for the wooden chair used by the first pope and his followers rises above the altar of the basilica at the visual and spiritual center of the apse. Yet in Lescot's scene, the elaborate seventeenth-century bronze sculpture, perhaps the most famous image in Saint Peter's, is obscured by the pilasters of Bernini's papal altar, and the simpler statue, dating from the early fourteenth century, is privileged. Its more human scale and accessibility invite the faithful to participate in more personal, even physical ways, in the same way, perhaps, as Lescot's low-key images of daily life in Italy make the culture more human, personal, and accessible.

Just as Holy Week occupied a central section of *Corinne* and Glorvina's relationship to Father John and Catholicism was extensively discussed in *The Wild Irish Girl*, Lescot uses religion here and in a large number of her Italian genre scenes (*Station de piferari devant une madone* [1810], *La Confirmation par un évêque grec dans la basilique de Sainte-Agnès* [1814], *Voeu à la madone pendant un orage* [1817], etc.) to reflect on the constructed nature of national identity and difference. For in each case, the female author or painter demonstrates the universal nature of Christianity and implicitly points to a larger context where the conception of divine love transcends divisions of nation and sect. Italian, French, or Irish, they argue, are all one in the eyes of God, and the diverse forms of worship are simply culturally inflected variations on a single theme. Saint Peter's Basilica can thus house both the French élite and the Italian peasants under a single, capacious roof, recalling John 14:2 ("In my Father's house are many dwelling places"), and in contrast to the violent scenes of Napoleonic conquest being produced during the period by Gros, Girodet, et alia, Lescot proposes another propaganda of sorts. Although socially connected to the world of Napoleon, both through the salons of the *merveilleuses* in Directory Paris and through Lucien Bonaparte (Lethière's patron) in Rome, Lescot nonetheless posits a subtle resistance to the discourses of empire in her paintings of occupied Italy. In depicting the culture of Rome, she shifts her gaze from the past to the present and from the (masculine) heroic to the (feminine) quotidian world of domesticity, ritual, and family.

With *Le Baisement des pieds de saint Pierre*, Lescot established her reputation both in Italy, where she displayed it at the Capitol, and in Paris, where she first exhibited it in a private showing for fellow artists at the Théâtre Italien some weeks before the Salon of 1812.[47] The former dancer was thus a canny promoter of her work, and her choice of venues—the Roman Capitol and the Théâtre Italien de Paris—further established the links between cultures that her canvas sought to promote, associating her as much with Italy as with France. The painting was purchased by the state in 1817 and displayed at the Luxembourg Palace, an honor limited to the most successful living artists.

Upon returning to France in 1816, Lescot continued to paint Italian scenes as well as portraits and historical "Troubadour" scenes, focusing on episodes from the Middle Ages and Renaissance. In 1820 Lescot married the architect Louis Haudebourt with whom she had a son, and unlike many female artists of the period, continued her career throughout the marriage. Between her return from Italy and her marriage, Lescot was named painter to the Duchesse de Berry, the fashionable daughter-in-law of Charles X, who was widowed in 1820 when her husband was assassinated as he left the Opera. Marie Caroline de Bourbon-Sicile (1798–1870) was the eldest daughter of Francis I, King of the Two Sicilies and married the younger son of the Comte d'Artois (later Charles

X) in 1816, giving birth to his son seven months after the Duc's death. Lively and informal, the Duchesse de Berry was an influential patron of the arts and the "undisputed leader of feminine fashion during the Restoration."[48] Raised in Naples in the court of King Ferdinand, the Duchesse de Berry may have been drawn to Lescot's scenes of Italian life, and in keeping with her patron's taste, Lescot also turned her attentions to the *genre troubadour* in small and highly polished scenes of French and British history. Her approach to the genre focused on women's roles in history, an orientation that may have appealed to the controversial Duchesse who attempted to shape French history herself in 1832. Following the Revolution of 1830 and the installation of the Orléans monarchy, the Bourbons were exiled to Britain. Disguised as a peasant, the Duchesse de Berry came back to France and led an attempt to overthrow Louis-Philippe and secure the throne for her son, Henri. The coup failed and she was imprisoned and ultimately exiled from France. Her abortive legitimist revolt, in which she played a leading role, demonstrates an unflagging faith in the power of women to participate in the political.

In looking at a final image by Lescot, taken from the life of Mary Queen of Scots, we find the artist's engagement with women's roles in history and art's role in its political representation. Mary Stuart was a popular figure among Troubadour painters, who frequently turned to British as well as French history for their subject matter. The French had long sympathized with the Catholic Queen: the daughter of James V of Scotland and Marie de Guise, she married François II in 1558 at fourteen, became Queen Consort of France in 1559, and was widowed a year later. Upon returning to Scotland, she became queen until she was forced to abdicate and was ultimately beheaded by her cousin, Elizabeth I of England. Mary's complicated tale of murdered husbands, rape, imprisonment, abdication, betrayal, and execution was portrayed in novels, plays, operas, paintings, and prints produced for popular consumption and reflected the renewed Romantic interest in the past. The fundamental conflict between Mary Stuart, the French Catholic Queen, and Elizabeth Tudor, the British Protestant Queen, emblematized many of the tensions between the two nations, playing out the differences perceived to be central to their constructed national identities.

In 1829, the Duchesse de Berry hosted the *Quadrille de Mary Stuart,* a fancy dress ball at which all of the guests were assigned roles and wore costumes of the period.[49] Playing the role of Mary Stuart herself, the Duchesse de Berry self-consciously alluded to the intersections between her own life and that of the sixteenth-century monarch, as both were widowed mothers of the (presumed) future king. What Caroline de Berry could not have known in 1829 was that her own fate would even more closely mirror that of Mary Stuart, while her son's would diverge radically from that of James VI. For Stuart, like Berry some three hundred years later, refused to accept her fate in exile. Escaping her prison in Loch Leven castle, Mary went to England to petition Elizabeth I for help in regaining the Scottish throne. Worried about the question of her own legitimacy—the same issue confronting the Bourbons—Elizabeth imprisoned Mary for nineteenth months before executing her for treason.[50] If the family of Charles X escaped the fate of Mary Stuart and the previous generation of Bourbons (Louis XVI and Marie-Antoinette, the Duchesse de Berry's aunt), Caroline's son, Henri Dieudonné, did not meet with the same luck as Mary Stuart's son James: where James VI of Scotland would go on to become James I of England, the Bourbons never regained the French throne and Henri would spend the rest of his life as the Comte de Chambord, the Legitimist Pretender.

Haudebourt-Lescot's watercolor, *Mary Queen of Scots Fainting on Being Forced to Abdicate* (figure 24), portrays the Stuart queen during her imprisonment as she is given a choice between abdication and death. In choosing an episode from British history, Lescot continues her engagement with a pluralistic vision of identity and nation, for the viewer's sympathy with the beleaguered queen transcends national difference, as noted above. Mary's hybrid identity, half-French, half-Scottish, was intended to build a bridge between the two cultures, and her marriage to François II had been orchestrated to unite the nations under a single rule. But Mary, despite her tragic fate, also embodies the powerful position of Queen, and not simply Queen Consort, for where the thrones in Scotland and England could pass to a daughter, in France they could not. While the image portrays the moment she is told she must choose between her position of power and her life, it is significant for Lescot, the Duchesse de Berry, and others that the choice was presented at all.

It is likely that Lescot's painting refers both to her patron's fascination with Mary Stuart and to Walter Scott's novel, *The Abbott* (1820), which recounts the Queen's imprisonment in Loch Leven castle. As Beth Wright has established, Scott was enormously popular in France in the 1820s and '30s, and influenced an entire generation's approach to literature, history, and narrative. Wright explains, "Scott helped the French to find new ways to imagine the past and provided a means of translating those historical insights into visual images."[51] His interest in folk culture and his "conception of the past as a web of cultural conflicts, whose persistent influence was evident even in their own time" (Wright 183) were consonant with Lescot's own approach to art and culture. The crossing of boundaries of word and image, past and present, Britain and France, are all presented in this small image. By including Margaret Erskine, Lady Lochleven, in the scene of abdication, Lescot collapses two separate episodes from the novel into a single frame. The mother of Mary's illegitimate half-brother, who is scheming to put her own son on the throne in place of Mary, Lady Lochleven embodies the forces conspiring against the Queen, adding to

Figure 24
Hortense Haudebourt-Lescot, *Mary Queen of Scots Fainting on Being Forced to Abdicate*. Salon of 1837. Watercolor on paper. 40.7 × 31.9 cm. Private collection. Bridgeman Art Library International, New York, NY.

the physical and psychological menace in a visually suggestive way. The tight composition opposes Mary, in white, against Margaret, in black, and all of the tension is drawn between the two powerful women. The upright and glowering matriarch in the background will triumph over the Catholic queen, who nonetheless is the focus of pity and devotion. In portraying a scene where the drama is entirely played out between influential women who represent political forces both as mothers and also in their own right, Lescot insists on women's political agency (even in Mary's ultimate "victimhood") and highlights the often occluded roles women have always played in shaping the nation. In choosing an episode from history, Lescot can also transcend the limits of her genre with implicit reference to events beyond the frame. For even as Scott's novel ends with Mary's escape from her prison, the nineteenth-century viewer would know that Mary's immediate sacrifices—her abdication, further imprisonment, and death—would ultimately defeat Lady Lochleven and her half-brother, for it is Mary's son who will rise triumphant and succeed not only to the throne of Scotland, but to that of England as well. Like the ending of *Corinne* and to a certain extent, *The Wild Irish Girl* as well, *Mary Queen of Scots Fainting* points beyond the immediate moment to a more hopeful future shaped by the efforts of women in history.

Haudebourt-Lescot would go on to exhibit more than 110 paintings at the Salons in the course of her thirty-year career, receiving medals in 1810, 1819, and 1827. Her work remained popular with the public and the critics and many of her images were reproduced through engravings and lithographs, the best of which were executed by the painter herself. Despite her association with the Duchesse de Berry, Lescot also received support from the July Monarchy and was one of the painters commissioned by Louis Philippe to decorate the galleries of Versailles with scenes from the history of France. Her salon became the gathering place for artists, authors, and aristocrats: Talma, Scribe, Rossini, Vernet, Drolling, and David d'Angers could be found there side by side with "everyone the court and the city considered most noble and brilliant—it was a rendezvous of the élite where everyone aspired to be admitted" (F. d'O. 320). Her obituary adds that it was even more chic to move from her salon to her atelier as one of her pupils. Lescot's students included a number of talented professional women artists (Mme de Herain, Mme Atala Varcollier, Mme Collin, Mlles Amic, Serret, and Fabre d'Olivet, the probable author of her obituary) who would go on to successful careers, as well as "*les grandes dames,* the queens of fashion and style, who wanted to add to their elegance the poetic charm of the arts" (F. d'O. 320). Hortense Haudebourt-Lescot was in many ways an exceptional woman—a successful female artist, the inventor of the Italian genre scene, and for more than forty years a popular denizen of society salons from the Directory through the July Monarchy. Yet with her paintings of Italian peasants, Scottish queens, and a wide variety of female Others, as well as her studio, open to women of every class and ability, she used art as means to forge new (imagined) communities of women and men based on commonalities rather than hierarchies of difference, thus participating in concrete as well as symbolic ways in the changing history and politics of the French nation.

Revolutionary Identities

Painting and Resistance in Owenson's *The Princess; or The Beguine*

The National Tale and Minor Literature:
IDENTITY AT THE MARGINS

With *The Wild Irish Girl*, Owenson introduced what would become the genre of the "national tale," a form developed primarily by women writers over the next several decades in tandem with the "historical novel," a genre associated with Walter Scott and a more "masculine" tradition. The national tale, Mark Mossman tells us, "embodies the strategy of political allegory"[1] in a narrative of cultural encounter that focuses on place and displacement, often negotiated through the experiences of a hero from the metropolitan/colonial center in the territory of the colonized periphery. Katie Trumpener explains that the genre addresses "questions of cultural distinctiveness, national policy, and political separatism,"[2] while Ina Ferris insists, following Owenson's own formulation, that the national tale is "founded on national grievances" which foreground the subjectivity of the subjugated Other of the "trampled-down nations."[3] The intersections between the politics of nation and those of gender are reflected both literally and allegorically in these tales that repeat the basic plot of *The Wild Irish Girl* in increasingly stylized ways. Although this plot initially comprised "the contrast, attraction, and union between disparate cultural worlds" Trumpener tells us (141), the union becomes increasingly problematized and ultimately impossible in Owenson's later works. She explains that the national tale's central political tendency "shifts gradually from a celebratory nationalism, which both recognizes cultural distinctiveness and believes in the possibility of transcultural unions, toward another more separatist position; continuing meditation on a history of cultural oppression makes rapprochement and reconciliation increasingly inconceivable" (146).

The national tale, relegated to a "minor genre" when recognized at all, is nonetheless integral in the development of the dominant form of the historical novel, and their interdependence reflects the dialogic nature of cultural representations of national identity in the early nineteenth century. Indeed *Waverley*, Scott's first work of historical fiction, was not published until 1814 and was clearly influenced by the political and national orientation of popular contemporary female novelists like Owenson and Edgeworth. But where the female-authored national tale sought to establish cultural legitimacy and a continuity between past and present, Scott's historical novels situate nationalism beyond the pages of the narrative "at a further stage of historical development" and only "through dislocation and collective suffering is a new national identity forged" (Trumpener 142). As gendered genres, the historical novel, depicting the nation through conflict and difference, rapidly took on the dominant position within the literary field, while the national tale, locating nation and culture in terms of broader connections and commonalities, was relegated to a secondary position. Writing from the literary as well as the national margins, Owenson used the national tale to give voice to a counter-discourse, exerting a feminist and pluralistic pressure on the political, national, and artistic centers.

In this sense, then, Owenson's national tales may be considered "minor literature," following Deleuze and Guattari's definition of the mode. As they explain, a minor literature does not come from a minor language, but rather it is that which a minority constructs within a major language, and its first characteristic is "the deterritorialization of language."[4] For Owenson and Irish authors to follow (Joyce, Beckett), English is at once the language of literature, the language in which they must write to be read, and also the language of the oppressor. Writing to give voice to a national consciousness, authors of minor literatures "deterritorialize" language in a variety of ways in order to foreground its extremities or limits, exposing and resisting the functions of power in language. In *The Wild Irish Girl*, Owenson's use of Irish or Gaelic (as well as Latin and French) throughout the English text and in the extensive footnotes, often without translation, destabilizes the dominant discourse by introducing a plurality of languages and registers. In *The Princess*, the narrative is similarly intertwined with passages and conversations in French, effectively interrupting English linguistic hegemony. The remaining characteristics of Deleuze and Guattari's "minor literatures" are "everything in them is political" and "everything takes on a collective value" (17). They explain: "It is a literature that produces an active solidarity in spite of skepticism; and if the writer is in the margins or completely outside his or her fragile community, this situation allows the writer all the more possibility to express another possible community and to forge the means for another consciousness and another sensibility" (17). Written by a female Irish author, doubly at the margins, Owenson's works manifest precisely these forms of political resistance and collectivity as they posit the existence and value of invisible histories, communities, and perspectives.

Challenging contemporary ideologies of nation and of gender, Owenson's national tales thus present a contestatory narrative of culture, identity, and difference through the disruption of the gendered division of the public and private spheres. Refusing the domestic ideologies that relegated women to the realm of hearth and home, the national tale represented women's active and participatory role in history, culture, and revolution. In *Mothers of the Nation*, Anne K. Mellor contends that despite—or perhaps because of—the dominance of women's domestic fiction in the Romantic period, "many women novelists offered an alternative vision of political governance, one grounded on a radical reform of the social construction of gender."[5] Female authors, including Owenson, Wollstonecraft, and Staël, actively participated in the Habermasian public sphere of civil society as they proposed and embodied alternate visions of society, gender, and the nation, both as politically engaged female writers and through the female characters in their fiction, who equally serve as models for the political role of women in national culture. Looking beyond the parochial and domestic, they offer "other ways of conceptualizing the locality of identity," Deidre Lynch tells us, in "communities that drew differently and disorientingly on the cultural flows of Empire."[6] If the national tale is didactic in its aims, it purports to educate the reader not only on the cultures of Ireland, Greece, India, Belgium, and elsewhere, but also on the contributions of women to national cultures of every variety.

Central to Owenson's vision of the national tale was the destabilization of accepted norms of identity and positionality, and through techniques of dislocation and displacement, she forces her readers to share the discomfort of her protagonists. Ferris finds in Owenson's national heroines an "ethic of estrangement through which the Irish novelist repositions the Staëlian heroine to expose the ambiguities of agency in colonial spaces" (78). Troubling the very assumptions of representation and subjectivity, Owenson crossed borders of gender, genre, and nation to body forth an alternative conception of a mobile and performative identity. Following the defeat of Napoleon in 1815, travel between Britain and France was once again possible and indeed was soon in vogue for the burgeoning middle class, many of whom had made their fortunes during the prolonged hostilities between the two nations. The Grand Tour, once the prerogative of the gentry, was now embraced (in modified forms) by a wide swath of English society; a cross-channel steam ship began service in 1816, and hotels were soon opened across the Continent to accommodate the swarms of British tourists. Travel accounts and guidebooks for the British tourist proliferated, and Owenson's interventions in the field share much with her national tales. Beginning with *France* (1817), followed by *Italy* (1821), and another volume entitled *France in 1829–1830,* the author of *The Wild Irish Girl* turned her gaze to European culture, geography, and politics. Unlike Staël's highly intellectual *De l'Allemagne,* Owenson's *France* and *Italy* focused on daily life and custom abroad, narrated through a liberal republican filter in what Raphael Ingelbien dubs the "travel-book-cum-radical-pamphlet."[7]

Thanks to the paradoxical *anglomanie* in France after Waterloo and to her literary acclaim with French readers, Owenson was welcomed into French society upon her arrival in 1816. In 1812, Owenson had married Sir Charles Morgan, and the former governess from Dublin acquired the title Lady Morgan. The English doctor's knighthood had only been bestowed shortly before the marriage, and the couple was regarded as arrivistes by London society, while the conservative British press endlessly mocked the pretensions of "Miladi." In France, however, the provenance of her title was of little interest, and Lady Morgan enjoyed great popularity for her wit and energy at the salons, soirées, and balls of Ultras and liberals alike. She befriended titled aristocrats and renowned intellectuals, leaders of the past and present from Mme de Genlis and Lafayette to Vivant Denon and Benjamin Constant, becoming such a "succès de société" that she was included in a chapter entitled "Certaines personnes de distinction" in Henri Bouchot's study *Le Luxe français: La Restauration* (1893). Bouchot notes, "One woman was especially in vogue in the early days of the Restoration: that was Lady Morgan,"[8] and goes so far as to include her portrait within the illustrated history of French society.

Owenson's *France* is a highly subjective examination of contemporary culture that gives equal weight to conversations with peasants, laundresses, and "Parisian society." Like all of her narratives, it is marked by heteroglossia, with lengthy sections in French and conversations transcribed "verbatim." Much like Lescot's paintings of the Italian peasants and their customs,[9] Owenson's *France* presents a series of vivid genre scenes that offer the reader a view of daily life through the lens of politics. The author announces her sympathies from the outset, beginning in Book I with "The Peasantry," and addressing topics such as "The Peasantry before the Revolution," "Conditions of the Peasantry arising out of the Revolution," "Rural Economy," "Peasant Dwellings," "Religious Processions," and "Costume." Here and throughout *France,* Owenson engages in social and political commentary, referring frequently to the Revolution, praising Napoleon's reign, criticizing the current Bourbon monarchy, and unabashedly addressing women's sexual and social freedoms. Her critique of the Restoration régime is direct and unapologetic, while her frequent comparisons between the French and Irish peasants focus on commonalities rather than the superiority of one or the other. In subsequent chapters, the author moves into "Society," turning her gaze to "Royalists," "Constitutionalists and Bonapartists," "Woman—Her former Influence and actual Position in French Society," and "Street Population of Paris," as well as to "Dinners," "Soirées," "Modern Artists," and "The French Theatre." Owenson establishes her social position as a mobile observer of the various ranks and venues of French life, equally at home in each, while locating her fixed political position as a republican and a feminist. As a female traveler in 1816, her engagement with contemporary politics was unusual and even audacious. The success of *France* with the British and liberal French public only increased the negative responses of her critics: Croker published a twenty-five page diatribe against the volumes in the *Quarterly Review,* and the French government issued an order forbidding her return to France.[10] Proving the dictum there is no such thing as bad publicity, *France* went into four editions in Britain, four in the United States, and two in France.

In 1818 Owenson's publisher, Henry Colburn, commissioned a similar volume on Italy which appeared simultaneously in Britain and France in 1821. If anything, Owenson's *Italy* was even more polemical than *France,* for Italy's fragmented, feudal state under the occupation of the Austrian Empire resonated with her vision of Ireland, as did the Romantic and picturesque landscape. Praised by Byron ("Her work is fearless and excellent on the subject of Italy"),[11] proscribed by the Pope, the Emperor of Austria, and the King of Sardinia (whom she called "the king of anchovies"), Owenson took her place alongside Staël, Byron, Keats, the Brownings, and countless other nineteenth-century defenders of the colonized Italian states. Shortly after the successful publication of *Italy* she began a study of Salvator Rosa. A fictionalized biography of the seventeenth-century painter, Owenson's first substantial foray into art criticism reflected her Staëlian belief in the interdependence of art and social structures, as well as a highly Romantic sensibility. Rosa's sublime landscapes and his status as "Painter, Poet, Musician, Philosopher"[12] appealed to Lady Morgan, but above all she admired his oppositional political engagement as "an Italian patriot, who, stepping boldly in advance of a degraded age, stood in the foreground of his times" (*Rosa* iii). Independent, rebellious, melancholy, and passionate, Rosa was an outsider in an era dominated by the more classicized canvases of Claude and Poussin. In *The Life and Times of Salvator Rosa,* Owenson makes unmistakable parallels between the political situation in Rosa's time and her own, while emphasizing the intersections between the Baroque genius's art and his politics.

In a new preface to an 1855 edition of the study she wrote, "Did Salvator live now, one might fancy him joining the ranks of the gallant defenders of national independence and civilization" (*Rosa* iv).

The Princess; or The Beguine:
REVOLUTIONARY IDENTITIES

Owenson's formulation of artistic identity, whether for painter or novelist, male and female alike, entailed "a spirit of independence" (*Rosa* iii) in both art and the politics of the nation. In *The Princess; or the Beguine* (1835), Owenson sets her final national tale in Belgium against the backdrop of the Belgian Revolution of 1830. Although most critics have insisted on Owenson's move away from Irish themes and subjects in the 1830s, Ingelbien demonstrates, conversely, that "Morgan's foreign subject matter was never at odds with the agenda of her Irish fiction; her defense of Ireland and her championing of continental radicalism complemented each other" (108). Indeed, the similarities between the rebellion of the Catholic Walloons against the domination of the Calvinist Dutch and the situation in Ireland are unmistakable, and Ingelbien notes that for Owenson, "Belgium's experience revealed potential lessons for Irish politics in the 1830s" (110) as she was able "to explore the paradoxes of a revolution that presented intriguing parallels with O'Connell's campaign for Repeal" (113). But of even greater interest for this particular study are the ways in which, in this late narrative of national and artistic identity, the mysterious heroine, who appears in the guise of a princess, a nun, a painter, and a patriot, demonstrates the ambiguities of gender and its performances in the revolutionary context. Perhaps Owenson's least read novel, *The Princess* offers her most developed consideration of the complexities of women's artistic and national identities in nineteenth-century Europe.

The title presents the first of many border crossings and ambiguities with its oscillation between two registers of female identity at opposing ends of the social spectrum. *Princess*, with its links to royalty and privilege, is uncomfortably paired with *Beguine*, a foreign word from the French and Dutch, denoting a member of a lay sisterhood of women devoting themselves to prayer and good works (though not under vows). If a Beguine is a nun of sorts who eschews worldly goods for celibacy and philanthropy, a Princess embodies the aristocracy, society, and frequently luxury. Much like *Corinne, ou l'Italie*, which serves as a model for this tale, *The Princess; or The Beguine* leaves the reader uncertain whether the two terms are synonymous (Corinne *is* Italy; the Princess *is* the Beguine) or mutually exclusive (one must choose *either* Corinne *or* Italy; the Princess *or* the Beguine). Though the answer is clear by the end of Owenson's novel, the initial blurring of terms and identities is central to the plot and meaning of the story. The epigraph at the beginning of chapter 1, taken from the letters of Madame de Sévigné, further establishes a cross-cultural context. Cited in French, the quotation from one of the most famous mothers of the seventeenth century (her letters were addressed to her beloved daughter), implies a female artistic lineage across the boundaries of time and nation.

The novel begins with a group of foolish British aristocrats at the opera, foregrounding from the very outset the ideas of performance and spectatorship. As they discuss the impending arrival of the Princess of Schaffenhausen, "so rich, and so odd . . . and then so *very clever*,—she speaks five languages and paints like a professional,"[13] the British express their ambivalence about the German visitor, while Owenson's own ambivalence about the wealthy fops is equally evident. In her absence, the Princess is invoked as somewhat "*louche*" (*PB* 1: 30), for not only is she "a woman of genius," but she is also sympathetic to the revolutionaries and "*la canaille*" (*PB* 1: 31). Her identity constructed through gossip, innuendo, and rumor, the Princess is a cipher: "more dazzling than appreciated, more imagined than understood. What she appeared was known even to the editors of the newspapers, and to the reporters for second-rate fashionable journals; what she really might be, had hardly yet been questioned by her most intimate associates" (*PB* 1: 60). The titular character is thus at once mysterious and suspicious, a princess paradoxically associated both with art and with revolution, but even before we "see" her in the text we are led to understand the disjunction between appearance and reality. Those who observe the Princess do not necessarily "know" or understand her. Throughout the novel she will be a shadowy and elusive figure, pursued by the British gentry and disappearing from sight almost as soon as she is glimpsed.

The male protagonist, Sir Frederick Mottram, is a variation on the Romantic Oswaldian type, from an overtly feminist perspective. Nervous, sensitive, shy, and impassioned, he is also a hypocrite whose insecurities shape his every move. Born the plebian son of a self-made man, Sir Frederick married a woman of a higher social class in a "*mariage de convenance*, the barter of rank for wealth" (*PB* 1: 63); now an inveterate snob, he is also aware of his inferiority. Sir Frederick's wife, Lady Frances, has become intimate with the Princess and in a reflection of Mottram's deeply rooted prejudices, "Even before he had seen her, he had learned to hate, with all the energy of wounded and implacable self-love, this fashionable and diplomatic sibyl" (*PB* 1: 62). While the final phrase recalls *Corinne* in pointed terms, Sir Frederick's hatred of this woman he has yet to meet takes Staël's paradigm to new levels of ferocity. Mixing national and gender politics in equal measure, the conservative Tory MP mistrusts this German woman of genius as much for her liberal views as for her foreign ways and unfeminine comportment; Lady Frances's friendship with the Princess (along with her infidelities) is one of Mottram's many reasons for desiring a separation from his wife.

When we are finally introduced to the Princess, the talented painter performs as well as creates works of art: "It was the peculiar character of the Princess of Schaffenhausen's countenance and person, to make a picture in whatever light or position she placed herself" (*PB* 1: 122). Always in costume, she evokes masterpieces of the past and on this particular evening, her "*ensemble* gave her the air of a picture by Hals or Velazquez" (*PB* 1: 123). As she confers with Lady Mottram about her unhappy marriage to Lord Frederick, the German artist sketches an image of the Englishwoman with a parakeet who has escaped its cage. The Princess, "seizing a pencil, with the aid of a little rouge borrowed from the adjoining toilette, produced a beautiful *croquis* of the beautiful subject. The resemblance, though flattering, was perfect. The bird was in the act of flying off; and a motto was written beneath, '*Qui me néglige, me perd*" (*PB* 1: 125). Thus, the Princess of Schaffenhausen is doubly associated with art, but if her performance of paintings serves to obscure her identity from others, her execution of her own original creations reveals truths, for the image exposes her inner thoughts and prefigures the end of the Mottram marriage. Art, in Owenson's formulation here, must be interpreted in order to signify, and appearance is by definition both mobile and deceiving.

The Princess centers on mobility of every sort—physical as well as social—and thus the greater part of the narrative follows the travels of three groups—Lady Frances and her aristocratic London friends; Sir Frederick Mottram and his Irish valet, Lawrence Fegan; and the comic Irish family of Sir Ignatius Dougherty—from Britain to the Continent. Although Sir Frederick's journey is the primary focus, the journeys of the other groups serve as important counterpoints and commentaries on class, race, and nation as they confront difference abroad. Sir Frederick, like Staël's Oswald, has lost his passion for life and is dying of ennui: "I am inert, listless, dissatisfied" he complains (*PB* 1: 154), and it is once again through the experience of foreign cultures that the Romantic hero may be intellectually and spiritually revived. Through a series of mix-ups, Mottram arrives in Ostend without his carriage, luggage, or even money and begins his Belgian education from an entirely difference position—foreign, penniless, powerless—than the one he normally occupies as a wealthy and well connected Member of Parliament in London. In certain ways, *The Princess* is a *Bildungsroman* in the tradition of Goethe's *Wilhelm Meister*,[14] but in an important inversion, the invisible hand secretly guiding the protagonist's adventures is not the Tower Society of enlightened male aristocrats, but a single woman in multiple personae, including Marguerite, the Beguine, and the Princess. The conservative politician, initially supportive of the Dutch opposition to Belgian freedom, begins to move toward the Belgian cause as he encounters the people and their culture directly; his first-hand experiences on the street without the buffer of wealth and status provide a new perspective that leads to empathy with the oppressed. Every bit as didactic as *Corinne,* Owenson's novel includes lengthy sections of travelogue devoted to the history, architecture, geography, and politics of Belgium, with the similar goal of educating the reader along with the protagonist.

At the same time, she destabilizes absolute knowledge as her narrator intones, "Among the many metaphysical refinements for which philosophy stands indebted to the Germans, there is none more luminous, and at the same time more sound, than their distinction between subjective and objective reality. The aspect of external nature borrows so much of its character, not only from the temperament and disposition, but from the caprices of feeling and passion of the beholder, that the evidence of the senses scarcely suffices to convince us of the identity of certain objects, when revisited under a change of fortunes or of moods" (*PB* 1: 262). This Romantic formulation, acknowledging the shaping force of emotion and experience on our perception of the world, signals the relativity of individual understanding. But Owenson takes the concept further through the device of the disguised heroine whose identity is impenetrable to Sir Frederick. Unable to perceive that the Princess is also the Beguine and Marguerite, he is also blind to the fact that she is the woman he had loved and abandoned in his youth. While critics complained that Sir Frederick's inability to recognize these women pushes the limits of verisimilitude, one could argue that is precisely the point. Like Balzac, Owenson disturbs the equivalence between *voir/savoir/pouvoir* (sight/knowledge/power) by denying Lord Mottram visual access to knowledge. He sees but he does not *see* what is before him, and metaphors of blindness and illumination are key to the tale. Lord Mottram, affiliated with the conservative and misogynistic forces of government and hegemony, is rendered impotent and ignorant, unable to read the world. It is only the Princess, as a visual artist who has also mastered invisibility, who controls access to representation, knowledge, and understanding. For indeed, in her performances of multiple identities and nationalities (German, Belgian, Irish), the Princess consciously embodies the constructed and subjective nature of identity, nationality, and ultimately even gender.

Early in his travels, Sir Frederick meets a young Flemish woman in a hooded cape who introduces him to some of the nation's most beautiful paintings. Importantly, clothes will serve as the Princess's primary modes of disguise. She depends on hoods, capes, and veils as costumes in her various performances, revealing in part the ways in which identities and perceptions are shaped by a sartorial vocabulary. If "clothes make the man," for woman in this novel these external trappings serve to obscure what lies beneath. Mottram is immediately intrigued by the hooded woman's intelligence and gentle manner, and as she teaches him about the art and history of Flanders's oppression, "Sir Frederick Mottram was slowly yielding himself to a cause for which he had hitherto felt no interest, through the medium of his imagination. The arts were mixing themselves with his political opinions . . . He was beginning to feel for Belgium; and feeling is a powerful step to conviction" (*PB* 1: 312). For Owenson, art (literary as well as visual) is a means to move and persuade, inciting political as well as aesthetic feeling.

One of the most pronounced aims of *The Princess* is a plea for the freedom of Belgium, and by extension Ireland, Italy, and the other colonized nations of the world. As Owenson clearly argues, women will play a central part in this political progress, and much of the novel is dedicated to examples of women's active engagement in culture, history, and national identity in the past and present day Belgium. Toward the end of the first of the three volumes of this triple-decker the narrator contends:

> The great movement of the age, the mighty struggle for conquest between past and present institutions, had produced in England, as elsewhere, an undercurrent of female agency, in which religion and politics, the church and the state, sought alike to sustain their power and advance their interests. In a moment of such crisis, no instrument was so humble, no means so indirect, as to be considered unsusceptible of advantageous employment: and it is the peculiar advantage of women's interference, that its sphere of action is all-pervading, and that its applicability commences there where all other agencies have no *prise* or lever to act upon. (*PB* 1: 323)

Owenson indicates that church and state, in their all-encompassing quest for domination, enlisted female agency to achieve their ends, and she defines the purview of women's influence as precisely where all other such powers end. In the course of the remaining two volumes, however, Owenson will demonstrate the ways in which women use this political and moral agency to advance an agenda in direct opposition to the "struggle for conquest," promoting instead a resistance to the very structures of power that seek to exploit them.

When in Bruges, Sir Frederick again sees a figure approaching in a mantle and hood "which might serve alike the purposes of devotion and concealment . . . She carried a large clasped volume which might either be the portfolio of the artist or the breviary of the devotee" (*PB* 1: 327-28). Like the oscillation between Princess and Beguine, this uncertain identity—is she an artist or a nun?—presents yet another aporia in the third incarnation of the title character as Madame Marguerite, a Belgian artist. In pairing these two vocations, Owenson invokes contemporary artistic brotherhoods such as the Nazarenes, who lived in monasteries and pursued "their ideal of a communal life that fused art and religion . . . replacing the model of the academic painter with the role of the monk-artist."[15] But where these male confraternities were devoted to a self-reflexive purity removed from the quotidian world, Owenson's artist, Marguerite, will be engaged in charity (like the Beguine) as well as art, working actively for the cause of freedom. Differences aside, the idea of a female sisterhood of artists is also posited by the evocation of religion and nuns, while aligning Marguerite (and the Beguine) with a higher power than Sir Frederick's self-interested politics. Importantly, however, Marguerite rarely speaks of God, Catholicism, or traditional spirituality; instead, she voices an anti-royalist stance, criticizing "absolute power" which she insists "like the sublime, borders on the ridiculous" (*PB* 1: 329). She explains to Mottram that a shift has occurred since the coronation of Charles X at Reims: "kings will no more be permitted to snatch their crowns from heaven, but must in future be contented to receive them from the people, as ours has done. You will however find, sir, in Belgium, images of another power, in our public edifices (quite as well worthy of attention as that of any royalty), the power of the nation" (*PB* 1:330). Intrigued by the Belgian artist, Sir Frederick is initially "displeased by the strong political colour of her opinions; and by a certain pedantry even in her own professional observations, which smacked of provincial notability." Before seeing her work, he dismisses her talent out of hand, deciding "This was doubtless the Angelica Kauffman or the Rosalba of some Flemish town" (*PB* 1: 340), in an echo of Henry Mortimer's dismissal of Glorvina's talents based on prejudice rather than experience.

Sir Frederick's education is not limited to Belgian politics and art; through his relationship with the hapless Fegan, an Irish valet who joins Mottram's service on the eve of his departure, the British lord comes to reconsider his views on class as well. Far from London and his zone of comfort, Sir Frederick must rely on Fegan not only for his labor but also for his companionship, and

> For the first time in his life, the haughty master of many servants was led to acknowledge their possible individuality. Accustomed to regard his domestics as machines mounted upon certain principles for his service, he had overlooked their moral characters as men; nor ever reflected that the *inconveniences* incidental to their administration, their follies, vices, and infidelities were in part the consequences of that total absence of sympathy and communion with which English masters treat their domestics. (*PB* 2: 2–3)

In an idealistic vein, Owenson thus proposes that class prejudice, like national prejudice, is based entirely in ignorance, and one need only to get to know the Other in order to love him. Attributing the serving class's "vices" to their treatment by their masters rather than an inherent inferiority, the author once again argues for equality and pluralism. In questions of nation and class, progress is achieved for Owenson when the oppressors can recognize the value and humanity of the oppressed, a message that implicitly applies to gender as well.

In a series of scenes in Book II, Owenson presents portraits of Marguerite at work, creating images of the image-maker or representations of the representer. With Sir Frederick as the focalizing observer, she is described in terms that elicit a work of art ("The bend of the long columned neck was in itself a study for a painter. The rounding of her statue-like shoulders was defined by a Vandyke of white cambric . . ." [*PB* 2: 73]), and render Marguerite the object of his constitutive gaze. But no sooner is the image proposed than it is refused by the author and her female artist who interrupts the fantasy. Sir Frederick stares at her, unseen, as she sits working on a drawing and framed by the window behind her: "There was a moment of perfect illusion, which a breath might have dissipated. Sir Frederick Mottram did not breathe, but the artist did; and there was a heaving of bosom-drapery, which transferred the admiration of the beholder from what appeared at first a living picture, to the most picturesque of living forms" (*PB* 2: 74). By insisting on her breath and her consciousness, as she returns his gaze, Owenson reminds the hero and the reader that the artist is a real woman, and the male viewer's fetishizing fantasy is destroyed. Indeed, Sir Frederick will continue to mistake art and representation—in the multiple performances of the Princess—for reality, unable to recognize the real woman behind the charades.

In a subsequent scene in her atelier, depicted in terms that evoke the myriad studios of contemporary painting and literature, Marguerite's paintings bring to mind an orphan taken in by Mottram's mother while he was away at Oxford. Returning from university, he had fallen in love with and then abandoned the foreign-born girl, sacrificing passion for ambition: "his after-life had been the expiation of the imprudent impulse, as it had been the penalty of his heartless desertion of its object. Distrust of woman, the habit of considering her through her position in life, as a *means*, and never as an *object*, had clung to him" (*PB* 2: 197). Redolent of the terms used to describe (and implicitly condemn) Mottram's treatment of the lower classes, the passage goes on to establish a parallel between the politics of gender and the politics of nation, both based in profound hypocrisy:

> The orthodox moralist, the pure and loyal church-and-state man, was a latitudinarian where the passions, or vanity, which so often passes for passion, were concerned. He had written one of his best papers in the Quarterly Review, on the superior morals of England while notoriously engaged in a *liaison* with the wife of his own friend, the Marquis of Montressor . . . Foreign demoralization was a frequent theme in his conversation, and his literary productions, when

he dabbled, like other party notabilities, in reviews and newspapers. But the domestic gallantry of England, the libertinism of some of her highest aristocratic *coteries* (comparable only to the society which flourished under Louis XV, and hurried on a revolution as inevitable as it was morally necessary), had never yet come under the ban of his opinion. (*PB* 2: 198–99)

The construction of difference and of England's moral superiority to other nations is here based entirely on false distinctions, and the man who wants to divorce his wife for her dalliances has himself strayed repeatedly. Owenson's dig at the *Quarterly Review,* one of her sharpest critics, is a pointed critique of its partisan leanings and its moral corruption.

Thus the "moralist" who despises the Princess for her turpitude considers taking the woman he admires, Madame Marguerite, along with him on his travels as a paid "*compagne de voyage*" (*PB* 2: 200), clearly seeing her as an object for sale for his pleasure or amusement. Yet having seen her in her atelier, having recognized her as a laboring subject rather than an idle object, his opinion begins to change. Sir Frederick's confrontation with "the desolate work-room" and the female artist's "struggling genius, with all its sublime but melancholy imagery, the eight years spent there in profitless labor . . . had cast over the character and position of this singular woman a halo of respect, and awakened a reverential admiration for her qualities, and a pity for her dreary position, which altered the whole nature of the sentiment she had hitherto inspired" (*PB* 2: 201–2). If she gains his respect, it is notably for her suffering, while his admiration is mixed with pity; had she been successful she would have been intolerable to the egotistical lord. Nonetheless, it is the evidence of her labor that makes her in some way *real* and thus human to Mottram. The description of Mme Marguerite constructs her as the Romantic artist *par excellence*—a misunderstood genius, struggling in an impoverished garret—and the following passage, recounted by an elderly gentleman to Sir Frederick, also reflects on Owenson's own career. He explains that the Belgian woman is "Not a fine artist, monsieur, but a fine genius. She has worked for bread more than for fame, and therefore wants finish; besides, she has indulged her taste more than consulted her interest. She has, too, a knack of painting a fool like a fool, and rogue—not to be mistaken" (*PB* 2: 253). Like Owenson herself, who began writing novels to escape her life as a governess and continue to support her father and sister, Marguerite paints to earn her living, and it is a means of female independence as well as expression. Owenson, like the fictional painter here, was frequently criticized for her shoddy style, poor spelling, and lack of finish, and clearly identifies with the attribution of these faults to "genius." The author and her artistic mirror portray subjects that criticize, rather than flatter, society. Like Owenson's overtly political novels, Madame Marguerite's "pictures have all a moral object . . . and our *noblesse* has never patronized her" (*PB* 2: 253). Outside of the mainstream, neither appreciated nor patronized by the powers that be, Madame Marguerite and Lady Morgan are artists who, like Salvator Rosa, embody Owenson's version of Romantic genius and freedom, following their own inspiration rather than social dicta. For each, artistic creation is an act of politically engaged labor.

In the final volume of *The Princess; or the Beguine,* Sir Frederick and Madame Marguerite engage in a lengthy debate that echoes those between Corinne and Oswald, but where Mme de Staël's characters discuss religion and literature, Owenson's engage directly with the contemporary politics of empire and nation. She aligns the characters' leanings with gender, class, and life experience: Sir Frederick's conservatism and Marguerite's liberalism are inextricable from their positions in society. Once again, Mottram's inability to perceive the other is highlighted. He proposes to the painter that "you non-conservatives" are not as far from his own position as one would imagine: "it is on the question of practicability that we most widely differ." He continues, "Our views of human nature . . ." but is interrupted by Marguerite who adds "Are formed upon the narrow experience of your exclusive circles, and they are forever misleading you" (*PB* 3: 25). The liberal viewpoint, linked to republicanism and political independence for the lower classes and oppressed nations, is ultimately tied to artistic identity as well by Owenson. When Sir Frederick offers the painter his arm she refuses his support: "I have gone through life without an arm to lean on; and I will not now risk my independence by taking the arm of a minister of state, even though he be *le plus aimable de tous les ministres possibles*" (*PB* 3: 26). In a prefiguration of the ending of the novel, politics is privileged even over love, and the heroine seeks not domesticity but social justice.

The conversation continues as they visit the library of the Dukes of Burgundy. Sir Frederick objects to women "meddling" in public affairs, while Marguerite maintains that they have always been singularly capable of managing both domestic and public functions, like Mme de Maintenon, able to "direct the affairs of Europe while they trace patterns for footstools." The Belgian painter explains, "The influence of women was, is, and ever will be exercised, directly or indirectly, in good or in evil! It is a part of the scheme of nature. Give her the lights she is capable of receiving; educate her (whatever her station) for taking her part in society. Her ignorance has often made her interference fatal: her knowledge, never" (*PB* 3: 39). Very much in keeping with contemporary feminist thought, Owenson argues for woman's education at every social level, insisting that her ignorance is more dangerous than any knowledge could be. Whether through direct intervention or in conversation with husbands, fathers, sons, and friends, women can and do participate in the public and political spheres. She goes on to offer her conservative interlocutor examples of the influence of Belgian women on culture and history, including Marguerite of Burgundy "who was to the Low Countries what Francis the First was to France" (*PB* 3: 39).

The Princess is Mme Marguerite's "patroness," commissioning from her copies of paintings, manuscript illuminations, and other Belgian masterpieces. Moreover, she tells Sir Frederick, they are collaborating on a book dedicated to "one of our great stateswomen, the Duchess Marguerite," who was "author, politician, sovereign, but *femme avant tout*" (*PB* 3: 46). The Princess of Schaffenhausen will write the text while Madame Marguerite will illustrate it, a fact that shocks Sir Frederick as it combines the talents of the woman he is growing to love with those of the woman he thinks he detests, though it will soon be revealed they are one and the same. This "joint" female production has a precedent in a book begun in the sixteenth century by Marie de Behercke, their guide to the library explains, and completed in the seventeenth by Wilhelma De Vaël. In art as well as politics, Owenson continues to demonstrate the role of women in the nation.

When he finally declares his love for Madame Marguerite, she rejects him out of hand, for as a married man he offers her nothing more than a life of "Infamy!" When Sir Frederick protests "What jargon," she coolly replies "You would call it so, if offered to your wife" (*PB* 3: 101), returning again to the hypocrisy of his double standard of class and gender. Perennially misreading the signs, Mottram refuses to believe she is not in love with him: "You cannot suppose that I am such a dolt as to believe that you have done this, all this, in a spirit of fanatical liberalism, to work a political conversion, and bring over a proselyte to a cause in which you have no interest beyond that of abstract opinion!" Marguerite responds, "Why not?" (*PB* 3: 102). She explains that "Belgium has been misrepresented to England" and Mottram is "among those who influence opinion" (*PB* 3:103). Sir Frederick is a man whom people listen to, his thoughts are read in the newspapers, and his voice is heard in the Parliament, so in persuading him, Marguerite argues, she can change the fate of Belgium's cause in Britain. By a similar token, Owenson's novel seeks to serve the same purpose and effectuate the same change. Owenson's female painter privileges politics over love and public over private concerns, thus taking on the very agency described earlier in the novel. Marguerite goes on to explain that she is also the Beguine who, in disguise, has haunted Sir Frederick in Bruges, Ghent, on the Kantur, and in the church of St. Beghé. By implication then, he has been doubly blind to her intentions and to her dual identity, as both the artist, Marguerite, and the Beguine, Soeur Greite. But even more strikingly, she recounts her life story and reveals that she is also Sir Frederick's cousin, the girl he abandoned so long ago, and indeed the Princess of Schaffenhausen as well. Marguerite's complicated history posits a portrait of hybrid and mobile identity: the daughter of an Irish father and a Polish mother, she was born in Belgium in a *Béguinage* (convent) and immediately orphaned. Raised by the Beguines, she is sent to a British family at fifteen to be a companion to their daughter. She is treated as a pet by the mother who discovers that she is her niece, and when the son—Sir Frederick—proposes marriage upon his return from Oxford to the foreign girl, she is turned out into the street. Unable to survive on her own in England, for they are mistrustful of a female artist and a foreigner, she returns to Europe where she ultimately becomes the Princess of Schaffenhausen. Her social mobility, from orphan to princess, rejected by a family who is now far lower than she in the ranks of the gentry, is mirrored both by her national hybridity as Irish/Polish/Belgian and by her many identities that reveal facets of her life and experience. In a similar fashion, Sir Frederick's own unstable identity is also revealed: his mother was an Irish actress and the much ridiculed Dogherty family not only are his Irish cousins, but also have inherited an ancient baronetage, thus rising from the bottom to the top of the social scale. His servant, Larry Fegan, is revealed to be the bastard son of Ignatius Dogherty and thus Sir Frederick's own cousin and a descendent of the Irish kings. The defining characteristics of national and social identities that in turn determine hierarchies of power and prestige are thus destabilized, rendering any pretensions of social or national superiority absurd.

When the Princess reveals herself to the rest of the protagonists, this final encounter is staged like a tableau, with the artist composing and performing the scene one last time for her audience. Significantly, each person sees something different: "Lady Frances saw before her the concealed mistress of her husband, a person who had doubly made her a dupe. Lord Allington regarded her as a political intrigante, endowed with great beauty and as much ability as he had ever 'coped withal.' Lord Aubrey thought she made Lady Frances look *fade;* and Mrs. St. Leger saw the heroine of a German romance, painted by a member of the romantic school" (*PB* 3: 330). Perception, as much as identity, is disrupted, for each person has seen what he or she wanted to see all along. The Princess explains that she has never been the person they took her for and hoped to exploit for their own ends. Having read them in ways they failed to reciprocate, she tells the group: "I have only played your own game. When you English oligarchs received me into the sanctum of your mysteries political and social, you had hoped to make use of me for your purposes: I availed myself of the hint, and worked for my own, which were those of my country" (*PB* 3: 379). Having converted Lord Mottram to her cause, her work is done, and so the Princess declares she will end as she began, as a Beguine. Rejecting marriage (for Sir Frederick proposes after Lady Frances runs off with a lover) and domesticity, she returns to the Belgian sisterhood, whose mission remains to minister to and improve society, "to repair its mischiefs, and to pour oil and wine into the festering wounds of outraged humanity" (*PB* 2:107).

Throughout the novel, the Princess has controlled her own representation through a series of performances that signal her understanding of and resistance to the dominant orders of signification. Identified as a painter in all of her incarnations, her vocation seems central to her mastery of the scopic regimes of meaning and interpretation. Indeed art is the one constant in these multiple personae, and serves as a means to independence and self-fashioning.[16] For the Princess, painting is an accomplishment she can turn into a profession "should the rapid changes of the times, and the loss of her Belgian estates, ever drive her upon living by the exertion of her own high endowments" *(PB* 1: 58), while it is precisely how she supported herself when evicted by the Mottrams as a young girl, and later as Madame Marguerite. It is also, of course, a direct link to the author, another female artist seeking to effectuate social and political change through her representations. Owenson and her character derive their authority from their ability as artists to recognize and move within the multiple registers of power and meaning, manipulating the representation of identity to reflect the constructed nature of gender, class, and nation in Belgium and Britain alike.

Critics from its publication to the present have complained that *The Princess* fails as a novel, for its heroine's multiple identities serve no purpose beyond confusing the reader. In 1835 Christian Isobel Johnstone reproduced almost thirty pages of the novel in *Tait's Edinburgh Magazine* only to conclude that the main character is "a kind of second-hand Corinne, and very inferior sort of Mrs. Macgillycuddy, without adequate motive of object for her endless shifts, subterfuges, and manoeuvres,"[17] while in 1990 James Newcomer contended that Owenson "does obfuscate to no particular end" and that "*The Princess* has been rightfully forgotten."[18] If we consider, however, the dialectic identity of the nameless heroine as the site of meaning, rather than meaninglessness, then *The Princess* may be read as Owenson's reflection on women's active intervention in national history and their resistance to the limiting narratives of gender and identity.

Angélique Arnaud's *Clémence*

Art, Revolution, and Saint-Simonianism

The Politics and Poetics of the 1830s:
THE SENTIMENTAL SOCIAL NOVEL AND SAINT-SIMONIANISM

In the 1842 *Avant-Propos* (preface) to *La Comédie humaine,* Balzac cast a retrospective gaze upon his oeuvre and offered what would become a working definition of the Realist aesthetic. Emphasizing the scientific and philosophical sources of his approach to the observation of society, he famously cited the zoological methods of Cuvier, Geoffroy Saint-Hilaire, and Buffon, claiming his overarching idea was located in "a comparison between Humanity and Animality."[1] His primary literary influence, Balzac explained, was Walter Scott, whose generic innovations "raised the philosophic value of the novel to the level of history" and he praised Scott's modernity, originality, and scope, insisting that like his Scottish predecessor, he would write "the history forgotten by so many historians, the history of manners (*des moeurs*)" (1: 10–11). Scott's historical novel thus helped shape the French Realist novel as developed by Balzac and Stendhal in the 1830s, and like the British historical novel, French Realism was gendered almost exclusively male.[2] But just as the historical novel emerged in (repressed) dialogue with the female-authored national tale, Realism too was dialogically generated in terms of and against sentimental fiction. Associated

171

with female authors and readers, the sentimental novel and the sentimental social novel competed directly with Realist fiction for cultural dominance during the 1830s and '40s, and, though mostly forgotten today, this subgenre played a significant role in shaping the literary field of the July Monarchy.

Indeed, following Bourdieu, Margaret Cohen contends that "a writer's practice is overdetermined by his or her competition with contemporaries responding to the same codes and constraints, as writers take positions in relation to each other, striving for literary recognition and/or economic success" (*Sentimental* 7). In France in the 1830s, Cohen tells us, "Balzac and Stendhal made bids for their market shares in a hostile takeover of the dominant practice of the novel when both started writing: sentimental works by women writers" (*Sentimental* 6). As the novel gained cultural capital, making the transition from light entertainment to the more elevated, socially engaged form that Balzac outlines above, male authors of the 1830s "associated the invention of realist codes with the masculinization of a previously frivolous feminine form in their polemic and in their poetics" (*Sentimental* 13). The sentimental social novel, which flourished from 1830 to 1848, was closely linked to Sand and her followers, who entered the field of cultural production in unprecedented numbers during the period. Maïté Albistur and Daniel Armogathe have noted that the July Monarchy produced as many *femmes écrivains* as the entire eighteenth century combined, though the "impérialisme masculin" of contemporary criticism recognizes only those "who did not stray too far from the style defined by men alone."[3] Importantly, the sentimental social novel focused on the condition of women in contemporary France and the conflicts between individual freedom and the structures of societal laws and mores. Where the sentimental novel of the previous decades envisioned harmony between the individual and the common good, Cohen argues that after 1830, as the genre developed into what she calls the sentimental social novel, society is represented as an oppressive force and social difference is represented as "a relation of power," while the protagonist "suffers because she or he occupies a dominated social position" (*Sentimental* 130–31). No less critical of society than the Realists, the women penning sentimental social novels nonetheless approached the questions of both power and social oppression from a distinctly different viewpoint. For Realist heroes like Eugène Rastignac and Julien Sorel, oppression and impotence are temporary conditions to be overcome, and beneath the sardonic pose of the narrator is the promise of success once the codes are mastered and illusions discarded. Paradoxically, while the sentimental social novelists were often linked to utopian religion and politics, their viewpoints reflect a fundamental pessimism vis-à-vis the contemporary world. The heroes and heroines of the sentimental social novel, almost always female and/or proletarian, are never able to transcend oppression based on their gender or class difference. Instead, as they hold fast to their ideals, they end up victims of laws and social divisions inimical to the individual freedoms of women and the proletariat.

In this sense, the sentimental social novel gives voice to a social critique no less pointed than that of the Realists, but where Balzac, Stendhal, and company accept the status quo as corrupt but immutable, the sentimental novelists of the July Monarchy militate for social change and, as authors, establish a clear political position. Cohen notes, "Sand's *Indiana*, Arnaud's *Clémence*, Tristan's *Méphis*, Marbouty's *Ange de Spola* and *Une Fausse Position* insist that women's flagrant inequality must be remedied with thoroughgoing legal and social transformation" (*Sentimental* 137). Where Owenson's politically oriented novels focused on the question of Ireland's national identity and independence from British domination, the novels of Angélique Arnaud and many of the other women writing social novels in the 1830s and 1840s engage with the internal politics of France, and specifically the questions of class and gender in French society. While they share both narrative strategies and social concerns, their very sense of the relationship between gender and nation is different. For Owenson, Ireland (or Belgium) shares the subaltern position of women: denied freedom and independent identity, both are oppressed by the hegemonic powers of masculine domination. For Arnaud, on the other hand, France is the metaphoric oppressor of women and thus the nation and its female populace are opposed rather than conflated. Nonetheless, both authors see a crucial role for women in the future of the nation, leading Ireland and France to a more just and morally elevated state. And each chooses the figure of the female painter to represent the role of the woman artist in the public sphere.

Angélique Arnaud (1797–1884), identified as a "socialiste, républicaine, libre penseuse,"[4] was perhaps most markedly a feminist and a Saint-Simonian, and this pair of closely tied movements played a significant role in shaping her aesthetics as well as her politics. Saint-Simonianism, based on the writings of the Comte de Saint-Simon and led by Prosper Enfantin, was a short-lived but influential utopian socialist movement that became popular in the early 1830s. Coinciding with the second generation of Romanticism, Saint-Simonianism combined religion and economics, spirituality and progress, in the quest for social change. Focusing on an ideal future rather than the idealized past of earlier Romantics, the Saint-Simonians advocated a new social order in which the collective good was valued over individual interests. Working toward a "new age" of equality and harmony, the Saint-Simonians eschewed militarism and class conflict for a paradigm of "association" or peaceful, communal cooperation. As Pamela Pilbeam explains, the primary objectives of the movement "from their formation in 1825, were the liberation of working people and of women."[5]

The first stage of Saint-Simonianism, led by "industriels" from the École Polytechnique, gave way around 1829 to a more spiritual phase in which women played a far greater role. Unlike the feminism of the Revolutionary period, shaped by Enlightenment ideas of essential gender equality (Olympe de Gouges, Etta Palm, Condorcet), the Saint-Simonians understood men and women to be fundamentally different, but in a reversal of traditional hierarchies, elevated female qualities to the highest value. The "natural" spirituality and emotion or sentiment of women was privileged over the "natural" reason or rationalism of men, and God was conceived as male *and* female, "FATHER and MOTHER of all men and women (*tous et toutes*)."[6] Accordingly, the New Christianity would be jointly led by the "couple-pope," in keeping with God's dual nature. Only a woman could announce the new morality for the new age, and thus the Saint-Simonians awaited a new female Messiah who would complete the doctrine. An empty chair on the dais of Saint-Simonian meetings represented the "attente de la Femme" (the wait for the Woman) and the departure of a large number of adherents to Egypt to search for the female Messiah in 1833–34 signaled the end of the movement's active functioning. On a more practical level, the Saint-Simonians strove to "empower women and called for their full participation in public life" (Moses and Rabine, 29). From 1829–33, women occupied positions of authority within the movement, theoretically sharing a limited amount of power with Saint-Simonian men within the hierarchies of leadership. Both priests and priestesses were proposed, workers' associations were to be headed jointly by *directeurs* and *directrices,* and the communal houses in Paris were overseen by *frères* and *soeurs*. Although they never came close to a truly equal role within the movement, and the gap between ideology and reality remained significant, the very presence of women on the platform along with the male apostles during meetings and sermons in 1830–31 carried enormous symbolic import for the movement's followers.[7] Working class women embraced Saint-Simonianism in large numbers after 1830, and many "were won over by the doctrine that women had a divine mission in the regeneration of society" (Pilbeam 83).

The reconfiguration of marriage and domestic family life was central both to Saint-Simonian philosophy and to much contemporary social debate of the time. Indeed Victor Considérant, the disciple of Charles Fourier (1772–1837) whose radical writings influenced both Saint-Simon and Enfantin, insisted that "Social reform is completely dependent on the question of the organization of the household."[8] More of a utilitarian than a humanitarian, Fourier saw woman's domestic servitude as an economic loss for society and believed that capitalism and marriage were the two primary sources of contemporary corruption. Admired by socialist feminist Flora Tristan, Fourier argued that social progress could begin only when women were liberated from the constraints of monogamy and domesticity: he wrote, "social progress and changes of historical period take place in proportion to the advancement of women toward liberty, and social decline occurs as a result of the diminution of the liberty of women . . . The extension of the privileges of women is the fundamental cause of all social progress."[9] Fourier's radical ideas on marriage and monogamy were toned down, if not radically revised, by Victor Considérant and the Fourierists of the 1830s, so when Enfantin proclaimed the principles of free love and sexual liberation to the Saint-Simonians in 1831, a rift emerged in the movement that never entirely healed. Enfantin and the other male leaders were imprisoned in 1832 for corruption of public morals, and soon thereafter women split off from Saint-Simonianism proper, forming their own associations based on the idea of the *femme nouvelle* (new woman).

The self-proclaimed *femmes nouvelles* of the 1830s continued to embrace the fundamental ideas of the Saint-Simonian movement in egalitarian, inclusive collectives that moved away from the rigid hierarchies established by Enfantin and the other male leaders. The *femmes nouvelles* identified themselves as workers, whether employed outside the home or as wives and mothers, and united gender and class analysis in their political writings. In 1832, Reine Guindorf and Désirée Veret founded *La Femme libre,* the first journal to be published entirely by women and for women, and although it lasted only two years, it gave voice and inspiration to a new generation of feminists. In the first year of publication, *La Femme libre* (Free Woman) changed its name to *Apostolat des Femmes* (a direct reference to its Saint-Simonian leanings), then *La Femme de l'avenir* (The Woman of the Future) and *La Femme nouvelle* (another Saint-Simonian reference) before settling on *Tribune des femmes* until its demise in 1834. The "Appel aux femmes" (Call to women) on the cover page of the first issue announced the journal's radical mission:

> When people everywhere are taking action in the name of *Liberty* and the proletariat is reclaiming its freedom, shall we women remain passive before this great movement of social emancipation taking place before our eyes? Are we so happy with our lot that we have nothing to demand? Woman until now has been exploited, tyrannized. This tyranny, this exploitation must cease. We are born free, like man, and one half of the human race cannot be, without injustice, enslaved to the other half. Let us understand, then, our rights; let us understand our power . . . We are free and equal to man.[10]

Recognizing the power arising from solidarity, the proletarian women writers of the *Femme libre* and its variants sought to "invent a new woman," Laure Adler tells us, and "to do it together."[11] Urging women to unite with one another regardless of class, the journal's authors published only under their first names in a pointed resistance to patriarchal authority. Sold for fifteen centimes a copy, *Femme libre* was targeted at a working class audience: under the loosened censorship laws of the July Monarchy, Adler notes, journals became a "lieu de lutte" (battleground) and "the best way to make oneself heard" (90).

Angélique Arnaud began her literary career submitting to feminist, socialist, and Saint-Simonian journals much like *La Femme libre,* and an article signed by "Angélique" and "Sophie Caroline" from an 1833 issue of the *Tribune des femmes* calling for an "Artists' and Workers' Saint-Simonian Assembly" may well have been her collaborative effort. A self-taught, petit bourgeois wife and mother from the provinces, Arnaud surmounted innumerable obstacles to become a published author, and her personal letters are frequently filled with self-doubt. Driven by her commitment to feminism and Saint-Simonianism, Arnaud used her fiction to promote progressive political views while at the same time asserting her personal independence from an unfulfilling marriage. In 1838 she sent Prosper Enfantin a copy of her first novel with a letter proclaiming "Your words gave birth to this book. It was your call that gave me enough independence to conceive it, enough courage to deliver my sentiments and thoughts to the world."[12]

In a collection of letters between Arnaud and fellow Saint-Simonians Caroline Simon and Charles Duguet,[13] we get a vivid sense of the close connection between her sense of mission and her writing. Early in the correspondence, she tells Simon of her frustrations with her domestic duties and her "need to write." Enervated by the demands of family life and teaching her two children, she laments "my thoughts agitate and dominate me like an order from the heavens . . . then my mind boils over and exalts like that of the ancient prophetess" (*Corr* 74). Comparing herself to a sibyl, Arnaud initially writes to earn enough money to afford a tutor for her children so she has more time to write. In 1833 she plans on composing an article for a Saint-Simonian journal on "la position d'une femme saint-simonienne" waiting for "la Mère" to proclaim "the new law" (*Corr* 87) and several months later she sends Caroline a copy of a poem she has written for an upcoming ceremony. Celebrating the anticipated arrival of the female Messiah, this "hymne de l'union" invokes the role of all women in redemption, proclaiming "Femmes vous sauverez le monde" (Women you will save the world) (*Corr* 115).

By 1834 Arnaud's orientation begins to shift away from religious fervor to a more political bent, and she observes to Simon, "we are walking in the darkness. The liberty, the equality of woman, this is what is undeniably sacred: but every application of this truth is awkward, even dangerous" (*Corr* 123). Sand's writings, and *Leila* in particular, come up frequently in the letters as a source of inspiration, and in November 1834 Arnaud responds to Duguet's proposal of Sand herself as a model for her "mission": "You told me, Charles, that you have conceived a mission for me like that of Madame Dudevant and this thought has troubled me more than once. It is quite true that sometimes I feel irresistibly called to tear away the veils that hide the wounds of our poor society, but I lack the talent, the health, and the inspiration that is born of an active life. Why did God allow such a large disproportion between our wishes and our strength?" (*Corr* 146). Acutely aware of the politics of gender, she later writes to Caroline Simon "I wanted to send you some reflections on the bias with which the world judges the works of Madame Sand on moral grounds. Reflections which inform a parallel between [Sand's] *Jacques* and [Balzac's] *Le Père Goriot*. Maybe this article, which is much more factual, would be suitable for the *Revue de Paris* or the *Deux Mondes;* but I have so little confidence in my success that I have no courage for the work" (*Corr* 165–66).[14] Arnaud's interest in comparing the works of Sand, a female sentimental social author, and Balzac, the quintessential Realist, reveals her intrinsic understanding of the differences in artistic production and reception between the two gendered genres. What is accepted by the critics as "real" in Balzac is taken as "immoral" in Sand, a bias that extends from fiction to the lives of the artists as well and clearly discourages the fledgling author. Some three years later, Arnaud will make unmistakable references to Balzac's *Le Père Goriot* in both the setting and the plot of *Clémence*, and her intertextual allusions highlight the differences between their works while at the same time laying claim to her own place in the field of cultural production.

As Arnaud's confidence grows, she admits she prefers the freedom of novel writing to composing articles for journals that want her to "contain herself within their frame" (*Corr* 173), and in an 1835 letter to Caroline she declares that she writes not only to support her family, but "for all of humanity" (*Corr* 181). She speaks increasingly of her life's mission as artistic creation: "my sweet Caroline, my morale is better than ever. Everything is harmonious in my circle where such serious upheavals have sometimes erupted. My mission is clearly defined. People from everywhere are asking for my writings and I feel within me an inspiration and confidence that guarantee success despite the difficulties that plagued my first steps" (*Corr* 185). In 1838 she published *La Comtesse de Servy,* followed by *Clémence* (1841) and *Coralie* (1843).[15] The final letters in the collection indicate that neither Simon nor Duguet liked the first novel, and the correspondence ceased in May of that year. Arnaud continued to write for the feminist press throughout the Second Empire and collaborated with Maria Deraismes as late as 1872 on the feminist journal *Avenir des femmes*. At Arnaud's funeral in 1884, Deraismes, one of the leading feminists of the day, recalled her as "the apostle of all the great causes . . . There is not a noble and humanitarian movement in the century with which Mme Arnaud was not associated" (*Corr* 54).

Clémence:
PAINTING REVOLUTION

Clémence begins with a "letter" addressed to Emile Souvestre, a socialist author and critic whose novels were among the first to celebrate the working classes.[16] In his influential essay, "Du Roman," which appeared in the *Revue de Paris* in 1836, Souvestre outlined the genesis of the novel as a newly dominant form. Proposing that "every age has its own poetics as well as its own history," Souvestre ties the novel to a modern sensibility.[17] Where ancient literary forms like the epic sought to create a sense of collectivity and "l'esprit national" as nations were forming (117), the "mission" of the novel in the age of the individual is the moral transformation and social advancement of the people (121–22). "Politics, morality, philosophy, criticism, history, all will be its domain" Souvestre proclaims (122), and he insists that the novel's subject matter must be "le vrai" and "le réel" (the true and the real). Although he singles out Scott and Balzac for praise (most notably *Eugénie Grandet*), it is above all George Sand who "launches" the novel, "sword in hand, against social prejudice" and pushes it "toward the true" (123). Thus, it is worth noting, Balzac's Realism did not hold exclusive sway over the real in 1830s fiction.

By invoking Souvestre at the outset, Arnaud establishes her own desire to engage in a "moral" and didactic form for the betterment of society. Arnaud's opening disclaimer similarly draws attention to the very aspects of the work that she pretends to disavow: "You will easily understand that I did not have the pretension to give my book the form of an historical novel. If politics are found there, it is in order to serve as a frame for the action and to facilitate the development of the characters: it also gave me the opportunity along the way to express the hope that a time of peace will follow the conflicts of our epoch, and to indicate how I conceive of the role of woman in the midst of political troubles and partisan hatred."[18] Against the background of France's national trauma (the Revolution of 1830), Arnaud seeks to intervene as a female author in moving the nation toward "a moral law more appropriate to human nature" (1: 3). Arnaud twice uses the verb *peindre* (to paint), a word associated with the documentation of the real. In referring to her own activity of writing in terms of painting ("à peindre ou à caractériser les événements" [1: 2] and "si je peins, au lieu d'inventer . . . n'est-ce pas pour moi un devoir, de produire de semblables modèles" [1: 4]), Arnaud further draws an implicit parallel between herself, as author, and Clémence, the heroine of the tale who is a painter.

As she continues in her prefatory dedication, Arnaud goes on to equate the jobs of the *moraliste* and novelist,[19] and while claiming Souvestre might find fault with her as an artist, she contends "you will approve of me as a moralist" (1: 4–5). Locating her lesson squarely in the realm of contemporary French politics, she explains "When civil law is insufficient for regulating certain relationships between people, it is on these relationships that the moralist must focus her solicitude" (1: 6), making clear reference to Napoleon's oppressive Code Civil that codified women's legal "nonexistence."[20] Arnaud's preface establishes that the novel to follow will be feminist in its orientation and also aimed at the working class, and in choosing to portray a female artist who lives in a Parisian boarding house and must work to support herself, she describes the lives of countless young women, "honest and poor . . . with no other support than a good conscience and a noble character" (1: 9). The novelist owes less to the privileged classes than to those "threatened existences," she tells us, and it is for these victims that the writer "should light the way, signal the pitfalls, and embellish the path that leads to an honorable end" (1: 9). Finally, she maintains, "today it should be less a question of restricting the liberty of woman than of teaching her how to use it with moderation and dignity. Precautions can guarantee purity. But one must have independence to be truly virtuous" (1: 9). In a move that signals a new confidence from the author of the earlier letters, she signs this politically charged prefatory letter "Angélique Arnaud." Following in Sand's admired footsteps, she announces her engagement with contemporary social concerns, but nearly a decade after the publication of *Indiana* the female author uses her own name rather than a male pseudonym.

Clémence recounts the artistic development and political awakening of a female painter in Restoration Paris. In a variant on the structure of the *Bildungsroman* of the period, Arnaud depicts her hero against the backdrop of contemporary events, while positing her journey from youthful optimism, through an impossible romantic attachment, to maturity and lost illusions. Here, however, the hero is a woman whose identity is generated neither by family nor by marriage, but through her profession and ultimately through her social engagement, as she comes to embrace the revolutionary cause. During her stay in a Parisian boarding house, Clémence falls in love with the mysterious Santa-Cortez, who is later revealed to be Horace Gramond, a leader of the uprisings that would result in the overthrow of the Bourbon Monarchy in July 1830. The ill-fated love becomes secondary to both characters' commitment to the greater good of the people and the nation, and both protagonists sacrifice their lives on the barricades in a sentimental ending that privileges public good over private happiness in a way that marks a distinct departure from the more cynical narratives of male Realists of the period.

Indeed, from the outset of the novel Arnaud enters into a dialogue with Balzacian Realism that allows her to foreground the themes of social "types" and social mobilities as they intersect with money, profession, and identity; working both within and against these discourses, the female author complicates the formulas by introducing gender, revolutionary politics, and social idealism into the mix, and ultimately positing an alternate version of development (*Bildung*) more in keeping with a Saint-Simonian vision. She begins *Clémence* with a precise evocation of time and place, setting the scene in a modest boarding house near the Boulevard des Italiens toward the end of the Restoration, a period of increased governmental suspicion when "the walls were said to have ears and *prudence* had even crept into the domestic sphere" (1: 12). Against the backdrop of this insular world, unmistakably reminiscent of the Maison Vauquer in *Le Père Goriot* (1834), Arnaud presents the various types, allowing the female characters (all of whom are single or widowed) to occupy center stage. The proprietor of the Hôtel du Lac, Madame Armand, is well known for her liberalism, and her boarders are like a family and "members of this little republic" (1: 13). While the male boarders include a collection of unsurprising types—a sensitive Romantic intellectual (Frantz), a serious and imposing Spaniard (Santa-Cortez), a foppish merchant, and a good-for-nothing aristocrat—Clémence is introduced through her exceptional status. Thus, like Corinne, Clémence's reputation precedes her, and even before her arrival at the Hôtel du Lac, Madame Armand describes the new boarder as "une femme hors de ligne" (an uncommon woman) (1: 32) who is at once beautiful and brilliant. Although her independence is emphasized, the first question asked by the male boarders is "Is she single, married, or a widow?" (1: 35). This query, also central to the response of both English- and Frenchmen upon meeting Corinne in Italy, reflects the dominant conception of women in terms of their marital status and/or sexual availability; highlighting these categories only to resist them allows both Staël and Arnaud to establish their heroines' identities in other terms. Clémence's friend Madame Palmer, another resident of the Hôtel du Lac, refuses to answer, telling the curious men "What matters is that she is beautiful and charming. The rest is of little importance to us" (1: 35), thus shifting the focus from her relationship to patriarchal structures to her individuality, though still highlighting her physical and social charms. Madame Palmer, formerly the Marquise de Mont-Brun, spent her youth at the court of Marie-Antoinette and at 60 is a representative in taste and manners of another era, yet she too resists consigning female identity to marital status. In keeping with the specific ethos of Arnaud's liberal novel, the aristocrat is neither the enemy nor the Other, and her empathy and open-mindedness humanize this member of the Ancien Régime. This theme of female solidarity across the lines of social class will be central to Arnaud's novel and to Clémence's role as an avatar of the nation's future.

Clémence's identity, as announced by Madame Armand, is located in her profession. Rather than giving her last name or family history, Madame Armand explains to her boarders that "Madame Clémence is a distinguished artist . . . she makes portraits that have the advantage of a perfect resemblance and genre paintings that are said to demonstrate infinite intelligence and taste" (1: 37). In choosing the figure of the female artist for the hero of her socially engaged novel Arnaud echoes many of Balzac's stories of the period but is less interested in the dynamics of the visual than she is in creating a character whose labor can at once provide her with a means of support and independence while at the same time promoting the causes of justice and liberation—here in the form of her participation in the Revolution of 1830. Proletarian painters also figured prominently in Flora Tristan's novel, *Méphis* (1838) and George Sand's *Horace* (1842), but in each case they were male. Nonetheless in Tristan's socialist tale, the idealistic artist paints the image of the "woman *guide of humanity*," an allegorical representation of "The Future" followed by people of all races and classes, demonstrating the role played by woman in society and its betterment, "the moral role reserved for her by Providence, in order to counterbalance the muscular forces of man."[21] The embodied nature of the painter and his or her production, at once an artist but also an artisan or craftsperson producing a material object, would have held a strong appeal for authors engaged in representing and addressing the working classes while at the same time making the case for the social/political role of art. In making her Saint-Simonian heroine a successful independent woman artist, Arnaud invokes not only Corinne but also the *femme nouvelle* of contemporary feminism.

Clémence, moreover, despite her humble birth now "earns a great deal of money" but is indifferent to wealth, spending her fortune with "magnificent indifference" (1: 37). Like innumerable male artists of myth and fiction, she operates outside of social convention, here defined in feminine terms: "She is capable of wiping her paintbrush with her cashmere shawl when the exaltation of art overtakes her, and of going out without gloves or hat if a thought strongly preoccupies her" (1: 37). An unconventional woman, she ironically depends on a more conventional woman—a *femme de chambre* (lady's maid)—to save her from her own distraction and "insouciance" (1: 37). The theme of social class—and the constructed nature of its boundaries—is further foregrounded in the painter's relationship to the Duchesse de Berry, who is Clémence's patron and protector. Although they share different political beliefs ("Clémence loves the princess and not her title"), their friendship transcends rank and once again demonstrates a female solidarity outside of social position. By invoking the Duchesse de Berry, Arnaud establishes Clémence's success with the most fashionable patron of the period, while at the same time invoking her real court painter, Hortense Haudebourt-Lescot. Following a topos found in "lives of the artists" from Pliny and Vasari through her own day, Arnaud describes the "discovery" of Clémence's talent by the Duchesse de Berry during a visit to the painter's native village. The young Clémence, "still a child" (1: 38), drew a portrait of the royal visitor that so impressed her that she begged to keep it.

As Madame Armand recounts, the princess was so struck by both the child's beauty and her natural talent that she offered to take her to Paris and pay for her training with the greatest masters, "but the artist, already proud and independent, refused to leave her family" (1: 39). Ernst Kris and Otto Kurz have traced the repetition of this myth through the centuries, noting that the motif of the gifted young painter being discovered by a noble patron who will sponsor and protect him reflects not only on the theme of the social standing of artists but also on the Freudian "family romance."[22] But it is almost without exception a male painter and a male patron, and Arnaud's self-conscious feminization of the topos signals her desire to establish a parallel history for female artists. Clémence's fierce independence and her refusal to accept her patroness's gifts without giving her "some albums or paintings" in return (1: 39) establishes a relationship based on mutual respect and equality between the women that will be central to the dénouement of *Clémence,* while at the same time delineating her noble character, another quality frequently found in the hagiographic myths of the artist circulating at the time.[23]

Like so many male artists in myth and fiction, Clémence has long eschewed love for her art, and when pressed by Mme de Mont-Brun on her solitude she protests "Is my heart not full enough? Are you no longer my mother? Is Frantz no longer my brother and friend? And my paintbrushes? And my colors? Isn't that enough for a complete happiness, an entire life?" (1: 47). In this sentimental tale, these substitutes for love, family, and marriage (the "mother" and "brother" are simply friends of the orphan) are eclipsed by her impossible passion for the mysterious Santa-Cortez, but in another bow to the real, Clémence also confesses that she remains distant from men after her friend's father attempted to rape her. Until her fatal attraction to the idealistic and unattainable revolutionary, Clémence seeks only friendship and fraternity with the opposite sex "and felt more and more irritated by the men who were not lofty enough to sense the purity of her soul" (1: 62).

Horace Gramond, disguised as the brooding and distant Santa-Cortez, leads the secret society of revolutionaries (*les carbonari*) who will go on at the end of the novel to overthrow the Bourbon Monarchy in July 1830. Like the artist, Santa-Cortez has no time for love as his life is consumed by his dedication to the political cause, and he keeps his distance from the young painter. But if both characters are equally committed to their work, it is Clémence's artistic production—the product of her labors—that mediates their unspoken attraction. When Clémence secretly observes Santa-Cortez leafing through an album of her drawings and copying one of her sketches she can read through the language of gestures and vision what words and conscious actions might obscure. Unable or unwilling to connect to the female artist directly, he looks to her art to know her. In this reversal of the gendered hierarchies of vision, the male character is the object of the appraising gaze of the female artist, and it is he, rather than she, who copies from another's image. Clémence "found a certain charm in watching him in this way, without being seen" (1: 71) and as an "unseen seer" she (and the reader) have access to hidden levels of meaning. By a similar token, it is only when she glimpses herself in the mirror in a state of disheveled distraction that Clémence realizes that "this man has the power to arouse in me chaos and confusion" (1: 91). When she admits her feelings to her friend Frantz, he proclaims that she is "not simply a divine artist, an angel wandering the earth . . . Clémence, you are also a woman! A woman! That is to say a being who can sigh, be moved, weep with passion, love . . ." (1: 110). In keeping with the conventions of the sentimental genre, but also with the elevated aspirations of Arnaud's Saint-Simonianism, Frantz tells Clémence that Santa-Cortez is "the greatest, most noble, most generous being that has been born in our era," adding "your name will be inscribed next to those of the women who were the inspiration and the strength, the joy, and the reward of the heroes of humanity" (1: 111–12). In keeping with Arnaud's feminism, Clémence will go beyond the women of the past to inspire not only Santa-Cortez but also a broad swath of humanity through both her art and her actions.

The novel is structured around a series of secrets and revelations that mirror those of *Le Père Goriot:* in Arnaud's novel, as in Balzac's, some inhabitants of the boarding house lead double lives, while others spy upon their mysterious neighbors, hoarding information like treasure and willing to sell what they know to the highest bidder. In these microcosms of society, men and women from disparate classes and backgrounds vie for power and love while trying to negotiate their own positions within the hierarchies. Yet where Balzac's wily protagonist, Vautrin, seduces men and women alike with his performance of affability, only to be exposed in the end as the criminal Jacques Collin, Arnaud takes the opposite tack. Santa-Cortez, like Vautrin, lives under a pseudonym and hides both his real identity (as Horace Gramond) and his real activities. Taken for a criminal, he is really a hero in the narrative, and despite his pure and elevated nature, he is unpopular with his fellow tenants who feel an "antipathy" for the severe and silent "foreigner." Both authors play with the registers of visible and invisible identities and the disjunction between seeing and knowing, but where Balzac hints at a world far worse than what we think we see, Arnaud shows her characters to be better than they are suspected of being. Where Rastignac's education as Vautrin's pupil and protégé is one in the corrupt ways of the world, Clémence is enlightened and elevated by Santa-Cortez/Gramond, and introduced to a world of higher meaning. Perhaps most significantly in this novel of initiation, the protagonist from the provinces is not an ambitious young man, but an ambitious young woman, and her trajectory follows a positive, if idealistic arc.

The reversal of gender roles hinted at early in the novel continues throughout the tale. Upon first meeting Santa-Cortez, Clémence refers to him in terms of a work of art, recalling the popular Pygmalion paradigm. Describing him as a sculpture, she remarks that the "statue" may not necessarily be as cold and inanimate as he appears, for she senses a "dark fire that belies the insensibility of marble" (1: 46). Later, she idealizes the secretive rebel, referring to him repeatedly as "an angel" and declaring her desire to protect him. When she discovers that he is secretly married, Clémence quickly shifts to a platonic love, and "more than ever she believed it was her destiny to save Santa-Cortez" (1: 202). If Rastignac climbs the ranks of Parisian society, casting off idealism to follow Vautrin's model of exploitation and deceit, as Clémence begins to follow Santa-Cortez's model of political engagement, she casts off personal fantasy for the greater good of working for *le peuple*. She reflects, "Gone are the dreams of a young woman, artist's fantasies, child's caprices! Goodbye to days idly spent, I am taking hold of the higher realms of life! I, too, will live for an idea! I, too, will ask why the people suffer, why there are classes of men condemned to serfdom, and parasitic classes that bring nothing to the masses and live like kings on the fruits of their brothers' labors" (1: 195).

Central to Clémence's new vision is the idea of regeneration, a concept embraced and aspired to by the Saint-Simonians. She proudly shows Frantz a painting that she has finished under this new "inspiration," and her symbolic aesthetic reflects equally on Clémence's own state. The artist explains she wanted to paint "humankind awakening and regenerating in the sunshine of a fecund thought" (1: 254). Using nature to suggest this revival, she sets the scene at dawn: "the field lit by the flames of the sunrise," "blossoming flowers," "dew-veiled grass" and a "silvery lawn" symbolize the rebirth of her "young Spartan." Her subject "for the first time understands the meaning of the word *homeland (patrie)*" and "his honorable future is inscribed in his gaze" (1: 254–55). The allegorical subject, like Clémence herself, has an "innocent heart" that will "never be troubled by a profane love" and will "tremble only at the sound of the name of Lacedemonia" (Sparta's city-state) (1: 255). Fusing Romantic imagery with Saint-Simonian politics, Clémence's painting is declared a "masterpiece" by Frantz and represents an idealistic vision of the role of art. Yet if the work of visual art functions allegorically, Arnaud's own novel is far more straightforward in its narration, signaling a distance between the painter's and the author's aesthetic. Where Clémence's *chef-d'oeuvre* remains tied to the single moment of awakening and the potentiality of the ideal, *Clémence* can also introduce the disjunctions and disappointments in the realm of the real. Nonetheless the painting and the novel share the desire to raise the political above the personal in both art and life. Moreover, Clémence's canvas, and by extension Arnaud's tale, demonstrate the active role women can play in social change: "the importance of their intervention and the happy influence their presence can exert everywhere that a useful thought brings people together" (1: 269). Frantz concurs, telling Clémence "if every woman were like you, the world would be regenerated in less than ten years" (1: 269).

As in so many sentimental novels of the period, marriage is an essential theme in Arnaud's *Clémence*. Santa-Cortez's relationship to his wife, Clara, is particularly complex for they are at once married and not married, again highlighting the tensions between appearance and reality. Abandoned by her first husband yet still legally married to him, Clara is the innocent victim of the law and the social system that make it impossible for her to live a respectable life as a deserted wife. Taking pity on her without actually loving her, Santa-Cortez lives with Clara in the guise of marriage to return to her a position of social legitimacy, but his act of generosity renders them both miserable—Clara because she loves him, Horace because he does not, and cannot, love her. Like Sand and others, Arnaud demonstrates how contemporary divorce laws make men suffer as much as women, and draws explicit parallels between the family and the state. Comparing Clara's marriage to the Restoration monarchy, Santa-Cortez reflects that the French people are like the abandoned wife, legally tied to the monarch by the charter, even after he has violated their trust and they no longer respect or love him. Given this analogy, the revolutionary ignores the law and protects the victim, yet ultimately this arrangement only creates more suffering, in part because Clara remains dependent and infantilized.

At the beginning of the second volume, Clémence is invited to the palace to join the Duchesse de Berry and her friends prepare costumes for *carnaval* in an episode that delineates the mobility of social identities. Caroline (as the Duchesse is known to her friends) admires the painter and her independent ideas, and goes so far as to think "I would have tried to be like her, if I hadn't been a princess" (2: 10). In the presence of the aristocrats, Clémence feels a surge of fierce pride and despite the enormous difference in social stature, she is comfortable for "the superiority of rank seemed to fraternize in good faith with the superiority of intelligence and talent" (2: 11). This conception of an aristocracy of sensibility is decidedly Romantic, once again elevating the artist to the higher ranks of society, but for Arnaud the idea of equality is key and the Duchess envies Clémence's "liberté" (2: 13). Caroline is planning one of her famous costume balls (see chapter 4), and as Clémence designs the dresses, the princess and her friends try to sew the gowns themselves. The Duchesse de Berry, a native of Italy, chooses the costume of an Italian peasant, self-consciously seeking a momentary reprieve from the weight of her position through the performance of an alternate identity. The image of the Italian *paysanne* was closely associated with Hortense Lescot, and here it functions as a way to demonstrate the constructed nature of difference between the classes who all ultimately aspire "to the pleasure of feeling free" (2: 13). As the conversation turns to politics, however, and the "winds of revolution" (2: 15), Clémence finds herself in an awkward position between two worlds. A chevalier comes to tell the princess and mother of the future king that the famous conspirator, Horace Gramond, has been discovered to be living in Paris under a false name (thus another mobile or performed identity) but the police were planning on arresting him shortly.[24] As Clémence begins to tremble, the courtiers mistake her fear for Santa-Cortez for terror at the thought of revolution.

Gathering her courage, Clémence admits to Caroline that although she would give her life for the princess and her son, she would never betray a man "threatened by the sword of the law" (2: 21). When asked directly if she is a liberal, Clémence affirms that she is, "in the good sense of the word," and while the women of the court recoil in horror, the Duchesse de Berry accepts her protégée's confession with grace and good will, noting there is nothing to fear from such honesty and admitting "I am delighted, after all, that someone can be a liberal and still like me" (2: 23). In this important scene, the mutual respect and affection between the princess and the painter carries more weight than abstract political principles, and Arnaud humanizes the aristocratic Other against whom the revolutionaries are conspiring. Thus, while opposing the system of the monarchy Clémence cannot forget that they too are human beings and friends. In some ways, the intimacy between Caroline and Clémence, Duchess and liberal, reflects themes also found in Owenson's *The Princess,* for above all the author here seeks to establish a common ground among women and the constructed nature of difference. While Caroline, dressed as a peasant, avows her empathy for Clémence, the painter is in the costume of a queen proclaiming her revolutionary views. Yet their fondness for each other is more important than their social or political positions.

These dual identities and dual loyalties are equally thematized in Clémence's exchanges with Santa-Cortez as she functions as an intermediary between the two extremes. Leaving the palace for the boarding house, she hurries back to the Hôtel du Lac to warn Santa-Cortez. Still dressed in the regal silk and velvet gown of a queen, Clémence sacrifices her reputation to enter the *carbonaro*'s room: knowing that anyone who sees her slipping out of his chambers at night will assume the worst, the painter decides that his life and the cause are worth more than the opinion of the boarders and once again the constructed nature of these social mores is highlighted. Once inside the shocked Gramond's room, the woman who just left the palace sees the revolutionary's bullets and cartridges spread out upon the table, and these parallel scenes demonstrate Clémence's trusted position on both sides of the political divide. Deeply indebted to her, Santa-Cortez asks how he can repay her for saving his life and sacrificing her name. As they gaze at each other in a "sublime look" with "a deeply felt sympathy," she asks him "Will you grant me your esteem and friendship?" (2: 38). He promises he will do so forever, and she adds "In as much as you are able, will you protect the person and freedom of the Duchesse de Berry in the public troubles?" (2: 39), to which he also agrees. In asking for both respect and clemency from Santa-Cortez, Arnaud's heroine delineates a vital role for women in social change. Clémence is an intermediary between the opposing factions, and while her warning allows the revolutionary leader to survive and thus continue his efforts to topple the monarchy, her injunction to save the life of the princess tempers the violence of the overthrow. Like the imagined female Messiah of the Saint-Simonians, Clémence brings a message of change combined with mercy. As an artist, she can "see" with a unique clarity, unclouded by personal partisanship.

After Santa-Cortez's escape, Clémence's "education" or *Bildung* concludes as she devotes herself fully to the political movement. Just as the question of gender was foregrounded upon her arrival at the bourgeois boarding house, the female artist also struggles to be accepted as an independent and self-defining individual by the all-male fraternity of revolutionaries. Thus, when Clémence asks her friend Frantz, one of the *carbonari*, to let her join the association and give her "a mission" (2: 44), he laughingly tells her she is too beautiful to risk her life; in Clémence's impatient response, Arnaud's feminist message is clearly announced. The painter proclaims that she does not want to be treated like a "frivolous woman or a child. I don't want any more of your praise; speak to me seriously, as you would to a man! . . . I want, like you, to smell the scent of the scaffold which heightens our courage; I want to utter those burning words which give life to nations while consuming the individuals that offer them; I want the daggers that graze your chest and *his* to reach mine as well" (2: 45). In keeping with a Saint-Simonian/socialist paradigm, Clémence seeks a brother- and sisterhood with her fellow believers and implores Frantz, "Come on, my friend, suffer more equality between us; let your pride as a man resign itself to it and your heart as a friend rejoice in it!" (2: 47–48). She asks him to take her to the secret meetings disguised as a man in the hopes that there her "mission will be revealed" (2: 48). Frantz, long in love with Clémence, "found an infinite charm in feeling more intimately tied to this woman" (2: 51) through shared commitment to an ideal rather than a romantic entanglement.

In a mirroring scene of performed and mobile identities, Clémence disguises herself as a male revolutionary, and *en travestie* attends a meeting where Gramond elaborates for his followers the aims of the insurrection: "the goal was the overthrow of a dynasty imposed by foreigners; the triumph of liberal ideas, from which would inevitably flow a less costly government for the people, a less illusory freedom of religion, an equality that would no longer be a vain word written in the charter, but which, with the help of larger institutions would move from a state of dogma to a state of practice and truth" (2: 64). As he glances out into the crowd, Gramond sees "a young man" in the shadows, "a celestial figure" whose appearance gives him pause, for although he doesn't realize that it is Clémence dressed as a man, her memory is invoked and soothes his soul. The passionate revolutionary orator undergoes "a rapid and striking transformation"; suddenly repulsed by the thought of the blood that must be spilled for the cause, he now urges his fellow rebels to have mercy: "You will be moderate and generous in victory . . . Do not lose sight, in the midst of the storms, of our mission of future enlightenment" (2: 67–68). Remembering his promise to spare the Duchesse de Berry, Gramond counsels against injustice and wanton violence, reminding the revolutionaries that the "axe must be converted into an olive branch" and "in the confusion that accompanies the beginning of all social reform, do not confuse abuse with principle" (2: 68). Arnaud's 1841 readership, nearly all of whom would have experienced the Revolution of 1830 first- or second-hand, would have recognized the disjuncture between the elevated rhetoric of the novel and the violent reality of the *Trois Glorieuses*. In proposing a fictitious narrative of how a woman might influence the revolution, Arnaud rewrites the past with an eye to a better future.

Ultimately, in keeping with Arnaud's Saint-Simonianism, Clémence comes to take on aspects of a messiah and Santa-Cortez begins to believe "in this woman as he believed in God . . . It seemed to him that at this moment Clémence's voice was the echo of a divine voice that vibrated in his own heart, and he looked at the young woman like predestined sister" (2: 85–86). Addressing the painter directly, Santa-Cortez tells her how "without abandoning her feminine delicacy and the peaceful instincts of her heart she could serve the cause of liberty. He praised the beautiful mission of the artist, which must be the echo of all sorrows and the prophecy of all hopes" (2: 86). This artist's mission applies equally to Arnaud and her project, which combines both hope and suffering in the name of liberty. For Clémence, art becomes a sacred calling and this higher inspiration enables her to "cross the border from talent to genius" (2: 101). Imitation of the great masters, imaginative fantasies, and tasteful finesse no longer suffice her ambition; rather the painter aspires to translate "the feeling of moral beauty that God had inscribed on the soul of the poet; to make it visible and palpable, through the transparency of material forms and to thus bring humans to the imitation of the divine model" (2: 101). As in the earlier scene in the novel, Santa-Cortez channels his feelings for the artist into the contemplation of her art, and the *carbonari* leader focuses his adoration on the images rather than on their creator.

In this novel centered on the fantasy of social and political equality, Clémence attains a parity of sorts with Santa-Cortez when she draws his final portrait and her artist's gaze dominates the powerful man. Arnaud elevates art and the artist to the level of a "divine power," and the revolutionary cedes his active stance to become the passive object of the artist's creative and forceful will (2: 109) in an image that posits art and politics as equally commanding forces. Yet soon thereafter, a crisis arises when Clara arrives in Paris with their daughter Porcia and Santa-Cortez willingly sacrifices the artist to protect the weaker and more vulnerable woman, telling himself that Clémence is strong enough to withstand the blow. Searching for solidarity with Clara, Clémence reaches out to her rival, only to be rejected repeatedly, and the novel's idealistic aspirations veer toward widespread failure, much like the revolution they reflect. The longed-for sisterhood Clémence seeks with Clara is impossible, as is her relationship with Santa-Cortez, who is finally revealed to be an egoist ready to sacrifice others to his own peace of mind. Like Ondine in *L'Atelier d'un peintre*, Arnaud's female painter finds herself "Alone, always alone" and her fate will be the same as the earlier Romantic figure. But where Desbordes-Valmore's character sought meaning in community and in love, Clémence, after much soul searching realizes that her art can be redemptive and give significance to her life. In a gender reversal of the courtly love paradigm, an impossible love inspires the female artist to heights of creativity. While she takes little pleasure in the crowds gathered around her tableaux at the Louvre (2: 167), Clémence finds satisfaction in the fact that her paintings can "aid in the process of bringing humanity to a state of greater perfection and happiness" (2: 181). Where Clara responds to her heartbreak by committing suicide, Clémence transcends personal suffering for the greater good.

The final chapters of the novel take place during the July Revolution. Clémence, who is slowly dying of consumption, regains some of her strength in order to participate in the epoch-changing events. Once again donning male clothes, she advances to the barricades where she finds Gramond asleep, exhausted by the combat. In a lengthy passage, Arnaud describes Clémence watching the sleeping revolutionary stretched out among the cobblestones in a scene that once again places the female character in the position of the active gazer and as she contemplates his face, unseen, Clémence feels the joy and suffering of her love revive once again in her soul. Emphasizing the composition and lighting of the scene, Arnaud creates her own tableau of the artist and the revolutionary on the barricades in a momentary state of grace. Toward dawn, Clémence sees a group of men approach and aim a gun at the sleeping leader. Jumping up, she throws her body in front of Horace, shielding him from the bullet and falling wounded into his arms. If Delacroix's famous *Liberty Leading the People* (1830) allegorized Woman as the image of triumphant revolution, Arnaud rewrites the image of woman and war, demonstrating heroic sacrifice and death. Although the bullet wound is slight, it is fatal to the weakened Clémence, who slowly expires with Horace Gramond/Santa-Cortez by her side. Horace himself, also moribund, asks Frantz to care for Porcia as a "brother to my daughter" (317). The child, whose name evokes Shakespeare's Portia and "the quality of mercy," will once again be the hope for the future as the female artist dies, a victim of her own success.[25]

Angélique Arnaud's novel represents the liberal political leanings of the sentimental social genre, influenced to a greater and lesser extent by the works of Sand and Balzac, aspiring to social change and idealism while actively resisting the masculine, individualist paradigms of Realism. Arnaud's Clémence, a *femme supérieure* who sacrifices her love and ultimately her life for the cause of *le peuple*, embodies revolutionary principles in her life as well as in her death. Her career as an artist privileging work over marriage, her understanding of her "mission" as a life outside of the domestic sphere, and finally, her engagement as a woman and an artist in shaping the political life and future of the nation, were singly and collectively radical, subverting contemporary gender roles in a variety of ways.

Although *Clémence* is forgotten today, Arnaud's subject and "moral" (as announced in her preface) reflected a vision of women's role in the public sphere that only became more pronounced over the course of the decade. Indeed, echoing Clémence, women played a crucial role both intellectually and even on the barricades in the Revolution of 1848, led by former Saint-Simonians Jeanne Deroin and Pauline Roland. As Daumier's 1849 caricature (Figure 25) makes clear in its image of a woman near her desk reading her radical pages to other women, the conflation of female socialists and female writers was firmly established by the end of the 1840s, and produced enough social anxiety to engender a series of ten of Daumier's satirical images under the title "Les Femmes socialistes" in *Le Charivari* from April to June 1849. Deroin, who published voluminously, lectured widely, and tried (unsuccessfully) to run for the National Assembly, was arrested in 1850 and imprisoned for subversion. By 1852 Roland was exiled to Algeria by Louis Napoleon's new regime, and Deroin had escaped to London, where she lived the rest of her life in exile. Thus, like Clémence, whose ambitious hopes to change the world for the better end in the poignant image of her death, the real *femmes socialistes* and feminists of the July Monarchy and Second Republic laid the groundwork for progress that would be realized only by generations to come.

Figure 25
Honoré Daumier, *Les Femmes socialistes*. Lithograph. *Le Charivari*, 17 May 1849. [What is woman in society today? Nothing! What should she be? Everything . . . yes, everything!—Bravo, that's even better than Jeanne Deroin's last speech].

Part III

The Portrait
Romanticism and the Female Subject

Margaret Gillies and the Miniature

Portraits of Radical Engagement

Portraits, Gender, and Identity

The portrait is the artistic genre most readily identified with women; from Dibutades to Cindy Sherman, female artists have employed the form to a variety of ends, and the nineteenth century was no exception. Historically tied to imitation or mimesis rather than imagination, portraiture was accorded little prestige within the hierarchies of the arts in Britain and France; as an art form that was almost always commissioned by the sitter, the portrait was further "debased" by its commercial associations. The private, intimate, and even domestic nature of the portrait made it a "suitable" genre for the female amateur, while large numbers of the women supporting themselves as artists were also portraitists by profession. Painted from a (usually) well-bred and fully dressed sitter rather than a lower class, naked model, and destined for the domestic interior of a private home rather than the Salon or gallery, portraiture theoretically allowed the female artist to retain her position outside of the public sphere.[1] Yet despite the mechanical implications of the "taking of a likeness," a portrait is rarely a simple or transparent representation of one individual by another. Closely linked to changing beliefs in the nature of identity itself, the portrait reflects contemporary epistemologies and ideologies of subjecthood, as well as efforts to subvert those ideologies. Definitions or constructions of self and other are played out in the intersubjective encounter between artist and subject which is often, implicitly, a political as well as an aesthetic transaction. In other words, the image that the viewer confronts is a representation of a relationship between the artistic self and the artistic other as much as it is a painted reflection of the "original" sitter. At the same time, the portrait is a process that produces both subject and object, the painter and sitter, at a certain moment in time.[2] If the sitter's pose is a performative self-fashioning, aimed at presenting a certain identity to the world, Richard Brilliant reminds us that we must also consider "the artist's collusive involvement in the fabrication of an identity for the subject that may, or may not, correspond to the subject's own representation of self."[3] The portrait thus reflects social relations and power struggles inextricably linked to historical concepts of identity, representation, and the body.

Portraits invoke visual conventions of dress, gesture, comportment, and accoutrement that allow the viewer to "read" the subject, and these codes are of course socially and historically determined. Indeed, "Portraits exist at the interface between art and social life and the pressure to conform to social norms enters into their composition because both the artist and the subject are enmeshed in the value system of their society" (Brilliant 11). As in any work that foregrounds identity and social norms, gender is central to the dynamics of the portrait at every level. Inscribed in the subject's performance of his or her identity, conventions of gender and subjectivity also subtend the relationship between viewers—that is, both the artist and the eventual audience—and the painted subject who is, in turn, the object of their gazes. The paradigmatic structure of male bearer of the gaze/female object of the gaze (Mulvey) is enacted in the vast panoply of portraits in eighteenth- and nineteenth-century France and Britain where male artists portray female sitters in poses and personae (mythic, allegorical, seductive, maternal, etc.) that affirm and consolidate contemporary constructions of femininity. More often than not, male desire and fantasy are projected onto the screen of the female portrait subject, for as Tamar Garb contends we almost always find "sexual dynamics at the heart of the making and viewing of modern female portraits."[4] When the artist and gazing subject is female, however, these conventions and constructions of gender, vision, and subject position are destabilized, if not subverted entirely. In the present chapter I will examine the artistic interventions of Margaret Gillies in the field of the nineteenth-century portrait in terms of her engagement in issues of social and artistic identity.

Margaret Gillies and the Radical Unitarians

Margaret Gillies (1803–87) was identified at her death as a "female pioneer,"[5] whose life and art directly inspired Anna Mary Howitt, Octavia Hill, and Mary

Ann Evans (George Eliot) and paved the way for generations of women to follow.[6] Embodying the sister arts, Margaret, a professional painter, and her sister Mary Gillies (1800–1870), a professional author, lived and worked together for fifty years: Mary writing fiction, poetry, reviews, children's literature, and translations, and Margaret painting miniatures, portraits, genres scenes, and watercolors. Committed to a liberal Unitarian ideal of the power of art and literature to elevate the heart and mind, the Gillies sisters collaborated on a number of radical journals of the 1830s and '40s, providing text and portrait illustrations for *The Monthly Repository, Howitt's Journal, The People's Journal,* and *A New Spirit of the Age,* among others. Even outside of the pages of the periodical press, their lives and their work reflected a proto-feminist vision of women's role in the world and a politicized desire to reshape the very definitions of gender, genre, and domesticity in nineteenth-century Britain through collaboration, cooperation, and progressivism.

Born to a well-connected and intellectual Scottish family, the Gillies sisters were raised by wealthy relations in Edinburgh after their mother's death in 1811. In the home of their uncle Adam, Lord Gillies, Mary and Margaret met Walter Scott, Lord Erskine (an influential animal rights advocate), Lord Jeffrey (a long-time editor of the *Edinburgh Review*) and "other men of note and wit for which the northern capital was then famous."[7] Exposed to the world of literature and ideas, the sisters had difficulty accepting the social roles assigned to them, and after Margaret refused a marriage proposal in 1819, they left their uncle's home together for London. Despite their family's objections, Margaret and Mary set up house together and began supporting themselves, primarily on the income from Margaret's portraits. By the early 1830s, the Gillies sisters had become actively involved in a radical circle of writers and reformers that grew out of the Unitarian ministry of William Johnson Fox. As they attended gatherings in his home, Margaret and Mary came to know the leading progressive thinkers of the day, including Harriet Taylor, John Stuart Mill, Leigh Hunt, Robert Browning, William Macready, and the Howitts,[8] while Bulwer Lytton, Charles Dickens, and William Godwin also numbered among Fox's frequent visitors. Margaret was introduced by Fox to Thomas Southwood Smith (1788–1861), a sanitary reformer, separated from his second wife, who became her lover in the mid-1830s and lived with her from 1838 until his death more than twenty years later. The unconventional household included the unmarried sisters, Southwood Smith, and Richard Hengist Horne (1803–84), a liberal author and editor who was Mary Gillies's romantic partner.[9] Living and working together in a spirit of collaboration and mutual inspiration, the couples eschewed marriage for artistic and spiritual partnerships that reflected the progressive social views that have come to be associated with the "radical Unitarians."[10] For the better part of thirty years, Margaret Gillies's painting was the principal means of support for the extended household, which variously included her father and step-mother, Mary Leman Grimstone Gillies; Southwood Smith; Horne; Gertrude Smith (Southwood Smith's granddaughter) and ultimately Gertrude's husband, Charles Lewes (son of G. H. Lewes).

An offshoot of the more traditional Unitarian church, the radical Unitarians held dissident views on women, marriage, and divorce that distanced them from the "official" branch of the denomination. Led by Fox, the radical Unitarians of the 1830s-1840s combined progressive politics and Christian ethics into a hybrid philosophy of social critique and reform influenced by German Romanticism and contemporary theories of social idealism, including Saint-Simonianism and Owenism. As they embraced the principles of freedom, progress, and labor, the group placed a strong emphasis on the power of education and art to help bring forth a cultural revolution that would include the emancipation of women, slaves, and the working classes. Recognizing the power of the press to reach a wide audience, the radical Unitarians and likeminded liberals promoted their programs of reform in the *Monthly Repository*, a journal edited by Fox from 1828–36. During this period, Harriet Martineau, John Stuart Mill, Harriet Taylor, Robert Browning, Ebenezer Elliott, Richard Horne, and many others contributed essays on political economy, housing, philanthropy, and reform, as well as poetry, fiction, translations, and art and book reviews.[11] Perhaps most strikingly, the *Monthly Repository* also published a steady stream of articles devoted to "Woman's Condition" and the inequities of marriage. Essays by Fox, Mary Leman Grimstone, and William Bridges Adams, among others, highlight the radical Unitarian understanding of the constructed nature of contemporary female identity, as the authors argue for the importance of education for women.

As the only visual artist in the radical Unitarian group, Margaret Gillies played a unique role in the promulgation of their ideas of progress and reform in British society. In one of her few surviving letters she wrote: "Artists in general seize every opportunity of painting the nobility of wealth and rank; it would be far more grateful to me to be able to paint what I conceive to be true nobility, that of genius, long, faithfully, earnestly, and not without suffering, laboring to call out what is most beautiful and refined in our nature and to establish this as our guide and standard of human action."[12] Gillies here announces her aesthetic of public engagement and her conception of the role of painting as a medium that could elevate the minds and feelings of the viewer. Turning away from the traditional subject matter of portraiture—the aristocracy of "wealth and rank"—Gillies instead embraces the Romantic "aristocracy of sensibility," that is, artists, philosophers, poets, for her portraits. Working primarily in the form of the portrait miniature, Gillies disrupted the boundaries of gender and genre by taking a distinctly personal artistic form, associated with the private sphere of domestic display and consumption, and inserting it into the "masculine" public arena of political engagement.

The Portrait Miniature:
THE POLITICS OF FORM

As developed in the sixteenth century, miniatures were closely linked to British royalty and rapidly became markers of status for members of the moneyed classes.[13] Diminutive, intimate images painted in watercolor on ivory, miniature portraits were exchanged between loved ones and frequently carried on one's person or exhibited in the more private quarters of the home. Although most miniatures were small enough to fit in a hand or be worn as adornment, by the late eighteenth century the size had increased to a more substantial scale to incorporate more ambitious compositions; Marcia Pointon explains that a miniature could also be "a painting too large to put in a pocket but small enough to be passed around a dinner table" (48). Yet unlike easel portraits, which "present a public self meant to face outward," Robin Jaffe Frank tells us, "portrait miniatures reveal a private self meant to face inward."[14] The association of the miniature portrait with what John Murdoch terms "personal adornment and private emotions"[15] tended to "feminize" the form, while its enormous popularity with eighteenth-century bourgeois consumers eager to acquire "the patina of established taste" (Frank 15) led to its commercialization and loss of cultural capital. By the beginning of the nineteenth century, the miniaturist was scorned by Academic painters as a profit-seeking artisan rather than an inspired artist.[16]

Looked down upon by denizens of "high art," the miniature portrait was a popular art form and pastime for middle- and upper-class patrons and amateurs in nineteenth-century Britain. The tension between its resolutely commercial nature, as art produced for commission, and its associations with the feminine created an indeterminate identity for miniature painting, oscillating between the masculine realm of labor and capital in the public sphere and a "ladylike" and "genteel domestic pastime."[17] Perhaps more than any other genre of the period, the miniature was deemed an "appropriate" profession for women seeking to support themselves in a respectable manner, not only because of its delicacy and imitative subject matter, but also because of its distance from the elevated ranks of academic art.

The popular vision of a female miniature painter of the 1820s and '30s is emblematized by Dickens's Miss La Creevy in *Nicholas Nickleby* of 1838. Dickens, whose aunt was a miniaturist, creates a comic portrait of an aging woman who supports herself through her art. At once foolish and good-hearted, Miss La Creevy's character is marked by her solitude, frivolity, artistic pretensions, and diminutive stature, personifying the very genre she works in. Gently mocking the miniature portrait's tendency to idealize the subject, Dickens paints a painter who portrays her subjects not as they are, but as they wish to be: "What with bringing out eyes with all one's power, and keeping down noses with all one's force, and adding to heads, and taking away teeth altogether, you have no idea of the trouble one little miniature is."[18] Miss La Creevy follows a formula she believes to have discovered at the Royal Academy, explaining to Kate Nickleby, "there are only two styles of portrait painting, the serious and the smirk; and we always use the serious for professional people (except actors sometimes), and the smirk for private ladies and gentlemen who don't care so much about looking clever" (121). The irony of the "we," associating the female miniaturist with her male counterparts at the Academy is no small part of Dickens's humor here, echoed by Kate, who "seemed highly amused by this information." The disjunction between La Creevy's portraits and their sitters is driven home when she reveals that the numerous images of military officers on display in her studio are "only clerks and that, who hire a uniform coat to be painted in" (121–22). Like the clerks posing as soldiers, Miss La Creevy represents the female miniature painter posing as a real artist, and the happy ending of the novel includes her marriage to Mr Linkinwater, a "superannuated bank clerk," after which, the reader can only assume she retires her paintbrush for domestic bliss.

The life and art of Margaret Gillies bore little resemblance to those of her fictional counterpart. As a miniature painter during the same decades as Dickens was publishing his novels, Gillies shared far more with the author, who used his art for social criticism and reform, than she did with the timid Miss La Creevy. Indeed, in 1843 Dickens happily sat for Gillies six or seven times for a miniature portrait exhibited at the Royal Academy in 1844 and later included as an engraving in Horne's *A New Spirit of the Age,* as part of the painter's project to adapt the genre to more inspirational ends.[19] During the 1820s, Gillies had become one of two female students instructed in miniature painting by Frederick Cruikshank, a popular Scottish portraitist in London who was himself a pupil of Andrew Robertson. Robertson (1777–1845) played an active role in attempting to revolutionize the very genre of miniature painting and to transform it from a frivolous and decorative art to a more serious art form. Moving to a rectangular, rather than oval format, Robertson increased the size of the ivory to allow for more complex compositions that might rival those of oil paintings. His technique was notable for its elaborate use of watercolor and masterful draftsmanship, and in his quest to "paint *pictures*" rather than "toys," as he qualified oval miniatures,[20] Robertson eschewed the flattering portraits of his contemporaries for unidealized images in the style of the Old Masters.

Although Robertson's influence on Gillies was indirect, the two Scottish miniaturists shared a desire to expand the purview of the miniature portrait, and like Robertson, Gillies sought to use the form for more serious ends. Translating the intimate form into the social sphere of public engagement, Gillies used the miniature for the broad dissemination of images of Fox, Dickens, William Wordsworth, Leigh Hunt, Jeremy Bentham, Ebenezer Elliott, William Macready, Southwood Smith, Horne, and other Unitarian, liberal, and/or Romantic thinkers both at the RA exhibition and in the pages of the radical press. Even more importantly, Gillies devoted a large number of her miniature portraits to images of influential women of the period, including Mary Howitt, Charlotte Cushman, Helen Faucit, Mary Leman Grimstone, and Harriet Martineau. As images of outspoken reformers, authors, and actors painted and exhibited by a woman, Gillies's portraits of progressives presented a female subject's intervention in the politics of identity, representation, and art in nineteenth-century Britain. Moreover, as she exhibited her work both in official expositions (Royal Academy, Society of British Artists, Royal Scottish Academy, Liverpool Academy) and in the pages of the *Monthly Repository, Howitt's Journal, People's Journal,* and *A New Spirit of the Age,* Gillies began to occupy a noteworthy place in the field of cultural production of early Victorian England as a female portraitist, a fact that was recognized by her contemporaries.[21] Through images, rather than words, Gillies allowed the faces and postures of Fox, Martineau, Howitt, and other notables to speak directly to the viewers, and in manifesting the "divine spirit" Gillies believed that her art, like its subjects, could benefit humanity. Through the miniature format, the painter calls attention both to her gender and to her subject matter, moving a "feminine" art form into the public realm and demonstrating the constructed nature of the boundaries that would separate them.

Gillies's *Harriet Martineau:*
A PORTRAIT OF RADICAL DIFFERENCE

An early portrait of Harriet Martineau (1802–76) reveals essential aspects of Gillies's engagement with the politics of gender and artistic identity in the 1830s. Martineau, who began contributing to the *Monthly Repository* in 1822, was a committed Unitarian whose influential writings on political economy and women's issues made her one of the most prominent women of the day. In 1832 she achieved broad public acclaim with the publication of *Illustrations of Political Economy,* a series of stories translating Priestly and Bentham's theories of utilitarianism and Adam Smith's theories of free trade into the language of everyday life, showing them in their practical social applications. By demystifying these important ideas for the common people, "illustrating" rather than theorizing, Martineau hoped to impart principles that would help them better manage their lives and finances. In moving from the arcane language of economics, comprehensible only to the initiated (*de facto* educated, upper-class men), to narrative, a more "feminine" discourse accessible to all, Martineau deliberately crossed the boundaries of gender and genre in order to educate and even liberate the oppressed lower classes.[22]

Gillies's first portrait of Martineau was painted at the artist's request in 1832, immediately following the success of *Illustrations of Political Economy*. The miniature, which remained in Gillies's possession, was reproduced in 1833 as an engraving that circulated widely and was chosen by Martineau as the frontispiece for her *Autobiography* (1857). Indeed, as with many of Martineau's portraits, the image took on iconic stature and continues to be found today in myriad books and websites, often unattributed. This notable pairing—the image of a female writer painted by a female artist—promoted both women's professional status while also promoting the more general idea of women in the field of cultural production. Just as Martineau made theories of political economy available to the non-elite through her stories, Gillies made the inspirational image of this female reformer available through the format of engraving. Where a painting on display at the Royal Academy would primarily be seen by a small, self-selected group of Londoners, an engraving, in its reproducibility, could circulate in the pages of broadsheets, newspapers, magazines, journals, and books on its own as a discrete entity, reaching a broad swath of the population both in Britain and abroad. Indeed Gillies, Martineau, and the radical Unitarians of the 1830s and '40s fought to effectuate social revolution through the distribution of their art and writing to the masses. As opposed to the singularity of the oil painting or miniature, the plurality of the engraving emblematized not only an expanded audience and expanded scope for art itself, but also the communitarian ideal that was central to both feminist and socialist movements of the period.

In the 1832–33 portrait of Martineau (figure 26), Gillies emphasizes her intellect rather than her beauty, portraying the writer as visionary, gazing off into the distance.[23] At once inspired and inspiring, Martineau projects an image of determination and focus, the set of her mouth and chin suggesting a woman who is confident in her mission and not easily deterred. Looking past the spectator, she is caught in a moment of absorption in her own thoughts. Gillies adopted a similar pose for several other portraits during this period, including those of Fox and Bentham, to indicate the elevated and spiritual nature of the subject's disposition. But where portraits of the male subjects are tightly focused on the head, bringing the figure to the front of the picture plane, Martineau's image is set further back, allowing us to see not only her face, but her torso as well. The distance protects the female subject from the intimacy of the images of Fox and Bentham, but if it is less immediate, Martineau's image is also less

Chapter 7: Margaret Gillies and the Miniature

Figure 26
Margaret Gillies, *Portrait of Harriet Martineau*, 1833. Engraving.
British Museum.

abstract, for there is a precisely rendered female body, with a woman's bust and narrow waist, beneath her head. In keeping with the conventions of the portrait genre, Martineau's clothes and hair are also carefully depicted, further requiring the viewer to read her as a woman as well as a political economist. The elaborate lace collar and fur cuff of her dark dress place Martineau in a certain social strata, while her lustrous and carefully groomed hair emphasizes her relative youth and attractiveness: although she is a woman of ideas, she is indisputably feminine in her self-presentation. Fox's and Bentham's disheveled hair and sketchy clothes draw the viewer's attention to their implied intellect and inner brilliance, for Gillies is clearly working within the discourses of Romantic genius. In the absence of a discourse of *female* Romantic genius, Gillies crafts an image that locates Martineau as both a woman and a visionary, expanding the possibilities of what a woman's identity might entail.

Indeed the question of gender and professional identity was central to contemporary portraits of Martineau, ranging from Maclise's malicious caricature of her in *Fraser's Magazine* in 1833 to Richard Evans' elegant and flattering oil exhibited in 1834, and these images provide a revealing context for Gillies's own intervention. Maclise's portrait of Martineau, included in "*Fraser's* Gallery of Illustrious Literary Characters," took part in the conservative periodical's larger effort to establish what Judith Fisher has called "genderized aesthetic norms" during the 1830s.[24] The caricatural, irreverent images of literary celebrities, accompanied by William Maginn's satirical text, function in dialectical opposition to Gillies's inspirational and socially engaged portraits in the progressive press (*The Monthly Repository, Howitt's Journal, The People's Journal*, etc.). For if both sets of images engaged with contemporary authors' "performance of gendered professionalism" (Fisher 105), *Fraser's* sought to establish a model of authorial "manliness," while Gillies hoped to legitimize women's position in the field of cultural and intellectual production. Thus, Maclise's portrait of a decidedly unattractive Martineau highlights the disjunction between her gender and her profession with an unmistakable emphasis on her lack of femininity. Placing her in a stark domestic interior, seated before a hearth with a cat suggestively arched upon her back, Maclise constructs the political economist as a "Utilitarian witch,"[25] while Maginn's text mocks her as a Malthusian whose teachings on population control are not surprising, since she is "too ugly to marry." The focus in this cruel parody falls not on Martineau as a writer per se, but on Martineau as a transgressive woman whose intrusion into the masculine realm of politics and authorship is visualized in ways that demonstrate her unfeminine and even threatening nature. Taking the opposite tack, Richard Evans portrays Martineau in his large oil portrait as an elegant society woman, wrapped in silks and furs, decorated in jewels, while seated in a luxurious interior; while her good looks, middle-class status, and femininity are privileged here, there is little beyond a hand placed on some papers upon the table to indicate Martineau's identity as a writer and economist.

In Gillies's portrait of the female author, Martineau is depicted as both a woman *and* a visionary writer. Yet the most striking aspect of the image is Martineau's right hand, which is cupped around her ear, foregrounding the fact that the sitter had been going progressively deaf since adolescence and relied on a trumpet to hear. Charlotte Yeldham reads the gesture as an allusion "to her receptivity to social problems"[26] and indeed the posture only increases the sense of Martineau's rapt attentiveness. The inclusion of a hand within a head and shoulders composition is unusual and the awkwardness of the hand, with fingers at once obscuring and emphasizing the ear, draws the viewer's attention to her gesture, and by extension to her disability, in a way that no other visual portrayal of the period did. Indeed, if Maclise, Evans, and Martineau's other portraitists framed the writer within or against traditional discourses of femininity, Gillies inscribes gender and difference in a way that focuses on the contemporary conflation of female identity and disability, only to refuse the assumed limitations of both.

Gillies's portrait of Harriet Martineau thus foregrounds the radical author's difference, locating it in both her gender and her disability, while at the same time suggesting Martineau's strength as a deaf woman who could hear what men would not and say what women could not. Where even sympathetic critics such as Samuel Smiles and William Howitt accounted for her powerful voice and intelligence by calling her "a woman with a manly heart and head"[27] and "a masculine intellect in female form,"[28] Gillies refutes the assumptions that these qualities could only belong to a man by painting Martineau as a woman who is no more crippled by her gender than she is by her deafness. By foregrounding the body as the site of difference, only to subvert the binaries of gender and ability/disability, Gillies reflects and repeats Martineau's own audacious border crossings. For indeed Martineau herself recognized that her deafness and her gender placed her in the realm of those "deemed unfit" for intellectual pursuits in the public sphere[29] and self-consciously sought to undermine the very norms that would condemn her to silence and passivity. Victorian science's determination that both women and the deaf were physiologically incapable of abstract thought, and thus intellectually inferior, allowed critics to attack her "fitness" for political economy on both fronts and in an emblematic jibe, conservative MP Lord Brougham derided the successful female author as "the little deaf woman from Norwich." As Susan Bohrer explains "By remarking upon her deafness and womanhood Lord Brougham defers to the stereotypes associated with both women and the deaf. As a woman and disabled, Martineau's work represents the transgression of the limits of her proper sphere . . . Since both Martineau's hearing impairment and her femininity should confine her to domesticity and a severely restricted intellectual capacity, her engagement within theoretical and political realms reveals how ignominious her trespass is."[30] Martineau's "trespass" as a deaf woman into the masculine world of political and economic writing was all the more powerful in its challenge to the assumption of muteness associated with both marginalized identities. In her writings, as in her life, Martineau used her disability as a form of resistance to these restrictive constructions, revising the tropes of deafness, Bohrer concludes, "to emphasize her own independence and intellectual prowess" and transforming "what Martineau's critics see as her greatest liabilities, her gender and her deafness" into "the foundation of her fortitude" (27; 36). Margaret Gillies's early portrait of Martineau anticipates the author's own self-portraits in *Letter to the Deaf* (1834) and *Life in the Sickroom* (1844), challenging the limiting, gendered discourses of domesticity and silence by presenting her as a model for the new age, celebrating rather than occluding her deafness, and thus privileging femininity and disability as sources of strength, authority, and inspiration for social progress and reform. Destabilizing the very norms of genius, creation, intellect, and political engagement, these visual and verbal representations by Gillies and Martineau "pose[d] the perilous possibility that the norm itself is neither universal nor true" (Bohrer 25). Just as Habermas suggests that the public sphere of the nineteenth century was structured by representation, Gillies, Martineau, and other radical thinkers, artists, and authors of the 1830s and '40s consciously worked to show the public a different view of itself than the one propagated by the dominant discourse.

The Collaborative Paradigm

No less socially engaged than her sister, Mary Gillies penned essays, biographies, and children's stories with the shared goal of ameliorating the social condition of women and the working classes. Much of what she wrote was collaborative and often pseudonymous, frequently composed with her romantic partner, Richard Hengist Horne, for publication in various journals, including *Howitt's* and *People's Journal*, as well as *A New Spirit of the Age*. Mary co-edited the *Monthly Repository* with Horne in 1836–37 and they collaborated extensively on *The History of Napoleon*, published in 1841 under Horne's name alone. Mary published *Memoirs of a London Doll* with illustrations by her sister in 1846, and the following year began publishing a series of articles and stories on "Associated Housing" in *Howitt's Journal* in which she most eloquently delineated her own theories of social progress and female identity. Like Martineau, Mary Gillies transformed theoretical ideas into narratives, and in these short pieces she shifts the focus from the lives of working men, a popular contemporary topic, to the life of the family in the modern city. In a series of tales mixing fiction and reportage she delineates the evils of contemporary living conditions for the working poor, with no clean water, heat, or light, and contrasts this "tale of misery" with her vision of "Associated Homes" of the future. Located in well-lit streets with good drainage, the homes are apartments within a building with central heat, light, running water, and waste disposal. As Mary Gillies highlights the importance of sanitation she also underlines a new understanding of the crucial role played by women and family in the well-being of the nation. The Associated Homes are conceived of as cooperative societies with a shared kitchen, where meals are prepared collectively and taken together, as the tenants work together, make their own rules, and share the responsibility of the establishment on equal footing. There are schools, a library, infant care, and workshops with the collective household, where multiple generations can live together in harmony. "A Labourer's Home" tells the story of John, a worker who lost his wife and five children to the squalor of their wretched living conditions; by the second installment he is enjoying the utopic conditions of a shared establishment and observes: "What is more to my feeling than all the rest is the great improvement that Associated Homes make in the condition of women. Women are raised by them from anxious toil-worn drudges, to their true place in the world. Now they can enjoy the boon of existence. Now we know what blessings to us are our daughters, our sisters and our wives; and our children will know what it is to have mothers."[31]

In advocating for a collective domesticity, not unlike that she shared with Margaret, Southwood Smith, and Horne, Mary Gillies resists the ideology of the private sphere by making it, in many ways, public both in its lived experience and in its larger realm of influence. As described in her series, meals and leisure activities such as reading, conversation, and singing move from the family parlor into the shared public space of the Associated Homes. Deconstructing the monolithic definitions of family and home, Gillies inserts women and their work into a far more public domain of shared labor rather than "natural" private duty or instinct. Childcare and the education of young children are also collectively, rather than individually, administered, leaving mothers more time to develop their own interests and skills. Gillies's subsequent articles indicate the advantages for every class of British society, and she concludes "that the whole of our social arrangements may be wonderfully improved and that this co-operative plan is the medium by which it will be elevated."[32] By changing the structure of domesticity and collapsing some of the boundaries between the private and public worlds, a more communal society would be created, improving the lot of not only women and children, but all of humanity. In moving from the isolation within the family domicile to the solidarity of communal labor, women are liberated from the oppression of the ideologies that fetishized the image of the angel of the house while denying the value of her efforts as true labor. As described by Mary Gillies, the hierarchical structure of gender in the private sphere is replaced by a more horizontal orientation in the Associated Home, placing women's and men's work on a parallel plane, each equally important to the collective well-being.

Margaret painted several portraits of artistic couples that reflect some of these same concepts, while further promoting her social vision. In 1839, poet

Thomas Powell wrote to Wordsworth on Gillies's behalf to request that she be allowed to come to Rydal Mount to paint his portrait. Powell describes the female painter as follows: "she is highly gifted; most enthusiastic; young: with a fine mind: and one very likely to interest you"; he further explains that she planned "to have the work engraved by one of the first artists of the day, and thus afford every Englishman an opportunity of having by his fireside a portrait of our 'great Bard.'"[33] Gillies was described by her friends (for Leigh Hunt and Southwood Smith also vouched for her) as the only artist capable of capturing a true likeness of the poet, and the Wordsworths welcomed her into their home in the fall of 1839 for several months. During her stay at Rydal Mount, Gillies executed three portraits of Wordsworth, as well as images of his wife Mary, Dora (their daughter), and several friends from the area including Isabella Fenwick and Kate Southey. The first of the three miniatures was completed in November and exhibited the following year at the Royal Academy and the Liverpool Academy to great acclaim. Both critics and poets praised the portrait while friends and family declared it "decidedly the best likeness that has ever been taken."[34] Elizabeth Barrett Browning considered it "exquisite," agreeing with Horne's assessment that Gillies captured the very soul of her subject.[35]

The image of Wordsworth shows the poet at nearly seventy, poised before a table with an open book and a window behind him. His gentle and contemplative look suggests poetic meditation or inspiration, while the idealized landscape framed by the arched window portrays his beloved Lake District. With his large nose and thinning hair, the author of "Intimations of Immortality" is shown at peace with old age in this affectionate representation of his elderly face. Wordsworth's pose performs the "inward gaze" that had come to be associated with Romantic genius, but also hints at spirituality and acceptance of what the future might bring. The revolutionary Romantic of the early decades of the nineteenth century here becomes a sober paterfamilias; the image was engraved in 1841 and included in *The People's Journal* in 1846. Another, simpler portrait of Wordsworth in profile was also executed during Margaret Gillies's visit, and the engraved image was featured in *A New Spirit of the Age* in 1844, accompanied by Elizabeth Barrett Browning's account of the poet.

Gillies's portrait of Mary Wordsworth, painted for the family rather than the public, is an intimate image of the poet's wife with a quill pen in hand. Like Wordsworth, she gazes off into the distance with a focused look of concentration on her face as she pauses in her composition. The elderly woman is elaborately swathed in a blue velvet gown, fur stole, and lace fichu, with a lacy bonnet covering her white hair. Her veined hands are vividly depicted, expressing an incipient energy and activity that complements the patient and intelligent smile hovering on her lips. Her head tilting forward slightly, as if listening or remembering, Mary projects calm, emotional engagement that bespeaks connection with others while at the same time her face and posture signal strength, diligence, and dignity. With no other props than her pen and paper, the portrait suggests a woman of serious purpose and commitment; the abstract background invokes no reference at all to her domestic or maternal duties. Where the poet's hands were idle in Gillies's portraits, the poet's wife, well known to be his amanuensis, hold the tools of inscription for posterity. Wordsworth composed two sonnets inspired by the miniature of Mary: the first, "To a Painter (Miss M. Gillies), 1841," compares art and memory, proclaiming "All praise the Likeness by thy skill portrayed; / But 'tis a fruitless task to paint for me," for his heart cherishes the image of "that inward eye" which sees the "bloom that cannot fade," untouched by Time.[36] The second, "Miss Gillies' Portrait of Mrs. Wordsworth, 1841," revisits his initial resistance to the representation of Mary's advanced age and pays tribute both to Gillies and to Mary for the beauty of the image of his wife in the present moment. He intones, "Though I beheld at first with blank surprise / This Work, I now have gazed on it so long / I see its truth with unreluctant eyes." The portrait, the poet proclaims, allows him to recognize that "Morn into noon did pass, noon into eve" unnoticed, but he now concedes "the old day was welcome as the young" and indeed is "More beautiful, as being a thing more holy." Although her body may age, the spirit is ageless, and Wordsworth pays tribute to "the eternal youth / Of all thy goodness, never melancholy; / To thy large heart and humble mind, that cast / Into one vision, future, present, past."[37] He indicates that Gillies, in capturing Mary's physical likeness has also located the deeper truth of her beauty that transcends the ravages of time. If he initially resists the portrait's portrayal of his wife's identity, the poet comes to see Gillies's gift for capturing a spiritual truth beyond the surface mimesis.

While still at Rydal Mount, Gillies began a double portrait of William and Mary together (figure 27). Combining the two earlier images with some changes, the new image was not completed until 1840. In bringing the two figures together in a single composition, Gillies transforms the image of the solitary Romantic poet into that of a partner or one of a pair; similarly, Mary's attentive face and poised hand are now read in terms of her work with her husband. Although their gazes do not meet, William appearing to compose a verse in his head and Mary waiting to transcribe the words, there is an ease and intimacy in their postures, as well as an air of familiarity, for indeed it was well known that Wordsworth dictated his poems to Mary. Their fruitful collaboration is witnessed by the stack of books on the table before them, and the past, present, and future alluded to in Wordsworth's sonnet above is represented in the bound volumes of earlier poems, the present moment of creation represented here, and the folio that Mary is filling which will someday be another book. The sublime landscape forming the background of the first

Part III: The Portrait

Figure 27
Margaret Gillies, *William and Mary Wordsworth*, 1839–40. Watercolor on ivory. 30 × 27 cm. Wordsworth Trust, Rydal Mount. Bridgeman Art Library International, New York, NY.

portrait of Wordsworth is here replaced by a markedly domestic setting with heavy curtains and carved columns that appear to evoke the library at Rydal Mount as engraved by William Westall in 1840.[38] Gillies thus presents an image of marriage as a partnership and the home as a potential site for intellectual collaboration. Although Wordsworth inarguable dominates the composition with his imposing presence, dwarfing the more delicate Mary, she nonetheless anchors the scene, providing balance to the larger figure in black and white, and Gillies unmistakably signals that they work together as partners in poetry as well as in life. Physically subordinated to her husband, Mary Wordsworth nonetheless plays an important role in the production of his art.

A second double portrait of William and Mary Howitt (1846) (figure 28) echoes the structure and sentiment of Gillies's portrayal of the Wordsworths. A close friend of the family, Gillies exhibited a single portrait of Mary Howitt at the RSA in 1847 and one of Anna Mary Howitt at the RA in 1849. As discussed in chapter 3, the Howitts were committed to liberal causes and social reform; William and Mary frequently collaborated on publications, including *Howitt's Journal,* and Mary was arguably as successful as her husband as an author, poet, translator, and editor. Gillies's miniature of William and Mary Howitt shows William standing magisterially before a table gazing off with a look of determination and clarity rather than the dreamy inspiration manifested on Wordsworth's face. His erect posture, with one hand on his hip and the other holding a small volume that rests upon the table, projects a masterful identity that seems to mirror closely the many characterizations of the reformer. Mary Howitt, like Mary Wordsworth, is seated on the right side of the painting, physically dominated by her husband, and like the poet's wife, Mary Howitt is writing with a quill pen. Her calm demeanor offsets the hint of impatience in William's stance, while her face and eyes communicate an intelligence and intensity that signal her own unshakeable commitment to reform. If Mary Wordsworth's contribution to the collective family good was the transcription of her husband's verse (as well as, of course, the care and nurturing of the family and their home), Mary Howitt was a well-regarded author in her own right, whose collaborations with her husband and daughters were complements to her own publications and translations. To any viewer of the period, the Howitts' partnership would have been well known, and Gillies's image of husband and wife together at a worktable would have evoked a sense of shared purpose and production. The coming together of their hands at the center of the canvas suggests the very heart of the Howitt home, depicted in this domestic scene of creative cooperation and mutual engagement. These miniatures and others like them reflected Margaret Gillies's vision of harmonious and productive affiliations of men and women working together to improve society and the belief, shared with her sister Mary, that the family could be the site of social as well as domestic labor. In seeking to elevate and inspire her viewers, Margaret Gillies consciously strove to represent women actively participating in culture and reform. Gillies's portraits of contemporary progressive "nobility" construct a collective image of female identity that reconciles and even naturalizes the association of women and artistic/social labor, presenting a counter-discourse to the ideologies that would oppose women and meaningful work. In a letter to Horne in 1870, around the time of her sister's death, Margaret reflected:

Figure 28
Margaret Gillies, *William and Mary Howitt*, 1846. Oil on ivory. 41.9 × 33 cm. Nottingham City Museums and Galleries.

"We think it is right for women to work and women do work and have worked always; but we think and the world is beginning to think, that their work should be acknowledged and respected—not merely accepted and despised."[39] Much of her effort in the course of her long career was directed toward gaining that acknowledgment and respect for women and their work.

Leigh Hunt and "The Feast of the Violets":
PORTRAITS OF GENDER PARODY

Although many of the ideas put forth by the Gillies sisters were supported by their fellow progressives in the 1830s and '40s, these idealized, if not utopic visions of sister- and brotherhood, collaborative labor, and solidarity as the hope for art and society were not necessarily embraced by all who espoused the liberal cause. Leigh Hunt (1784–1859), the Romantic poet and publisher, was renowned for his radical politics and reformist views. A friend of Shelley and Byron, Hunt founded a series of journals, including *Examiner* (which he published from jail from 1812–15), *The Liberal* (published along with Shelley and Byron from Italy), and the short-lived *Leigh Hunt's London Journal,* which carried the subheading "To Assist the Enquiring, Animate the Struggling, and Sympathize with All." Like Gillies and the radical Unitarians, Hunt believed "The great use of the arts is thus to humanize and refine, to purify enjoyment, and, when duly appreciated, to connect the perception of physical beauty with that of moral excellence."[40]

But if Hunt shared the radical Unitarian belief in social reform, his sympathies did not extend to women's issues, and like many of his fellow Romantics, Hunt betrayed a deep discomfort with the incursion of women into the field of cultural production. In 1837, as he took over as editor of the *Monthly Repository* from Richard Hengist Horne and Mary Gillies, Hunt published "Blue-Stocking Revels: or, The Feast of the Violets," a satirical poem aimed at contemporary female authors and artists. "Blue-Stocking Revels" is introduced as a distaff version of Hunt's "Feast of the Poets" (1812/14) which satirized male poets of the day, but where the earlier verse attacked Wordsworth, Southey, and others on poetic and political grounds, the "Feast of the Violets" focuses almost exclusively on ideologies of gender and containment. The disjunctive dialogue between the two poems is made manifest in their respective titles. "Blue-Stocking Revels" reduces women to a dismissive, mocking metonymy and highlights frivolity, while the subtitle ("Feast of the Violets") invokes "Feast of the Poets" while foregrounding the difference between male and female subjects. Hunt refuses women artists the designation *poets* applied to their male counterparts; instead, they are metaphorically represented by a diminutive flower (and symbol of reticence), which also serves as a synecdoche for their stockings, thus doubly reducing them to fragments which suggest neither art nor intellect, but rather "sweet, knowing ankles!"[41] By the same token, Apollo, who narrates both poems, muses early in the 1837 verse, "I've dined / With the Poets: 'tis now highly proper I find, / To descend (and with finger-tips here he fell trimming / His love-locks celestial) and sup with the Women" (35), making the distinction between poets and women eminently clear, while introducing the themes of desire and seduction entirely absent from the poem of 1812.

Before introducing the eponymous Blue-Stockings, the poem's narrator first offers a list of those "who form'd the spectators" (37), thus emphasizing the structure of a collective male gaze on the parade of women, whose positions as objects rather than subjects is here established. The men watching the revels include "Poets," "Wits," "Translators," "Artists," "Musicians," "husbands, friends and relations," but also "Physicians" (37). Hunt parenthetically adds "(they say that the godhead / To Knightson, Smith and Elliotson, specially nodded)" and in a footnote adds "With regard to 'Smith,' it may be allowed me to mention, considering the numerous respectable Smiths existing, doubtless in the medical as in all other professions, that the name of the most eminent of them, Dr Southwood Smith, is here intended" (37–38). By naming Smith, still married to his wife but living with Gillies (who is mentioned several pages later), Hunt includes the lovers of the "Blue-Stockings," thus foregrounding the private over the public personae of these artists while implicitly condemning the double transgressions of the boundaries of gender and linking female artists with promiscuity.

As the women enter the festivities, Hunt emphasizes their grace, beauty, and gowns rather than their talent, and indeed the very premise of the poem focuses on social rather than artistic accomplishment. Even "Genius," so crucial to the Romantic aesthetic, is reinterpreted here, and rather than inspiring great art, thought, or feeling, it is a force that physically transforms each woman—"The plain became handsome, the handsomest more so" (38). In a footnote Hunt explains "It hardly need be observed, that the word 'Genius,' here used in its mythological sense, does not, of *necessity*, imply that higher order of faculty, which gifts the possessors with something peculiar to them, and leaves a gap when they are gone" (38). In other words, in keeping with contemporary theories of gender and genius, Hunt makes clear that women are not susceptible to this higher form of inspiration.

In Canto II, "The Presentations and Ball," the female authors are introduced "not in stern order of fame" (39), but alphabetically, effectively placing all on the same plane. Hunt's comic descriptions of the women mock any pretensions to great art; using apostrophe, amusing end rhymes, and deep irony, he reduces his subjects to absurd caricatures. He recites:

> Miss Aikin judicious;—discreet Mrs. Austin,
> Whose English her German you'll never find lost in;
> And Madame d'Arblay, mighty grave all the while,
> Yet at heart smitten still betwixt fun and a style,
> And longing to tell us more ladies' distresses
> 'Twixt lords and vulgarians, and debts for their dresses.
> So deep was her curtsey, the hoop that she wore
> Seem'd fairly conveying her right through the floor. (39)

Elizabeth Barrett is warned not to "make things too verbal," while Apollo takes Leticia Landon to task for her grief-filled poetry: "Ever bent upon weeping for evil, instead / Of o'ermastering with roses its weak fountainhead" (43). Throughout the cantos, Hunt offers advice to the women, through the voice of Apollo, promising to "enlighten" them and counseling them (in his own doggerel) "to take better lyrical measures" (43). His list includes nearly all of the female poets and novelists of the day, though he readily admits to not having read most of their work.

Hunt is especially sharp with reform minded authors, including Martineau, Mary Howitt, and Mary Leman (Grimstone) Gillies, all of whom shared many of his sympathies and causes. Howitt is reduced to one of "These Muse Quakeresses" (43), while Martineau and Leman Gillies are satirized for "preaching," as the Romantic poet refuses these women the right to moral authority outside of the domestic sphere. Scolding them for their presumptuous theorizing, Hunt urges the progressive female authors to abandon their lofty poses and be "less didactic and blue" (42). In the midst of this litany of authors, Hunt introduces a stanza devoted to the "reigning female artists" (41). Apollo first asks after Lady Dacre, known for her animal sculptures:

> Then he asked after Margaret Gillies and Mee,
> Seyffarth, Carpenter, Robertson, Barrett, and Sharp,
> The Corbeaus, the Chalons;—in short, more than his harp
> Has strings to outnumber, or haste can disclose;
> And looked at the gall'ries, and smiled as they rose:
> For they all sat together, in colours so rare,
> They appeared like a garden, enchanting the air. (41)

Margaret Gillies's inclusion on this brief list of prominent female visual artists stands as testimony to her reputation in the late 1830s, although the very inclusion of women artists at all with the "Blue-Stockings" reflects the general tendency to see all women's artistic production under a single rubric. The short catalogue of painters and sculptors lacks the specificity of much of the rest of

Hunt's poem, and for better or worse he does not single any out for specific comment. Instead, the female visual artists are collectively referred to in terms of their visual effect. Turning the tables on the visual arts, Hunt reduces their very bodies to the pleasing colors of a garden and thus transforms them metaphorically into flowers—beautiful, silent, decorative, and natural. Returning to the gendering of the genres, Hunt perpetuates the "feminine" associations of painting, and if he has little criticism of the group, it is perhaps because he cedes them little power, refusing them representation itself.

Canto III, "The Supper," concludes "Blue-Stocking Revels" with an airy parade of female authors of the past, beginning with Sappho ("As brown as a berry, and little of size; / But lord! With such midnight and love in her eyes!" [50]) and including women from Marguerite de Navarre and Aphra Behn to Mesdames Genlis, Riccoboni, and Staël. They are followed by Homer, Chaucer, Cervantes, Dante, and Petrarch, and in keeping with Hunt's vision of the women in sexually coded terms, the Blue-Stockings see the female authors of the past as their rivals and swoon over the famous men. As the party winds to an end, with the women tipsy with wine and desire ("I'm told that Miss Edgeworth became so vivacious, / The damsels from boarding-school whispered "My gracious!""), each guest is presented with a "parting dish" with a cover decorated by "Angelica," in a clear reference to Kauffman whose designs appeared on walls, furniture, and china during this period.

> The sides were all painted, not only with Muses
> And Loves, but with Lares, and sweet Household Uses:
> Good Temper was laying a cloth for Good Heart,
> And the Graces were actually making a tart!
> Each cover for knob had a ruby, heart-shap'd;
> And the whole stood on legs, with white elegance drap'd,—
> Legs bewitching, most feminine, tipp'd with a shoe;
> And the stockings (mark that!) were a violet blue. (54)

The porcelain vessel doubly marks the domestic world that Hunt believes women should return to, and the allegorical figures of female virtue are accompanied by Graces—usually associated with artistic inspiration—who are instead cooking. The violet-stockinged legs supporting the cover make clear the metaphorical transformation at hand, as Hunt turns the container into woman herself, in a direct reference to the womb. The "most feminine" and "bewitching" violet stocking is one who is good tempered, kind hearted, loving, and maternal, unlike Blue-Stockings, who are, by inference, neither domestic nor maternal.

Not content merely to suggest, Hunt has cupids fly under the table and slip violet stockings on the legs of all the guests, leaving them "Mute, curious, respectful" (55) at the turn of events. Associating "*blue*-stockings" with "the masculine, vain, and absurd" (56), Hunt decrees that "all real women, ev'n though they may speak / Not with Sappho's eyes only, but even her Greek" (56) take their hue from the bashful violet, "the queen of the sylvan retreat." Apollo warns the women that the choice is theirs, for the stockings will change color according to their behavior, in turn determining whether they "will be loved or hated" (56). Ignoring all questions of talent, art, or expression, Hunt's poem reasserts the boundaries of art and gender by basing woman's success not on the quality of work, but on her performance of femininity:

> Remaining *true violet*,—glimpses of heaven,—
> As long as you're wise, and your tempers are even;
> But if you grow formal, or fierce, or untrue,
> Alas gentle colour! Sweet ankle, adieu!
> Thou art chang'd: and Love's elf, at the changing, looks *blue*.
> Seize the golden occasion then.—You who already
> Are gentle, remain so; and you, who would steady
> Your natures, and mend them, and make out your call
> To be men's best companions, be such once and for all. (56–57)

Importantly, he delineates only competition between the women, who vie with each other for Apollo's attention, bicker, snicker, and gossip about one another, and in short refute the idealized images of artistic sisterhood with an equally overdetermined image of fractious fragmentation.

Hunt concludes his poem with the admonition, "UNAFFECTEDNESS, GENTLENESS, LOVINGNESS.—This / Be your motto. And now give your teacher a kiss" (57). Thus the champion of liberal causes defines women's roles as "men's best companions," and while not explicitly condemning the existence of the "Blues" per se, he mocks the works, the tenor, and the comportment of female authors and artists as unfeminine, unseemly, and uninteresting. Hunt's "violet-stockings," gentle, unassuming, and unambitious, are not in fact artists at all, but adoring wives and mothers who subordinate their opinions, independence, and creativity to men, thus subordinating art to love. The poem ends when the narrator awakens from his dream, and indeed the "Blue-Stocking Revels" displays more than a hint of anxious fantasy about suppressing the threat of female artistic production and restoring traditional gender roles.

A year after "Blue-Stocking Revels" appeared in *Monthly Repository*, Margaret Gillies painted Hunt's portrait (figure 29) and exhibited the painting at the RA in 1839.[42] The image portrays Hunt in a sinuous, almost flaccid pose, leaning on a pillar and gazing into the distance, much like most of her artist subjects. His long hair, wrinkled cloak, and rumpled collar lend Hunt an air of Romantic

Figure 29
Margaret Gillies, *Leigh Hunt,* 1839. Watercolor and gouache on ivory. 22.5 × 14.9 cm. © National Portrait Gallery, London.

dishevelment that emblematizes his lack of interest in worldly considerations. Gillies pays particular attention to her sitter's face and hands, which are painted with careful detail, while his body disappears beneath the voluminous folds of cloth. This idealized portrait shows Hunt looking much younger than his fifty-five years, and the adolescent dreaminess in his soft cheeks, clear eyes, and smooth, tapered hands suggest the youthful spirit of the poet and reformer. Yet there is an air of self-indulgence in his face and pose: Hunt's mouth and brow project a patronizing look of superiority that may reflect his attitude toward the female artist so clearly enunciated in "Blue-Stocking Revels." The portrait captures a likeness without making the subject particularly likeable, and unlike the contemporaneous portraits of Wordsworth, Southwood Smith, Horne, and the Howitts, despite his serious expression the foppish Hunt lacks gravitas, and inspires neither respect nor admiration. Indeed, the unresolved visual tension between the highly polished facture of the face and hands, and the loose, sweeping treatment of Hunt's clothes suggests to the viewer other contradictions. As painted by Gillies, Hunt's body lacks form and solidity, indicating a lack of groundedness and connection with the material world. The undulating lines of the massive sleeve echo his languid pose, as his hands dangle limply before him. The portrait suggests a kind of impotence in the body that floats beneath the dreaming head, unable to carry out the fantasies the Romantic Hunt envisions. Similarly, the youthful, unlined face is crowned with gray: the roots of his hair, illuminated by an unidentified light source, stand in stark contrast to the dark, flowing locks below and the boyish demeanor.

The inconsistency between Hunt's chronological age and his (self-) presentation or performance of Romantic, poetic identity, render this portrait an image of a dreamer at odds with the material world and its exigencies. Indeed, the almost childlike appearance of the poet and publisher here anticipates Dickens's own portrait of Leigh Hunt as the "airy, improvident, and objectionable" Harold Skimpole, the self-described "child" ("I am a child you know!") in *Bleak House* who takes no responsibility for his finances, family, or friendships, borrows money from all and sundry, and embodies a self-indulgent solipsism that also haunts this painting. As Mr Jarndyce explains to Esther and Ada, he is "not a child in years. He is grown up—he is at least as old as I am—but in simplicity, and freshness, and enthusiasm, and a fine guileless inaptitude for all worldly affairs, he is a perfect child . . . He has been unfortunate in his affairs, and unfortunate in his pursuits, and unfortunate in his family; but he don't care—he's a child!"[43] Skimpole's debts and his pursuit by creditors throughout the novel reflected Hunt's own perennial destitution and time spent in debtor's prison, while Skimpole's remorseless sponging off of Jarndyce, Esther, and Richard echoed Hunt's dependence on the charity of his friends and fellow poets throughout his life, only to manifest his ingratitude in unflattering portraits of those who supported him in *Lord Byron and his Contemporaries* (1828).

In many ways a knowing and canny portrait, Gillies's image of Hunt captures the essence of a weak and self-indulgent Romantic who never lived up to the ideals he espoused. In her commitment to art, social reform, and progressive politics, Gillies shared much with Hunt and her affection for the puerile poet is clear in the gentleness of this critique. Yet unlike her admiring portraits of Wordsworth, Dickens, Howitt, Fox, and others, Gillies does not elevate her subject to a position of an inspiring visionary; instead, she portrays a man who embodies some of the contradictions of Romanticism itself. In her reflection on Hunt's insubstantiality, Gillies also reflects perhaps on the paradoxes of a Romanticism that espoused artistic liberty only to remain too often inaccessible and disconnected from real social needs and responsibilities. In his mocking attack on female artistic identity in the pages of *The Monthly Repository*, portraying women authors and painters as weak, vain, and trivial, sexual rather than intellectual beings, Hunt exposed his immaturity and distance from the ideal that Gillies and her sisters in art envisioned, but at the same time made manifest some of the troubling tenets of an artistic movement that left little room for the female subject. Margaret and Mary Gillies, Harriet Martineau, Mary Howitt, and the early feminists of the 1830s and '40s actively sought to reconfigure the boundaries of gender and genre in British culture, establishing through their writings, paintings, and lives new models of female identity as politically, intellectually, and ethically engaged in the labor of social progress and reform. Margaret Gillies's portraits of her contemporaries played a key role in the visualization of models of inspiration, but also provided a subtle but unmistakable resistance to the gendered discourses of Romanticism.

Bronté's Portraits of Romantic Resistance

The Tenant of Wildfell Hall

The Brontës and the Visual Arts

The visual arts played an important role in the lives and education of the Brontë family from their earliest youth. Although, as discussed above, painting and drawing were included in most young girls' education as suitable pastimes and accomplishments (or, in the case of the Brontës, important skills for a governess), for Charlotte art was her first chosen career. Before moving to writing as her vocation, Charlotte saw her future as a professional painter, probably of miniatures, and in 1834 she exhibited two drawings at the summer show of the Royal Northern Society for the Encouragement of the Fine Arts in Leeds (where Rolinda Sharples had also shown her work). The exhibition included images by Turner, and Charlotte's professional ambitions are underscored by the fact that her drawings were both marked for sale. The oldest of the surviving Brontës, Charlotte influenced her younger siblings in myriad ways, and it is worth noting that the earliest extant example of her art is an illustrated story she wrote for Anne. Like Charlotte, Branwell, Emily, and Anne sketched illustrations for their stories, journals, and letters throughout their lives, and alongside the copying that constituted artistic training of the period, the Brontës individually and collectively paired their own words and images in a wide variety of hybrid creations.

The collaborative paradigm, so important in the written works of the Brontës from the composition of Gondal and Angria forward, also pertained to their drawing and painting. Thus, just as they wrote childhood stories together and would later read their writings to one another, they also sat as models for each other. Anne, the youngest and most docile, was perhaps the most willing participant as there are today four portraits of her by Charlotte, one by Emily, and two by Branwell.[1] Upon her return from Roe Head in 1832, Charlotte spent two years at home teaching her sisters not only how to write, but also how to draw. Her artistic accomplishment was well known enough for Smith Elder to invite her to illustrate the second edition of *Jane Eyre* in 1848. Anne would thus have seen first-hand in her sister Charlotte a woman who envisaged a career first as a professional painter and later as a professional writer. In stark contrast to the popular image of her retiring modesty, Charlotte embraced the Romantic cult of genius and saw her art as a means "to be for ever known."[2]

If Charlotte's ambition outstripped her artistic skills in painting and drawing, her only brother, Branwell, had superior talent but little motivation. In 1834 it was decided that he would become a professional painter, and William Robinson, a former student of the renowned portraitist Sir Thomas Lawrence, was hired as his master. Unlike his sisters, Branwell was trained in oil painting and under the tutelage of Robinson would have been exposed to the theory and practice of contemporary "high art." Yet despite his facility and training, Branwell lacked the drive to pursue the career his sister longed for with the necessary energy and determination. His bid for a place at the Royal Academy in London was aborted and he settled for a career as a provincial artist in Bradford, only to give that up as well before he ultimately found a job as a tutor at Thorp Green with Anne. In this reverse trajectory, Branwell ended up in the very profession that his sisters sought to escape. Despite his training and the privileges of his gender, Branwell failed as a professional painter; despite their lack of training and the interdictions presented by their gender, Charlotte, Emily, and Anne found success as professional writers.

Like her siblings, Anne had some talent for painting and drawing, as well as a gift for observation of nature and people. In *Agnes Grey*, the protagonist includes art among her accomplishments, much as Jane Eyre did, and the fictive governesses draw and paint both as part of their teaching and for personal enjoyment. But with *The Tenant of Wildfell Hall*, Anne makes a dramatic—and controversial—departure from her sisters when she creates a female hero whose art serves as a means of financial support and personal liberation from an oppressive marriage. Helen Huntingdon, among the most overlooked of the Brontë protagonists, is also the only professional artist among them and in this sense shares a distinctive quality with Charlotte, Emily, and Anne not found in Jane Eyre, Catherine Earnshaw, Agnes Grey, Lucy Snowe, Caroline Helstone, or Shirley Keeldar. Importantly, Helen's rebellion against her lot takes the form also employed by the Brontë sisters: the secret creation of art sold under a false name. And like the Brontës with their writing, Helen enjoys her painting but sees it not simply as a pastime, but as a profession, creating landscapes—much as they created novels—for public consumption. Here, as in no other novel by Charlotte, Emily, or Anne, artistic creation plays a central role in the self-creation of the heroine.

As Lucasta Miller demonstrates in *The Brontë Myth*, the public personae of the Brontë sisters were self-conscious constructions begun with the invention of Currer, Ellis, and Acton Bell. But as the real identity of the three authors became known, a more complex mythology developed, spearheaded by Charlotte's perspicacious grasp of the social implications of their identities. The figure of the nineteenth-century "authoress," almost always conflated with her heroines, was vulnerable to personal attacks on her morality. Thus, as the critics assailed the Brontë novels as "coarse," "offensive," and even "revolting,"[3] Charlotte and her supporters took care to separate the woman from the artist, attributing the unmistakable transgressions of social mores in their novels to their isolated upbringing on the moors. Miller explains that the myth of the shy spinster, "which eventually inspired the saintly heroine of Elizabeth Gaskell's *Life of Charlotte Brontë*, was a quiet and trembling creature, reared in total seclusion, a martyr to duty, and a model of Victorian femininity, whose sins against convention, if she had unwittingly committed any, could be explained away by her isolated upbringing and the suffering she had endured."[4] Like any myth, there is a kernel of truth to this image, but Miller, Stoneman, and others have revealed a Charlotte Brontë who was as ambitious and savvy as she was inventive.

Charlotte's "Biographical Notice of Ellis and Acton Bell," which appeared in 1850 (following Emily's death in December 1848 and Anne's death in May 1849) gives a vivid sense of the early construction of the Brontë myth, both in the desire to separate the authors from authority and in the centrality of their collective identity as sisters. Appended to a new edition of *Wuthering Heights* and *Agnes Grey*, Charlotte's "Biographical Notice" announces once again that the works of Currer, Ellis, and Acton Bell were not "the production of one person."[5] Yet, they are initially described as "we," and their formation as siblings and authors is shared. Currer Bell explains that "he" and his two sisters (thus revealing Ellis and Acton's true gender but still veiling her own) had grown up "Resident in a remote district, where education had made little progress, and where, consequently, there was no inducement to seek social intercourse beyond ourselves and our own domestic circle." Charlotte, in the persona of Currer, goes on to say that "we were wholly dependent on ourselves and each other, on books and study, for the enjoyments and occupations of life" (30).

This hermetic image of domestic isolation elides, of course, the Brontës' actual engagement with the world, via journals and periodicals, boarding schools, travel, and jobs, but as a fictional construct serves to promote an idea of Romantic genius blossoming almost *ex nihilo*. Yet unlike previous myths of Romantic artistry, they are neither male nor solitary, but instead three women living and working together (for, indeed, despite Currer/Charlotte's pose, there was little doubt at this point of her gender as well).

The "Biographical Notice" rehearses the publication history of their volumes, beginning with *Poems* by Currer, Ellis, and Acton Bell, emphasizing again the collective nature of their endeavor and the conflict between "the dream of one day becoming authors" and their aversion to "personal publicity," for "we had a vague impression that authoresses are liable to be looked at with prejudice; we had noticed how critics sometimes use for their chastisement the weapon of personality, and for their reward, a flattery which is not true praise" (31). But in the remainder of the Notice, Charlotte shifts her focus away from authorship to the personal, sketching out her sisters' natures and their weaknesses in a bid for sympathy and exoneration. Thus, in declaring *The Tenant of Wildfell Hall* "an entire mistake," Charlotte takes pains to separate the novel from its author, insisting "nothing less congruous with the writer's nature could be conceived" (34). Emphasizing Anne's "brief, blameless life" and her Christian melancholy, Charlotte denies Anne the very power of creation and self-determination when she pathologizes her ill-advised "choice of subject" (as Gaskell and Martineau would subsequently pathologize Charlotte's own novels after her death), attributing it to the harm she suffered when "called on to contemplate, near at hand, and for a long time, the terrible effects of talents misused and faculties abused" (34). By reducing the story to a reflection of personal experience and trauma, Charlotte removes *The Tenant* from the realm of the political. Anne's deliberate realism and her pointed critique of marriage and the patriarchy are not read in terms of her artistic and/or aesthetic decisions, but rather through the lens of biography, thus rendering this resolutely feminist novel a *roman à clef* about Branwell's descent into alcoholism and addiction. While Arthur Huntingdon's debauchery may well have been modeled after her brother's, *The Tenant of Wildfell Hall* is ultimately the story of Helen Huntingdon and her own journey from child to wife to independent woman.

The final pages of the "Biographical Notice" evoke the deaths of Emily and Anne, thus effectively diminishing the threat of these "authoresses" and rendering them tragic, Romantic figures. "Two unobtrusive women," Emily and Anne manifested "retiring manners and habits" (35) that stand in implicit contrast to their passionate and headstrong heroines. Where Emily's simplicity and lack of worldly wisdom left her "unadapted to the practical business of life,"

Anne was "long-suffering, self-denying, reflective, and intelligent . . . Neither Emily nor Anne was learned; they had no thought of filling their pitchers at the well-spring of other minds; they always wrote from the impulse of nature, the dictates of intuition, and from such stores of observation as their limited experience allowed them to amass" (36). Thus, the profoundly original sisters are transformed into paragons of Victorian womanhood, their disturbing novels subordinated to their mythologized lives.

Charlotte's objections to *The Tenant of Wildfell Hall*, voiced here and in letters, led her to suppress its publication after Anne's death. While she consistently couched her discomfort with Anne's radical tale in terms of its "unfortunate" subject,[6] she does not specify what precisely it is about the subject that she does not like. Although it has been understood by critics to be the disquieting image of the alcoholic husband, at once abusive and unfaithful to his young wife, the strength of Charlotte's resistance to *The Tenant* and her active effort to keep it out of print, hint at perhaps more personal motivations behind this response. Anne's novel, moving from the image of unmarried virgins to unhappily married women, entered a more threatening arena of female identity for the reading public, only exacerbated by the decision to make Helen an artist. As Charlotte carefully crafted a Romantic Brontë persona for herself and for her sisters—for at some level the Bells/Brontës also functioned as one—Anne subverted the image of the innocent and socially unengaged authoress with her Realist study of the consciousness of a female artist that announced its criticism of the status quo. With *The Tenant*'s Helen Huntingdon, Anne threatened to expose not only herself, but also her sisters, as female authors whose works emerged from financial necessity and social rebellion, rather than spontaneous expression of genius. Anne's final novel, maligned by her family as well as the critical press, worked at counter-purposes to Charlotte's project of protective myth-making. *The Tenant of Wildfell Hall* and its hero, Helen Huntingdon, participated instead in the ongoing construction of a new image of the female artist in the mid-nineteenth century as neither accidental nor apologetic, but instead as a woman whose identity is deliberately chosen and defiantly located in an unromanticized world of contemporary reality.

The Tenant of Wildfell Hall:
PORTRAITS OF RESISTANCE

Much attention has been lavished on the "clumsy" narrative structure of *The Tenant of Wildfell Hall*, which uses a framing technique to tell the story of the woman painter from two distinct perspectives.[7] This "awkward split narrative" juxtaposes male and female voices in such as way as to reflect what Rachel

Carnell has identified as "the intractable cultural rift between public and private spheres."[8] Gilbert Markham's framing narrative takes the form of a series of letters to his friend and brother-in-law, J. Halford, Esq., while Helen Huntingdon's contained narrative takes the form of a diary written before her marriage to Markham. This familiar gothic strategy, shared by Emily in *Wuthering Heights,* serves to highlight the multiple versions of truth and reality, effectively destabilizing the gendered ideologies of domesticity, while at the same time demonstrating the shaping role played by gender in experience and perception. For indeed, as contemporary feminist critics concur, the jarring bipartite structure lies at the heart of Brontë's social commentary in the novel. I will argue, however, that the tension between Gilbert's epistolary narrative, written as a "man speaking to men," and Helen's journal, addressed to herself, further generates aesthetic and artistic as well as political critique. These contrastive "self-portraits," set off in their formal "frames," function within the thematics of painting to give the reader insight into Brontë's vision of the role of women's representation of women in art and literature.

In keeping with Naomi Jacobs, I will read the framing and framed narratives in *The Tenant* as "competing works of art," and like Jacobs, concur that "We cannot see or experience the buried reality of the 'framed' story without first experiencing the 'framing' narrative. There is no other way in."[9] Gilbert's self-portrait frames Helen's in a way that provides a dialectic image of each—only through the contrast between the two voices and their constructed representations of self and other does a clear "picture" emerge of the two characters. Gilbert's "techniques of representation" are fully evident only when the reader "sees" Helen's own, both in her narrative and in her painted portraits, and the tensions between these three distinct forms of representation subtend Brontë's meaning. For if *The Tenant* proposes a critique of the female condition in Victorian Britain, Brontë's target is both the injustice of the laws oppressing married women[10] and the social structures that uphold them by obscuring the reality of this oppression with constructed, romanticized fantasies of gender and domesticity. Brontë's embedded narratives reflect a belief that art, representation, and narrative play no small role in the perpetuation of dominant ideologies and what Rancière identifies as the "police order," establishing the "borders between the visible and the invisible, the audible and the inaudible, the sayable and the unsayable" (*PA* 89). If Gilbert's version of events, filtered through the consciousness of an indulged and privileged "country gentleman," put forth a skewed and inaccurate picture of Helen, it is only her corrective self-portrait that renders visible the reality of women's experience. Rancière's borders, suggested by the "frames" of the double narrative, are crossed by the readers who synthesize their own portraits of the characters and come to see what was invisible to Gilbert: the real existence of the married woman.

Chapter 8: Brontë's Portraits of Romantic Resistance

Gilbert's epistolary self-portrait thus begins (and ultimately ends) Brontë's novel of the female visual artist. As discussed in chapter 7, the portrait as an artistic form reflects contemporary ideologies of subjecthood, as identity is performed and represented for an audience. Here, in a closed homosocial circuit, Markham paints his own image through words exclusively for Halford's consumption, and this structure mirrors the macrocosm of nineteenth-century art and fiction focalized through a male subject and addressed to a male audience (the popular female reader notwithstanding). The intimate and familiar missive proposes "a full and faithful account of certain circumstances connected with the most important event of my life" and is penned to "atone" for not having shared confidences with Halford on a previous occasion. Tying narrative to sin and redemption, this opening letter establishes intimacy between men, while Markham's voice—at once ruminative and slightly melancholy, identifies him as a Romantic narrator. As he sets the scene of his own composition he explains, "It is a soaking, rainy day, the family are absent on a visit, I am alone in my library, and have been looking over certain musty old letters and papers, and musing on past times" (8). Markham's Romantic subjectivity, established at the very outset of the novel, will stand in stark contrast to Helen's own voice in the middle section of the tale and play an important role in Brontë's own counterdiscourse.

Gilbert's retrospective narrative is shaped by teleology ("the most important event of my life") and the distancing mechanisms of memory: while the letter is dated June 1847, the story takes place twenty years earlier, in 1827, immediately placing his claims to "a full and faithful account" in question. Lacking immediacy, Gilbert's version of the story is told with the end in mind, while the constitutive relationship between self and other within the narrative (Gilbert and Helen) is dominated by that without (Gilbert and Halford), as the narrator portrays himself with an eye to his audience. What Markham sees, how he sees it, and how he subsequently represents what he has seen to his male reader will be central to the ironic portrait that Brontë herself offers of the character. As Andrea Westcott contends, Markham "shapes his past to portray himself in the most advantageous light," and Brontë "presents an intentionally mixed portrait of her 'hero,' a critique of the ideal country gentleman."[11] In a larger sense, Gilbert represents representation from the dominant male perspective, with its attendant self-reflexive prejudices and inevitable blindness. As a Romantic viewer and reader of the world, he can see and read Helen only through Romanticism's distorting and unrealistic lens.

Gilbert begins his self-portrait with the disjunctive lessons of his father, who urged him to a life as a gentleman farmer, and his mother, who instilled in him greater ambitions. Though he followed the paternal dictum, his mother's encouragement leaves him convinced that he is "hiding his light under a bushel" (9) by abandoning higher aims and "great achievement" for life in the country. Thus, accepting the patriarchal role "not very willingly" (9), Markham feels superior to his own situation and to those around him (again, a Romantic position), and when his mother and sister begin their tale of a new woman in the neighborhood, Gilbert and his brother, Fergus, can barely contain their contemptuous amusement. As his sister Rose recounts the rumors circulating about the new tenant living alone at the abandoned Wildfell Hall, Helen is introduced as an invisible presence who is both as yet unseen and in many ways incomprehensible. Relegating the news to the realm of the feminine, Markham filters the introduction of the new neighbor through his mother and sister, who are troubled by "the apparent, or non-apparent circumstances, and probable or improbable history of the mysterious lady" (13). Even after meeting her, they cannot locate her within the traditional confines of class and gender, for she displays a shocking "ignorance on certain points" of "household matters, and all the niceties of cookery, and such things, that every lady ought to be familiar with," and worse still, "had not even the sense to be ashamed of it" (13). The reader's first introduction to Helen, before she is even named, is to a woman removed from the world of domesticity who actively rejects the expectations of local society; indeed, when Mrs Markham assures the young widow that she will be married again, she responds, "almost haughtily, 'I am certain I never shall'" (14). Unable to see parallels between his own distaste for farming and the widow's for domesticity, Gilbert portrays Helen's difference in unsympathetic ways that reflect his mother's judgment as much as his own.

Markham's response to his mother's account of the stranger reveals above all his own view of the world. He observes: "Some romantic young widow, I suppose . . . come there to end her days in solitude, and mourn in secret for the dear departed" (14), a radical misreading of Helen and her situation that not only marks the reader's own horizon of expectation, but also sets up a contrast between the perspectives of the two central characters. When he does finally see her in church, he notes her hardness, her thin, compressed lips and reads in them "no very soft or amiable temper" (15), an observation many critics have noted might just as easily be attributed to the pugnacious Markham himself. Despite her avowal that she is not interested in remarriage, Gilbert, like his mother, can see women only as potential wives and he reflects as he gazes upon her "I would rather admire you from this distance, fair lady, than be the partner of your home" (15). Yet rapidly the tables turn, and Helen answers his gaze "with a momentary, indefinable expression of quiet scorn, that was inexpressibly provoking to me" (15). Their preliminary exchange establishes Helen's position as a viewing subject who answers and even resists the Romantic Markham's gaze with her own direct and challenging vision. The scene proposes Helen's "provoking" usurpation of Gilbert's presumed domination as master of the gaze, while the lexicon ("indefinable expression" and "inexpressible") indicates a visual dynamic that Gilbert is unable or unwilling to decipher. The Romantic narrator cannot find words to describe the woman who refuses to inhabit the object position and instead returns his look with her own defiant stare.

In a similar fashion, Wildfell Hall is presented through the romanticizing filter of Gilbert's consciousness as he passes it one day on a hunt. What is for Helen a refuge is perceived by her neighbor as a Gothic ruin, complete with ghosts. In an echo of Wuthering Heights and Thornfield Hall, her sisters' fictional dwellings,[12] Gilbert comes upon the "gloomy" Hall and "withered" garden and muses "to my young imagination, they presented all of them a goblinish appearance, that harmonized well with the ghostly legends and dark traditions our old nurse had told us respecting the haunted Hall and its departed occupants" (20). Gilbert, a Romantic reader, approaches the building as if it were a structure in one of Currer or Ellis Bell's novels, a world further associated with childhood and nursery tales. As this novel progresses, however, his imaginative fantasies of youth will be confronted with Helen's realist vision of the far more frightening experiences of adulthood. Indeed, as he is lost in daydreams, "leaning on my gun, and looking up at the dark gables, sunk in an idle reverie, weaving a tissue of wayward fantasies" (20), a noise awakens him. Looking up, he encounters Helen's son, Arthur, the reality of her living child interrupting his childish dreams of Romantic specters.

On his first visit to Wildfell Hall, the narrator and his sister are escorted not into the sitting room, as they expected, but instead into Mrs Graham's studio:

> To our surprise, we were ushered into a room where the first object that met the eye was a painter's easel, with a table beside it covered with rolls of canvass, bottles of oil and varnish, palette, brushes, paints, etc. Leaning against the wall were several sketches in various stages of progression, and a few finished paintings—mostly of landscapes and figures. (42)

Through the accumulation of visual signifiers, the reader learns, along with Gilbert, that the tenant of Wildfell Hall is a painter, while her greeting—"I must make you welcome in my studio, said Mrs Graham; there is no fire in the sitting room today"—hints at a substitution of art for domesticity. The very fact that Helen Graham has a studio of her own, testifies to her professionalism and dedication, for as discussed in chapter 1, few women in Britain could boast such a space devoted to art. Even as she entertains her uninvited neighbors, Mrs Graham remains standing beside her easel, "not facing it exactly, but now and then glancing at the picture upon it while she conversed, and giving it an occasional touch with her brush, as if she found it impossible to wean her attention entirely from her occupation to fix it upon her guests" (42). As Gilbert and his sister, Rose, become an audience watching her paint, her art takes precedence over convention. Eschewing the role of hostess, Helen Graham follows her own inclinations and desires, continuing her engagement with the painting rather than subordinating her work to her social "duty."

The painting on the easel is an early morning view of Wildfell Hall, "very elegantly and artistically handled," but when Gilbert approaches the canvas, he observes that she has attached another name and place to the painting. Mrs Graham explains that she hopes to keep her whereabouts concealed from friends who might recognize her style. Significantly, the image of Wildfell Hall represented and circulating under a false name prefigures Helen's own hidden identity (Helen Huntingdon) and assumed moniker (Graham is her mother's maiden name), while both the building and its occupant are misread as Romantic, mysterious figures by viewers who project their own fantasies. In perhaps the closest evocation of the Brontës' own artistic modus operandi, young Arthur refutes the Markhams' assumption that his mother is an amateur, painting for her own amusement. She claims that she cannot afford such a luxury and Arthur adds "Mamma sends all her pictures to London . . . and somebody sells them for her there, and sends us the money" (43). A female artist who sends her creations to London to be sold under a pseudonym mirrors Anne's own endeavor and that of her sisters, much as *Agnes Grey* and *Jane Eyre* had shared their authors' experiences as governesses. But in the transition from governess to painter, Anne exchanges an acceptable occupation for an unmarried woman of the middle class for a more controversial one. Where a governess, though paid for her labor, remained in a subordinated position within the domestic sphere and devoted herself to the education of children, a female artist entered the public sphere through her production, competing with men, albeit indirectly, with her creative or expressive output. Here, Helen's anonymity is chosen, rather than imposed, and the tinge of shame or dishonor so eloquently evoked in Emily Osborn's *Nameless and Friendless* (figure 30) comes from the perception of vulnerability that clearly links the sale of the body of art to sale of the female artist's body. Indeed the very question of sexuality is also raised here, for like the woman in Osborn's painting, Helen has a child and is thus ineligible for a position as a governess. Whether a spinster, a widow, a fallen woman, or, in Helen's case, a married woman in search of (illegitimate) income, a professional female artist embraced a level of independence in her labor considered dangerous and even threatening, for her work could circulate independently of its producer and thus free of the identifying markers of gender, class, and marital status. Through the simple adoption of a pseudonym, the female artist could separate her gender from her art, inducing much of the anxiety seen in the reviews of Currer's, Ellis's, and Acton Bells's novels. Indeed, if a woman could produce a novel or a painting and sell it as the work of a

Figure 30
Emily Osborn, *Nameless and Friendless*, 1857. Oil on canvas. 86.4 × 111.8 cm. Private collection. Bridgeman Art Library International, New York, NY.

man, undetected, then some of the most fundamental beliefs about gender and identity were subverted or even destabilized.

Helen's paintings, as first presented in this chapter on "The Studio," are primarily landscapes and portraits, "a sad dearth of subjects" (43) she proclaims, limited not only by her lack of training in other genres, but also, importantly, by her unromantic desire to paint from experience rather than imagination. Like the Impressionists to follow, Helen paints Wildfell Hall in different lights and weather and, in this theme and variation, highlights the changefulness of perception. In an "obscure corner," Gilbert finds a portrait of a small child sitting in the grass with his lap full of flowers, an image he recognizes as Arthur "in his early infancy."[13] When he lifts it up he discovers another picture with its face to the wall: "It was a portrait of a gentleman in the full prime of youthful manhood—handsome enough, and not badly executed; but if done by the same hand as the others, it was evidently some years before; for there was far more careful minuteness of detail and less of that freshness of colouring and freedom of handling that delighted and surprised me in them" (44). Although this portrait of the father, hidden behind that of the son, will only be positively identified later in the story, Gilbert and the reader can gather as much from the likeness. The layers of images, with the son superimposed over the father, point to layers of meaning both in Helen's paintings and in Brontë's novel that call for interpretation, comparison, and retrospective consideration. They also point to Helen's self-appointed role as the creator of her husband's image; if the image of her child corresponds to traditional conflations of artistic and maternal (re)production, the portrait of the child's father foregrounds the female painter's subjectivity, heretofore invisible in the tale. Not only is Helen the mysterious and romanticized object of Gilbert's fantasies; she is also a representing subject who shapes the image of her husband as well as of her son.

The detailed description of the hidden portrait reveals multiple insights into the subject of the painting, the artist herself, and the viewer, demonstrating some of Brontë's own narrative strategies. Examining the picture, Gilbert observes:

> I surveyed it with considerable interest. There was a certain individuality in the features and expression that stamped it, at once, a successful likeness. The bright, blue eyes regarded the spectator with a kind of lurking drollery—you almost expected to see them wink; the lips—a little too voluptuously full—seemed ready to break into a smile; the warmly tinted cheeks were embellished with a luxuriant growth of reddish whiskers; while the bright chestnut hair, clustering in abundant, wavy curls, trespassed too much upon the forehead, and seemed to intimate that the owner thereof was prouder of his beauty than his intellect—as perhaps he had reason to be;—and yet he looked no fool. (44–45)

Gilbert, who has devoted considerable time in these early pages to reading—or misreading—Helen's physiognomy, now turns his attention to her interpretation of another man's face. The interest he claims indicates the gradual transition from curiosity about Mrs Graham to romantic inclination, for here he is confronting a rival for her affection. Although he has been critical of his neighbor, finding her "too hard, too sharp, too bitter for my taste" (39), Markham readily admits to the success of her painting, a testimony to her talent. Helen has captured not simply the features of this unidentified gentleman, but the character and personality—qualities that have escaped Gilbert in his own examination of her, thus marking her as a better "reader" of faces than the male protagonist.

The image of "youthful manhood" is later revealed to be her husband, Arthur Huntingdon, and is our first introduction to the villain of the tale. Significantly, our perception is mediated through the visions of both Helen and Gilbert, and art is closely tied to truth and revelation. The subject's mocking, irreverent nature is read in his eyes and his smile, while his voluptuous lips and luxuriant hair on his face and head communicate animal appetites and virility. Helen's portrait communicates his vanity and intelligence, allowing the viewer to perceive the simultaneous attraction and threat of his overt sexual potency. The successful image shows the strengths and weaknesses of her subject, marking its resemblance to Brontë's own intent, signaled in her Preface, to depict things "as they really are." If every portrait reveals as much of the painter as it does of her subject, this image also manifests Helen's youthful desire for the dangerous figure of Huntingdon, while on a symbolic level it indicates her later desire to contain and control this figure who retains legal and social rights over her body, her property, and her life.[14] The painting delineates the complex relationship between Helen and Arthur, and even as Arthur remains absent from the narrative, he is present to his wife in numerous ways. Ironically, the very artifact that she keeps to remind herself of what she is escaping belongs not to its creator, but to her husband, thus embodying the laws of coverture that Brontë is contesting.

The fact that Gilbert finds Helen a better painter now than she was when she executed the earlier portrait, demonstrates that professionalism has granted her more "freedom" and "freshness" in her work than was possible in her subordinate positions as a ward or wife. Implicitly, independence has improved, rather than diminished her art. Both then and now, the very act of representation has allowed Helen to take the subject position, giving her at least a vestige of power over the object of her gaze as well as her audience. The symbolic role of the painting is thus played out as Helen removes it from Gilbert's hands and refuses to explain to him whom it portrays. Retaining control over representation, she also controls the system of interpretation and will not relinquish the key to the signified.

Part III: The Portrait

As the novel progresses, Helen and Gilbert's relationship continues to be mediated through art. On a trip to the shore with a picnic party, Helen quits the group to sketch in solitude on "a narrow ledge of rock at the very verge of the cliff which descended with a steep, precipitous slant, quite down to the rocky shore" (62). Her position alone on the edge of the precipice defines both her social and psychological states, but importantly, it is a spot she has chosen, for it allows her access to a sublime scene at once terrifying and inspiring. Gilbert, ever in pursuit of her company, follows her uninvited and when he asks if he may watch her draw, she resists, ever jealous of her independence. She allows him to join her only when he promises to look at the scene, rather than at her, and she continues to work, absorbed by the seascape and her labor. Here, Brontë uses the aesthetic categories of the sublime and the beautiful to highlight the different temperaments of her two protagonists, while further destabilizing the gendered associations of art. Following Burke's influential formulations, the experience of the sublime is induced by contemplation of size, force, and magnitude that dwarf our very existence and engage the imagination, suggesting a power greater than our own; in this dangerous and intellectual capacity, the sublime was almost inevitably gendered male. The beautiful, for Burke, is conversely linked to qualities that bring sensations of pleasure and inspire love: smallness, smoothness, delicacy, and grace, most often associated with the feminine. Yet as they sit on the ledge overlooking the wild sea, it Helen who focuses on the sublimity of the scene while Gilbert shifts his gaze to the beautiful, turning away "from the splendid view at our feet to the elegant white hand that held the pencil, and the graceful neck and glossy raven curls that drooped over the paper" (63).

Where Gilbert is idle, Helen is happily and gainfully employed ("few people gain their livelihood with so much pleasure in their toil as I do" [80]); where he is a Romantic dreamer, she is a realistic pragmatist, and where he is innocent and ignorant, she is experienced in the ways of the world. Much like Corinne and Oswald before them, Helen and Gilbert represent the inversion of gendered stereotypes of male strength and female weakness, while at the same time raising the unspoken question of female purity. In a redux of *Corinne*, there is an impediment to the love between this female artist and her suitor that Helen postpones telling him for fear he will blame her. And like Corinne she gives her lover a written text to explain her past, unsure whether or not after reading it he will not "willingly resign [her] as one no longer worthy of regard" (97). Gilbert, in turn, reproduces Helen's diary in his narrative, taking care however to alter the order and saving the beginning for a later chapter. This purposeful rewriting of her story for his own ends prefigures the end of the novel and in some sense reveals Gilbert's ultimate inability to read and fully understand Helen.

The shift from Gilbert's letter to Helen's diary brings with it other significant narrative changes. Where the former was addressed from one man to another, the latter is self-addressed from a woman to herself and not meant for others' eyes. Where Gilbert's epistle is written from a present moment looking back at an entire story, Helen's diary charts her story as it progresses. Dated 1821, the journal begins six years before Gilbert's framing narration, returning to a time when Helen, at 18, is still a young girl dependent on her aunt and uncle. Her voice here is humorous, insightful, lively, and opinionated, while its warmth and passion stand in stark contrast to Gilbert's vision of Helen. From the outset, Helen's independence is marked by her rebellion against convention and hierarchy. When her aunt reports to Helen Mr Boarham's request for her hand, she responds: "I hope my uncle and you told him it was not in your power to give it. What right had he ask *any* one before me?" (130), later adding "in such important matters, I take the liberty of judging for myself" (133).

The headstrong young woman falls instead for Arthur Huntingdon, and once again her art provides an important gauge of the power relationship between the protagonists. On a hunting party at Helen's uncle's house, Arthur looks at her drawings after dinner and "hearing him pronounce, sotto voce, but with peculiar emphasis concerning one of the pieces, 'THIS is better than all!'—I looked up curious to see what it was, and, to my horror, beheld him complacently gazing at the *back* of the picture—it was his own face that I had sketched there and forgotten to rub out" (146). Mirroring the scene at Wildfell Hall, a hidden image of Arthur is discovered against her will, but here Arthur wields the power and tucks the picture into his waistcoat. These works of art (and others like them, for nearly all of her drawings bear traces of his image) reveal aspects of Helen's inner life—her love and her past—against her conscious will. Even where she erased her sketches, pentimenti remain, and Helen's art expresses thoughts, desires, and meanings at odds with social expectations that she hopes to keep hidden. In this sense, the art works function as metonymies for their creator, rendering visible and concrete precisely that which cannot be seen. Again, we see the importance of interpreting the work of art to find the artist's hidden meanings, and by extension, Brontë's own creation, the novel we are reading, must be considered in the same terms.

Arthur both understands and demonstrates this function, giving him leverage over Helen in his ability to penetrate her paintings to read her innermost thoughts. Helen devotes a long section in the diary to describing the "masterpiece" she is working on in highly Romantic terms that reflect her youth and innocence. The scene in a forest glade depicts a young girl gazing at a pair of turtledoves and is seen by Huntingdon through an open window, thus doubly framed by Helen and Brontë. The interloper aptly analyzes her image as "a very fitting study for a young lady.—Spring just opening into summer—morning just approaching noon—girlhood just ripening into womanhood—and hope just verging on fruition. She's a sweet creature! But why didn't you make her hair black?" (150). Her future husband gently mocks Helen's transparent translation of her own dreams and fantasies, and reads the artist herself in her painted figure: "Sweet innocent! She's thinking there will come a time when she will be wooed and won like that pretty hen-dove, by as fond and fervent a lover; and she's thinking how pleasant it will be, and how tender and faithful he will find her" (151).

After penetrating her meaning, Huntingdon goes further and begins rummaging through her portfolio of unfinished sketches which she allows no one to see. Ignoring her protests, he grabs the "bowels" of the portfolio from her hand, metaphorically violating Helen and once again finding his own image hidden inside, this time in the form of a carefully finished miniature portrait. Again he slips it into his waistcoat pocket, but this time she responds in defiant anger. Asserting her rights of privacy and ownership, Helen cries: "I *insist* upon having that back! It is mine, and you have no *right* to take it. Give it me directly—I'll never forgive you if you don't" (152). Setting the stage for future conflicts, Helen makes it clear that she will not be bullied and her belief in her rights is stronger than her desire for Arthur or his admiration. Taking the miniature away from its subject, she rips it in two and throws it in the fire in order to thwart him. Arthur's "mute amazement" at her reckless independence marks a shift in power, as Helen regains control of her own creation and demonstrates her willingness to sacrifice her own treasure—and indeed, his own image—to resist his domination.

Helen's consignment of her romantic head of Arthur to the flames prefigures the death of her own Romanticism during their marriage. As she loses her illusions, she comes to see Arthur's cruelty and degradation, to which she will not submit quietly. Helen actively resists her husband's desire to turn her into a "household deity" and voices her resistance in no uncertain terms: "I am tired out with his injustice, his selfishness and hopeless *depravity*—I wish a milder word would do—; I am no angel and my corruption rises against it" (256). Brontë's Helen refuses the idealized role of the angel of the house, and in so doing voices a critique of marriage and the idealization of female suffering. When she witnesses her husband's unfaithfulness, Helen moves from resistance to hatred ("it is not enough to say that I no longer love my husband—I HATE him!" [297]) and they enter a new phase of conjugal life with "no love, friendship, or sympathy between them" (307). Helen will be his wife "in name only," implicitly refusing him the "right" to her body or soul. Echoing Indiana's speech to her husband in Sand's groundbreaking novel, Helen distinguishes between her duties as a wife and her prerogatives as a human: "for as long as I discharge my functions of steward and housekeeper, so conscientiously and well, without pay and without thanks, you cannot afford to part with me. I shall therefore remit these duties when my bondage becomes unbearable" (308).[15] Highlighting the parallel between wives and slaves, Brontë, through Helen, portrays a woman who refuses to accept her role as victim of an abusive husband and of a social structure that subordinates her life to his. When Arthur contends that she drives him to depravity with her "unnatural, unwomanly conduct" she again refuses to accept the role assigned her. After she has done all in her power to help him, she absolves herself of responsibility: "he may drink himself dead, but it is NOT my fault" (309).

Helen's decision to leave the marriage is motivated by her desire to protect her son from his father, for she deems it "better far that he should live in poverty and obscurity with a fugitive mother, than in luxury and affluence with such a father" (226). While Arthur's comportment is indeed repugnant, Helen's response was even more shocking, as she makes clear that "the world's opinion and the feelings of my friends must be alike unheeded here" (336) for her own sense of duty lies outside of acceptable social mores and legal parameters. Ready to break the laws of country and society, Anne Brontë's Helen transgresses the boundaries of her class, her gender, and her nation in a manner far closer to one of Sand's heroines than to those of her sisters. Like Indiana, Helen carefully plans her escape from her husband, determining how she will finance the movement from legitimate wife to outlaw, for in each case the flight is not conceived in a moment of passion, but is rather a deliberate and thoughtful response to an intolerable situation. But where Indiana leaves Delmare for her lover Raymon, trading one man for another, Helen runs away and supports herself through art. From the beginning, her scheme of freedom depends on her painting, and thus art is closely tied to independence. Hoping at first to find asylum in New England, she reflects:

> I would support myself and [my son] by the labor of my hands. The palette and easel, my darling playmates once, must be my sober toil-fellows now. But was I sufficiently skillful as an artist to obtain my livelihood in a strange land, without friends and without recommendation? No; I must wait a little; I must labor hard to improve my talent and to produce something worth while as a specimen of my powers, something to speak favourably for me. (337)

As Helen begins her move away from dependent wife to independent woman, she shifts her attitude toward painting from idle amusement to paid profession and recognizes the need for improvement in her skills before she can support herself and her child through her craft. The canvases will be her ambassadors, entering the world as testimony to her talents and "powers" and will "speak" where she cannot. Resolutely unromantic, she does not hope for "brilliant success"; her goal now in painting is to achieve "some degree of security," food for her child, and "money for the journey, the passage, and some little to support us in our retreat" (337). Thus, her professional aspirations begin before she leaves home, and Helen paints pictures that her servant Rachel will sell to dealers while she is still living with Huntingdon.

The threatening nature of her endeavor and its close association with Helen's rebellion is made clear when Arthur discovers her plan by reading her diary. (The fact that both husbands read Helen's diary is noteworthy, drawing another parallel between Arthur and Gilbert.) Reversing the earlier scene with his portrait, here it is Huntingdon who takes the upper hand. Entering her studio, in a second violation of her private space, he casts all of her painting materials—"palette, paints, bladders, pencils, brushes, varnish"—into the fire, just as she had thrown the miniature of his head into the hearth several years earlier. In a deliberate evocation of hell, Helen notes "I saw them all consumed—the palette knives snapped in two—the oil and turpentine sent hissing and roaring up the chimney" (350) as her husband destroys the tools she was using to forge her freedom. Telling a servant to burn all her easels, canvases, and stretchers, Arthur takes all of her money and jewels as well, so she cannot escape and "disgrace him" by supporting herself and their son by the "labour of [her] hands . . . a low, beggarly painter" (351). This metaphoric rape, anticipated by Arthur's earlier violations of her portfolio, reminds the reader that as his wife, Helen belongs to Huntingdon, just as her possessions—paintings, artistic tools, money, jewelry—are in fact his possessions, and the parallel between woman and object is central to Brontë's protest.

Trapped once again in her marriage and deprived of artistic agency, Helen sees herself as "a slave, a prisoner" (352). She counsels her young friend Esther to abandon romantic fantasy and enter into marriage only for affection and esteem. Helen contends, "You might as well sell yourself to slavery at once, as marry a man you dislike. If your mother and brother are unkind to you, you may leave them, but remember you are bound to your husband for life" (359). When she finally escapes Huntingdon, she adopts her mother's maiden name (Graham), thus freeing herself both from her marriage and from her immediate patriarchal identification.

With her arrival at Wildfell Hall, Helen's own narration catches up with Gilbert's and the reader is presented with their differing versions of similar scenes and circumstances. Thus, the edifice first presented through the filter of Gilbert's Romantic imagination as gothic and foreboding, is for Helen something entirely different. The house and its surroundings "might have struck me as gloomy enough at another time, but now, each separate object seemed to echo back my own exhilarating sense of hope and freedom: infinite dreams of the far past and bright anticipations of the future seemed to greet me at every turn" (376). The mocking portrait of Arthur Huntingdon that Gilbert happened upon in Helen's studio is also an unstable signifier, whose meaning changes both for the characters and for the readers in the course of the novel. Painting, as an activity, is the means to Helen's independence, while the concrete artifact—the painting as object—stands as a constant reminder of what she has left and why. If the first portrait of Arthur, the miniature that she destroyed, symbolized Helen's willingness to sacrifice her idealized vision of her lover, this later portrait, painted during their first year of marriage and carried along mistakenly into her new life, symbolizes her awakening to the reality of her husband and the subjectivity of perception.

Helen muses on the contrast between her feelings when she painted the image and when she gazed upon it six years later: "How I had studied and toiled to produce something, as I thought, worthy of the original! What mingled pleasure and dissatisfaction I had had in the result of my labours!—pleasure for the likeness I had caught; dissatisfaction, because I had not made it handsome enough. Now, I see no beauty in it—nothing pleasing in any part of its expression" (377). The painted image is a gauge not only of its subject and its author, but also ultimately of its viewer as well, and the same portrait—unchanging in its representation—is perceived in entirely different ways by Arthur, Gilbert, and Helen, each of whose readings are shaped by their sensibilities, desires, and experiences. Helen's own metamorphosis, chronicled in her journal through words, is thus perceptible to herself, as to the readers, when she becomes her own audience. Importantly, though, she retains her position as observing subject while Arthur remains the object of the evaluative gaze.

The passage continues: "The frame, however, is handsome enough; it will serve for another painting" (377), linking Helen's endeavor to Brontë's own. For indeed, *The Tenant of Wildfell Hall*, like *Sisters in Art*, *Elle et lui*, and other contemporaneous novels in this study, presents a model for a new image of the female artist, and Helen is both the subject and the object of artistic representation. Helen's mobility, her resistance, and her independence designate the female painter as a woman with agency and resilience, whose creations may be generated by necessity as well as inspiration and whose desires may be professional as well as romantic. The narrative frame, like that of the painted portrait, may be suited for other subjects, and unlike the Romantic artist, neither Helen nor Brontë makes any claim for uniqueness or singularity. Instead, as Brontë seems to indicate, the frame will fit any number of women artists, whose invisible presence will be seen differently by those who have experienced Helen's life through the pages of the book.

While she cannot fully escape from Arthur, for indeed she remains his wife even in her absence, his portrait remains a reminder of the bond she is legally unable to break. Nevertheless, Helen retains a level of mastery over the past not only because it is an image she herself has shaped, but also because she uses it for her own ends. She explains, "The picture itself I have not destroyed, as I had first intended; I have put it aside; not, I think, from any lurking tenderness for the memory of past affection, nor yet to remind me of my former folly, but chiefly that I may compare my son's features and countenance with this, as he grows up, and thus be enabled to judge how much or how little he resembles his father" (377). Thus her art plays a corrective role, holding up a negative image against which future lives might be shaped. Similarly, *The Tenant* itself must be read in a socially corrective vein, providing readers with images or models of marriage, of art, and of gender.

Indeed the images of her son embody a final level of critique through contrastive portraits, pointing to other forms of female intervention and creation. Mothers and sons are central to both the framing narrative and the framed, and the dyad of Helen and young Arthur are mirrored by Gilbert and Mrs Markham, as alternative images of maternal influence. In an echo of *Indiana*, Brontë draws a direct connection between an indulgent mother and a self-indulgent son, delineating an arena of women's power and influence despite their legal and social subjugation. In describing Raymon de Ramière, the man who seduces and abandons both Indiana and her maid, Sand attributes his moral weaknesses to his adoring mother:

> The character of her son, impetuous yet cold, calculating yet passionate, was the result of her limitless love and her generous tenderness for him. He would have been better with a mother who was less kind; but she had let him become used to taking advantage of all of the sacrifices she made for his sake; she had taught him to seek and protect his own happiness and well-being as ardently and as strongly as she did for him. Because she thought she was made to protect him from all suffering and to subordinate all of her interests to his, he had become used to believing that the entire world was made for him and would be placed in his hand at his mother's word. By dint of her generosity, she had only succeeded in making a selfish, egotistical heart. (*Indiana* 223)

Similarly, Gilbert's mother cossets and adores him, encouraging in him the "self-conceit" (9) that leads him to see himself as superior to his station as a country gentleman and to the marriageable women in the neighborhood. Like Mme de Ramière, Mrs Markham teaches her son that, within a marriage, husband and wife have proper roles: "it's your business to please yourself, and hers to please you" (54), a formula she also follows as his mother.[16] Gilbert's egotism, pride, and blindness to the plight of the other, are attributable to the lessons he learned as a child, and even he is forced to admit "Perhaps, too, I was a little bit spoiled by my mother and sister" (32). Implicitly establishing a parallel between Gilbert and Arthur, Brontë moreover traces the weaknesses of Helen's first husband to misguided maternal solicitude. Even before she marries Arthur, Helen vows "his wife shall undo what his mother did" (166). Attributing Arthur's sins to "his madly indulgent mother," she later writes in her diary "If ever I am a mother I will zealously strive against this *crime* of over indulgence—I can hardly give it a milder name when I think of the evils it brings" (214). Helen's decision to leave Arthur is predicated on her desire to save their son from his father's corrupting influence, privileging ethical duty over legal obligation, and as Antonia Losano and others have noted, Helen's son Arthur is her most vivid creation. Demonstrating woman's ability to conceive and produce both artworks and children, Helen transcends the classically gendered structures of artistic production and reproduction by succeeding at both. As Losano explains, "Helen succeeds in rearticulating the Aristotelian and traditional dynamic of both aesthetic and sexual generation by claiming the right to be the master framer and form-giver rather than the passive vessel. By the end of the novel, Brontë has put Helen in control of her son, her artwork, her now deceased husband's property (which originally came from Helen's family anyway), and her erotic life" (94).

The remainder of the novel is narrated once again from Gilbert's point of view. Even as he recounts Helen's misfortunes and noble sacrifice, as she returns to nurse Arthur through his final illness, the focus falls almost entirely on Markham's feelings, while the misunderstandings arise from his pride and self-absorption. Brontë exposes the feminized nature of the Romantic persona, as her male hero weeps and suffers in passive sway to his love for the independent and self-determined Helen. Gilbert's self-indulgent Romanticism, clearly evident in the first part of the novel, is all the more noticeable following Helen's own more restrained and clear-headed narration. Reversing the traditional gender hierarchies, Brontë allows Helen dominance over Gilbert, first emotionally, and then financially, when she inherits a fortune upon her uncle's death, thus making her far wealthier than he. Despite his love for her, Gilbert feels he cannot ask for her hand due to the inequality in their status, so in the end it is Helen who proposes, offering Gilbert a rose in a gesture that echoes Jane Eyre's proposal to Rochester.

In Anne's novel, however, the hero is metaphysically, rather than physically, blind, and when Gilbert is unable to understand Helen's gesture, she throws the flower out of the window, once again signaling her independence in a move that recalls her immolation of Arthur's portrait. At the same time, Gilbert's continual misreadings present a contrast to Arthur's astute analyses, and while Markham may love her more than Huntingdon, he may understand her less well. Indeed, as Helen controls symbols and meanings, tearing out the final pages of her journal so that Gilbert could not read what she thought of him, he remains almost entirely incapable of penetrating her thoughts, feelings, and intentions, blinded by his Romantic self-absorption. Just as she chose Arthur Huntingdon against her family and friends' advice, so too does Helen marry Gilbert against her aunt's wishes, as the older woman maintains "Could she have been contented to remain single, I own I should have been better satisfied" (470).

The novel ends not only with the marriage of Gilbert and Helen, but also with her silence. Gilbert will continue to speak for her and about her, but within his own Romantic narration there is no room for the voice or feelings of the female artist. Elevated to the realm of his domestic fantasy, Helen is a wife and mother embedded in Gilbert's world as symbolized by the closing of the letter to Halford with his declaration of their collective marital bliss. Where nineteenth-century critics were troubled by Brontë's "coarse" subject matter, twentieth-century critics have been almost universally disturbed by the conclusion of the novel, which pairs Helen with the "unimpressive" Gilbert in "a lightweight ending"[17] But if we consider the novel in terms of Helen's own artistic prescriptions and aesthetic—and read Helen Huntingdon and Anne Brontë as sister artists—then the two narratives that comprise *The Tenant of Wildfell Hall* must be understood and interpreted contrastively. The story that Gilbert tells at the beginning and end of the novel portray a Romantic version of Helen that is distinctly at odds with the woman found in her own self-narration. The gaps between how Gilbert sees Helen and how she, and the readers, see her, serve to remind us of the subjectivity of portraiture, in both its execution and its reception, much as the portrait of Arthur served to remind Helen of the changes both she and her first husband had withstood. Just as Helen saw only what she wanted to see when she fell in love with Arthur, so too is Gilbert's vision shaped by his desires and fantasies, presenting his readers with an image that bears the shaping trace of his Romanticism. By framing their narratives in distinctly different styles, Brontë offers a critique of the laws that deprived a married woman of her rights and independence in a way that also links politics, gender, and aesthetics. Gilbert's egoism and conservative view of women as wives, sisters, and mothers are reflected in a Romanticism that continues to privilege male emotion and values while obscuring female identity. We cannot truly perceive or understand Helen as an artist or a woman until she is given her own voice, a voice whose unflinching realism gives the reader a fully developed portrait of the artist as a young woman. Thus Brontë makes it clear that Romanticism, an essentially masculine construct, is antithetical to a fully developed understanding of the female artist. Instead, only a female voice in a Realist mode can give life and expression to the new figure of the female artist, as Brontë herself has done, thus illustrating the need for sisters in the sister arts.

From Margin to Center

Sand's Portraits of Difference

From the early 1830s until the close of the nineteenth century, perhaps no woman embodied the persona of the "female artist" more vividly than George Sand. Revered and reviled in Britain and America as well as in France, Sand was a public figure whose visibility was in some ways the paradoxical product of her initial quest for invisibility: assuming a pseudonym and male garb to hide her gender, Aurore Dudevant became the most famous woman in France, renowned almost as much for her literary and sartorial *travestie* as for her novels.[1] As such, Sand's was a self-consciously constructed identity, negotiated through the near constant interplay between her own work and innumerable portraits of the artist in words and images. From early self-portraits and correspondence to her magisterial *Histoire de ma vie* (1855),[2] Sand herself crafted an image that was confirmed, complemented, and contradicted in innumerable portraits of her by contemporary male authors, artists, and photographers. Unlike most of the other women authors and painters in this study, Sand was included in the *confraternité* of the leading artists of the period and was friends and/or lovers with the most influential poets, novelists, painters, and composers of the Romantic era, including Balzac, Musset, Flaubert, Delacroix, Liszt, and Chopin, among others. Despite her success and popularity, however, Sand faced many of the same challenges confronting other woman artists, and like Desbordes-Valmore, Howitt, Owenson, Arnaud, and Brontë, she turned to the figure of the female painter in her fiction to foreground questions of creation, representation, subject position, and gender. In the course of her long career, Sand created a series of characters whose relationship to the visual arts, ranging from vocation to profession, illustrates not only the changing role of women in the field of cultural production during this period, but also the author's evolving vision of her own craft and her artistic persona.[3]

Portrait of the Artiste Manquée:
VALENTINE

In *Valentine* (1832), one of her earliest novels, we find Aurore Dudevant establishing the authorial voice and persona of George Sand. The story begins with a visual evocation of the Berrichon countryside:

> The southeastern part of Berry encompasses several leagues of singularly picturesque countryside. The great road from Paris to Clermont that passes through it is bordered by the most thickly settled lands, and it is difficult for the traveler to suspect the beauty of the neighboring area. But for those who would branch off of the highroad, in search of shade and silence, and follow one of the many twisting and narrow paths, cool, calm landscapes soon appear, tender green fields, melancholy streams, clumps of alders and ash trees—an entire scene of sweet and pastoral nature.[4]

Creating an initial parallel between author and painter, she goes on to set the scene with a narrative focus on the landscape, fields, streams, and cottages, the colors and composition of "cette nature suave et pastorale" in a manner that will become the signature style of her pastoral novels. With her emphasis on the undiscovered nature of "these forgotten countrysides" (193), Sand's narrator immediately establishes her authority vis-à-vis a reader presumed to be ignorant of the ways of this corner of the world. As she describes the sorrowful streams and ruined towers invisible to those who do not diverge from the road from Paris to Clermont, she also focuses on the peasants and their language, translating words, phrases, and attitudes which again would be foreign to her readers,[5] and from the outset the novel proposes an alternative vision to the Parisian center, validating the margin and by extension those who can master its discourses. While not unusual for a Romantic text, this narration sets up a subject position negotiated through both a vision of and familiarity with the rural landscape that will be shared by the heroine of the story, Valentine.

Like *Indiana*, published six months earlier, *Valentine* presents a counter-discourse to the popular marriage plot, positing the resistance of the eponymous heroine to the social and institutional strictures of matrimony. In this second novel, however, Sand adds the themes of class, education, and social mobility to the equation, further complicating the questions of female identity and rebellion. At the same time, she introduces the "double structure of the mother-grandmother," which would play a central role both in her childhood and in her novels.[6] Valentine, like Sand herself, is an aristocratic daughter at odds with the world of her birth. Raised by her ambitious mother and decadent grandmother and eager to escape their sway, Valentine rejects the *arts d'agrément* deemed appropriate for girls of her class in favor of practical training in art, and painting becomes the first marker of difference between the heroine and the other women in the tale. The three main characters, Valentine, Athénaïs, and Bénédict, are distinctively shaped by their educations, which are at odds with their social rank. Where Valentine seeks useful skills to transcend the limitations of noble birth, her friend Athénaïs is an upwardly mobile *paysanne* who eschews the practical as debasing and uses her family's wealth to transform herself into a *bourgeoise* by learning embroidery, music, and other parlor skills of the wealthy. Bénédict, Athénaïs's fiancé who ultimately becomes Valentine's lover, is also a peasant who has been corrupted by a frivolous Parisian education. Alienated from his natural tendencies and blighted by ennui, Bénédict has no métier or profession; his lack of occupation causes others in the *bourg* to scorn him, for "he didn't know how to be useful, even to himself" (*Valentine* 202).

Separated from her sister Louise, who was seduced and abandoned with an illegitimate son, Valentine reflects that female education for women of her class is "misérable," for "they teach us a little bit of everything, without allowing us to learn anything in depth" (*Valentine* 220), leaving women like her sister innocent and ignorant, unprepared for anything but being rich. She explains to Bénédict that in examining the lives of her mother and grandmother, products of "emigration and Empire, Coblenz and Marie-Louise," she has learned that she must protect herself from "the misfortunes of the one and the prosperities of the other" (*Valentine* 220). Implicitly linking the political and the personal, Sand makes it clear that in a world where women continue to be legally and socially infantilized, one must learn from the past and forge new paths to independence. To this end, Valentine has developed her skills as a painter in the belief that "whatever the times and the fashions, a person who knows how to do something well can support herself in society" (*Valentine* 220). In this very desire for self-sufficiency rather than dependence upon a husband or family, Valentine again marks her difference from other women in the novel and specifically from her foremothers, while setting the stage for her subsequent subversions of matriarchal as well as patriarchal orders.

Yet, like that of Sand herself in 1832, Valentine's vocation as an artist is more closely tied to independence than to aesthetics, and represents the heroine's

245

resistance to her past, her family, her contemporaries, and to roles prescribed for women. Reflecting on the instabilities of the world, Valentine contends that "our rank, our fortune, mean nothing," words that might also apply to Sand's own experience as she separated from Casimir and confronted the challenge of earning a living in Paris. Arriving at writing less from inspiration than from financial motivation (indeed she tried painting before moving to a literary career),[7] Aurore Dudevant picked up the pen from necessity rather than from an overwhelming need for artistic expression. As she wrote to Jules Boucoiran in 1831 shortly after arriving in the capital, "I am embarking on the stormy seas of literature. I need to survive [Il faut vivre]," later adding, "I dream simply of increasing my well-being with some profits, and since I have no ambition at all to be well known, I never will be. I will not attract the envy and hatred of anyone."[8] Her immediate success notwithstanding, Aurore did not immediately consider herself an Artist writ large, and her initial anxieties of transgression and retribution upon entering the public sphere are voiced in Valentine's rationale for choosing painting. Despite her natural talent in music, Valentine maintains that it would not suit her as a career, for it puts a woman 'trop en évidence' on the stage or in salons. Painting, Valentine avers, "gives one more freedom; it allows a more secluded existence, and the pleasures that it brings become twice as precious in solitude" (*Valentine* 220), a sentiment which echoes Sand's own confession in 1831 that she chose writing because she could "hide from view," for "of all conditions, that of the author is the most free and the most obscure" (*Corr.* 1: 801). This compromise position, wherein the female artist might gain financial independence while retaining personal integrity removed from the spotlight, may not be reflected in Sand's later ethos, but at the outset of her career this impulse to present a nonthreatening image of a female artist surfaces in prefaces and characters alike.[9] Sand was a canny crafter of her public persona, and we cannot discount the author's desire to couch her own ambition in palliative terms and images. But whether a political move or one that reflects personal uncertainties, Sand's earliest image of the female artist is one of cautious independence far removed from the vexing questions of creation, genius, and competition. Indeed, although Valentine never progresses beyond her avocation as a painter, it is her aspiration to use art as a means toward a productive life of financial self-sufficiency that marks her difference from her friends and relations.

He Paints, She Paints:
PORTRAITS OF DIFFERENCE IN *ELLE ET LUI*

Sand's dual portraits of a male and female painter in *Elle et lui* provides significant, yet almost entirely ignored, insights into the author's late aesthetic and her evolving conception of female artistic identity. Since it first appeared in 1858, Sand's critics have focused on the personal, rather than the artistic aspects of the story. Identified from its very début as a *roman à clef* about the author's ill-fated love affair with Musset, *Elle et lui* prompted a volley of other texts, including Paul de Musset's *Lui et elle* (1860), Louise Colet's *Lui* (1860), Mathurin de Lescure's *Eux et Elles: Histoire d'un scandale* (1860), and Spoelberch de Lovenjoul's *La Véritable histoire de Elle et lui* (1897), all of which attempted to set the record straight on who exactly victimized whom in this clash of artistic titans. In the twentieth century, the focus continued to fall on the novel's correlation to history, and the Editions de l'Aurore volume (1986) provides a three-page chart mapping events in the fictitious story against the timeline of Sand and Musset's affair, trip to Venice, and eventual rupture.[10] Barely mentioned in any of the major studies of Sand that have recently appeared,[11] *Elle et lui* has been relegated to the margins of Sandinalia as a somewhat embarrassing attempt on the part of the author to take revenge on her dead lover. In keeping with Henry James's dismissive quip in his article on "*She and He*," this "Sandian enterprise" continues to be read more as "the intellectual and especially financial exploitation of a store of erotic reminiscences"[12] than as an independent work of fiction.

But as Roberta White observes, "When a woman novelist portrays a woman artist painting in her studio, the reader is invited to reflect upon women's creativity and their struggles to attain a space in which to create,"[13] and thus this novel of two painters must be read not simply in terms of the personal, but also (and primarily) in terms of the aesthetic and by extension, the political. In *Elle et lui*, the dynamics of artistic production and the fate of the female artist reflect the dramatic changes in Sand's own artistic identity, closely linked to the rise of the *femme auteur* of the period. Indeed, the two decades following the publication of *Valentine* produced more female authors in France than the entire preceding century,[14] while Sand herself penned more than thirty novels between 1832 and 1858, claiming her undisputable place as an author in the public sphere. The cautious formulations of *Valentine* are accordingly supplanted here by a far more confident vision of the role of the female artist, in keeping with the author's own position in the field of cultural production of mid-nineteenth-century France. Where Valentine espoused painting as a possible vocation, in *Elle et lui*, Thérèse is a successful professional portraitist who has realized Valentine's fantasy as she supports herself through her art. Thus, a life in art is no longer a means to an end that may or may not be possible (and in Valentine's case, it was not), but rather it is a full-fledged identity, and the focus shifts from the question of whether a woman *can* be an artist (that is, painter or author) to what the role of the female artist might be within the larger sphere of art and society. Where *La Princesse de Clèves* served as intertext for *Valentine*, evoking the anodyne image of female authorship in the distant figure of Mme de Lafayette (whose threat was effectively neutralized by her presumed co-author, La Rochefoucauld), in *Elle et lui* Sand engages with and challenges contemporary male authors and aesthetics, moving from the female margins to the center of the contestatory field. Through the trope of the portrait, she stages resistance to male power, representation, and the myths of genius, proposing alternative paradigms of subjectivity and artistic production. In Rancière's terms, the female artist (author/painter) had achieved a level of visibility and recognition, however contested, by 1858, in no small part due to Sand's own interventions. Yet if she was visible, the female artist remained to some extent incomprehensible as a creator in her own right, and in *Elle et lui* Sand establishes female artistic identity and legitimacy based not in women's reflections of the masculine model but instead in artistic and aesthetic *difference*.

Much like *The Tenant of Wildfell Hall*, Sand's novel uses the epistolary form to proffer contrasting portraits of artistic difference in the figures of the two painters. *Elle et lui* begins with a letter from Laurent addressed to "Ma chère Thérèse," in which he discusses professional questions of art, portraiture, and commissions, thus mixing intimacy and aesthetics from the very outset of the story. Treating Thérèse as his artistic peer, he recounts his refusal to paint the portrait of a wealthy traveler, Dick Palmer, who will play an important role in the ménage à trois to follow. Laurent explains:

> Certain painters, incapable of inventing anything, can faithfully and pleasingly copy the living world. They are assured success, as long as they can present the model in its most favorable aspect and have the skill to dress it becomingly while dressing it fashionably; but when one is nothing but a poor history painter, unskilled and contested, as I have the honor of being, one cannot do battle with the professionals. I promise you I have never conscientiously studied the folds of a black suit and the particular idiosyncrasies of a given physiognomy. I am an unhappy inventor of attitudes, types, and expressions. Everything must obey my subject, my idea, my dream. (*Elle* 40)

These opening words announce Laurent's Romantic identity, as he defines himself in opposition to the world of popular success. His lamentation of debased inferiority ("pauvre . . . apprenti . . . contesté") ironically signals his aesthetic superiority within the praxis of Romantic values. As a history painter, he practices the most elevated artistic genre, associated not only with erudition and imagination but also with the training available only to elite men of the period. His disdain for portraiture, linked to imitation and languishing near the bottom of these hierarchies, further reflects the gendered values of art that will be subverted in the novel. Devalued for its association with *métier* rather than genius, the portrait is for Laurent (and for his masculine cohort) a feminized genre, here practiced by Thérèse, his artistic interlocutor. Laurent scorns the real for the ideal, insisting that he can paint only the world of his own fantasy; a self-proclaimed "poet and creator," his art reflects nothing so much as himself.

Refusing to paint Palmer's portrait, Laurent refers the commission to Thérèse, and the image of the female artist that emerges in his letter reflects once again Laurent's own narcissistic vision. As he recounts the conversation to Thérèse, he tells her: "you know that for me you are not Mlle Jacques, who paints lifelike portraits that are very much in vogue, but a superior man disguised as a woman, and who, without ever having drawn an academic nude, divines and makes a viewer divine an entire body and soul in a bust, in the manner of the great sculptors of antiquity and the great painters of the Renaissance" (*Elle* 41). Sand was famously characterized as a woman who was a man by innumerable artistic acquaintances, including Balzac, Musset, and Janin, revealing the implicit assumption that an artist was necessarily a man and thus a "real" woman could not be a "real" artist.[15] *Elle et lui* in turn engages directly with this paradigm, proposing an alternative image of art, gender, and the "real." Here, as in no previous novel on this theme, the focus falls on *two* esteemed painters and the differences between female success and male failure. In Thérèse's response to her friend, an immediate contrast arises between the frivolous and Romantic Laurent and the more practical and grounded Thérèse when she explains to him the numerous ways in which he has misread the situation. Although he insists Palmer is a "perfect specimen of English manhood" (*Elle* 39), Thérèse explains, "As for your Englishman, he is American"; moreover, she intones, "you took him for a grocer and you were mistaken. He is a man of judgment and taste, who knows what he is talking about" (*Elle* 42). From the outset, then, Laurent is blind to what is before him, unable to read people and situations, while the more prosaic Thérèse can see what he cannot, and these metaphors of vision will define each artist's engagement with the world.

Like her artistic foremother, Corinne (and to a lesser extent, Helen Huntingdon), Thérèse is a woman with a mysterious past, without family or husband, who establishes a place in society based on her talents. A gifted portraitist, Thérèse has gained both celebrity and critical acclaim for her paintings: considered a "master" by "people of taste," the female visual artist "quickly gained a reputation of the first order and a handsome income" (*Elle* 51) shortly after her arrival in Paris from parts and family unknown. Thérèse is an "anomaly" as a woman who is "young, beautiful, intelligent, absolutely free, and living alone of her own volition" (*Elle* 51); like Corinne, she falls in love with a younger man who is unable to commit to her and the relationship is doomed from the outset. But unlike Mme de Staël's heroine, Thérèse does not die at the end of the novel, condemned to the ambivalent reward of seeing her genius carried on by the daughter of her sister and her former lover. Instead, Sand's novel resists the privileging of genius while shifting toward an entirely different set of aesthetic and ethical values for the female artist. Through the defining contrast with Laurent, Thérèse embodies artistic difference in ways that highlight success and productivity for the female artist, rather than failure and death, through images of portraiture and maternity. Reversing Corinne's tragic demise, at the end of *Elle et lui,* Thérèse leaves Laurent and begins a new life with her son, concluding the tale with a revelatory distinction between maternal solidarity and artistic solitude, production and sterility, happiness and suffering.

Deciphering the complex metaphors of art, maternity, gender, and genre through the dueling discourses of the real, as embraced by Thérèse, and the ideal, as pursued by Laurent, an interesting paradox emerges. For if Sand's critics have consistently used the counter example of the male-centered Realism of Balzac and Flaubert—her aesthetic sibling rivals—to define Sand's (sentimental social) Idealism, less attention has been focused on Sand's contentious relationship with Romanticism or on the aesthetic, rather than amorous, clashes between Sand and Musset. In reading *Elle et lui* through the lens of the aesthetic, it becomes evident that the relationship between Laurent and Thérèse maps out artistic difference in terms that further our understanding of Sand's own definition of the ethics of art, the real, and the ideal, while clearly demarcating what Isabelle Naginski has called Sand's "reformulation" of Romanticism "in the feminine."[16]

The aesthetic dialogue between the lovers began long before Sand's late response to Musset's *La Confession d'un enfant du siècle* (1836) which gave *his* version of their affair and its dissolution a mere year after the fact. Indeed, the liaison that began in 1833 between this pair of "enfants terribles"[17] and finally ended in 1835 after much suffering on both parts gave birth to another pair of novellas that may also be read in terms of an ongoing artistic conversation and/or rivalry between Sand and Musset. The much discussed trip to Venice in 1834, where Musset fell ill and accused his mistress of betraying him with his physician, Dr. Pagello, had aesthetic as well as amorous consequences for both authors, for it also inspired Sand's *Les Maîtres mosaïstes* (The Master Mosaicists) of 1837 and Musset's *Le Fils du Titien* (Titian's Son) of 1838. These historical novels, centering on Renaissance artists in Venice, served as vehicles for the authors to elaborate their evolving visions of art, love, social engagement, and family. Read in tandem, *Les Maîtres mosaïstes* and *Le Fils du Titien* provide a retrospective illumination of the frequently elided aesthetic tensions between Sand and Musset, while setting the stage for the more direct discourse in *Elle et lui.*

Sand's tale, like Musset's, reflects the *style troubadour* popular in the 1820s and '30s (see, for example, Haudebourt-Lescot in chapter 4). Inspired by episodes from Gothic and Renaissance history, this nostalgic, anecdotal genre romanticized the archaic in narrative images that served to legitimize the art of the present through the patina of the past. Troubadour paintings and stories frequently focused on the lives of Renaissance artists, including Leonardo, Poussin, Titian, Tintoretto, and Raphael, using the filter of history to reflect upon contemporary aesthetic issues.[18] Set in Venice in 1563, *Les Maîtres mosaïstes* is notable in Sand's oeuvre as the only work based entirely on real historical characters and events.[19] The story centers on the brothers Francesco and Valerio Zuccato, a pair of mosaicists who reproduce the works of Titian and Tintoretto on the walls and ceiling of Saint Mark's basilica. Their rivals, the Bianchini brothers, are as dishonest and shoddy as the Zuccati are honest and hardworking. Through a series of deceptions, the Bianchini succeed in having Francesco and Valerio imprisoned for defrauding the state by substituting painted wood for their commissioned mosaics. Eventually attracting the sympathy of the Doge, the Zuccati, who had remained loyal to each other and to their apprentices, are acquitted and triumph over the Bianchini in a later competition. Unlike Balzac's *Chef-d'oeuvre inconnu*, which shares many similarities with Sand's novella, in *Les Maîtres mosaïstes* virtue is rewarded, as is solidarity among artists and brothers.

The more famous and prestigious artists, Titian and Tintoretto, play a secondary role to the mosaicists here, and one of the principal themes is the elevation of artisanal labor to the same status as fine art. The Zuccati's artistic production is entirely within the public sphere for collective consumption and religious contemplation, and Sand defines the ideal not in the Romantic realm of personal fantasy of the individual [male] genius, but in a public engagement, solidarity between artists, and honest commitment to labor. The story ends on the optimistic note of an impending wedding between Valerio Zuccato and Marietta Robusti, Tintoretto's talented daughter who would become a nineteenth-century icon for the woman artist. Thus Sand points to an idealized future of art in the union of male and female creators, high and low art, all placed on an equal footing with an equal commitment to the public and private spheres.

In *Le Fils du Titien*, following directly on the heels of Sand's Venetian tale, Musset picks up where his mistress left off. Set in the same locale some seventeen years later, Musset's story answers the positive vision of Tintoretto's gifted and productive daughter with a darker look at Titian's son. Titian, who also played an important role in Sand's story, has died, along with his oldest son, and the story recounts the career of his second son, nicknamed Pippo. Deliberately severing the family connections so important to Sand's narrative, Musset creates an orphaned Romantic hero whose love for wine, women, and gambling precludes his artistic production. Unlike the dedicated Zuccati, Pippo is an oil painter of potential genius who lacks both inspiration and ambition. Like many Romantic heroes of the nineteenth century, he is overwhelmed by the mediocrity and crass commercialism of contemporary art and thus cannot engage in the artistic process. Where Sand praises artisanal production that copies masterpieces for the masses, Musset privileges a high art that ultimately remains theoretical, for by the end of the story both of Pippo's two canvases are destroyed. Titian's son, burdened by his father's reputation, squanders both his fortune and his genius as he dedicates his life to personal pleasure in an effort to distance himself from the shadow of comparison.

In a more typical formulation, the female character in Musset's tale is not an artist but a model and a lover, in this case the beautiful aristocrat Beatrice Loredano, widow of a *procurato*. She longs to become Pippo's muse and make him as great a painter as his father, and so insists he paint her portrait. When the image is nearly complete, Pippo destroys his own work by scratching out the eyes and mouth of the painted Beatrice as Venus, both physically and metaphorically denying her vision and expression. This violation of an ambitious female who pushes the artist to abandon decadent indulgence for a more disciplined production may reveal Musset's lingering hostility towards Sand, who frequently urged him to work harder and herself remained prolific and successful throughout their troubled relationship.[20]

Silencing the female and denying her the subject position associated with sight and speech, Musset's Pippo symbolically negates both Sand and her creations, celebrating instead a Romantic aesthetic of impotence and incompletion. In the end, although he does finish the portrait, it is his final painting as he abandons art for love. For Musset, as for the majority of nineteenth-century authors, love and art were mutually exclusive, and here the artist chooses happiness over sacrifice for his genius. Sand's forward-looking ending in *Les Maîtres mosaïstes* is counter-balanced here by the absolute closure of *Le Fils du Titien*, where the master Renaissance painter is dead, his only surviving son dedicates his life to idleness, and his only remaining painting is ultimately destroyed by Beatrice's family. Less nihilistic than Romantic, Musset's story refuses the idealizing image of solidarity and artistic commitment to the greater good found in Sand's coterminous text, proposing instead a vision of art closely tied to suffering and impossibility. Where Sand links art and love (both fraternal and erotic) as a means to unite the personal and the public, Musset insists they are antithetical, while both remain firmly ensconced in the realm of the private.

In returning to *Elle et lui*, penned twenty years later, we find many of the same issues rehearsed in an expanded form. Retaining the trope of painting, Sand moves her narration from the distant to a more immediate past: the 1830s. Abandoning the historical filter, her protagonists are fictitious rather than fictionalized versions of real artists, thus forcing the reader to consider the aesthetic differences between Laurent and Thérèse in terms that are not mediated by their ultimate canonization. Perhaps most importantly, Sand foregrounds the questions of gender and creation present but not fully developed in *Les Maîtres mosaïstes* and *Le Fils du Titien*.

As part of her larger project of destabilizing the binaries of gendered identities, Sand creates a male hero who is weak and childlike, a victim of the whims of fancy and caprice, who rejects the real world for his own fantasy—in a word, "feminine" in the nineteenth-century understanding of the word. Laurent embodies the very essence of the Romantic artist whose genius is as much a source of suffering as it is of art, and who, as Margaret Waller has so convincingly argued, uses his impotence as a means of domination.[21] Conversely, Thérèse is strong, independent, and mature; forced by circumstance to support herself, she has no choice but to embrace the reality principle with a sober lack of emotionalism frequently associated with the masculine. This pair of painters reverses the positions that Balzac assigned to male and female artists in the passage famously quoted by Sand in *Histoire de ma vie*. There she reported that he said:

> You look for man as he should be; I take him as he is. Believe me, we are both right. These two paths lead to the same end. I also like exceptional beings: I am one myself. I need them to make my ordinary characters stand out, and I never sacrifice them unnecessarily. But these vulgar characters interest me more than they interest you. I exaggerate them, I idealize them in an inverse sense, in their ugliness or stupidity. I give their deformities terrifying or grotesque proportions. You could not do that; you are wise not to want to look at beings and things that would give you nightmares. Idealize toward the pretty and the beautiful; that is a woman's job.[22]

Yet aesthetically, it is Laurent who seeks the ideal in *Elle et lui* and Thérèse who casts a cool realist's eye on the world. Indeed, Palmer does not want Thérèse to paint his portrait, for the commission is intended for his adoring mother in America, and she will not like it "if it is too real" (*Elle* 52). Instead, he insists that Laurent execute the likeness because he is "un maître idéaliste" (*Elle* 52). How, then, are we to resolve the apparent contradiction between the clearly flawed character of Laurent, who nonetheless seems affiliated with the ideal, and the positive character of Thérèse, so closely akin to Sand yet aesthetically and emotionally linked to the real?

The key to unraveling the complex tissue of imbrications and contradictions between real and fictional aesthetics lies once again in difference and in the problematics of representation, gender, and maternity in the field of cultural production in nineteenth-century France. As signaled by the intended recipient of the portrait above, mothers, both absent and present, biological and metaphorical, play a critical role in the negotiations of artistic production and identity in *Elle et lui*. Thérèse is the illegitimate daughter of a wealthy banker who seduced his own daughter's tutor and placed the baby in a convent, where she is raised collectively by a sisterhood of nuns. Married off by her father to a Portuguese count, Thérèse is doubly disenfranchised when, just as she is about to give birth, she discovers that she has been disinherited by her father and deceived by her bigamist husband: "She thus found herself ruined precisely at the moment when she became a mother, and at the very same moment she saw an exasperated woman arrive at her home who was reclaiming her rights and wanted to make a scene; this woman was the first, the only legitimate wife of her husband" (*Elle* 71). Motherhood here initially signals an end rather than a beginning. Shortly after the birth, Thérèse's husband kidnaps her son and then reports that the child has died on the trip to America, leaving her bereft of all legitimate contacts with the patriarchal order. In the paradoxical position of being a daughter who is not a daughter, a wife who is not a wife, and a mother who is no longer a mother, Thérèse crafts a new identity as an independent artist and supports herself through her own labors.

Yet maternity, always a complex theme *chez* Sand, remains central in the novel, tied both to difference and to substitutions as well as legitimacy. If Laurent represents certain constructions of power and dominance in relation to Thérèse—he is male, she is female; he is a history painter, she is a portraitist; he is well-born, she is illegitimate; he is a "genius," she paints to earn a living—he is nonetheless infantilized throughout *Elle et lui,* while Thérèse is consistently transformed into a mother figure for her lover, an unhealthy and unproductive substitution for both that further mirrors many of the author's own relationships. As in so many of Sand's novels, the maternal love affair pairs a strong but sacrificing woman with an infantile and self-centered man whose narcissistic needs deny her very subjectivity. As Françoise Massardier-Kenney notes, in Sand's oeuvre "being like a mother does not mean so much being in the position of a protector who can control the relation . . . but being the target of an immature and demanding bond where the mother figure is effaced behind the love that consumes the masculine figure."[23] Through her relationship with Laurent, Thérèse destroys her reputation in Paris, but more significantly sacrifices her work, her independence, and her income, for "until then she had gained enough money through her work to lead a comfortable life; but it was possible only because of her ordered habits, her ordered expenses, and the same order in her occupations. The spontaneous life that charmed Laurent brought her financial difficulties. She hid it from him, not wanting to refuse him the sacrifice of her precious time, which is the entire capital of the artist" (*Elle* 94).

If the practical Thérèse needs time and order to produce her work, Laurent needs "stimulation coming from outside of him: a magnificent music emanating from the ceiling, an Arab steed entering through the keyhole, an unknown literary masterpiece in his hand, or better yet, a naval battle in the Genoan harbor, an earthquake, or any kind of delicious or terrible event which would tear him away from himself and under whose spell he would feel exalted and renewed" (*Elle* 96); he needs, in other words, all the clichés of Romantic inspiration. When they travel to Italy, Laurent is struck by impotence in the presence of the great masters while Thérèse, motivated by financial exigency, spends her days copying portraits by Van Dyck for a dealer who will have them engraved. Scorning her diligence, Laurent insists that he "had never felt inclined to copy anything. He was too much of an individualist and too passionate for this kind of study" (*Elle* 95).

The radical differences between the two modes of artistic inspiration and production of Laurent and Thérèse reflect the contemporary gendering of genius that was especially prevalent in the Romantic ethos. From Aristotle to Kant and beyond, western culture had defined genius as a distinctly male form of mental strength, eternally at odds with Nature and the feminine. The link between artistic genius and male fertility emerged from the stoic conception of *logos spermatikos* and was later confirmed in Tissot's *De la santé des gens de lettres* (1766) where "the animating nervous fluid that produces genius is made analogous to male semen."[24] These beliefs, reinforced by popular theories of nineteenth-century physiology, precluded the possibility of female genius, *Corinne* notwithstanding. Where men could create works of art through the 'productive' imagination, women could merely reproduce reality—in the form of portraiture, still life, or children, in an act of imitation or copying. As Carolyn Korsmeyer reminds us, "genius was ferociously guarded as a male preserve."[25]

Working both within and against this ideology, Sand creates two artists who follow these parameters—Laurent as a male genius and Thérèse as a female *copiste*—while at the same time creating a counter-discourse that ultimately privileges the act of imitation over that of the imagination. For indeed Laurent's Romantic fancies are associated not so much with originality as with falsehood and a refusal of the real that leads to isolation and sterility. In a pivotal scene, the lovers spend the night in the forest, and as Laurent sits atop a rock, gazing at the stars in a Lamartinian mode, it becomes clear that there is no room for a real woman—or reality *tout court*—in the world of Romantic *isolement*. Where Thérèse knows the names of the stars, Laurent does not want to hear them, preferring to make up his own; and where she knows the way out of the forest, he insists on going his way and the couple becomes hopelessly lost (*Elle* 87). His fantastic dream that night in the ravine turns into a nightmare that he recounts in detail, but "it was difficult to know, when Laurent was speaking like this, if he was recounting something that he had really experienced or if he had combined in his head an allegory born of his bitter reflections and an image glimpsed while half-asleep" (*Elle* 91). Later Thérèse muses that "aspiration to the sublime" had become a contemporary "disease" of the epoch, blighting "the normal conditions of happiness as well as the ordinary duties of life." Existence with the "unreasoning genius" of her Romantic lover has hurled her "into that awful circle of human hell" where suffering is exalted at the expense of joy and peace (*Elle* 172). Rejecting this manufactured misery of Romantic genius, which leads to artistic aporia for her, Thérèse terminates her relationship with Laurent to return to her art and "aspire henceforth to the *true*." Thérèse's aesthetic focuses not on the interior imaginings of the artist but on representing the real world, in all of its beauty and pain.

Thus, if Laurent is a "maître idéaliste" his type of idealism is not shared by the author, who makes a pointed effort to critique his solipsistic fantasies as she aligns the narrative voice and the reader's sympathies with the reality-based Thérèse. Yet *Elle et lui,* far from embracing a purely Realist aesthetic, demonstrates how the female painter's revised Romantic vision can and must reflect the material realities of society in order to appeal to a non-elite audience and model an ethics of solidarity, labor, and love. In a central allegory, Laurent recounts a story, that he professes he does not understand, of a young man who falls in love with a statue on a tomb. Eventually going mad with passion, the man opens the sarcophagus to uncover the beautiful woman behind the stone, but finds instead a mummy. His reason returns and he embraces the skeleton, proclaiming "I love you better like this; at least you are something that has lived, while previously I was taken with a stone that had never been aware of its own existence" (*Elle* 98). The sharp distinction between art and life, between an aesthetics of ideal beauty that appeals to the head and an aesthetics of ideal love that appeals to the heart is figured forth here in this Pygmalion reversal and prefigures the fate of the two characters at the end of Sand's tale. As Thérèse writes to her own mother, with whom she has resumed a clandestine relationship, "this child would like his mistress to be something like the Venus de Milo, animated by the breath of my patron Saint Thérèse, or perhaps more accurately he wants a woman who can be Sappho today and Joan of Arc tomorrow" (*Elle* 129). Looking alternatively and collectively for a mother, a work of art, a saint, and/or a goddess, Laurent remains unable to love a *real* woman, and Thérèse sadly notes "perhaps you will never be a complete man or a complete artist" (*Elle* 55).

Laurent's failure as an artist and a man in Sand's universe is encapsulated in his misguided portraits of Thérèse. Following his confession in the opening letter that he sees her as a man disguised as a woman, Laurent draws a pair of images of his friend and lover that again reflect his inability to truly see the woman artist as anything but an extension of his own consciousness. Upon their return from the night in the forest, Laurent transforms their experience into a caricature, parodying their exhausting night with an image of "his wild, distraught look" and Thérèse's "torn gown and body shattered with fatigue" (*Elle* 92); beneath the drawing of his mistress he includes the caption "her heart as torn as her dress." His ability to mock her distress, turning their painful adventure into an ironic cartoon, indicates Laurent's emotional blindness. The separation between form and content reveals the Romantic artist's lack of human connection: where Thérèse recognizes the brilliant draftsmanship in the drawing, which reveals, "despite its buffoonery, the hand of a master," she also reflects "there are certain sorrows of the soul that will never have a humorous side" (*Elle* 92). Laurent's "portrait" of his lover reveals his own callousness and immaturity, while portraying Thérèse in a manner that focuses on exaggerated surfaces and emotions rather than depth or understanding. Later, he sketches a "pensive and melancholy" image of Thérèse in an album that she later finds is filled with dozens of drawings of other women, former lovers who inhabit Laurent's memory and imagination like "phantoms of the past," appearing on the blank pages of the album "perhaps in spite of himself" (*Elle* 98). Tearing her portrait out of the book, Thérèse throws it into the fire in a violent move that recalls Helen Huntingdon's immolation of Arthur's portrait. But here, in Thérèse's destruction of her lover's image of her, we discover both the destructive nature of Laurent's art and his love, and Thérèse's rejection of this form of representation. In representing Thérèse, he represents every woman and any woman, but not the real woman, and in each of his images of her throughout the novel Laurent reproduces his own projected fantasies. Whether descriptions, caricatures, drawings, or paintings, Laurent's portraits of Thérèse represent a Romantic male gaze and what Naomi Schor has called "male representational narcissism" which reflects "the very foundations of the representational system elaborated by patriarchal society."[26] Within these paradigms of social and scopic power, the male artist ultimately, always, represents the male self, while the female subject, as Other, is elided into a caricature of powerlessness through "the twin excesses that are the hallmarks of male misogyny: idealization and demonization" (115).

Finally, *Elle et lui* proposes an alternate model of representation that subverts the dominance of the male phallic gaze. Turning one final time to the idea of the portrait, Sand concludes the novel with an image of the fusion of art and life. After spending the night in her studio praying to be delivered from the torture of her relationship with Laurent, Thérèse opens the door to a young boy who "resembled someone she knew but whose name she could not remember" (*Elle* 178). Taking him into the garden, she is struck by the uncanny similarity between the child "and a face she had recently painted by looking into the mirror, to send to her mother, and that face was her own" (*Elle* 178). The reflection of her own face is of course that of her son, who is not dead and is reunited with Thérèse, completing the matriarchal line disrupted but not severed by fathers, husbands, and lovers. Seeing her own face in that of her child and collapsing maternity with self-portraiture, Thérèse, one could argue, falls victim to a variant of Laurent's own Romantic narcissism. But at the same time, even as Thérèse represents Sand's own idealized (and narcissistic) self-portrait, the female painter bodies forth for the author an ethics of connection in the novel that privileges life over art, the child over the painting, as she turns from the representation to the real. Within Sand's schema, Thérèse's portrait of herself, painted for her mother, becomes an emblem of her own motherhood in its reflection of her (absent) son; conversely, as her son reflects back both Thérèse's own face and her portrait, the female artist's creation transcends the limitations of the self in the embodied Other. In a deliberate refusal of the schema that posited art and maternity as mutually exclusive productions, Sand asserts that the woman artist can do both: Thérèse succeeds both as a portraitist and as a mother, her gender allowing her a privileged rather than denigrated position as a creator. Rejecting her infantile lover for her son, Thérèse leaves Laurent for good as "the mother had irrevocably killed the lover." Although she may not be a Romantic genius, she is also spared the suffering and isolation it entails, and Thérèse retires to Germany to savor "her child, her happiness, her work, her joy, her life" (*Elle* 179).

The female artist and mother has the final words of the novel, in a letter addressed to Laurent. Forgiving him his sins against her, she returns one final time to the themes of the real, the ideal, and love. Thérèse writes "You aspired with all of your might to ideal happiness and you grasped it only in your dreams. But your dreams, my child, are your reality, they are your talent and your life" (*Elle* 180). Admitting that love with a real woman is impossible for Laurent, she adds "The women of the future, those who will contemplate your work from century to century, those are your sisters and your lovers" (*Elle* 180). Returning to the allegory of the statue, it becomes clear that Laurent, the embodiment of Romantic genius, will remain disconnected from life, from humanity, and from love, his only communion coming in the posthumous appreciation of his creations. Thérèse's fate, directly reflecting her aesthetic and Sand's, links life and art, maternity and creation, in a fusion of the ideal and the real that privileges an ethics of intersubjective connection over the more intellectual elitism of genius.

Finally, then, if *Elle et lui* is inseparable from the circumstances that generated it, and from the intertexts of Sand's love affair with Musset, its disastrous ending in Italy, Musset's own version of it in *La Confession d'un enfant du siècle*, and the subsequent revisions of this *liaison dangereuse*, it nonetheless surpasses the simple designation of "revenge novel." A rejection of the masculinist aesthetics of Musset's Romanticism every bit as important as her dialogic battles with the Realism of Balzac and Flaubert, *Elle et lui* presents a cogent object lesson in Sand's utopic/Idealist aesthetic. By centering her tale on a female artist, Sand of course invited comparisons between herself and the saintly, virtuous Thérèse at the personal as well as aesthetic levels. Making the dual case for the important role of the female artist in society and for her own blameless role in love affairs of the past, Sand moves from her earlier androgynous model to the maternal, linking Thérèse's artistic production and reproduction to signal her superiority. In this way, Sand continues her interrogation of the very notion "that a male artist's gender simply engenders his writing," or his painting, music, or other art form. Instead, as Leland Person, Jr. contends, Sand's novels (as interpreted by Henry James) "suggest, rather, that the artist constructs a gender identity in the act of engendering the work of art—indeed, that he knows his own gender only in retrospect, by reading or viewing what he has created."[27] In *Elle et lui,* Thérèse's retrospective gaze upon her production finds the double inscription of the feminine in her joint production of canvases and offspring, while the emptiness at the heart of Laurent's impotent search for originality leaves his gender floating in the indeterminate realm of future production, to be read by "les femmes de l'avenir." Expanding upon the paradigms established in *Les Maîtres mosaïstes* and *Le Fils du Titien,* written on the heels of their amorous dissolution, Sand defines her own difference from Musset, Romanticism, and the masculinist order of the past through the visual arts, where the much maligned and "feminized" genre of portraiture serves as the template for successfully connecting art and life while doubling as a mirror, rather than a substitute, for successful maternal creation.

The Mother as Muse:
SAND'S MATERNAL LEGACY

Although frequently idealized, the maternal was inevitably a vexed category for Sand, tied to loss and absence as well as art and identity in her life and works.[28] If Thérèse successfully fuses motherhood and painting at the end of *Elle et lui,* it is only after the unsuccessful relationship with her lover has failed, and the substitution of profession and parenthood with her son for a romantic/sexual relationship with Laurent reflects an ongoing either/or formulation precluding the female artist from combining love and artistic professional identity. In a late story included in the *Contes d'une Grand-mère* (1873), Sand turns to the form of the fairy tale to craft her final image of a female painter, while at the same time inscribing her fantasy of art, love, and the maternal that points to a happier future for the female artist.

Le Château de Pictordu, an allegorical *Bildungsroman* set in the eighteenth century, traces the artistic development of Diane, the motherless daughter of a famous painter, Flochardet. As the story opens, Diane and her father are on a journey when they encounter an accident in their carriage. They take shelter in the ruins of a mysterious castle (the Château de Pictordu) where Diane first meets her muse in the form of the "veiled woman,"[29] who comes to her in a dream and introduces the young girl to gods, goddesses, and nymphs come to life from murals and statues on the castle grounds. The encounter inspires her to return to her secret passion for drawing the next day, despite the fact that her father has only discouraged her from art and "laughed with all his might" (*Château* 54) at her efforts. As a wealthy society painter, Flochardet wants his daughter to be a "a real young lady, that is to say, a pretty person knowing how to dress and prattle pleasantly" (*Château* 54), and although he loves her, he does not truly see her, for like so many artists in nineteenth-century fiction, he is yet another painter who is blind to much before him. Her stepmother similarly misunderstands Diane, turning the child into a pretty doll, dressing and grooming her until she falls sick from boredom and repression. Diane is saved by Dr Féron, who recognizes the girl's need of a real education and takes her under his wing. He teaches her about antiquity and nature, encourages her secret obsession with painting and drawing, and most importantly recognizes that she is a born artist, though her father "could not see it" (*Château* 66). Flochardet, renowned for his flattering portraits of wealthy women, is nonetheless devoid of originality and authenticity; he is unable to appreciate Diane's gifts because they are utterly foreign to his way of seeing. Féron determines that he must shelter her from her father's lessons, which would "distort her vision and ruin her feeling for art" (*Château* 66).[30]

As she grows older, Diane becomes increasingly alienated from her stepmother, and when the veiled lady comes to her again in a dream, the faceless woman reveals that she is Diane's mother and only Diane can restore her face. The final chapters of the story are devoted to the girl's quest to draw the face of her mother. She gradually learns to accept the difference between her father's vision and her own, realizing that they see with different eyes and she cannot follow the father's path if she is to find her mother and ultimately herself. When the doctor offers to show her a miniature of her mother, Diane has another dream where she and the veiled lady search through piles of cameos looking for her face. She finally discovers in her hand a shining carnelian with the profile of an ideal beauty carved in white that grows from the size of a ring to fill her palm. The fairy cries "Finally! Here I am! It is really me, your muse, your mother" (*Château* 80), but when she begins to take off her veil the dream disappears and Diane is left with the fleeting memory in her mind's eye.

At 15, Diane discovers her father is bankrupt, his fortune dissipated by his spoiled second wife. She calls out to her mother to help her save her father, and as she is sketching, she hears the voice of her mother whisper "I am here. You have found me" (*Château* 86). When she looks down, she sees that she has drawn a silhouette that turns out to be the exact image of her mother in the unseen portrait. When she finally opens the miniature she sees that "it was the muse, it was the cameo, it was the dream, and it was her mother; it was reality found through poetry, feeling, and imagination" (*Château* 89). Having discovered her mother and her muse, Diane goes on to develop as an artist, painting alongside her father but in an entirely different way, and her efforts save his life and his fortune. Yet she reaches a point where she needs to make a transition to the future in order to continue to grow as a woman and an artist. Feeling the conflict between her love for her father and her desire to transcend the limits of her family circle, she hears the voice of her mother and muse a final time. In her last intervention she tells her daughter:

> Leave the care of your future to the maternal soul that watches within you and over you. Together, we will find the path to the ideal . . . Do not think that you must choose between duty and a noble ambition. These two things are made to go together, one helping the other. Moreover, do not think that vanquished anger and pain endured are the enemies of talent. Far from exhausting talent, they stimulate it. Remember that through tears you found the face you were looking for, and be assured that, when you suffer with courage, unbeknownst to you, your talent and strength also grow. The health of the mind is not found in repose, it is only found in victory. (*Château* 108)

Following this rallying cry, Diane can find her true vocation and lives a life at once "very noble, very happy, and very rich in exquisite works of art" (*Château* 112). She marries the doctor's nephew and uses her wealth and talent to establish an atelier for poor girls, where she teaches them to paint for free.

This allegory of the life of the female artist, with its rejection of the oppressive law of the father and return to the Lacanian realm of the maternal imaginary, is at once Sand's most abstract and certainly her most idealized meditation on gender and creativity. Unlike her earlier novels, where the protagonists mirrored aspects of her own life and artistic development in concrete social and aesthetic terms, *Le Château de Pictordu* reflects the larger psychological issues confronting the female artist in her search for identity. At the end of her life, secure in her position as an author and a woman in her self-styled persona as the "Bonne Dame de Nohant," Sand created her most optimistic portrait of the artist as a young woman. Addressed to her beloved granddaughters and by extension to the generations of women to come, Sand announces her own role as mother and muse to future female artists. In a notable departure from the other authors in this study, Sand eschews the metaphors of sisterhood for those of motherhood, replacing an image of collective or collaborative feminist labor for one closer perhaps to the masculine model of generational inspiration and influence (à la Harold Bloom), with its implicit hierarchies of authority and power. Yet if Sand, at the end of her life, constructs herself as a *grand-mère* to subsequent generations of women artists, it is in an idealist mode that proposes a model of female (artistic) identity formulated in terms of difference. Although Sand never considered herself a feminist, here she acknowledges the centrality of gender and the need for artistic mothers as well as fathers as women construct artistic identity. *Le Château de Pictordu,* as an allegory of artistic development, presupposes future generations of female artists by setting out the path for girls to follow. The novel proposes that they pursue their passions, seek an education in the history of the human and natural worlds, and resist the forces of a society that would turn them into *poupées* (dolls). The "genie" of Pictordu informs young girls that they cannot follow the itineraries set out by their fathers, for these will not be consistent with their own visions. Instead, they must find their own voices and visions, despite obstacles and derision from the patriarchal order. Suffering can bring strength; love and ambition, far from being opposed, can indeed go hand in hand; and a woman can be a daughter, wife, mother, teacher, and artist all at once. It is only in shifting the gaze from the masculine model, and in looking inward and to the real and metaphoric mothers and muses that girls and women may come to a noble and happy end as writers and painters in their own right.

Like all identities—gender, national, political, social—artistic identity is necessarily both a construction and an ongoing performance, subject to the multifarious forces of context and culture. In the fifty-year course of Sand's career, the figure of the female artist in France was transformed from an anomaly to an established—if contested—fixture in the field of cultural production. In tracing the development of her narratives of female artistic identity, from the aesthetic and social uncertainty of *Valentine,* to the dialogic assertion of legitimacy and difference in *Elle et lui,* and finally to the hopeful image of future generations of female artists in *Le Château de Pictordu,* we can better understand the ways in which the aesthetic, the political, the personal, and the maternal intersect in Sand's own authorial voice and persona, and perhaps more importantly, evaluate the role her novels played in the larger construction of female artistic identity in the popular imagination in the nineteenth century.

Conclusion

Art is not what you see, but what you make others see.

—Edgar Degas

In late 1856, not long after her image as *Boadicea* appeared, Barbara Leigh Smith joined forces with several other women to establish the Society of Female Artists, and the organization held its first exhibition the following year. In 1860 the first female student was admitted to the Royal Academy School (albeit amid great controversy),[1] and in 1876 Ellen Clayton published her two-volume compendium of *English Female Artists,* thus gesturing toward a collective history and identity for British women painters. Emily Osborn's 1888 portrait of Leigh Smith for Girton College portrayed the college's founder seated in front of an easel, paintbrush in hand, in a gesture that acknowledged the important links between feminism, education, and women artists in nineteenth-century England. In France, the Académie Julian opened joint classes for men and women in 1868, offering serious training for female artists first in the mixed atelier and later in separate but still rigorous studios. By 1890 Rodolphe Julian was running four ateliers for female painters in Paris, as art instruction for women became, in Gabriel Weisberg's phrase, "both a business and a cause."[2] The Union of Women Painters and Sculptors was established in Paris in 1881, sponsoring the *Salon des femmes* and the *Journal des femmes artistes* while at the same time, Tamar Garb explains, serving a political as well as artistic function as "a major campaigning body for women artists."[3] It was not, however, until 1897 that women were finally admitted to the Ecole des Beaux-Arts. By then, photographs, etchings, and paintings of women in the atelier regularly appeared not only at the Salon or RA exhibits, but in newspapers, journals, and the popular press, carving a space for this once anomalous figure in the public imagination.

After 1860 in France as in Britain, women's professional artistic training thus began to move from the margins to the forefront of the public's consciousness as a political and social as well as an aesthetic issue. Professional women painters also entered new realms of fame and legitimacy in the second half of the nineteenth century. After winning a gold medal at the Salon of 1848, Rosa Bonheur gained international fame in 1853 for her painting of *The Horse Fair*, a monumental image purchased by the London art dealer Ernest Gambart for 40,000 francs. Gambart, in turn, displayed the painting in London (including a private showing for Queen Victoria), Glasgow, Liverpool, and Manchester, charging a shilling per visit and establishing Bonheur's reputation, according to the popular press, as a "female Landseer" and "the greatest painter of rural scenes in France, perhaps in the world."[4] In 1857, *The Horse Fair* traveled to New York, where it was eventually bought by Cornelius Vanderbilt for $53,000 and donated to the Metropolitan Museum of Art. By the 1860s, Rosa Bonheur had become a "household name," Gretchen van Slyke affirms, "in France, across the English Channel, and even across the Atlantic Ocean."[5] Van Slyke adds, "By the end of the century engravings of [*The Horse Fair*] were hanging on schoolroom walls throughout Great Britain and the United States" (xii) and Bonheur served as a "model and mentor" to women on both continents, from American girls playing with their Rosa Bonheur dolls (van Slyke xii) to her "soeurs de pinceau" (sisters of the brush) in France and England (Garb 1994, 3). Bonheur's studio became a sought-after destination for men and women alike, prompting the Empress Eugénie to pay a visit in 1863; two years later the Empress named Bonheur the first female Chevalier of the Legion of Honor, as she insisted "genius has no sex." Portraits of the artist at work appeared at the Salon in images by Edouard Dubufe (*Portrait de Rosa Bonheur*, 1857), George Achille-Fould (*Rosa Bonheur dans son Atelier*, 1893), and Anna Klumpke (*Portrait de Rosa Bonheur*, 1898) among others, and each depicts the female painter in terms that reflect her professionalism, success, and artistic authority; in Klumpke's luminous image of the artist shortly before her death, the rosette of the Légion d'honneur hangs on her chest at the center of the composition, testimony to Bonheur's achievement in a world once exclusively open to men. The only woman included in Nicaise de Keyser's *Les Grands Artistes de l'école française du XIXe siècle* (1878), Bonheur was posthumously memorialized by Gaston Leroux-Veunevot in a life-sized statue, palette and brushes in hand, in 1910, in a concrete and symbolic representation of her status as the most renowned female artist of the nineteenth century.

Nor was Bonheur's artistic acclaim an anomaly. Mary Cassatt, Berthe Morisot, and Eva Gonzalès achieved success in the 1870s not only in the traditional Salon, but perhaps more importantly as members of the avant-garde, exhibiting with the Impressionists at the Salons des Refusés and participating in the stylistic and ideological challenge to the artistic status quo that would ultimately signal the end of the *Académie*'s hegemony. Manet's controversial painting of Eva Gonzalès at her easel (*Portrait of Mlle E.G.*, 1870) portrayed his student at work on a still life of flowers that looks more like one of Manet's canvases than her own; yet if the scene functions more as "a cipher for his own creative identity," as Tamar Garb claims,[6] than for Gonzalès's artistic vision, the image is nonetheless notable in its serious depiction of a readily identifiable female artist in the studio, representing contemporary art in material and metaphoric ways. On the other side of the Channel, Antonia Losano has shown, the number of British women identifying themselves as painters doubled between 1851 and 1871 and continued to rise through the end of the century (2), while the second generation of Pre-Raphaelite women artists—Lucy Madox Brown, Emma Sandys, Marie Spartali, Julia Margaret Cameron—achieved a level of acceptance and visibility in the 1860s–1880s that Anna Mary Howitt and her cohort had been unable to attain. The figure of the female painter continued to appear in Victorian literature and served, Losano contends, to demonstrate the ways in which women might "mine the liberatory potential of art as a source of emotional, spiritual, or financial satisfaction and tap the potentially radical transformative power of the woman artist to make significant changes in social, cultural, and political arenas" (3).

Nineteenth-century female artistic identity, negotiated through paintings and novels as well as petitions, campaigns, and pamphlets, continued to be inextricably linked to the feminist cause in their shared battle for the right to work and the right to representation, in every sense of the word. But even as women artists (authors and painters equally) became associated through their labor with feminism—for the very act of writing or painting as a professional was in a sense a militant gesture—it was above all their *art* that played a formative role in transforming the cultural habitus (Rancière's distribution of the sensible) in such a way as to enable French and British society to imagine, envision, and ultimately even understand or accept a professional female subject entering the field of cultural production and representing the world. Indeed, as Janet Wolff so cogently reminds us, "culture is central to gender formation. Art, literature, and film do not simply represent given gender identities, or reproduce already existing ideologies of femininity. Rather they participate in the very construction *of* those identities."[7]

The figure of the female painter remained a powerful image of artistic identity in the novel well into the twentieth century, and perhaps the most famous of all—Virginia Woolf's Lily Briscoe—gives voice to many of the same issues as her nineteenth-century predecessors, while at the same time embodying Woolf's own Modernist concerns and new directions for the female artist. Woolf's engagement with the sister arts was personal as well as theoretical: her sister Vanessa Bell, often considered a model for Lily,[8] was a successful Modernist painter who illustrated some of Virginia's works, while the Bloomsbury Group, to which they both belonged, included artists, authors, critics, and intellectuals in its ongoing discussions of aesthetics, politics, and philosophy. In *To the Lighthouse* (1927), appearing nearly seventy years after *Elle et lui*, the female artist remains politically charged, and the image of a woman representing her view of the world, indeed struggling to find and express "her vision," was perhaps no less radical in 1927 than it was a century earlier. Woolf's novel foregrounds many of the same questions of gender, art, and identity that Desbordes-Valmore, Howitt, Owenson, Arnaud, Brontë, and Sand wrestled with in their own works, while at the same time offering a critique of the patriarchal structures of society and of representation, much as her predecessors had done. An astute reader of nineteenth-century women's fiction, Woolf maintained that "a woman writing thinks back through her mothers,"[9] and Lily Briscoe emerges from a collective history of real and fictitious women painters and authors fighting for visibility, reflecting not only Virginia Woolf's (and perhaps Vanessa Bell's) aesthetic battles, but also those of generations of women before them. But if Lily is a central character in *To the Lighthouse*, the passage of time is a central theme, and by the end of the novel, as Lily finally finishes her painting, Woolf points to the possibility of new models of female art and identity, and the eventual shift from Mrs Ramsey's domestic ideal to Lily's independence as a female artist.

From the outset of *To the Lighthouse*, the tension between gender and artistic expression is articulated through the character of Charles Tansley, whose injunction "Women can't paint, women can't write" echoes throughout the narrative in Lily's consciousness, reflecting the voice of the patriarchy while linking the two genres (painting and literature) as equally inaccessible to women.[10] Although set in the years immediately preceding and following World War I, the values of the nineteenth-century remain dominant, and the subject of Lily's painting, and by extension Woolf's novel, is the reinterpretation of the image of Mrs Ramsey and her son James, "mother and child then—objects of universal veneration" (55–56) in both formal and thematic terms. If Lily hopes that they "might be reduced to a shadow without irreverence" (56), so too does Woolf shift her narrative to reflect the formal nature of perception and the stream of human consciousness; yet at the same time, Mrs Ramsey represents traditional subject matter and traditional roles for women, both of which are subverted by author and painter for a new vision/version of what art might be and what women might be or do. Intimacy is here achieved not through love or physical contact, but in the very act of becoming visible to the other, and in keeping with Rancière's formulations, when Lily allows William Bankes to examine her painting and "it had been seen" she feels "This man had shared with her something profoundly intimate" (57). For Lily Briscoe, as for Woolf, the importance lies less in the painting as physical artifact than in its manifestation of her personal vision, a way of seeing and representing the world that signals a break with earlier modes and mores.

For Lily, as for Desbordes-Valmore's Ondine, Howitt's Alice Law, Owenson's Marguerite, and Arnaud's Clémence, identity and meaning come from their artistic production and profession rather than marriage and maternity. Although Mrs Ramsey constantly urges Lily to marry, in the pivotal scene at the dinner table, in the midst of the small talk, domestic negotiations, and social tensions, Lily "remembered all of a sudden as if she had found a treasure, that she had her work. In a flash she saw her picture" (87) and "her spirits rose so high at the thought of painting tomorrow that she laughed out loud at what Mr Tansley was saying" (95). Placing a saltcellar on the table cloth to remind herself of her picture, Lily contemplates her inner landscape while Woolf presents her reader with a series of refracted still lifes and portraits, and both artists reflect the interpenetration of the interior and exterior worlds, giving new resonances to the psychological "truths" of these "feminine" genres. Indeed the domestic and quotidian world of summerhouses, dinner parties, boat trips, and children on the lawn is endowed with new value as Woolf, through Lily's painting and her own narrative, locates meaning not in the object itself, but in the very act of representing perception and the accurate reflection of experience.

In the final section of the novel, following Mrs Ramsay's death, Lily returns to the Isle of Skye with the Ramsays and tries to resume the painting she had begun ten years earlier. The canvas serves as a "barrier" to ward off Mr Ramsay's "neediness," and in the absence of the original subjects—Mrs Ramsay and James, mother and child—Lily returns to her vision, "that line there, that mass there" (153) resisting, even refuting, the chorus "Can't paint, can't write" that continues to echo in her mind. In a scene that establishes the formal and stylistic connections between author and painter, Woolf describes Lily's *act* of painting, rather than the painting itself, in rhythmic, lyrical terms that mirror Woolf's own prose, as each attempts to capture the inner process of perception, "making of the moment something permanent" (165). Woolf's Lily Briscoe thus departs from earlier female painters in the novel in her commitment to an inner vision outside of the studio or society, and in her personal engagement with expression. In none of the previous novels examined here did the female author privilege the fictitious painter's *style* and *form* in such a way as to draw inevitable parallels between her prose and the visual artist's painting, and here the political act of women's artistic creation lies in her presentation of a woman's *vision*. As Woolf would later contend in *Three Guineas*, although men and women may "see the same world," they nonetheless "see it through different eyes."[11] For Lily Briscoe then, it is less a question of being "seen as an artist" (as it was, one could argue, for the artists in the earlier novels), but rather of finding a way to express her vision, even if it is only she who will see it. Her identity as an artist, denied by Tansley and Mrs Ramsay, ultimately comes not from society but from herself. The passage of time, rendered palpable in the novel, is reflected in Lily's movement toward the successful translation of her vision as she recognizes that "nothing stays; all changes; but not words, not paint. Yet it would be hung in the attics, she thought; it would be rolled up and flung under a sofa; yet even so, even of a picture like that, it was true" (182–83).

In the act of painting, Lily performs artistic identity, at once representing her vision of Mrs Ramsay and moving beyond the limitations imposed by her subject, finding freedom in the absence of her metaphoric mother. As she applies pigment to canvas she reflects: "And one would have to say to [Mrs Ramsay], It has all gone against your wishes. They're happy like that; I'm happy like this. Life has changed completely. At that all her being, even her beauty, became for a moment, dusty and out of date" (178). Thus, Lily Briscoe embodies the next generation of women, moving beyond the seductive beauty of Mrs Ramsay's maternal ideal, turning away from social mandates refusing their expression ("Can't paint, can't write") that reflect the "dusty and out of date" values of a previous century, for new ways of being and seeing. Value and meaning for Woolf's Lily Briscoe come from a painting no one may ever see that nonetheless represents her point of view, a woman's consciousness. In the final lines of the novel, Woolf affirms Lily's success as an artist:

> [S]he turned to her canvas. There it was—her picture. Yes, with all its greens and blues, its lines running up and across, its attempt at something. It would be hung in the attics, she thought, it would be destroyed. But what did that matter? she asked herself, taking up the brush again. She looked at the steps; they were empty; she looked at the canvas; it was blurred. With a sudden intensity, as if she saw it clear for a second, she drew a line there, in the centre. It was done, it was finished. Yes, she thought, laying down her brush in extreme fatigue, I have had my vision. (211)

Tansley's words remain vivid reminders of the continuing social and ideological barriers faced by women artists well into the twentieth century, and the fact that Lily's painting would indeed more than likely end up in an attic or under a couch reminds us of the vast strides that remained to be achieved before women would hold a place of equality with men in the field of cultural production.¹² Yet Woolf's canonical Modernist novel centering on a female painter and her "vision" stands as testimony to the ongoing struggle for visibility undertaken by her nineteenth-century predecessors and the continuing resonance of these issues of gender, genre, representation, and female subjectivity in fiction and painting.

In *The Future of the Image,* Jacques Rancière affirms that "the images of art are, as such, dissemblances."¹³ Whether visual or verbal, the artistic image reflects regimes of representation, giving form to what is sayable or visible; more radically, however, the image can also confer "a new visibility" and "educate a new gaze" (*Future* 14), allowing the reader or viewer to see what had not previously been "seen." The images of the female painter in the novels and paintings produced in Britain and France during the first half of the nineteenth century served to construct both an identity and even a cultural presence for a formerly invisible and inconceivable figure. From Marceline Desbordes-Valmore and Hortense Lescot to Anne Brontë and Margaret Gillies, the authors and painters in *Portraits of the Artist as a Young Woman* offered up images that reflected art and gender identity not simply as they were, but as they might be, opening the door for future generations of women artists to continue the ongoing struggle for voice and visibility in the public sphere.

Introduction

1. Elizabeth Fries Lummis Ellet, *Women Artists in All Ages and Countries*, v. Ellet notes that Ernst Guhl had published *Die Frauen in der Kunstgeschichte* in Germany in 1858.

2. Léon Lagrange, "Du Rang des femmes dans les arts," 39. All translations throughout this study are my own unless otherwise noted.

3. See Mary Sheriff, *The Exceptional Woman*.

4. In *Women, Art, and Power*, 145–78.

5. See, in particular, Nochlin's *Women, Art, and Power* (1988), *The Politics of Vision* (1989), and *Representing Women* (1999). Nochlin's exhibition, co-curated with Ann Sutherland Harris, "Women Artists: 1550–1950," at the Los Angeles County Museum in 1976, and the catalogue for the exhibition (*Women Artists: 1550–1950*) were also foundational in the reassessment of women's art history.

6. Griselda Pollock, *Vision and Difference*, 13.

7. Pollock, *Differencing the Canon*, 33.

8. Tamar Garb, *Sisters of the Brush*, 1.

9. Deborah Cherry, *Painting Women*, 53.

10. Cherry, *Beyond the Frame*, 1–2.

11. Abigail Solomon-Godeau, *Male Trouble*, 9.

12. Antonia Losano, *The Woman Painter in Victorian Literature*, 1.

13. W. J. T. Mitchell, in condemning prevalent modes of interdisciplinary study, notes "these methods have been mainly associated with the work of literary scholars moonlighting in the visual arts," although "they have a certain hidden institutional presence in art history as well." *Picture Theory*, 84.

14. See, in particular, "The Visual Impulse in Prose: Border Crossings and the Anxieties of Interdisciplinarity," in Wettlaufer, *In the Mind's Eye*, 9–22.

15. Wendy Steiner, *The Colors of Rhetoric*, 18.

16. See Wettlaufer, *Pen vs Paintbrush* and "Composing Romantic Identity: Berlioz and the Sister Arts."

17. These include Balzac's *La Vendetta* (1829), Marceline Desbordes-Valmore, *L'Atelier d'un peintre* (1833), Sydney Owenson, *The Princess* (1835), Angélique Arnaud, *Clémence* (1841), Anne Brontë, *The Tenant of Wildfell Hall* (1848), Dinah Craik, *Olive* (1850), Anna Mary Howitt, "The Sisters in Art" (1852), William and Mary Howitt, "Margaret von Ehrenberg, The Artist-Wife" (1853), and George Sand, *Elle et lui* (1858). Delphine Gay de Giradin's 1854 one-act comedy, *La Joie Fait Peur,* also focused on a female painter. Several other female authors penned novels about male painters, including Flora Tristan, *Méphis* (1838), Marie d'Agout, *Nelida* (1846), and Mary Anne Hardy, *The Artist's Family* (1857). For discussion of the figure of the female painter later in the century in Britain, see Losano, *The Woman Painter in Victorian Literature*.

18. It is noteworthy that Lagrange's article was reprised in *The Crayon*, an American art journal that promoted Ruskin's teachings and Pre-Raphaelite painting and writing. See "Woman's Position in Art," *The Crayon* 8 (February 1861): 25–28.

19. Jacques Derrida, "The Law of Genre," 56.

20. Fredric Jameson, *The Political Unconscious*, 106.

21. See Judith Butler, *Gender Trouble: Feminism and the Subversion of Identity.*

22. John Frow, *Genre*, 1–2.

23. Baudelaire reflected in one of the fragments collected in *Mon Coeur mis à nu*, "Glorifier le culte des images (ma grande, mon unique, ma primitive passion)." See Baudelaire, *Oeuvres complètes* 1: 701.

24. See Richard Altick, *The Shows of London;* Kate Flint, *The Victorians and the Visual Imagination;* and Linda Shires, *Perspectives: Modes of Knowing and Viewing in Nineteenth-Century England,* for discussion of the role of the visual in nineteenth-century Britain. Jonathan Crary's *Techniques of the Observer* and Andrea Goulet's *Optiques* trace the relationship between vision, optics, art, and literature in France during the period.

25. Jean-Louis Comolli, "Machines of the Visible," 122–23.

26. On the effect of technical advances on book and newspaper illustration in France, see Ségolène Le Men, "Book Illustration." On the illustrated book in Britain, see Richard Maxwell, ed., *The Victorian Illustrated Book.*

27. For discussion of the "unseen seer," see Richard Burton, "The Unseen Seer, or Proteus in the City," and Michel Foucault, *Discipline and Punish,* for discussion of the panopticon. Balzac's *L'Histoire des Treize* and Dickens's *Great Expectations* are two of the many novels of the period that thematize the anxieties of being observed by an invisible force.

28. Walter Benjamin, "The *Flâneur.*" Benjamin notes that the nineteenth century was distinguished "by a marked preponderance of the activity of the eye over the activity of the ear," while the activity of the *flâneur,* a "characteristic product of modern life," was entirely motivated by "the crucial issue of seeing." See Benjamin, *Charles Baudelaire: A Lyric Poet in the Era of High Capitalism,* 37–38.

29. David Peters Corbett, *The World in Paint,* 15. Also see Hal Foster, ed., *Vision and Visuality,* and Martin Jay, *Downcast Eyes.*

30. Laura Mulvey, "Visual Pleasure and Narrative Cinema," 19. Mulvey's categories have been disputed (see, for example, E. Ann Kaplan, "Is the Gaze Male?"), as has her assumption of a heterosexual norm of desire. If these structures are taken to reflect nineteenth-century *ideologies* of vision and visuality, it is also important to understand that they in no way preclude female viewing subjects.

31. Jacques Rancière, *The Politics of Aesthetics,* 13. Referred to hereafter in the text as *PA*.

32. Eric Méchoulan, "On the Edges of Jacques Rancière," 4.

33. Kristin Ross, "On Jacques Rancière," 245.

34. Rancière, *The Future of the Image,* 7.

35. See Rancière's *La Nuit des prolétaires* (Nights of Labor) for discussion of the workers of the 1830s and '40s who reclaimed the night for their own intellectual labors, composing journals, poetry, and newspapers, and appropriating access to the world of thought denied to the proletariat.

36. Within Rancière's thought, "equality" (*l'égalité*) has no *a priori* foundation or content and is not necessarily associated with the distribution of rights; it is instead found in acts of subjectivization. I use it here both in the usual sense of the word and in Rancière's as well.

37. Richard Terdiman, *Discourse/Counter-Discourse,* 149.

38. See Raymond Williams, "The Romantic Artist," in *Culture and Society,* for a discussion of the construction of an alienated artistic identity as a response to the rise of bourgeois markets and the commodification of art.

39. Michael Wilson, *Rebels and Martyrs,* 7.

40. Abigail Solomon-Godeau, "Male Trouble," 294.

41. For discussion of the nineteenth-century woman reader, see Kate Flint, *The Woman Reader, 1837–1914,* and James Smith Allen, *Popular French Romanticism: Authors, Readers, and Books in the 19th Century.*

42. Herbert Sussman, *Victorian Masculinities,* 114.

43. Christine Battersby, *Gender and Genius,* 3.

44. Honoré de Balzac, *Lettres à Madame Hanska,* 1: 585.

45. "Les Jeunes France," *Figaro* (30 août 1831), 1.

46. David Scott, *Pictorialist Poetics,* 12.

47. Murger wrote in his Preface to *Scènes de la vie de Bohème,* "Bohemia neither exists nor can exist anywhere but in Paris," xxiv. The idea quickly caught on in England and in 1851 Dickens noted in *Household Words,* "The Parisian Bohemians of today are a tribe of unfortunate artists of all kinds—poets, painters, musicians, and dramatists—who haunt obscure cafés in all parts of Paris, but more especially in Quartier Latin." In *Household Words* 4 (15 November 1851): 190–92.

48. George Du Maurier, *Trilby,* 27. Du Maurier's *Trilby* also began as a serial before becoming a best-selling novel, and later a play and series of films.

49. For an overview of other novels focusing on the figure of the artist, see Bo Jeffares, *The Artist in Nineteenth-Century English Fiction,* and Theodore Bowie, *The Painter in French Fiction.*

50. Trilby, the title character in Du Maurier's novel, becomes a famous singer, but only under the influence of her mesmerizing manager, Svengali. When no longer under his hypnosis, Trilby cannot sing a note, and thus the female artist in this novel of bohemia is a vehicle for male talents and energies which she independently lacks. Trilby's true role in the novel is that of the love object of the male painters. Du Maurier illustrated his own novels, as did Thackeray, thus providing both visual and verbal portraits of the artists and their mistresses.

51. Jerrold Seigel, *Bohemian Paris,* 5.

52. Carlyle, *On Heroes and Hero Worship,* 152. See Fred Kaplan, "'Phallus-Worship'

(1848): Unpublished Manuscripts III—A Response to the Revolution of 1848," for discussion of Carlyle's dislike of Sand and the French novel, "in his eyes the most pernicious embodiment of the sexual-material corruption that seemed to be increasingly dominating western culture" (21).

53. Sussman contends, "This community of male artists, a 'Priesthood' in Carlyle's terms, becomes both oppositional to the hegemonic male sphere and yet its very image through the occupation with communicating masculine wisdom, excluding the female, and bonding through shared labor" (141).

54. Carol Christ, "'The Hero as Man of Letters': Masculinity and Victorian Nonfiction Prose," 20.

55. See "De la poésie classique et de la poésie romantique," in *De l'Allemagne,* 1: 211–14.

56. See Alan Richardson, "Romanticism and the Colonization of the Feminine," 13–25.

57. Theresa Kelley and Paula Feldman, *Romantic Women Writers: Voices and Counter-Voices,* 7.

58. See, for example, Dorothy Mermin's reading of Christina Rossetti's "Song: When I Am Dead, My Dearest," in "The Damsel, The Knight, and the Victorian Woman Poet."

59. Although the term "feminism" was not used until much later in the nineteenth century, I will use the term throughout this discussion to denote what would today be considered feminist thought. Early French feminist Olympe de Gouges, author of the *Declaration of the Rights of Woman* (1791), was guillotined in 1793, and British feminist Mary Wollstonecraft, author of *Vindication of the Rights of Woman* (1792), was discredited following her death for her unconventional lifestyle.

60. Elizabeth Eger, *Brilliant Women: 18th-Century Bluestockings,* 32.

61. For discussion of the French *salonnières* see Benedetta Craveri, *The Age of Conversation,* and Evelyn Bodek, "Salonnières and Bluestockings."

62. Frédéric Soulié, *Physiologie du bas-bleu,* 6. In French grammar, the pronoun must agree with the antecedent in gender and number. Thus, if the antecedent is a feminine noun such as *la blanchisseuse* (the laundress), the pronoun would be *elle* (she), but if the antecedent is a masculine noun such as *le bas-bleu,* the pronoun must be *il* (he), even if the referent is female.

63. Leigh Hunt, *Blue-Stocking Revels,* 56.

64. Thus, for example, nineteenth-century French historian Jules Michelet called Britain "the anti-France" in *Le Peuple,* 240. See also Linda Colley, *Britons: Forging the Nation,* and Tombs, *That Sweet Enemy: The French and the British.*

65. Margaret Cohen and Carolyn Dever, "Introduction" to *The Literary Channel: The Inter-National Invention of the Novel,* 2.

66. Doody, *The True Story of the Novel,* 269.

67. DeJean, "Transnationalism and the Origins of the (French?) Novel," 38.

68. Diderot, "Eloge de Richardson," 35.

69. Kendrick, "Balzac and British Realism," 5.

70. McMurran, "National or Transnational? The Eighteenth-Century Novel," 51.

71. Patrick Noon, *Crossing the Channel: British and French Painting in the Age of Romanticism,* 7.

72. Stephen Bann, "Print Culture and the Illustration of History," 29.

73. Scheffer's house and studio are currently home to the Musée de la Vie Romantique in Paris and serve as a museum for Sand's belongings (paintings, furniture, jewelry) as well.

Chapter 1

1. Austen, *Pride and Prejudice*, 39.
2. Ann Bermingham, *Learning to Draw: Studies in the Cultural History of a Polite and Useful Art*, 180, 184.
3. Deborah Cherry, *Painting Women: Victorian Women Artists*, 9.
4. For discussion, see Charlotte Yeldham, *Women Artists in Nineteenth-Century France and England*; Cherry, *Painting Women*; and Gen Doy, *Women and Visual Culture in 19th-Century France*.
5. The *Académie Royale* admitted fifteen women as members between 1663 and 1783; following the Revolution, no women were admitted to the *Académie*'s various incarnations until the twentieth century. The British Royal Academy included Angelica Kauffman and Mary Moser among its founding members in 1768, but no other women were admitted until 1922. In both cases, the female members of the academies had limited privileges and were never accorded the same status as the male academicians.
6. Linda Nochlin, "Why Have There Been No Great Women Artists?" in *Women, Art, and Power*, 159–60.
7. In this study, "Salon" will refer to the official art exhibition of the French *Académie Royale de peinture et de sculpture*, while "*salon*" will denote an art critical review of the exhibition. The *livret* was the booklet distributed at the Salon with the names of the artists and the titles of their paintings.
8. Mary Sheriff, *The Exceptional Woman*, 2. See Sheriff for extensive discussion of Vigée-Lebrun as an exceptional woman. Also see Fraisse, *La Raison des femmes*.
9. See Thomas Cole and Mary Pardo for discussion of "The Origins of the Studio."
10. Philippe Junod, "L'Atelier comme autoportrait," 85, 88, 96.
11. See Crow, *Emulation: Making Artists for Revolutionary France*; Ockman, *Ingres's Eroticized Bodies*; and Solomon-Godeau, *Male Trouble: A Crisis in Representation*.
12. Susan Siegfried, *The Art of Louis-Léopold Boilly*, 96.
13. Yeldham, *Women Artists*, 48.
14. The sole exception is Delécluze's peculiar discussion of Mme de Noailles at several junctures in *Louis David: Son école et son temps*, in which the female student is portrayed less in terms of her art than in terms of her class, and as a troubling source of desire for the author's alter ego, Étienne. For discussion see Solomon-Godeau, *Male Trouble*, 46–48. For a memoir of Girodet's studio, see P. A. Coupin's Introduction to the *Oeuvres posthumes de Girodet*.
15. Solomon-Godeau, *Male Trouble*, 47.
16. See Marie-Juliette Ballot, *Une Elève de David: La Comtesse Benoist*.
17. Margaret Oppenheimer, *The French Portrait: Revolution to Restoration*, 35.
18. Bruun Neergaard, *Sur la situation des Beaux-Arts en France, ou Lettres d'un Danois à son ami* (Paris, an IX/1801) 13: 39–40.
19. In *Nouvelles des arts* an X (1801), critic Charles Landon noted the "essaim de jeunes et charmantes artistes" (swarm of young and charming female artists) displaying their work at the Salon.
20. R. J. Durent, *Journal des arts*, 5 octobre 1812. Durdent's Salon review was reprinted as *Galerie des peintres français du Salon de 1812* (Paris, 1813).
21. Auricchio, *Adélaïde Labille-Guiard*, 1.
22. See Sheriff, 186–89.

23. See Greer, *The Obstacle Race*, 262–69, for a brief discussion of Labille-Guiard's career and several of her students.

24. Joachim Lebreton noted in his obituary of Labille-Guiard that the painter "was always tormented by our society's lack of institutions that could offer resources for earning an honest living to women without fortune." *Notice sur Mme Vincent, née Labille, peintre* (Paris: an XI).

25. Victor Stoichita, *The Self-Aware Image*, 39–40.

26. See, for example, Ripa's *Iconologia* and the allegorical representations of Art.

27. Labille-Guiard divorced her first husband, Nicolas Guiard, in 1792 when it became legal to do so. She did not marry Vincent, her partner for more than twenty years, until 1800.

28. See Mulvey, 19.

29. Morowitz and Vaughan, "Introduction," *Artistic Brotherhoods in the Nineteenth Century*, 11.

30. Nina Athanassoglou-Kallmyer, "*Imago Belli:* Horace Vernet's *L'Atelier* as an Image of Radical Militarism."

31. See Charles Gabet, *Dictionnaire des Artistes de l'école française au XIXe siècle*, 325–26.

32. See Francis Haskell, *An Italian Patron of French Neo-Classical Art.*

33. Marc Gotlieb, "Creation and Death in the Romantic Studio," 150.

34. While Germaine Greer identifies the woman in this scene as a "female student assistant," a contemporary drawing by Cogniet of his sister in a recent Sotheby's sale so closely resembles the woman in Amélie's painting as to leave little doubt that it is a self-portrait. See Germaine Greer, "'A tout prix devenir quelqu'un': The Women of the Académie Julian," 42.

35. Susan Sidlauskas, *Body, Place and Self in Nineteenth-Century Painting*, x.

36. In another painting of Cogniet's atelier, attributed to Amélie, the studio is shown from the reverse angle, looking toward the large windows. In this second composition, the same active/passive dynamic is repeated, with Léon sitting on a ramp and contemplating an unseen work while Amélie is busy painting at an easel.

37. Caroline (Thévenin) Cogniet was also known as Catherine, while Rosalie, born in 1820, was Anne-Marie-Reine Thévenin.

38. For discussion of the legend of Zeuxis selecting models for Helen of Troy and Kauffman's version of the scene, see Elizabeth Mansfield, *Too Beautiful to Picture.*

39. Sass's School of Art in Bloomsbury, where Anna Mary Howitt studied, is a notable, if not unique, exception. Run by Francis Cary after 1842, Sass's offered artistic training at a fairly high price to British women, including Eliza Fox, Adelaide Claxton, and Henrietta Ward. Fox would later hold classes for women interested in drawing the nude model in her home.

40. See Sir Joshua Reynolds, *Discourses on Art.*

41. Holger Hoock, *The King's Artists: The Royal Academy of Arts and the Politics of British Culture*, 78.

42. See Yeldham, *Women Artists* 1: 167–68 and 236–41.

43. Quoted from Ellen Sharples's diary in Katharine McCook Knox, *The Sharples*, 13. Knox affirms that Ellen's copies are often indistinguishable from her husband's original portraits, posing difficulties in attribution for contemporary scholars.

44. *Diaries of Ellen and Rolinda Sharples*, June 1803.

45. Quoted from Ellen Sharples's diary in Kathryn Metz, "Ellen and Rolinda Sharples: Mother and Daughter Painters," 6.

46. See Greenacre, *The Bristol School of Artists*.

47. See Metz, 4.

48. Ellen Sharples wrote that she was always "exceedingly agitated when attempting original portraits but not so Rolinda, who conversed with a person sitting for a portrait with as much ease as if unemployed and made her sitters equally at ease." Quoted in Knox, 25.

49. See Metz, 7–8.

50. Quoted in Metz, 9. Ellen Sharples compiled Rolinda's notes into her own diary, creating a journal of sorts of her daughter's life as well.

51. See the entry for Rolinda Sharples in *The Concise Grove Dictionary of Art* (Oxford: Oxford University Press, 2002).

52. See Caroline Davidson, *Women's Worlds: The Art and Life of Mary Ellen Best*, 14–16.

53. Lynne Walker, "Women Patron-Builders in Britain," 121.

54. The paintings are identified by Simon Howard in Davidson, 36. What were formerly believed to be a pair of Tintorettos are now ascribed to Paulo Fiammingo.

55. Benham's articles appeared in the *Literary Gazette* (19 October 1850): 773–76, and *Art-Journal* (November 1850): 360–61. Howitt's pieces were published in *Athenaeum* on 19 October, 2 November, and 7 December 1850; 1 March and 12 April 1851. Anna Mary's letters from Munich ran in Dickens's *Household Words* from November 1850 through May 1851. Edited by her mother, Anna Mary's narrative appeared unsigned, as did all work in *Household Words*.

56. Mary Howitt, who played an active role in editing and promoting Anna Mary's German letters, wrote to her daughter in December 1850: "Mrs. Gaskell is much pleased with your writings. She says you do not make the reader see the things with your eyes, but you present the scene itself to him. She hopes, on your return, you will collect and publish your letters in a volume—a sort of '"Art Life in Munich."' *Autobiography*, 201. In reviews of her paintings, AMH is frequently referred to as "Author of *An Art-Student in Munich*." In William Michael Rossetti's "Art News from London," in *The Crayon*, for example, he begins his review of her painting *Sensitive Plant* by referring to Howitt as "the authoress of a vivid and picturesque book, 'The Art Student in Munich.'" *The Crayon* 1.16 (18 April 1855): 263.

57. Howitt, *An Art Student in Munich*, vii.

58. In the preface to *An Art Student in Munich* Howitt wrote: "Should some readers, however, cavil at what they may deem a certain *couleur-de-rose* medium through which all objects seem to have been viewed, the writer would simply reply, that to her it appears more graceful for a Student of Art to present herself in public as the chronicler of the deep emotions of job and admiration called forth in her soul by great works of the imagination, than as the chronicler of what in her eyes may have appeared defects and shortcomings" (vii).

Chapter 2

1. A notable exception is Mme Riccoboni's *Histoire d'Ernestine* (1765) chronicling the love affair between a young German painter and the French aristocrat who is the subject of the portrait she is finishing.

2. For discussion, see Bowie, *The Painter in French Fiction,* and Newton, "The Atelier Novel: Painters as Fictions."

3. For discussion of the *paragone* or competition between the arts, see Leonardo, "The Works of the Eye and Ear Compared," and d'Este, *Le Paragone.*

4. Johnson, "The Lady in the Lake," 627–28.

5. Danahy, "Marceline Desbordes-Valmore et la fraternité des poètes," 386.

6. Quoted in C. A. Sainte-Beuve, *Memoirs of Madame Desbordes-Valmore,* 177.

7. Barbey d'Aurevilly, "Marceline Desbordes-Valmore," 145.

8. In a letter dated 2 August 1833, Victor Hugo wrote to Marceline Desbordes-Valmore, "Vous êtes la femme même, vous êtes la poésie même." Quoted in Louis Aragon, "Deux poems inédits de Marceline Desbordes-Valmore et une lettre inédite de Victor Hugo," 8.

9. Sainte-Beuve, "Madame Desbordes-Valmore," in *Portraits contemporains* 2: 115–37.

10. Baudelaire, 2: 146–47.

11. Richardson, "Romanticism and the Colonization of the Feminine," 13.

12. Desbordes-Valmore began acting in Rouen to earn money for the family and was well received in Paris at the Opéra Comique and Odéon. She married fellow actor Prosper Valmore in 1817, published her first book of poetry in 1817, and finally left the stage in the 1820s.

13. Boutin, "Marceline Desbordes-Valmore and the Sorority of Poets."

14. As Sainte-Beuve recounts it, Lamartine mistakenly believed that Desbordes-Valmore had dedicated a poem to him in a keepsake album and wrote his own poem to her as thanks for her verse. The inscription "To M. A.D.L." was actually meant for Aimé de Loy rather than Alphonse de Lamartine. See *Memoirs of Madame Desbordes-Valmore,* 162–68.

15. Alphonse de Lamartine in *Les Oeuvres poétiques de Marceline Desbordes-Valmore* 2: 818–20.

16. Desbordes-Valmore, *Oeuvres poétiques* 1: 224–26.

17. Gretchen Schultz provides a reading of various theories of Desbordes-Valmore's "sincerity" in her poetic voice and disclaimers in *The Gendered Lyric,* 43–45.

18. In a letter to M. Duthilloeul accompanying a copy of Lamartine's poem, Desbordes-Valmore astutely observes: "I have copied these beautiful verses with tears in my eyes, forgetting that they were addressed to so obscure a person as myself. But no: they were composed for the poet's own glory,—to show how full his heart is of sublime and gracious pity." Quoted in Sainte-Beuve, *Memoirs of Madame Desbordes-Valmore,* 167.

19. The most pronounced of these "biographical" readings may be found in Boyer d'Agen's edited version of *L'Atelier d'un peintre,* published in 1922. Retitling Desbordes-Valmore's novel *La Jeunesse de Marceline,* he excises nearly a third of her story and recasts the novel as autobiography, thus denying the poet her creation. Subsequent interpretations have focused on the story as a reflection of the Parisian art world during the Napoleonic and Restoration periods. Thus, Stephen Bann reads *L'Atelier d'un peintre* almost entirely in terms of its possible *mise en scène* of the early career of Paul Delaroche. See Stephen Bann, "The Studio as Scene of Emulation: Marceline Desbordes-Valmore's *L'Atelier d'un peintre.*"

20. For discussion of Desbordes-Valmore's relationship to Balzac, see "Marceline et Balzac," in Ambrière, *Le Siècle des Valmore* 1: 447–60.

21. See Wettlaufer, *Pen vs. Paintbrush.*

22. Nesci, *La Femme mode d'emploi,* 28.

23. Bolster, *Stendhal, Balzac et le féminisme romantique,* 9.

24. Honoré de Balzac, *Lettres à Madame Hanska* 2: 183.

25. Stendhal, "Appendice sur le Rouge et le noir," 511.
26. For further discussion, see Cohen, *The Sentimental Education of the Novel*.
27. Balzac, *La Vendetta*, in *La Comédie humaine* 1: 1040.
28. In traditional versions of the myth, Diana, goddess of the moon, falls in love with the beautiful shepherd, Endymion, as he tends his flocks on Mt. Latmus. The goddess is so infatuated with the slumbering mortal that she asks Jupiter to let him sleep forever so that he would be ever available for her amorous nocturnal visits. The topos was popular with rococo painters, including Lagrenée, Van Loo, Boucher, and Fragonard. For discussion of Balzac's interpretation of Girodet's *Endymion*, see Wettlaufer, "Girodet/Endymion/Balzac: Representation and Rivalry in Postrevolutionary France," *Word & Image: A Journal of Verbal/Visual Enquiry* 17.4 (2001): 401–11.
29. Gérard Genette, *Paratexts*, 2.
30. Marceline Desbordes-Valmore, *L'Atelier d'un peintre: Scènes de la vie privée*, 8.
31. By 1830, popular interest in the hagiography of artists was so great that journals such as *L'Artiste* and *Le Magazin pittoresque* regularly included critical accounts of the lives and works of the Old Masters. Studies including Quatremère de Quincy's *Histoire de la vie et des ouvrages de Raphael* (1824) were regularly used as sources. See Francis Haskell, "The Old Masters in Nineteenth-Century French Painting," for further discussion.
32. Revolutionaries destroyed a large number of churches in 1789. While Constant Desbordes did indeed inhabit a studio in an abandoned Couvent des Capucines, it was during a period where he was estranged from his niece, and Marceline never lived there with him. Thus, though based in fact, it is clear that the author has chosen this locale for its symbolic resonance.
33. Girodet was in fact the friend and neighbor of Constant Desbordes. He opened a studio for women in 1819 and trained a number of professional women painters, including Constance Jaquet and Rosalie Renaudin. Fanny Robert, deaf and mute from birth, was also a pupil and executed a portrait of her teacher now in the collection of Smith College. See Jean Adhémar, "L'Enseignement académique en 1820: Girodet et son atelier," and F. L. Bruel, "Girodet et les dames Robert."
34. Desbordes-Valmore's daughter, Ondine, later took lessons in Haudebourt-Lescot's studio, probably in 1838.
35. Dibutades is credited with the "invention" of drawing when she traced her lover's profile on the wall; she was a popular mythic figure in eighteenth- and early-nineteenth-century art. See Pliny's chapter on "Modeling" in *Historia naturalis*, for the original version of the tale.
36. Castiglione's *The Book of the Courtier* (1513–27) is written in dialogue form and gives voice to a range of female characters. In Book II, Giuliano de' Medici proposes that the female courtier should engage in the same moral training and intellectual pursuits as her male counterpoint. The ensuing debate on female equality resonates throughout the text.
37. Sir Philip Sydney, *Astrophil and Stella*, 165. See also Terry Castle, "Lab'ring Bards: Birth Topoi and English Poetics 1660–1820."
38. Susan Stanford Friedman, "Creativity and the Childbirth Metaphor: Gender Difference in Literary Discourse," 74.
39. For discussion of maternity in Desbordes-Valmore's poetry, see Aimée Boutin, *Maternal Echoes: The Poetry of Marceline Desbordes-Valmore and Alphonse de Lamartine*. Boutin does not discuss *L'Atelier d'un peintre*.

40. Griselda Pollock, *Differencing the Canon*, 35.

41. Abel de Pujol's story is recounted in the chapter entitled "Un Elève de David," connecting the fictional atelier with the real, while referring to two historical painters who also trained female students in their studios. The novel is set about ten years before Grandpierre-Deverzy's 1822 painting was executed.

42. Bertrand-Jennings, *Un Autre mal du siècle*, 87.

Chapter 3

1. Cherry, *Beyond the Frame*, 9.
2. Morowitz and Vaughan, "Introduction," *Artistic Brotherhoods in the Nineteenth Century*, 1.
3. Mary Ann Clawson, *Constructing Brotherhood: Class, Gender, and Fraternalism*, 45.
4. Rosenfeld, "Pre-Raphaelite 'Otherhood' and Group Identity in Victorian Britain," 72.
5. Sussman, *Victorian Masculinities*, 115.
6. Prettejohn, *The Art of the Pre-Raphaelites*, 18.
7. Anna Mary Howitt was invited to publish in *The Germ* (the PRB journal) in 1850 and participated in the Portfolio Club with Rossetti and Millais in 1854.
8. Jan Marsh has used the term "Pre-Raphaelite Sisterhood" to refer to the models and muses of the Pre-Raphaelite Brotherhood—Elizabeth Siddal, Emma Brown, Annie Miller, Fannie Cornforth, Jane Morris, and Georgiana Burne-Jones (*Pre-Raphaelite Sisterhood*). In her very helpful study *Pre-Raphaelite Women Artists*, co-edited with Pamela Gerrish Nunn, Marsh argues for the inclusion of women among the Pre-Raphaelites, while Nunn's essay, "A Pre-Raphaelite Sisterhood?" takes up the case, maintaining that, had they kept painting, Anna Mary Howitt, Jane Benham Hay, and Joanna Boyce "would have made a triumvirate to equal that of DG Rossetti, WH Hunt and JE Millais." *Pre-Raphaelite Women Artists*, 66.
9. The *Athenaeum*'s review of Howitt's *Margaret Returning from the Fountain*, for example, referred to "the Pre-Raphaelite school to which Miss Howitt, perhaps unconsciously, inclines" (19 March 1854): 346.
10. See, for example, Holman Hunt, *Pre-Raphaelitism and the Pre-Raphaelite Brotherhood*, which makes no mention of any of the women who participated in the movement.
11. See Nina Auerbach, *Communities of Women: An Idea in Fiction* and Sharon Marcus, *Between Women: Friendship, Desire, and Marriage in Victorian England* for further discussion.
12. For discussion of Howitt's life and art, see Pamela Gerrish Nunn, *Canvassing*, and Nunn and Jan Marsh, *Women Artists and the Pre-Raphaelite Movement*.
13. Howitt also joined Eliza Fox's cooperative art classes for women held at Fox's home in the late 1840s.
14. Mary Howitt, *An Autobiography*, 189.
15. Linda H. Peterson, "Collaborative Life Writing as Ideology: The Auto/biographies of Mary Howitt and her Family," 177.
16. See Linda Peterson, "Mother-Daughter Productions: Mary Howitt and Anna Mary Howitt in *Howitt's Journal, Household Words* and Other Mid-Victorian Publications," for further discussion of Anna Mary's professionalization as an illustrator of her parents' works.
17. 1844 letter from Mary Howitt to her sister Anna Harrison, quoted in Amice Lee,

Laurels and Rosemary, 164. Lee, a granddaughter of Anna Harrison, compiled this study primarily from letters between the sisters passed down through the family.

18. Anna Mary's translation of Hans Christian Andersen's *The Red Shoes* appeared in the 11 September 1847 issue of *Howitt's Journal* (171–73). Her sister, Margaret, fifteen years her junior, worked as a professional translator before becoming a nun toward the end of her life.

19. Edward Bateman, who proposed before she left for Germany, wanted to marry in 1852. Anna Mary, in love with Bateman though nervous about the impact of marriage on her career, preferred to remain in Munich, and ultimately the engagement was broken. In a letter of 25 October 1850 written to Barbara Leigh Smith from Munich, Anna Mary happily reveals that Bateman "had as great a horror of marriage seemingly as you or I," in Lenore Ann Beaky, "The Letters of Anna Mary Howitt to Barbara Ann Smith Bodichon" 2: 145. By 1854, she is clear in her determination that she prefers to remain unmarried. She writes to Barbara, "I wonder myself how anyone has the energy to think of getting married. To me, in my 'used up' state of mind even the preparations to say nothing of what would probably come after—would be a profound bore and worry! Is this not an unusual state of mind for a woman to be in!!!!!" (Beaky 2: 175). Following her nervous breakdown in 1856, Anna Mary married Alaric Alfred Watts, the son of close family friends, in 1859.

20. Letter from Anna Mary Howitt to Anne Leigh Smith, dated November 1854, in Beaky 2: 185.

21. Carl Ray Woodring, *Victorian Samplers: William and Mary Howitt,* 115.

22. For further discussion of Leigh Smith's life and work, see Pam Hirsch, *Barbara Leigh Smith Bodichon,* and Sheila Herstein, *A Mid-Victorian Feminist: Barbara Leigh Smith Bodichon.* I will use the name Leigh Smith rather than Bodichon here, as Barbara's marriage in 1857 and her removal to Algeria marks an unofficial end to the sisterhood.

23. "Domestic Life," *The English Woman's Journal* II (October 1858): 75.

24. The Victoria Press, named in honor of the Queen, was run entirely by women compositors. After its successful launch, Parkes wrote to Leigh Smith, "Here are women in the trade at last! One dream of my life!" Quoted in Hirsch, 192.

25. Under British law, any income a woman earned for her work was legally her husband's. Despite Leigh Smith's active campaigning throughout the 1850s and '60s, the Married Woman's Property Act was not passed until 1893.

26. Barbara Leigh Smith, *Women and Work,* 6–7.

27. Regenia Gagnier, *The Insatiability of Human Wants,* 1. She explains that in market society, identities become tied to "whether [individuals] make nails, automobiles, books, contracts, breakfast, hotel beds, music, speeches, or babies" (3).

28. Jane Rendall, *The Origins of Modern Feminism,* 135. Rendall is quoting Bessie Raynor Parkes, original emphasis included.

29. Carolyn Maibor presents these ideas in *Labor Pains* in relation to Emerson, Hawthorne, and Alcott.

30. Bessie Raynor Parkes, "What Can Educated Women Do?" 151.

31. Jennifer Ruth, *Novel Professions,* 4 and 34. Also see Poovey, *Uneven Developments,* for discussion of the role of the novel in the construction of the professional writer in Victorian England.

32. Leigh Smith and Parkes wore Balmoral boots with colored laces and skirts shortened several inches above the ankle for ease of walking during their European tour in 1850,

when this sketch was probably made. They also refused to wear corsets in the belief "that women should be freed from the fetters of contemporary clothes." See Hester Burton, *Barbara Bodichon*, 39. A drawing of Parkes in the boots and shortened skirt, very much in the same mode as "Ye Newe Generation," is also found in the Barbara Leigh Smith Bodichon papers held at Girton College, Cambridge.

33. Beaky 2: 145.

34. Mary and Margaret Gillies were veritable "sisters in art," Mary being an author and Margaret a successful painter who inspired and encouraged Anna Mary. Intimate friends of the Howitt family, the Gillies sisters lived and worked together until their deaths and may have shaped Anna Mary's conception of a productive sisterhood. Mary wrote frequently about Associated Homes for *Howitt's Journal* and elsewhere, and Margaret painted portraits of contemporary intellectuals and radicals, including William and Mary Howitt (see chapter 7).

35. Matthew Rowlinson, "Reading Capital with Little Nell."

36. Charles Dickens, *Master Humphrey's Clock*, 15.

37. The exchange of woman for painting recalls Balzac's *Le Chef-d'oeuvre inconnu* (1831), as does the opening scene of the novel, where Wood's entry into the Silvers's shop followed by Lizzy echoes Frenhofer's arrival at Mabuse's studio followed by the young Poussin. Like her French contemporaries, George Sand and Marceline Desbordes-Valmore, Howitt appears to be writing against the overt misogyny of Balzac's fiction and reclaiming the subject position for the female character.

38. Here I am thinking specifically of the pair of original illustrations of Nell in chapter 1 of *The Old Curiosity Shop* (London: Penguin, 2000). The first, by Daniel Maclise, shows the child in the shop with her grandfather and the narrator (10), and the second, by Samuel Williams, corresponds to the narrator's dream of Nell asleep in a room chock-a-block with curiosities (21). Both highlight the contrast between the old and musty objects and the youthful innocence of Nell, portending her ultimate demise.

39. Letter from Dante Gabriel Rossetti to William Michael Rossetti, dated 23 May 1854. In *Ruskin, Rossetti, Preraphaelitism*, ed. W. M. Rossetti, 7–8. Rossetti's drawing is unlocated.

40. Griselda Pollock and Deborah Cherry have argued that Siddal functions within Pre-Raphaelitism "as a symbol of the whole movement" and was treated by both the artists and critics as "woman as sign" rather than a signifying subject. See "Woman as Sign in Pre-Raphaelite Literature," in Pollock, *Vision and Difference*, 91–116. In *Painting Women*, Cherry contends that Siddal's poetry, drawings, and watercolors "addressed the desires of women and for women, women looking and the look of women" (191), issues also central to Howitt's story. Siddal's own artistic production began in 1852, the same year *Sisters in Art* was published.

41. Charles Tennyson writes, "Alfred had many talks with Mary Howitt about the education and social position of women" and planned on "composing a poem on these subjects." In *Alfred Tennyson*, 202.

42. Beaky 2: 123.

43. Letter dated 5 January 1848, in Beaky 2: 127.

44. Alfred Tennyson, *The Princess*, Prologue, 127; I, 129; II, 79–80.

45. "The woman's cause is man's: they rise or sink / Together, dwarfed or godlike, bond or free" (*The Princess* VII, 242–43). Donald E. Hall observes, "Even judged by the modest feminist ideals of his period, Tennyson's poem is clearly reactionary; its sexual politics may

be covert, but *The Princess* dramatizes a harsh and relentless oppression of women," in "The Anti-Feminist Ideology of Tennyson's *The Princess*," 49.

46. William Howitt, "Literary Notices. *The Princess, a Medley*, by Alfred Tennyson," 28.

47. Quoted in Woodring 107.

48. AMH to Barbara Leigh Smith c. 1850. Cambridge University Library Association, ms. 7621.

49. Letter to Barbara Leigh Smith dated 10 February 1851, in Beaky 2: 157.

50. Aside from Silver's fortune, Alice's school is endowed with Dr Falkland's "matchless anatomical museum," Giuseppe's casts, and Mrs Cohen's house and gardens in Wimbledon for a country studio. All who encounter the women offer their economic and intellectual support of the project in this utopian tale.

51. In 1855 Howitt exhibited *The Sensitive Plant*, a diptych based on Shelley's poem of the same name, and her image of *Margaret at the Well*, from Goethe's *Faust*, also engaged a literary theme. *Boadicea*, however, was notably ambitious in its epic historical theme.

52. Joanna Boyce also exhibited an *Elgiva* in 1855 that was praised by Ruskin for its portrayal of the noblewoman's despair. Like Howitt, Boyce selected a heroic female subject from British history who was a political victim, but her image of gentle sorrow was more palatable to the critics than Howitt's wrathful Boadicea.

53. See Tacitus, *The Annals*, Book XIV, 31–37.

54. Howitt exhibited one final image, *From a Window*, at the Society of Female Artists exhibition in 1858. As described in "The Society of Female Artists," *The Athenaeum* (3 April 1858), the scene is "a poetical autumn sunset seen from a window" (439).

55. The earlier painting, taken from *Faust*, was in fact entitled *Margaret at the Well*. Gretchen, a diminutive form of Margaret, is also used by Goethe in the text.

56. The entire text of the review of *Boadicea* can be found in "Fine Arts," *The Athenaeum* (7 June 1856): 718.

57. Letter dated 15 January 1855, in Beaky 2: 202.

58. Lee, *Laurels and Rosemary*, 217.

59. Lee, 217.

60. John Ruskin, *The Works of John Ruskin* 14: 54.

61. Pamela Gerrish Nunn, "The Woman Question: Ruskin and the Female Artist," 175.

62. In a letter of 1855 in which he hoped to persuade Siddal to accept his offer of support, Ruskin admitted "Perhaps I have said too much of my wish to do this [i.e., buy her artwork] for Rossetti's sake." In *Ruskin, Rossetti, PreRaphaelitism*, 63.

63. Ruskin to Siddal, May 1855, in *Ruskin, Rossetti, PreRaphaelitism*, 89.

64. Mrs. Harry Coghill, ed., *The Autobiography and Letters of Mrs Oliphant*, 36.

65. William Michael Rossetti, *Some Reminiscences*, 171.

66. Beaky 2: 228.

67. Peterson, "Collaborative Life Writing," 195.

68. Marlene Tromp, "Spirited Sexuality: Sex, Marriage and Victorian Spiritualism," 68.

69. Alex Owen, *The Darkened Room: Women, Power and Spiritualism in Late Victorian England*, 6.

70. Anna Mary Howitt Watts, *Pioneers of the Spiritual Reform*, 268.

71. Rachel Oberter, "Spiritualism and the Visual Imagination in Victorian Britain," 279.

Notes to Chapter 4

72. Thornycroft's wife, Mary Thornycroft, was one of the most successful female sculptors in Britain and the mother of a "dynasty" of children, including three daughters, who also pursued careers in art. See McCracken, "Sculptor Mary Thornycroft and Her Artist Children."

Chapter 4

1. W. J. T. Mitchell, "Space and Time," 112.
2. Peter Sahlins observes that national identity is "contingent and relational: it is defined by the social or territorial boundaries drawn to distinguish the collective self and its implicit negation, the other." *Boundaries*, 271.
3. See Rancière, *On the Shores of Politics*.
4. Appiah, *Cosmopolitanism*, 4.
5. Mellor, "Embodied Cosmopolitanism," 294.
6. Although she came to be known as Lady Morgan following her marriage in 1812, I will use the name Sydney Owenson here, as I will be primarily discussing her earlier work, published under the name Owenson before her marriage.
7. John Claiborne Isbell, *The Birth of European Romanticism*, 5.
8. Moore, "Acts of Union," 114.
9. Ellen Peel and Nanora Sweet, "*Corinne* and the Woman as Poet in England," 215. Peel and Sweet refer here to *Corinne* and *Aurora Leigh*.
10. W. Hepworth Dixon recounts that Owenson was identified with the fictional Princess of Innismore, "and until her marriage she was always known in society by the sobriquet Glorvina." *Lady Morgan's Memoirs* 1: 277.
11. Quoted in Gutwirth, *Madame de Staël, Novelist*, 259.
12. See Patrick Vincent, *The Romantic Poetess*, 97–121.
13. In a letter of 1808, Owenson recounts that she and Lady Stanley "sat up till two this morning talking of *Corinne*" (*Memoirs* 1: 324), and ten years later she identifies Staël as a writer "of genius, governed by principle . . . from whose works I had received infinite pleasure, and (as a woman, I may add) infinite pride" (*France* 2: 383–84). In turn, Staël was reported to have had Owenson's *The Princess* read to her on her deathbed (Campbell, *Lady Morgan*, 149). Nonetheless, the two women never met.
14. See Gutwirth, *Twilight of the Goddesses*.
15. Susan Tenenbaum, "*Corinne*: Political Polemics and the Theory of the Novel," 160.
16. Mme de Staël, *Corinne, ou l'Italie* (Gallimard, 1985), 28. Translations are my own. For an excellent version of the novel in English, see *Corinne, or Italy*, translated by Sylvia Raphael.
17. Owenson, *The Wild Irish Girl*, 5.
18. I use the term "hybridity" in terms of Staël's work to signal a cultural and national mixture that is at once subversive and productive. For discussion of hybridity as "cultural mixture and border crossing," see Deborah Kapchan and Pauline Turner Strong, "Theorizing the Hybrid." It is interesting to note that Owenson herself was the daughter of an Irish Catholic father and an English, Protestant mother, echoing Corinne's divided heritage.
19. For discussion of gender and nation see Anne McClintock, "No Longer in a Future Heaven: Gender, Race and Nationalism."

20. J. Th. Leerssen, "How *The Wild Irish Girl* Made Ireland Romantic," 99.
21. Kari Lokke, "Children of Liberty: Idealist Historiography in Staël, Shelley and Sand," 505.
22. April Alliston, "Transnational Sympathies, Imaginary Communities," 145.
23. Larousse, *Grand Dictionnaire universel du XIXe siècle* (Paris, 1873), entry for "Haudebourg-Lescot."
24. Landon, *Salon de 1810*, 104.
25. See Landon, *Annales du Musée et l'école moderne des Beaux-Arts. Salon de 1831*, 139–40.
26. Béraud, *Annales de l'école française des Beaux-Arts*, 156.
27. Blanc, "Appendice: Mme Haudebourt-Lescot" 3: 47. Blanc adds that Haudebourt-Lescot is part of the family of "petits peintres," a denigration that reflects not only on her gender but also on her status as a genre painter, one of the least prestigious forms within Blanc's institutional hierarchies.
28. Valabrègue, "Les Femmes artistes du XIXe siècle: Madame Haudebourt-Lescot," 103–4.
29. Sparrow, *Women Painters of the World*, 180.
30. F. d'O., "Nécrologie. Madame Haudebourt-Lescot," 320.
31. Quoted in F. d'O, "Nécrologie. Madame Haudebourt-Lescot," 320.
32. Letter quoted in Henri Lapauze, *Histoire de l'Académie de France à Rome*, 83–85.
33. *Lettres à David, sur le Salon de 1819 par quelques élèves de son école*, 33.
34. See Richard Brettell and Caroline Brettell, *Painters and Peasants in the Nineteenth Century;* Pierre Gassier, *Léopold Robert et les peintres de l'Italie romantique;* and Laurence Chesneau-Dupin, *Jean-Victor Schnetz, 1787–1870: Couleurs d'Italie*, for discussion of these male painters of the Italian genre scene, landscape, and peasants. In all of these studies Haudebourt-Lescot is mentioned in passing, but not analyzed in any depth.
35. In a peculiar twist, this portrait of Haudebourt-Lescot was identified as an image of Aurore Dudevant (George Sand) in an article by Lyndon Orr entitled "Famous Affinities of History: The Story of George Sand," in *Munsey's Magazine* 43.4 (July 1910): 495. Haudebourt-Lescot painted an early portrait of Sand that was in the collection of Antonin Proust. The image, unlocated today, is reproduced in "Lettres familières de George Sand," *Revue encyclopédique* (1893), 855.
36. Melissa Calaresu, "From the Street to the Stereotype: Urban Space, Travel, and the Picturesque in Late Eighteenth-Century Naples," 189.
37. Michel de Certeau, *The Practice of Everyday Life*, 19.
38. Neil McWilliam, "Country Life," 79.
39. While Greuze spent two years in Italy and produced some Italian scenes, his most influential work was centered on the French domestic genre scene. For discussion, see Richard Wrigley, "Genre Painting with Italy in Mind."
40. Barker, "Putting the Viewer in the Frame," 108.
41. Kirshenblatt-Gimblett, "Objects of Ethnography" in *Exhibiting Cultures*, 432.
42. In *Maestà di Roma: D'Ingres à Degas, les artistes français à Rome*, ed. Olivier Bonfait, 478.
43. The configuration of the French visitors in Lescot's scene resembles the groups of painters in Capet's 1808 portrait of Labille-Guiard in intriguing ways.
44. Lescot was rumored to have been the model for Canova's famous *Terpsichore*.
45. *Peintures pour un Château*, 110.

46. L. Jaud, *Les vies des Saints*, 18 janvier.
47. "Necrologie. Madame Haudebourt-Lescot," *Journal des Artistes*, 41.
48. Lourdes Font and Michele Majer, "*La Quatrième Unité:* Costume and Fashion in *Genre Historique* Painting," 215.
49. For a description of the ball and the costumes worn by the court, see Reiset, 367–72, and Bouchot, *Le Luxe français: La Restauration*, chapter 4, "Les Fêtes de Madame," 77–104. Eugène Lami executed a series of watercolors of the *Quadrille de Marie Stuart* that were turned into a commemorative lithograph album distributed to the guests (Bouchot 98).
50. Elizabeth I was not recognized as the legitimate heir of Henry VIII by many Catholics, thus making Mary Stuart the legitimate ruler in the minds of some.
51. Wright, "Walter Scott and French Art," 182.

Chapter 5

1. Mossman, "Disability, Ireland, and *The Wild Irish Girl*," 543.
2. Katie Trumpener, *Bardic Nationalism*, 132.
3. Ina Ferris, *The Romantic National Tale*, 50. Ferris quotes Owenson's "Prefatory Address" to the 1846 edition of *The Wild Irish Girl*.
4. Gilles Deleuze and Félix Guattari, "What Is a Minor Literature?" 18.
5. Anne K. Mellor, *Mothers of the Nation*, 105.
6. Deidre Lynch, "Domesticating Fictions and Nationalizing Women," 64.
7. Raphael Ingelbien, "Paradoxes of National Liberation: Lady Morgan, O'Connellism, and the Belgian Revolution," 110.
8. Henri Bouchot, *Le Luxe français: La Restauration*, 130.
9. In her discussion of contemporary artists in Paris, Owenson makes several mentions of the young women painters working at the Louvre (*France* 2: 21, 27), and in her lengthy note on ateliers she has visited, Mlle Lescot is the only female artist she names. She writes, "Among the female artists (and there are many of considerable talent), Mademoiselle Lescot holds a distinguished rank, for her admirable representations of the interior of churches, &c. &c. &c." (*France* 2: 37).
10. Croker complained in his screed against Owenson and *France:* "Our charges (to omit minor faults) fall readily under the heads of—Bad taste—Bombast and Nonsense—Blunders—Ignorance of the French Language and Manners—General Ignorance—Jacobinism—Licentiousness and Impiety" ("*France* by Lady Morgan," 264).
11. Quoted in Campbell, *Lady Morgan*, 179.
12. Owenson, *The Life and Times of Salvator Rosa*, iii.
13. Owenson, *The Princess; or The Beguine* 1: 30. Referred to hereafter in the text as *PB*.
14. In an early letter to her father, Owenson admitted that her first novel, *St. Clair*, was written "in imitation of *Werther*." Quoted in Campbell, *Lady Morgan*, 39.
15. Mitchell B. Frank, "The Nazarene *Gemeinshaft:* Overbeck and Cornelius," 52.
16. The Princess's use of costume to perform multiple identities shares much with Théophile Gautier's *Mademoiselle de Maupin*, which also appeared in 1835.
17. Christian Isobel Johnstone, "Lady Morgan's Princess," 113.
18. James Newcomer, *Lady Morgan the Novelist*, 78.

Chapter 6

1. Honoré de Balzac, "Avant-Propos," *La Comédie humaine* 1: 7.
2. Unlike Britain, where female Realist authors were not uncommon, there are few, if any, female French Realists. For discussion see Margaret Cohen, *The Sentimental Education of the Novel*. There she posits a definition of the sentimental social novel as a subgenre which developed as an alternative preferred by female authors to the Realist novel.
3. Albistur and Armogathe, *Histoire du féminisme français*, 253.
4. Quoted from a biographical entry in the dossier Angélique Arnaud at the Bibliothèque Marguerite Durand in Paris, in Bernadette Louis, ed., *Une Correspondance saint-simonienne*, 30.
5. Pamela Pilbeam, *French Socialists before Marx*, 77.
6. Enfantin's words, quoted in the *Tribune des femmes* 1: 193, 194, 222. Also see Claire Goldberg Moses and Leslie Rabine, *Feminism, Socialism, and French Romanticism*, 34.
7. The empty chair of the Female Messiah would remain forever unoccupied and signals the real absence of female power within the movement. For further discussion of women's roles in Saint-Simonianism, see Claire Goldberg Moses, *French Feminism in the Nineteenth Century*, 41–116.
8. Quoted in Jonathan Beecher, *Victor Considérant and the Rise and Fall of French Romantic Socialism*, 127.
9. Charles Fourier, *Oeuvres complètes* 1: 132–33.
10. Jeanne-Victoire, "Appel aux femmes," *La Femme libre* 1.1 (1832): 1–3.
11. Laure Adler, *A l'Aube du féminisme: Les premières journalistes*, 43.
12. Letter of 10 mai 1838 from Angélique Arnaud to Prosper Enfantin, quoted in Louis, *Une Correspondance saint-simonienne*, 31. Referred to hereafter in citations as *Corr*.
13. Caroline Simon (1802–53) and her husband Léon Simon were ardent Saint-Simonians who rose to the upper ranks (or "degrees") of the order and at one point directed a communal Saint-Simonian residence. In 1832 the couple separated, and Caroline's affair with Charles Duguet, a lawyer who joined the movement in 1829, resulted in an illegitimate son. Duguet left for Egypt in 1833 on Enfantin's apostolic mission to find the female Messiah. Duguet introduced Arnaud and Simon, who began their correspondence during his absence, and if Caroline was his lover, Angélique cherished a platonic love for him during this period.
14. See Georges Lubin, "Qui fut Angélique Arnaud," for two letters from Sand to Arnaud praising her work.
15. Arnaud published two more novels in the 1870s: *Une Tendre dévôte* (1874) and *La Cousine Adèle* (1879), as well as numerous political articles and pamphlets. Arnaud's final book was a collaborative study with her daughter Laure, on the Saint-Simonian musicologist François del Sarte.
16. Souvestre (1806–54) published widely during his short career and was a frequent contributor to the *Revue des Deux Mondes*. His more radical socialist/feminist/proletariat novels include *Echelle des femmes* (1835), *Riche et pauvre* (1836), and *Confessions d'un ouvrier* (1851). For further discussion see Glen Shortliffe, "Populism in the Novel before Naturalism."
17. Emile Souvestre, "Du Roman," 117. "Du Roman" also served as the preface to Souvestre's 1836 novel, *Riche et pauvre*.

18. Arnaud, *Clémence* 1: 1–2.

19. "In tracing what I conceive as the moralist's duties here, I have indicated the task of the novelist: for the novelist must show himself to be essentially a moralist if he does not want to descend to the condition of a childish story teller or an unworthy speculator" (7).

20. Married women, for example, were required to take on their husbands' nationalities and could not sign legal documents or even dispose of their own property without their husbands' permission. The 1816 prohibition of divorce is a theme in *Clémence* as well as in many of Sand's novels. For discussion of the Napoleonic Code and its effect on French women's rights, see Moses, *French Feminism in the Nineteenth Century*, 18–20.

21. Flora Tristan, *Méphis* 1: 100.

22. See Kriz and Kurz, *Legend, Myth, and Magic in the Image of the Artist*, 26–38.

23. Variations on the lives of the Old Masters were popular in the periodical press during the Romantic period, as contemporary authors and artists constructed a new image of artistic identity in the age of commercial production. For some of the more enduring myths of the artist, see Margot and Rudolf Wittkower, *Born under Saturn*.

24. The betrayal of Santa-Cortez to the police by Madame Gervois, a frustrated and flirtatious middle-aged occupant of the Hôtel du Lac, closely echoes Mlle Michonneau's betrayal of Vautrin to the authorities in *Le Père Goriot*.

25. Portia, the heroine of *The Merchant of Venice*, delivers her famous oratory "The quality of mercy is not strained / It droppeth as the gentle rain from heaven / Upon the place beneath. It is twice blest: / It blesseth him that gives and him that takes," in Act IV, scene i, dressed as a man in court, arguing against the technicalities of the law.

Chapter 7

1. While portraits were certainly included in the Salon and Academy exhibitions, the vast majority were intended exclusively for private consumption.

2. See Angela Rosenthal, "She's Got the Look," for the portrait as process. Also see Hans Gadamer, "The Ontology of the Work of Art and Its Hermeneutic," for discussion of the "occasionality" of the portrait.

3. Richard Brilliant, *Portraiture*, 90.

4. Tamar Garb, *The Painted Face: Portraits of Women in France, 1814–1914*, 19.

5. Lady Lindsay, "Some Recollections of Miss Margaret Gillies," 265.

6. Gillies was a friend of Anna Mary's parents, William and Mary Howitt, for many years, and the younger painter refers frequently to Gillies in her letters. Evans came to know Mary and Margaret Gillies in the 1860s when Charles Lewes, son of Evans's partner, George Henry Lewes, married Gertrude Hill, who lived with the Gillies sisters and her grandfather, Thomas Southwood Smith (Margaret's partner), from the time she was two until after her marriage. Social reformer Octavia Hill, Gertrude's sister and another of Southwood Smith's granddaughters referred to Gillies as "Aunt Margaret" (see *Life of Octavia Hill*), and Lewes and Eliot called the Gillies sisters "the Aunts."

7. Obituary for Margaret Gilles, *The Times* (London [26 July 1887]): 7. William Gillies, father of Margaret and Mary, was a London merchant who met with considerably less success than his brothers. Adam, Lord Gillies, served as Judge of the Court of the Exchequer in Scotland; another brother, John Gillies, was a scholar and historian who

translated Aristotle's *Ethics, Politics,* and *Rhetoric* and was appointed Historiographer Royal of Scotland. See Roget, *A History of the "Old Water-Colour" Society* 2: 372.

8. The Gillies sisters remained close friends of the Howitt family well into the 1870s. In her *Autobiography,* Mary Howitt described Mary and Margaret Gillies as follows: "the one an embodiment of peace and an admirable writer, but whose talent, like the violet, kept in the shade; the other, the warm hearted painter" (183).

9. Horne edited *Monthly Repository* with Mary Gillies in 1836–37 and went on to edit *A New Spirit of the Age.* He and Mary co-wrote several books for children, though Horne is better known for his long-term correspondence with Elizabeth Barrett Browning. In 1852 he left for Australia with William Howitt and his sons.

10. See Kathryn Gleadle, *The Early Feminists,* 33–70, for an overview of the movement.

11. For a history of the *Monthly Repository* and its authors, see Francis Mineka, *The Dissidence of Dissent: The Monthly Repository, 1806–1838.*

12. Letter from Margaret Gillies to Leigh Hunt dated 17 July 1838, in Luther Brewer, *My Leigh Hunt Library* 2: 232.

13. For discussion of the place of the miniature in English cultural history, see Marcia Pointon, "Surrounded with Brilliants."

14. Robin Jaffe Frank, *Love and Loss: American Portrait and Mourning Miniatures,* 1.

15. John Murdoch et al., *The English Miniature,* 192.

16. Martin Archer Shee lambasted miniature painters in his *Rhymes on Art* (1805), disparaging them as "graphic dunces" who "degrade the pencil" (31–32). In a lengthy note he intoned, "from the prompt means of subsistence which miniature painting affords to every manufacturer of a face, it will always be the refuge of imbecility: a refuge for the poor and disappointed in art; where all who want the vigour that impels to higher game, or the means to support a longer pursuit, will sit down with humbled expectations, consoled by the reflection, that if fame be more confined, their profit is less precarious" (32–33).

17. Katherine Coombs, *The Portrait Miniature in England,* 104.

18. Charles Dickens, *Nicholas Nickleby,* 121.

19. The sittings began in July 1843 and continued through the fall. In a letter to Margaret Gillies of 23 October 1843, Dickens wrote, "Would you like me to ask Mr. Maclise to look in, during the sitting? He has a mighty knowledge of my face, and expressed himself much struck with the 'spirit' of your portrait." In *The Letters of Charles Dickens* 3: 584–85.

20. Andrew Robertson, *Letters and Papers of Andrew Robertson.* For discussion of Robertson and the "New Style" of miniature painting, see Coombs 112–15.

21. Canon Ainger, a friend of Gillies in the final years of her life, noted that by 1839, "It becomes evident that Miss Gillies's reputation as a miniature painter was growing, and notably in the circles of poets and artists." In "Margaret Gillies," 65.

22. Caroline Roberts contends that Martineau "toppled the hierarchy of 'masculine' and 'feminine' language, initially taken for granted by her contemporaries" through "her imposition of 'feminine' discourse on 'masculine' preserves and modes." See *The Woman and the Hour,* 15–16.

23. Gillies painted more portraits of Martineau, but none was after the live model, as Martineau severed ties with Gillies because of her irregular living situation. Martineau would later complain about the unauthorized circulation of her likenesses.

24. Judith L. Fisher, "*Fraser's* 'Portraits' and the Construction of Literary Celebrity," 105.

25. See Patricia Marks, "Harriet Martineau: Fraser's Maid of [Dis]Honor," 28–34.
26. Yeldham, *Margaret Gillies RWS*, 21.
27. Samuel Smiles, "Harriet Martineau," *Brief Biographies*, 499.
28. William Howitt, "Harriet Martineau," *People's Journal*, 141. Howitt's article is accompanied by another of Gillies's portraits of Martineau.
29. Harriet Martineau, *Society in America*, 228.
30. Susan Bohrer, "Harriet Martineau: Gender, Disability and Liability," 25.
31. Mary Gillies, "Associated Homes," *Howitt's Journal* (1847): 174. The first installment of the tale, "A Labourer's Home," appeared in *Howitt's Journal* (1847), 61–64.
32. Mary Gillies, "Associated Homes for the Middle Class," *Howitt's Journal* (1847): 272. These same principles were embraced in Anna Mary Howitt's *Art Student in Munich* (see chapter 3).
33. Letter from Thomas Powell to William Wordsworth dated 20 July 1839. Quoted in Yeldham, *Margaret Gillies RWS*, 34–35.
34. Letter from Dora Wordsworth to Isabelle Fenton, quoted in Yeldham, *Margaret Gillies*, 36.
35. Letter in *Elizabeth Barrett to Miss Mitford*, ed. Miller, 148.
36. Wordsworth, *Sonnets*, 122.
37. Wordsworth, *Sonnets*, 123.
38. For Westall's engraving, see Hebron, *William Wordsworth*, 107.
39. Quoted in Yeldham, *Margaret Gillies*, 4.
40. Hunt, "Utility and Beauty," *London Journal* 23 (3 September 1834): 183.
41. Hunt, "Blue-Stocking Revels," 33.
42. A letter from Gillies to Hunt indicates that the poet had written to the painter to inquire about the prices of her miniature portraits. She replied that "my prices for miniatures are from ten guineas to twenty according to the size" but offered to paint Hunt for free. Given the constant financial woes of Hunt and his family, this generous act might be taken as an act of charity; by working without a commission, however, Gillies was free to paint the subject as she saw fit.
43. Dickens, *Bleak House*, 117. Dickens wrote of his characterization of Hunt as Skimpole, "I suppose it is the most exact portrait that was ever painted in words! . . . It is an absolute reproduction of a real man." *Bleak House*, 955.

Chapter 8

1. See Alexander and Sellars, *The Art of the Brontës*, for discussion of the artistic training and production of Charlotte, Branwell, Emily, and Anne, along with excellent reproductions of their identified work.
2. Letter from Charlotte Brontë to Robert Southey, 29 December 1836, quoted in Miller, *The Brontë Myth*, 3.
3. Review of *Tenant*, in *Spectator* (8 July 1848). See Miriam Allott, *The Brontës: The Critical Heritage*, 250. These words appear throughout the contemporary reviews of all of the Brontës' novels found in Allott's collection.
4. Miller, *The Brontë Myth*, 4.
5. Charlotte Brontë, "Biographical Notice of Ellis and Acton Bell," in Emily Brontë, *Wuthering Heights*, 30.

6. In a letter of 31 July 1848 to W. S. Williams, following the publication of *The Tenant of Wildfell Hall*, Charlotte wrote, "For my own part I consider the subject unfortunately chosen—it was one the author was not qualified to handle at once vigourously and truthfully—the simple and natural—quiet description and simple pathos are, I think, Acton Bell's forte. I liked 'Agnes Grey' better than the present work." In *The Brontës*, ed. T. J. Wise and J. A. Symington, 2: 241.

7. George Moore was among the first to call the narrative "clumsy" in his *Conversations in Ebury Street* (1924), and the phrase has resonated ever since.

8. Rachel Carnell, "Feminism and the Public Sphere in Anne Brontë's *The Tenant of Wildfell Hall*, 1.

9. N. M. Jacobs, "Gender and Layered Narrative in *Wuthering Heights* and *The Tenant of Wildfell Hall*," 207. Jacobs does not further develop the artistic metaphor.

10. In "The Case of Helen Huntingdon," Ian Ward presents an excellent overview of a married woman's legal status in Britain during the period when the novel is set. This "Divine Right of Husbands" (153) over their wives' lives and property was a focal point of the Victorian feminist movement and central to Barbara Leigh Smith's reform efforts in the Married Woman's Property campaign.

11. Andrea Westcott, "A Matter of Strong Prejudice: Gilbert Markham's Self Portrait," 214.

12. Edward Chitham contends that "Wildfell Hall is an old mansion which mocks Wuthering Heights, even in its initials." *A Life of Anne Brontë*, 142. Jill Matus traces similar intersections in "'Strong family likeness': *Jane Eyre* and *The Tenant of Wildfell Hall*."

13. The theme of children and flowers, developed in Helen's diary as she paints this portrait, is also reflected in one of Anne Brontë's paintings, *Portrait of a little girl with a posy*, of 1843. Helen's painting, as described by Gilbert ("It was a little child, seated on the grass with its lap full of flowers. The tiny features and large, blue eyes, smiling through a shock of light brown curls, shaken over the forehead as it bent above its treasure, bore a sufficient resemblance to those of the young gentleman before me to proclaim it a portrait of Arthur Graham in his early infancy" [44]), bears more than a passing resemblance to Brontë's own work. See *The Art of the Brontës*, plate XX.

14. In "The Voicing of Feminine Desire," Elizabeth Langland reads *The Tenant* as "a narrative of exchange" (112) that gives voice to repressed feminine desire, the expression of which "depends on transgression and exchange" (122). My reading of the portraits reflects this vision of desire and transgression.

15. Indiana similarly fulfills her domestic duties for her husband while refusing him domain over her body or soul. She tells Delmare, "I know that I am the slave and you are the lord. The law of the land has made you my master. You can tie up my body, bind my hands, control my actions. You have the right of the powerful and society confirms it in you; but you have no power, sir, over my will . . . You can silence me, but you cannot stop me from thinking." *Indiana*, 232.

16. As Gilbert's sister Rose complains when Gilbert is late to tea: "if it had been *me* now, I should have had no tea at all—if it had been Fergus, even, he would have had to put up with such as there was, and been told to be thankful, for it was far too good for him; but *you*—we can't do too much for you.—It's always so—if there's anything particularly nice at table, Mamma winks and nods at me to abstain from it, and if I don't attend to that, she whispers, 'Don't eat so much of that, Rose, Gilbert will like it for his supper'—*I'm* nothing at all—in the parlour it's 'Come Rose, put away your things, and

let's have the room nice and tidy against they come in; and keep up a good fire; Gilbert likes a cheerful fire.' In the kitchen—'Make that pie a large one, Rose, I dare say the boys'll be hungry;—and don't put too much pepper in, they'll not like it I'm sure'—or, 'Rose, don't put so many spices in the pudding, Gilbert likes it plain,' or 'Mind you put plenty of currants in the cake, Fergus likes plenty.' If I say, 'Well Mamma, *I* don't,' I'm told I ought not think of myself—'You know Rose, in all household matters, we have only two things to consider, first, what's proper to be done, and secondly, what's most agreeable to the gentlemen of the house—any thing will do for the ladies.'" Mrs Markham affirms her daughter's characterization of their household priorities, adding "And a very good doctrine too . . . Gilbert thinks so, I'm sure" (53).

17. Margaret Smith, Introduction to *The Tenant of Wildfell Hall,* xx.

Chapter 9

1. See Catherine Nesci's chapter on Sand, "Le Flâneur travesti dans *Histoire de ma vie,*" in *Le Flâneur et les flâneuses* for further discussion.
2. Anne McCall notes, "dans le cadre de la *Correspondance,* les envois d'autoportraits et de portraits picturaux de sa personne deviennent un outil puissant non point pour faire valoir sa supposée beauté mais pour sonder son identité troublée." See "Image furtive, idée fixe," 56.
3. For discussion of Sand's relationship to painting and contemporary painters (most notably Delacroix), see Godeau, ed., *George Sand, une nature d'artiste.*
4. George Sand, *Valentine,* 193.
5. With the *vous* of direct address, Sand proposes an encounter in the second paragraph between her reader ("vous") and a berrichon peasant: "Le caractère grave et silencieux du paysan n'est pas un des moindres charmes de cette contrée. Rien ne l'étonne, rien ne l'attire. Votre présence fortuite dans son sentier ne lui fera même pas détourner la tête, et, si vous lui demandez le chemin d'une ville ou d'une ferme, toute sa réponse consistera dans un sourire de complaisance, comme pour vous prouver qu'il n'est pas dupe de votre facétie. Le paysan du Berri ne conçoit pas qu'on marche sans bien savoir où l'on va" (193). Throughout the text she includes italicized words and definitions, such as "*pâtoir* (c'est le mot de pays)" (194), further emphasizing the "foreignness" of this world of peasants and pastures.
6. See Lukacher, *Maternal Fictions,* 61–108. Sand was raised by her aristocratic grandmother after her father's death, and the ambivalent maternal figure will be discussed below.
7. For discussion of Sand's own artistic skills, see Sophie Martin-Dehaye, *George Sand et la peinture.*
8. George Sand, *Correspondance* 1: 777, 801.
9. The first preface to *Indiana,* for example, employs this self-effacing strategy. There she writes, "il faudrait répondre à la critique qu'elle fait beaucoup trop d'honneur à une œuvre sans importance; que pour se prendre aux grandes questions de l'ordre social, il faut se sentir une grande force d'âme ou s'attribuer un grand talent, et que tant de présomption n'entre point dans la donnée d'un récit fort simple où l'écrivain n'a presque rien créé." See Sand, *Indiana,* 37.
10. See Thierry Bodin's *Présentation* in George Sand, *Elle et lui,* 29–31.

11. *Elle et lui* is, for example, mentioned only in passing or not at all in Naomi Schor's *George Sand and Idealism,* Isabelle Hoog Naginski's *George Sand: Writing for Her Life,* David Powell's edited collection *George Sand Today,* and Françoise Massardier-Kenney's *Gender in the Fiction of George Sand.*

12. Henry James, "She and He," 738. For discussion of James's fascination with Sand's affair with Musset, see Peter Collister, "Taking Care of Yourself: Henry James and the Life of George Sand."

13. Roberta White, *A Studio of One's Own: Fictional Women Painters and the Art of Fiction,* 13.

14. Albistur and Armogathe, *Histoire du féminisme français,* 253.

15. In an 1833 letter to Sand, Musset called her "mon cher Monsieur George Sand, qui est désormais pour moi, un homme de génie" (Musset, *Correspondance,* 69), while critic Jules Janin observed two years later, "George Sand, chez lui, c'est tour à tour un capricieux jeune homme de dix-huit ans, et une très jolie femme de vingt-cinq à trente ans; c'est un enfant de dix-huit ans qui fume et qui prise avec beaucoup de grace, c'est une grande dame dont l'esprit et l'imprévu vous étonnent et vous humilient," in *La Mode* (septembre 1835), 181. And as Balzac so famously observed of his friend and rival in 1838, "Elle est garçon, elle est artiste, elle est grande, généreuse, dévouée, *chaste,* elle a les grands traits de l'homme, *ergo* elle n'est pas femme." *Lettres à Madame Hanska* 1: 585.

16. Isabelle Naginski, *George Sand: Writing for Her Life,* 14.

17. Jeanne Fuchs, "George Sand and Alfred de Musset," 207. Fuchs points out that when they met, Sand, twenty-nine, and Musset, twenty-three, were already famous for *Indiana* and *Les Caprices de Marianne* and notorious for their unorthodox behavior. They became lovers shortly after they were introduced by Sainte-Beuve at a dinner party given by Buloz in June 1833.

18. For discussion of Troubadour painting, see Tscherny and Stair Sainty, *Romance and Chivalry.* A prime example of this tendency in literature is Balzac's *Le Chef d'oeuvre inconnu* of 1831/37, which focuses on the artistic initiation of Poussin in the early seventeenth century while rehearsing Balzac's nascent Realist aesthetic in the nineteenth.

19. See Henry Lavagne, "Les Maîtres mosaïstes: Entre l'Histoire et l'histoire d'art, les 'écarts' de la romancière," 155–62.

20. Musset complained, "I worked all day long, and in the evening I wrote ten lines and drank a bottle of brandy; she drank a liter of milk and wrote half a volume." Quoted in Brem, *George Sand: Un Diable de femme,* 38.

21. See Margaret Waller, *The Male Malady: Fictions of Impotence in the Nineteenth-Century French Novel.*

22. George Sand, *Oeuvres autobiographiques* 2: 161–62.

23. Massardier-Kenney, 149.

24. See Battersby, *The Gender of Genius,* 86.

25. Korsmeyer, *Gender and Aesthetics,* 29.

26. Naomi Schor, "The Portrait of a Gentleman," 125–26.

27. Leland S. Person, Jr., "Henry James, George Sand, and the Suspense of Masculinity," 526.

28. Following the death of her father when she was four, Sand was raised by her mother, Sophie Delaborde, a *femme du peuple,* and her wealthy aristocratic paternal grandmother, Mme Aurore Dupin de Francueil, the illegitimate daughter of the Maréchal de Saxe and

granddaughter of the King of Poland. The two women shared little but their love for the child and competed with one another for her affection; Sand would later observe that they were "as different in their natures as they were in their educations and their habits. They were truly the two extremes of our sex" (*Story of My Life,* 468). As Maryline Lukacher has shown, "the double structure of the mother-grandmother" was a source of gendered anxiety that was played out both in Sand's life and in her novels (where female doubles, often from disparate classes, are frequently found), while "the idea of 'two mothers' gives a new twist to the Freudian theories of castration anxiety and the uncanny" (11). Ultimately, her mother ceded Aurore to her grandmother in exchange for a financial settlement, and their relationship was fractured, though not entirely severed, by the force of the grandmother's will and Sophie's choice of money (for herself and for her daughter) over maternity. Sand in turn played a maternal role with many of her friends and lovers (most notably Musset and Flaubert) and had a famously troubled relationship with her own daughter. For discussion of "the intertwined issues of missing maternal origins, mourning, and a coming to writing" in Sand's work, see Janet Beizer, "Writing Origins: George Sand and the Story of Our Life," in *Thinking through the Mothers,* 57–101.

29. George Sand, *Le Château de Pictordu,* 41.

30. In the original manuscript, the sentence concluded, "et la rendrait folle ou idiote" (and would make her mad or an idiot), giving an even more powerful sense of the deleterious effect of the father's lessons on Diane. See *Château de Pictordu,* 308n32.

Conclusion

1. Laura Herford gained admission to the Royal Academy Schools following a "brilliantly orchestrated campaign" when she submitted a drawing with her initials rather than her full name. See Cherry, "Artists and Militants," in *Beyond the Frame,* 9.

2. Gabriel Weisberg, *Overcoming All Obstacles,* 16.

3. Garb, *Sisters of the Brush,* 7.

4. Quoted from the British press reviews of Bonheur's *Horse Fair* in Lepelle de Bois-Gallais, *Biographie de Rosa Bonheur,* 45. The first quotation is from the *Illustrated Daily News* (21 July 1855), and the second from *Daily News* (19 July 1855).

5. Gretchen van Slyke, *Rosa Bonheur: The Artist's (Auto)Biography,* xii.

6. Garb, *The Painted Face,* 99. For discussion of the painting, see "Framing Femininity in Manet's *Portrait of Mlle E.G.,*" 58–99.

7. Wolff, *Feminine Sentences,* 1.

8. See, for example, Diane Gillespie, *The Sisters' Arts: The Writing and Painting of Virginia Woolf and Vanessa Bell.*

9. Woolf, *A Room of One's Own,* 93.

10. Woolf, *To the Lighthouse,* 51. "Women can't paint, women can't write" is repeated several more times in the text, including pp. 88, 93, 162, 163, and 200.

11. Woolf, *Three Guineas,* 4.

12. As the activist Guerrilla Girls remind us, female artists remain today an underrepresented, often invisible presence in the world of high art. In an open letter to the Broad Foundation, on the opening of the Broad Museum of Contemporary Art in Los Angeles in 2008, the Guerrilla Girls deplored the fact that 87 percent of the artists shown in the opening exhibit were male, and 97 percent were white. They wrote: "To open such

an important project like BCAM with a show that is so white (97%) and so male (87%) gives the impression that the contemporary art world is not diverse, and that the government of L.A. county and the trustees of the museum don't care, or are asleep at the wheel . . . Women have been graduating from art schools in the same number or greater than men for decades. Why not work with the Broad Education Foundation to find out what happens to them in the art market?" See http://www.guerrillagirls.com/posters/dear-estelibroad.shtml

13. Rancière, *The Future of the Image*, 7.

Bibliography

Adams, William Bridges. "On the Condition of Women in England." *Monthly Repository* 7 (1833): 217–31.
Adhémar, Jean. "L'Enseignement académique en 1820: Girodet et son atelier." *Bulletin de la société de l'histoire de l'art français* (1933): 270–79.
Adler, Laure. *A l'aube du féminisme: les premières journalistes (1830–1850)*. Paris: Payot, 1979.
Agoult, Marie d.' *Nelida*. 1846. Trans. Lynn Hoggard. Albany: SUNY Press, 2003.
Ainger, Canon. "Margaret Gillies." *Hampstead Annual* (1899): 59–69.
Albistur, Maïté and Daniel Armogathe. *Histoire du féminisme français du moyen âge à nos jours*. Paris: des femmes, 1977.
Alexander, Christine and Jane Sellars. *The Art of the Brontës*. Cambridge: Cambridge University Press, 1995.
Allen, James Smith. *Popular French Romanticism: Authors, Readers, and Books in the Nineteenth Century*. Syracuse: Syracuse University Press, 1981.
Alliston, April. "Transnational Sympathies, Imaginary Communities." In *The Literary Channel*. Ed. Cohen and Dever. 133–48.
Allott, Miriam, ed. *The Brontës: The Critical Heritage*. London: Routledge & Kegan Paul, 1974.
Altick, Richard. *The Shows of London*. Cambridge: Harvard University Press, 1978.
Ambrière, Francis. *Le Siècle des Valmore: Marceline Desbordes-Valmore et les siens*. 2 vols. Paris: Seuil, 1987.
Anderson, Benedict. *Imagined Communities: Reflections on the Origin and Spread of Nationalism*. London: Verso, 1991.
Appiah, Kwame Anthony. *Cosmopolitanism: Ethics in a World of Strangers*. New York: Norton, 2006.
Aragon, Louis. "Deux poems inédits de Marceline Desbordes-Valmore et une lettre inédite de Victor Hugo." *Europe* (July 1948): 1–8.
Armstrong, Nancy. *Desire and Domestic Fiction: A Political History of the Novel*. Oxford: Oxford University Press, 1987.
Arnaud, Angélique. *Clémence*. 2 vols. Brussels: Hauman, 1841.
———. *La Comtesse de Servy*. Paris: Charpentier, 1838.
———. *Coralie l'inconstante*. Paris: Berquet et Pétion, 1843.
———. *La Cousine Adèle*. Paris: Dentu, 1879.
———. *François del Sarte, ses découvertes en esthétique, sa science, sa méthode*. Paris: Delagrave, 1882.

Athanassoglou-Kallmyer, Nina. "*Imago Belli:* Horace Vernet's *L'Atelier* as an Image of Radical Militarism under the Restoration." *The Art Bulletin* 68.2 (June 1986): 268–80.
Auerbach, Nina. *Communities of Women: An Idea in Fiction.* Cambridge: Harvard University Press, 1998.
Auricchio, Laura. *Adélaïde Labille-Guiard: Artist in the Age of Revolution.* Los Angeles: J. Paul Getty Museum, 2009.
Austen, Jane. *Pride and Prejudice.* London: Penguin, 1996.
Balayé, Simone. "Madame de Staël, Napoléon, et la mission de l'écrivain." *Europe: Revue littéraire mensuelle* 480–81 (1969): 124–37.
Ballot, Marie-Juliette. *Une Elève de David: La Comtesse Benoist, l'Emilie de Demoustier, 1768–1826.* Paris: Plon, 1914.
Balzac, Honoré. *La Comédie humaine.* 12 vols. Paris: Gallimard-Pléiade, 1976–81.
———. *Lettres à Madame Hanska.* 4 vols. Paris: Le Delta, 1967–71.
Bann, Stephen. "Print Culture and the Illustration of History: An Anglo-French Perspective." *Crossing the Channel.* Ed. Patrick Noon. 28–37.
———. "The Studio as Scene of Emulation: Marceline Desbordes-Valmore's *L'Atelier d'un peintre.*" *French Studies* 61.1 (2007): 26–35.
Barbey d'Aurevilly, Jules. "Marceline Desbordes-Valmore." *Le XIXe siècle: Les Oeuvres et les hommes.* 3e série, *Les Poètes.* Geneva: Slatkine Reprints, 1968. 145.
Barker, Emma. "Putting the Viewer in the Frame: Greuze as Sentimentalist." In *French Genre Painting in the Eighteenth Century.* Ed. Philip Conisbee. Washington, DC: National Gallery of Art, 2007. 105–27.
Battersby, Christine. *Gender and Genius: Towards a Feminist Aesthetics.* Bloomington: Indiana University Press, 1989.
Baudelaire, Charles. *Oeuvres complètes.* Ed. Claude Pichois. 2 vols. Paris: Gallimard, 1975–76.
Beaky, Lenore. "The Letters of Anna Mary Howitt to Barbara Ann Smith Bodichon." 2 vols, Diss. Columbia University, 1974.
Beecher, Jonathan. *Charles Fourier: The Visionary and His World.* Berkeley: University of California Press, 1986.
———. *Victor Considérant and the Rise and Fall of French Romantic Socialism.* Berkeley: University of California Press, 2001.
Beizer, Janet. *Thinking through the Mothers: Reimagining Women's Biographies.* Ithaca: Cornell University Press, 2009.
Benjamin, Walter. "The Flâneur." In *Charles Baudelaire: A Lyric Poet in the Era of High Capitalism.* London: Verso, 1983. 33–66.
———. "The Work of Art in the Age of Mechanical Reproduction." In *Illuminations: Essays and Reflections.* New York: Schocken, 1969. 217–51.
Béraud, Antony. *Annales de l'école française des Beaux-Arts.* Paris: Pillet Aîné, 1827.
Bermingham, Ann. *Learning to Draw: Studies in the Cultural History of a Polite and Useful Art.* New Haven: Yale University Press, 2000.
Bertrand-Jennings, Chantal. *Un Autre mal du siècle: Le romantisme des romancières, 1800–1846.* Toulouse: Presses Universitaires du Mirail, 2005.
Blanc, Charles. "Appendice: Mme Haudebourt-Lescot." In *Histoire des Peintres de toutes les écoles. Ecole Française.* 3 vols. Paris: Jules Renouard. 47–48.
———. "Le Salon des arts unis." *Gazette des Beaux-Arts* (1 February 1861): 189–92.
Blom, Ida, Karen Hagemann, and Catherine Hall, eds. *Gendered Nations: Nationalisms and Gender Order in the Long Nineteenth Century.* Oxford: Berg, 2000.
Bloom, Harold. *The Anxiety of Influence.* Oxford: Oxford University Press, 1973.
Bodek, Evelyn. "Salonnières and Bluestockings: Educated Obsolescence and Germinating Feminism." *Feminist Studies* 3 (1976).
Bohrer, Susan. "Harriet Martineau: Gender, Disability and Liability." *Nineteenth-Century Contexts* 25.1 (2003): 21–37.

Bolster, Richard. *Stendhal, Balzac et le féminisme romantique*. Paris: Minard, 1970.
Bonfait, Olivier, ed. *Maestà di Roma: D'Ingres à Degas, les artistes français à Rome*. Rome: Electa, 2003.
Bouchot, Henri. *Le Luxe Français: La Restauration*. Paris: La Librairie Illustrée, 1893.
Bourdieu, Pierre. *Distinction: A Social Critique of the Judgment of Taste*. Cambridge: Harvard University Press, 1987.
———. *The Field of Cultural Production*. New York: Columbia University Press, 1993.
Boutin, Aimée. "Marceline Desbordes-Valmore and the Sorority of Poets." *Women in French Studies* (2001): 165–80.
———. *Maternal Echoes: The Poetry of Marceline Desbordes-Valmore and Alphonse de Lamartine*. Newark: University of Delaware Press, 2001.
Bowie, Theodore. *The Painter in French Fiction*. Chapel Hill: University of North Carolina Press, 1950.
Brem, Anne-Marie. *George Sand: Un diable de femme*. Paris: Gallimard, 1997.
Brettell, Richard and Caroline Brettell. *Painters and Peasants in the Nineteenth Century*. New York: Skira, 1983.
Brewer, Luther, ed. *My Leigh Hunt Library*. 2 vols. Cedar Rapids: Torch Press, 1932.
Brilliant, Richard. *Portraiture*. Cambridge: Harvard University Press, 1991.
Brontë, Anne. *Agnes Grey*. 1847. Oxford: Oxford University Press, 1998.
———. *The Tenant of Wildfell Hall*. Oxford: Oxford University Press, 1992.
Brontë, Charlotte. "Biographical Notice of Ellis and Acton Bell." In Emily Brontë, *Wuthering Heights*. 30–36.
———. *Jane Eyre*. 1847. London: Penguin, 2006.
Brontë, Emily. *Wuthering Heights*. 1847. London: Penguin, 1965.
Bruel, F. L. "Girodet et les dames Robert." *Bulletin de la société de l'art français* (1912): 76–93.
Bruson, Jean-Marie and Anne Foray-Carlier. "Les plaisirs de la ville." In *Au temps des merveilleuses: la société française sous le Directoire et le Consulat*. Paris: Musée Carnavalet, 2005. 112–24.
Bryson, Norman. *Word and Image: French Painting of the Ancien Régime*. Cambridge: Cambridge University Press, 1981.
Burke, Edmund. *A Philosophical Enquiry into the Origin of our Ideas of the Sublime and Beautiful*. Notre Dame: University of Notre Dame Press, 1968.
Burton, Hester. *Barbara Bodichon*. London: John Murray, 1949.
Burton, Richard. "The Unseen Seer, or Proteus in the City: Aspects of a Nineteenth-Century Parisian Myth." *French Studies* 42 (1988): 50–88.
Butler, Judith. *Gender Trouble: Feminism and the Subversion of Identity*. New York: Routledge, 1990.
Buzard, James. *The Beaten Track: European Tourism, Literature and the Ways to 'Culture' 1800–1918*. Oxford: Clarendon, 1993.
Calaresu, Melissa. "From the Street to the Stereotype: Urban Space, Travel, and the Picturesque in Late Eighteenth-Century Naples." *Italian Studies* 62.2 (2007): 189–203.
Campbell, Mary. *Lady Morgan: The Life and Times of Sydney Owenson*. London: Pandora, 1988.
Carlyle, Thomas. *On Heroes, Hero Worship, and the Heroic in History*. 1841. Garden City, NY: Doubleday, 1963.
Carnell, Rachel. "Feminism and the Public Sphere in Anne Brontë's *The Tenant of Wildfell Hall*." *Nineteenth-Century Literature* 53.1 (1998): 1–24.
Castiglione, Baldesarre. *The Book of the Courtier*. London: Penguin, 1976.
Castle, Terry. "Lab'ring Bards: Birth Topoi and English Poetics 1660–1820." *Journal of English and Germanic Philology* 78 (1979): 193–208.
Certeau, Michel de. *The Practice of Everyday Life*. Berkeley: University of California Press, 1984.
Cherry, Deborah. *Beyond the Frame: Feminism and Visual Culture, Britain 1850–1900*. London: Routledge, 2000.
———. *Painting Women: Victorian Women Artists*. London: Routledge, 1993.
———. "Women Artists and the Politics of Feminism 1850–1900." *Women in the Victorian Art World*. Ed. Orr. 49–69.

Chesneau-Dupin, Laurence. *Jean-Victor Schnetz, 1787–1870: Couleurs d'Italie*. Musée du Château de Flers, 2000.
Chitham, Edward. *A Life of Anne Brontë*. Oxford: Blackwell, 1991.
Christ, Carol. "'The Hero as Man of Letters': Masculinity and Victorian Nonfiction Prose." *Victorian Sages and Cultural Discourse: Renegotiating Gender and Power*. Ed. Thaïs Morgan. New Brunswick: Rutgers University Press, 1990. 19–45.
Chu, Petra. "Portrait of the Artist as a Young Man: Self-Invention and Promotion in the Early Self-Portraits of Gustave Courbet." In *Images de l'Artiste–Künstlerbilder*. Ed. Griener and Schneemann.
Clawson, Mary Ann. *Constructing Brotherhood: Class, Gender, and Fraternalism*. Princeton: Princeton University Press, 1989.
Codell, Julie F. "Artists' Biographies and the Anxieties of National Culture." *Victorian Review* (2001): 1–35.
Coghill, Mrs. Harry, ed. *The Autobiography and Letters of Mrs Oliphant*. New York: Dodd Mead, 1899.
Cohen, Margaret. *The Sentimental Education of the Novel*. Princeton: Princeton University Press, 1999.
——— and Carolyn Dever, eds. *The Literary Channel: The Inter-National Invention of the Novel*. Princeton: Princeton University Press, 2002.
——— and Christopher Prendergast, eds. *Spectacles of Realism: Gender, Body, Genre*. Minneapolis: University of Minnesota Press, 1995.
Cole, Thomas and Mary Pardo, eds. *Inventions of the Studio, Renaissance to Romanticism*. Chapel Hill: University of North Carolina Press, 2005.
———. "Origins of the Studio." In *Inventions of the Studio*. 1–35.
Colley, Linda. *Britons: Forging the Nation 1707–1837*. New Haven: Yale University Press, 1992.
Collier, Peter and Robert Lethbridge, eds. *Artistic Relations: Literature and the Visual Arts in Nineteenth-Century France*. London: Yale University Press, 1994.
Collister, Peter. "Taking Care of Yourself: Henry James and the Life of George Sand." *Modern Language Review* 83 (1988): 556–70.
Comolli, Jean-Louis. "Machines of the Visible." In *The Cinematic Apparatus*. Ed. Teresa de Lauretis and Stephen Heath. London: Macmillan, 1980. 121–42.
Connolly, Claire. "'I Accuse Miss Owenson': *The Wild Irish Girl* as Media Event." *Colby Quarterly* 36.2 (2000): 98–115.
Coombs, Catherine. *The Portrait Miniature in England*. London: V & A Publications, 1998.
Corbett, David Peters. *The World in Paint: Modern Art and Visuality in England, 1848—1914*. University Park: Pennsylvania State University Press, 2004.
Coupin, P. A., ed. *Oeuvres posthumes de Girodet-Trioson*. 2 vols. Paris: Renouard, 1829.
Craik, Dinah Mulock. *Olive*. 1850. Oxford: Oxford University Press, 1996.
Crary, Jonathan. *Techniques of the Observer: On Vision and Modernity in the Nineteenth Century*. Cambridge: MIT Press, 1990.
Craveri, Benedetta. *The Age of Conversation*. New York: New York Review Books, 2005.
Croker, John Wilson. "*France* by Lady Morgan." In *Quarterly Review* 33 (April 1817): 260–85.
———. "Private Correspondence." *Freeman's Journal* (15 December 1806).
Crow, Thomas. *Emulation: Making Artists for Revolutionary France*. New Haven: Yale University Press, 1995.
Danahy, Martin. "Marceline Desbordes-Valmore et la fraternité des poètes." *Nineteenth-Century French Studies* 19.3 (1991): 386–93.
Davidson, Caroline. *Women's Worlds: The Art and Life of Mary Ellen Best 1809–1891*. New York: Crown, 1985.
DeJean, Joan. "Transnationalism and the Origins of the (French?) Novel." *The Literary Channel*. Ed. Cohen and Dever. 37–49.
Delaborde, Henri. "Les Dessins de M. Ingres." *Gazette des Beaux-Arts* (1 March 1861): 257–69.

Delécluze, E.-J. *Louis David: Son Ecole et son temps.* 1855. Paris: Macula, 1983.
Deleuze, Gilles and Félix Guattari. "What Is a Minor Literature?" In *Kafka: Toward a Minor Literature.* Minneapolis: University of Minnesota Press, 1986. 16–27.
Derrida, Jacques. "The Law of Genre." *Critical Inquiry* 7.1 (Autumn 1980): 55–81.
Desbordes-Valmore, Marceline. *L'Atelier d'un peintre: Scènes de la vie privée.* Lille: Miroirs, 1992.
———. *La Jeunesse de Marceline.* Ed. Boyer d'Agen. Paris: NRF, 1922.
———. *Les Oeuvres poétiques de Marceline Desbordes-Valmore.* Ed. M. Bertrand. 2 vols. Grenoble: Presses Universitaires de Grenoble, 1973.
Dickens, Charles. *Bleak House.* London: Penguin, 1971.
———. *Great Expectations.* London: Penguin, 2002.
———. *The Letters of Charles Dickens.* Vol. 3, 1842–43. Ed. Madeline House, Graham Storey, and Kathleen Tillotson. Oxford: Clarendon Press, 1974.
———. *Master Humphrey's Clock.* London: Chapman and Hall, n.d.
———. *Nicholas Nickleby.* London: Penguin, 2003.
———. *The Old Curiosity Shop.* Harmondsworth: Penguin, 2000.
———. "The True Bohemians of Paris." *Household Words* 4 (15 November 1851): 190–92.
Diderot, Denis. "Eloge de Richardson." *Oeuvres esthétiques de Diderot.* Paris: Garnier, 1968. 29–48.
Dixon, W. Hepworth, ed. *Lady Morgan's Memoirs.* 2 vols. London: Allen, 1863.
"Domestic Life." *The English Woman's Journal* II (October 1858): 75.
Doody, Margaret. *The True Story of the Novel.* New Brunswick: Rutgers, 1996.
Doria, Arnauld. *Gabrielle Capet.* Paris: Les Beaux-Arts, 1934.
Douglas, Mary. *Purity and Danger: An Analysis of the Concepts of Pollution and Taboo.* London: Ark, 1985.
Doy, Gen. *Women and Visual Culture in Nineteenth-Century France 1800–1852.* London: Leicester University Press, 1998.
Du Maurier, George. *Trilby.* 1894. Oxford: Oxford University Press, 1998.
Duncan, Carol. "Art Museums and the Ritual of Citizenship" in *Exhibiting Culture: The Poetics and Politics of Museum Display.* Ed. Karp and Lavine. 88–103.
Durdent, R. J. *Galerie des peintres français du Salon de 1812, ou Coup-d'oeil critique sur leurs principaux tableaux et sur les différent ouvrages de sculpture, architecture, et gravure.* Paris: Journal des arts, 1813.
Edgeworth, Maria. *Castle Rackrent.* 1800. Oxford: Oxford University Press, 1995.
Eger, Elizabeth and Lucy Peltz. *Brilliant Women: 18th-Century Bluestockings.* London: National Portrait Gallery, 2008.
Eley, Geoff and Ronald Grigor Suny, eds. *Becoming National: A Reader.* Oxford: Oxford University Press, 1996.
Ellet, Elizabeth Fries Lummis. *Women Artists in All Ages and Countries.* New York: Harper, 1859.
Este, Lauriane Fallay d.' *Le Paragone: Le Parallèle des arts.* Paris: Klincksieck, 1992.
Facos, Michelle and Sharon Hirsh, eds. *Art, Culture and National Identity in Fin-de-Siècle Europe.* Cambridge: Cambridge University Press, 2003.
F. d'O. "Nécrologie. Madame Haudebourt-Lescot." *L'Illustration* (18 janvier 1845): 320.
Ferris, Ina. "Narrating Cultural Encounter: Lady Morgan and the Irish National Tale." *Nineteenth-Century Literature* 51.3 (1996): 287–303.
———. *The Romantic National Tale and the Question of Ireland.* Cambridge: Cambridge University Press, 2002.
"Fine Arts." *The Athenaeum* (7 June 7 1856): 718.
Fisher, Judith L. "'In the Present Famine of Anything Substantial': *Fraser's* 'Portraits' and the Construction of Literary Celebrity; or 'Personality, Personality Is the Appetite of the Age.'" *Victorian Periodicals Review* 39.2 (2006): 97–135.
Flint, Kate. *The Victorians and the Visual Imagination.* Cambridge: Cambridge University Press, 2000.
———. *The Woman Reader, 1837–1914.* Oxford: Clarendon Press, 1993.

Font, Lourdes and Michele Majer. "*La Quatrième Unité:* Costume and Fashion in *Genre Historique* Painting." In *Romance and Chivalry.* Ed. Tscherny and Sainty. 194–217.
Foster, Hal, ed. *Vision and Visuality.* Seattle: Bay Press, 1988.
Foucault, Michel. *Discipline and Punish: The Birth of the Prison.* New York: Vintage, 1979.
———. *History of Sexuality.* Vol. 1. *An Introduction.* New York: Vintage, 1990.
———. *The Order of Things: An Archaeology of the Human Sciences.* New York: Vintage, 1973.
——— and Colin Gordon. *Power/Knowledge. Selected Interviews and Other Writings, 1972–1977.* New York: Pantheon, 1980.
Fourier, Charles. *Oeuvres complètes de Charles Fourier.* 12 vols. Paris: Anthropos, 1966–68.
Fox, William Johnson. "A Political and Social Anomaly." *The Monthly Repository* VI (1832): 637–42.
Fraisse, Geneviève. *La Raison des femmes.* Paris: Plon, 1992.
Frank, Mitchell B. "The Nazarene *Gemeinshaft:* Overbeck and Cornelius." In *Artistic Brotherhoods in the Nineteenth Century.* Ed. Morowitz and Vaughan. 48–66.
Frank, Robin Jaffee. *Love and Loss: American Portrait and Mourning Miniatures.* New Haven: Yale University Press, 2000.
Friedman, Susan Stanford. "Creativity and the Childbirth Metaphor: Gender Difference in Literary Discourse." In *Speaking of Gender.* Ed. Elaine Showalter. New York: Routledge, 1989.
Frow, John. *Genre.* London: Routledge, 2006.
Fuchs, Jeanne. "George Sand and Alfred de Musset: Absolution through Art in *La Confession d'un enfant du siècle.*" In *The World of George Sand.* Ed. Natalie Datlof, Jeanne Fuchs, and David Powell. New York: Greenwood Press, 1991.
Gabet, Charles. *Dictionnaire des Artistes de l'école française au XIXe siècle.* Paris: Vergne, 1831.
Gadamer, Hans-Georg. "The Ontology of the Work of Art and Its Hermeneutic Significance." In *Truth and Method.* London: Continuum, 1989. 101–69.
Gagnier, Regenia. *The Insatiability of Human Wants: Economics and Aesthetics in Market Society.* Chicago: University of Chicago Press, 2000.
Galichon, Emile. "Description des dessins de M. Ingres." *Gazette des Beaux-Arts* (15 March 1861): 343–62.
"Gallery of Illustrious Literary Portraits, No. XLII. Miss Harriet Martineau." *Fraser's Magazine* 8 (November 1833): 576.
Garb, Tamar. *The Painted Face: Portraits of Women in France, 1814–1914.* London and New Haven: Yale University Press, 2007.
———. *Sisters of the Brush: Women's Artistic Culture in Late Nineteenth-Century Paris.* New Haven: Yale University Press, 1994.
Garval, Michael. *A Dream of Stone: Fame, Vision, and Monumentality in Nineteenth-Century French Literary Culture.* Newark: University of Delaware Press, 2004.
Gaskell, Elizabeth. *The Life of Charlotte Brontë.* Harmondsworth: Penguin, 1997.
Gassier, Pierre. *Léopold Robert et les peintres de l'Italie romantique.* Neuchâtel: Musée des Beaux-Arts, 1983.
Gautier, Théophile. *Mademoiselle de Maupin.* 1835. Paris: Garnier-Flammarion, 1966.
Genette, Gérard. *Paratexts: Thresholds of Interpretation.* Cambridge: Cambridge University Press, 1997.
Gillespie, Diane. *The Sisters' Arts: The Writing and Painting of Virginia Woolf and Vanessa Bell.* Syracuse: Syracuse University Press, 1988.
Gillies, Mary. "Associated Homes." *Howitt's Journal* (1847): 61–64, 174, 272.
Giradin, Delphine Gay. *La Joie Fait Peur.* Paris: Levy Frères, 1867.
Gleadle, Kathyrn. *The Early Feminists: Radical Unitarians and the Emergence of the Women's Rights Movement, 1831–51.* New York: St. Martin's Press, 1995.
Glen, Heather, ed. *The Cambridge Companion to the Brontës.* Cambridge: Cambridge University Press, 2002.
Godeau, Jérôme, et al. *George Sand: Une Nature d'artiste.* Paris: Musée de la vie romantique, 2004.
Goncourt, Edmond and Jules Goncourt. *Histoire de la société française pendant le Directoire.* Paris: Gallimard, 1992.

Gotlieb, Marc. "Creation and Death in the Romantic Studio." In *Inventions of the Studio*. Ed. Cole and Pardo. 147–83.
Goulet, Andrea. *Optiques: The Science of the Eye and the Birth of Modern French Fiction*. Philadelphia: University of Pennsylvania Press, 2006.
Greenacre, Francis. *The Bristol School of Artists. Francis Darby and Painting in Bristol, 1810–1840*. Bristol: City Art Gallery, 1973.
Greer, Germaine. *The Obstacle Race: The Fortunes of Women Painters and Their Work*. 1979. London: Tauris Parke, 2001.
———. "'A tout prix devenir quelqu'un': The Women of the Académie Julian." In *Artistic Relations*. Ed. Collier and Lethbridge. 40–58.
Griener, Pascal and Peter Schneemann, eds. *Images de l'artiste–Künstlerbilder*. Bern: Peter Lang, 1998.
Grimstone, Mary Leman. "Female Education." *Monthly Repository* IX (1835): 106–12.
———. "Sketches of Domestic Life." *Monthly Repository* IX (1835): 145–53; 225–34, etc.; X (1836) 14–25, etc.
Guerlac, Suzanne. "Writing the Nation (Mme de Staël)." *French Forum* 30.3 (2005): 43–56.
Gutwirth, Madelyn. *Madame de Staël, Novelist: The Emergence of the Artist as Woman*. Urbana: University of Illinois, 1978.
———. *Twilight of the Goddesses: Women and Representation in the French Revolutionary Era*. New Brunswick: Rutgers University Press, 1992.
———, Avriel Goldberger, and Karyna Szmurlo, eds. *Germaine de Staël: Crossing the Borders*. New Brunswick: Rutgers University Press, 1991.
Hagstrum, Jean. *The Sister Arts: The Tradition of Literary Pictorialism and English Poetry from Dryden to Gray*. Chicago: University of Chicago Press, 1958.
Hall, Catherine. "The Rule of Difference: Gender, Class, and Empire in the Making of the 1832 Reform Act." In *Gendered Nations*. Ed. Blom, Hagemann, and Hall. 107–136.
Hall, Donald. "The Anti-Feminist Ideology of Tennyson's *The Princess*." *Modern Language Studies* 21.4 (1991): 49–62.
Hardy, Mary Anne (Lady Duffus). *The Artist's Family: A Novel*. 3 vols. London: T. C. Newby, 1857.
Harkness, Nigel. *Men of Their Words: The Poetics of Masculinity in George Sand's Fiction*. London: Legenda, 2008.
Harris, Ann Sutherland and Linda Nochlin. *Women Artists: 1550–1950*. Los Angeles County Museum of Art. New York: Knopf, 1976.
Haskell, Francis. *An Italian Patron of French Neo-Classical Art*. Oxford: Clarendon, 1972.
———. "The Old Masters in Nineteenth-Century French Painting," *Art Quarterly* 34 (1971): 55–85.
———. *Past and Present in Art and Taste*. New Haven: Yale University Press, 1987.
Hawthorne, Nathaniel. *The Marble Faun*. 1860. London: Penguin, 1990.
Hebron, Stephen. *William Wordsworth*. London: British Library, 2000.
Herstein, Sheila. *A Mid-Victorian Feminist: Barbara Leigh Smith Bodichon*. New Haven: Yale University Press, 1985.
Higonnet, Anne. *Berthe Morisot's Images of Women*. Cambridge: Harvard University Press, 1992.
Hill, Octavia. *Life of Octavia Hill as Told in Her Letters*. Ed. C. Edmund Maurice. London: Macmillan, 1913.
Hirsh, Pam. *Barbara Leigh Smith Bodichon: Feminist, Artist and Rebel*. London: Chatto and Windus, 1998.
———. "Charlotte Brontë and George Sand: The Influence of Female Romanticism." *Brontë Society Transactions* 21 (1996): 209–18.
Honour, Hugh. "Canova's Three Graces." In *The Three Graces: Antonio Canova*. Edinburgh: National Gallery of Scotland, 1995.
Hoock, Holger. *The King's Artists: The Royal Academy of Art and the Politics of British Culture 1760–1840*. Oxford: Clarendon Press, 2003.

Howitt, Anna Mary. *An Art Student in Munich*. Boston: Ticknor, Reed and Fields, 1854.

———. *The Sisters in Art*. *The Illustrated Exhibitor and Magazine of Art* 2 (1852): 214–16, 238–40, 262–63, 286–88, 317–19, 334–36, 347–48, 362–64.

Howitt, Mary Botham. *An Autobiography*. Ed. Margaret Howitt. London: Isbister, 1891.

Howitt, Mary and William Howitt. "Margaret von Ehrenberg: The Artist-Wife." In *Stories of English and Foreign Life*. London: Bohn, 1853. 1–148.

Howitt Watts, Anna Mary. *Pioneers of the Spiritual Reformation*. London: Psychological Press Association, 1883.

Howitt, William. "Harriet Martineau." *The People's Journal* (14 March 1846): 141–43.

———. "Literary Notices. *The Princess, a Medley*, by Alfred Tennyson." In *Howitt's Journal* 3 (1848): 28.

Huet, Pierre Daniel. *Lettre-traité de l'origine des romans*. 1760. Paris: Nizet, 1971.

Hunt, Holman. *Pre-Raphaelitism and the Pre-Raphaelite Brotherhood*. 2 vols. London: Macmillan, 1905.

Hunt, Leigh. "Blue-Stocking Revels: or, The Feast of the Violets." *Monthly Repository* XI (July 1837): 33–57.

———. *The Feast of the Poets, and other pieces in verse*. London: Cawthorn, 1814.

———. "Utility and Beauty—Spirit of the Fine Arts." *Leigh Hunt's London Journal* 23 (3 September 1834): 183.

Ingelbien, Raphael. "Paradoxes of National Liberation: Lady Morgan, O'Connellism, and the Belgian Revolution." *Eire-Ireland* 42.3–4 (2007): 104–25.

Isbell, John Claiborne. *The Birth of European Romanticism: Truth and Propaganda in Staël's 'De l'Allemagne.'* Cambridge: Cambridge University Press, 1994.

Jacobs, Naomi. "Gendered and Layered Narrative in *Wuthering Heights* and *The Tenant of Wildfell Hall*." *Journal of Narrative Technique* 16 (1986): 204–19.

Jal, Auguste. *L'Ombre de Diderot ou le Bossu du Marais. Dialogue critique sur le Salon de 1819*. Paris: Coréad, 1819.

James, Henry. "*She and He:* Recent Documents." In *Henry James' Literary Criticism: French Writers, Other European Writers*. Ed. Leon Edel. New York: Library of America, 1984.

Jameson, Fredric. *The Political Unconscious: Narrative as a Socially Symbolic Act*. Ithaca: Cornell University Press, 1981.

Janin, Jules. "Galerie Contemporaine." *La Mode* (septembre 1835): 178–81.

Jaud, L. *Les vies des saints pour tous les jours de l'année*. Tours: Mame, 1950.

Jay, Martin. *Downcast Eyes: The Denigration of Vision in Twentieth-Century French Thought*. Berkeley: University of California Press, 1994.

Jeanne-Victoire. "Appel aux femmes." *La Femme libre* 1.1 (1832): 1–3.

Jeffares, Bo. *The Artist in 19th-Century English Fiction*. Atlantic Highlands: Humanities Press, 1979.

"Jeunes France, Les." *Figaro*. 30 août 1831.

Johnson, Barbara. "The Lady in the Lake." In *A New History of French Literature*. Ed. Denis Hollier. Cambridge: Harvard University Press, 1989: 627–28.

Johnstone, Christian Isobel. "Lady Morgan's Princess." In *Tait's Edinburgh Magazine*, n.s. 2 (February 1835): 85–114.

Junod, Philippe. "L'Atelier comme autoportrait." In *Images de l'artiste–Künstlerbilder*. Ed. Griener and Schneemann. 83–97.

Kapchan, Deborah and Pauline Turner Strong. "Theorizing the Hybrid." *Journal of American Folklore* 112 (445): 239–53.

Kaplan, E. Ann. "Is the Gaze Male?" In *Feminism in Film*. Ed. E. Ann Kaplan. Oxford: Oxford University Press, 2000. 119–38.

Kaplan, Fred. "'Phallus-Worship' (1848): Unpublished Manuscripts III—A Response to the Revolution of 1848." *The Carlyle Newsletter* 2 (March 1980): 19–23.

Karp, Ivan and Steven Lavine, eds. *Exhibiting Cultures: The Poetics and Politics of Museum Display*. Washington: Smithsonian Institute Press, 1991.

Kelley, Theresa and Paula Feldman, eds. *Romantic Women Writers: Voices and Counter-Voices*. Hanover: University of New England Press, 1995.
Kendrick, Walter M. "Balzac and British Realism: Mid-Victorian Theories of the Novel." *Victorian Studies* 20 (1976): 5–24.
Kirschenblatt-Gimblett, Barbara. "Objects of Ethnography." In *Exhibiting Cultures*. Ed. Karp and Lavine. 386–443.
Knox, Katharine McCook. *The Sharples: Their Portraits of George Washington and His Contemporaries*. New York: Da Capo, 1972.
Korsmeyer, Carolyn. *Gender and Aesthetics*. London: Routledge, 2004.
Krieger, Murray. *Ekphrasis: The Illusion of the Natural Sign*. Baltimore: Johns Hopkins University Press, 1991.
Kris, Ernst and Otto Kurz. *Legend, Myth, and Magic in the Image of the Artist*. New Haven: Yale University Press, 1979.
Lacey, Candida Ann, ed. *Barbara Leigh Smith Bodichon and the Langham Place Group*. London: Routledge & Kegan Paul, 1986.
Lagrange, Léon. "Du rang des femmes dans les arts." *Gazette des Beaux-Arts* 8 (octobre 1860):30–43.
Lamoureux, Johanne. "La Mort de l'artiste et la naissance d'un genre." In *Images de l'artiste*. Ed. Griener and Schneemann. 183–98.
Landon, C. P. *Annales du Musée et l'école moderne des Beaux-Arts. Salon de 1831*. Paris: Pillet Ainé, 1831.
———. *Nouvelles des arts*. Paris, 1801.
———. *Salon de 1810*. Paris: Pillet Ainé, 1829.
Langland, Elizabeth. "The Voicing of Feminine Desire in Anne Brontë's *The Tenant of Wildfell Hall*." In *Gender and Discourse in Victorian Literature and Art*. Ed. Antony Harris and Beverly Taylor. DeKalb: Northern Illinois University Press, 1992. 111–23.
Lanser, Susan L. "Writing Women into Romanticism." *Feminist Studies* 23.1 (1997): 167–90.
Lapauze, Henri. *Histoire de l'Académie de France à Rome*. Paris: Plon, 1924.
Lavagne, Henry. "Les Maîtres mosaïstes: entre l'Histoire et l'histoire d'art, les 'écarts' de la romancière." In *George Sand: L'Ecriture du roman*. Montreal: University of Montreal Press, 1996. 155–62.
Le Breton, André. *Le Roman français au 19e siècle*. Paris: Boivin, 1901.
Lebreton, Joachim. *Notice sur Mme Vincent, née Labille, peintre*. Paris, an XI.
Lee, Amice. *Rosemary and Laurels: The Life of William and Mary Howitt*. Oxford: Oxford University Press, 1955.
Leerssen, J. Th. "How *The Wild Irish Girl* Made Ireland Romantic." In *The Clash of Ireland: Literary Contrasts and Connections*. Ed. C. C. Barfoot and Theo D'haen. Amsterdam: Rodopi, 1989. 98–117.
Lemaire, Gérard-Georges. *Histoire du Salon de peinture*. Paris: Klincksieck, 2004.
Le Men, Ségolène. "Book Illustration." In *Artistic Relations*. Ed. Collier and Lethbridge. 94–110.
Leonardo. "The Works of the Eye and Ear Compared." *Leonardo on Painting*. Ed. Martin Kemp. New Haven: Yale University Press. 20–46.
Lepelle de Bois-Gallais, F. *Biographie de Mademoiselle Rosa Bonheur*. Paris: Gambart, 1856.
Lettres à David, sur le Salon de 1819 par quelques élèves de son école. Paris: Pillet Ainé, 1819.
Licht, Fred. *Canova*. New York: Abbeville, 1983.
Lindsay, Lady. "Some Recollections of Miss Margaret Gillies." *Temple Bar: A London Magazine for Town and Country Readers* 81 (1887): 265–73.
Lokke, Kari. "Children of Liberty: Idealist Historiography in Staël, Shelley and Sand." *PMLA* 118.2 (2003): 502–20.
Losano, Antonia. *The Woman Painter in Victorian Literature*. Columbus: The Ohio State University Press, 2008.
Louis, Bernadette, ed. *Une Correspondance saint-simonienne. Angélique Arnaud et Caroline Simon (1833–1838)*. Paris: Côté-Femmes, 1990.

Lubin, Georges. « Qui fut Angélique Arnaud ? Avec deux lettres inédites de George Sand. » *Pays Gannatois* 42 (octobre 1978): 7–9.
Lukacher, Maryline. *Maternal Fictions: Stendhal, Sand, Rachilde, and Bataille.* Durham: Duke University Press, 1994.
Lynch, Deidre. "Domesticating Fictions and Nationalizing Women: Edmund Burke, Property, and the Reproduction of Englishness." In *Romanticism, Race, and Imperial Culture, 1780–1834.* Ed. Alan Richardson and Sonia Hofkosh. Bloomington: Indiana UniversityPress, 1996. 40–71.
M. T. [John Wilson Croker]. "Private Correspondence." *Freeman's Journal* (15 December 1806).
Maginn, William. "Miss Harriet Martineau." *Fraser's Magazine* (November 1833): 576.
Maibor, Carolyn. *Labor Pains: Emerson, Hawthorne, and Alcott on Work and the Woman Question.* London: Routledge, 2004.
Mansfield, Elizabeth. *Too Beautiful to Picture: Zeuxis, Myth, and Mimesis.* Minneapolis: University of Minnesota Press, 2007.
Marcus, Sharon. *Between Women: Friendship, Desire, and Marriage in Victorian England.* Princeton: Princeton University Press, 2007.
Marks, Patricia. "Harriet Martineau: *Fraser's* Maid of [Dis]Honour." *Victorian Periodicals Review* 19 (1986): 28–34.
Marsh, Jan. *Pre-Raphaelite Sisterhood.* London: Quartet, 1985.
——— and Pamela Nunn. *Pre-Raphaelite Women Artists.* London: Thames and Hudson, 1998.
———. *Women Artists and the Pre-Raphaelite Movement.* London: Virago, 1989.
Martin-Dehaye, Sophie. *George Sand et la peinture.* Royer, 2006.
Martineau, Harriet. *Autobiography.* Ed. Maria Weston Chapman. 3rd ed. London: Smith, Elder, 1877.
———. *Illustrations of Political Economy.* London: C. Fox, 1832–34.
———. "Letter to the Deaf." *Miscellanies.* 2 vols. Boston: Hilliard, Gray, 1836. 248–64.
———. *Life in the Sick Room.* London: Bowles and Crosby, 1844.
———. *Society in America.* London: Saunders and Otley, 1837.
Massardier-Kenney, Françoise. *Gender in the Fiction of George Sand.* Amsterdam: Rodopi, 2000.
Matthews-Kane, Bridget. "Gothic Excess and Political Anxiety: Lady Morgan's *Wild Irish Girl.*" *Gothic Studies* 5.2 (2003): 7–19.
Matus, Jill. "'Strong family likeness': *Jane Eyre* and *The Tenant of Wildfell Hall.*" In *The Cambridge Companion to the Brontës.* Ed. Glen. 99–121.
Maxwell, Richard, ed. *The Victorian Illustrated Book.* Charlottesville: University Press of Virginia, 2002.
McCall, Anne. "Image furtive, idée fixe: George Sand auto-portraitiste et para-portraitiste dans la *Correspondance.*" *George Sand Studies* 11.1–2 (1992): 55–66.
McClintock, Anne. "'No Longer in a Future Heaven': Gender, Race, and Nationalism." In *Dangerous Liaisons: Gender, Race, and Postcolonial Perspectives.* Ed. Anne McClintock, Aamir Mufti, and Ella Shohat. Minneapolis: University of Minnesota Press, 1997. 89–112.
McCracken, Penny. "Sculptor Mary Thornycroft and Her Artist Children." *Woman's Art Journal* 17.2 (1996–97): 3–8.
McMurran, Mary Helen. "National or Transnational? The Eighteenth-Century Novel." *The Literary Channel.* Ed. Cohen and Dever. 50–72.
McWilliam, Neil. "Country Life." *Oxford Art Journal* 9.1 (1986): 76–81.
Méchoulan, Eric. "On the Edges of Jacques Rancière." *SubStance* 33.1 (2004): 3–9.
Mellor, Anne K. "Embodied Cosmopolitanism and the British Romantic Woman Writer." *European Romantic Review* 17.6 (2006): 289–300.
———. *Mothers of the Nation: Women's Political Writing in England, 1780–1830.* Bloomington: Indiana University Press, 2000.
Mellor, Anne K., ed. *Romanticism and Feminism.* Bloomington: Indiana University Press, 1988.
———. *Romanticism and Gender.* London: Routledge, 1993.

Mermin, Dorothy. "The Damsel, the Knight, and the Victorian Woman Poet." *Critical Inquiry* 13 (Autumn 1986): 64–80.

———. *Godiva's Ride: Women of Letters in England, 1830–1880.* Bloomington: Indiana University Press, 1993.

Metz, Kathryn. "Ellen and Rolinda Sharples: Mother and Daughter Painters." *Women's Art Journal* 16.1 (Spring–Summer 1995): 3–11.

Michelet, Jules. *Le Peuple.* Paris: Calmann-Levy, 1946.

Miller, Betty, ed. *Elizabeth Barrett to Miss Mitford. The Unpublished Letters of Elizabeth Barrett Browning to Mary Russell Mitford.* London: John Murray, 1954.

Miller, Lucasta. *The Brontë Myth.* New York: Knopf, 2003.

Miller, Nancy K. "Performances of the Gaze: Staël's *Corinne, ou l'Italie.*" In *The Novel's Seductions.* Ed. Szmurlo. 84–94.

Mineka, Francis. *The Dissidence of Dissent: The Monthly Repository, 1806–1838.* Chapel Hill: University of North Carolina Press, 1944.

Mitchell, W. J. T. *Picture Theory: Essays on Verbal and Visual Representation.* Chicago: University of Chicago Press, 1994.

———. "Space and Time: Lessing's *Laocoon* and the Politics of Genre." In *Iconology: Image, Text, Ideology.* Chicago: University of Chicago Press, 1986. 95–115.

Moore, George. *Conversations in Ebury Street.* London: Heinemann, 1924.

Moore, Lisa L. "Acts of Union: Sexuality and Nationalism, Romance, and Realism in the Irish National Tale." *Cultural Critique* 44 (Winter 2000): 113–44.

Morowitz, Laura and William Vaughan, eds. *Artistic Brotherhoods in the Nineteenth Century.* Aldershot: Ashgate, 2000.

Morse, Deborah D. "'I speak of those I do know:' Witnessing as Radical Gesture in *The Tenant of Wildfell Hall.*" In *New Approaches to the Literary Art of Anne Brontë.* Ed. Nash and Suess. 103–26.

Moses, Claire Goldberg and Leslie Wahl Rabine. *Feminism, Socialism, and French Romanticism.* Bloomington: Indiana University Press, 1993.

Moses, Claire Goldberg. *French Feminism in the Nineteenth Century.* Albany: State University of New York Press, 1984.

Mossman, Mark. "Disability, Ireland, and *The Wild Irish Girl.*" *European Romantic Review* 18.4 (2007): 541–50.

Mulvey, Laura. "Visual Pleasure and Narrative Cinema." In *Visual and Other Pleasures.* Bloomington: Indiana University Press, 1984. 14–26.

Murdoch, John, Jim Murrell, Patrick Noon, and Roy Strong. *The English Miniature.* New Haven: Yale University Press, 1981.

Murger, Henry. *Scènes de la vie de bohème.* Paris: Gallimard, 1988.

Musset, Alfred de. *La Confession d'un enfant du siècle.* Paris: Garnier-Flammarion, 1993.

———. *Correspondance.* Paris: Presses Universitaires de France, 1985.

———. *Le Fils du Titien.* In *Nouvelles.* Vienna: Manz, n.d.

Myrone, Martin. *Body Building: Reforming Masculinities in British Art, 1750–1810.* New Haven: Yale University Press.

Naef, Hans. *Die Bildniszeichnungen von J-A-D Ingres.* Bern: Benteli, 1977–80.

Naginski, Isabelle. *George Sand: Writing for Her Life.* New Brunswick: Rutgers University Press, 1991.

Nash, Julie and Barbara Suess, eds. *New Approaches to the Literary Art of Anne Brontë.* Aldershot: Ashgate, 2001.

"Necrologie. Madame Haudebourt-Lescot." *Journal des Artistes.* 2e série. 2 février 1845. 40–42.

Neergaard, Bruun. *Sur la situation des beaux-arts en France, ou Lettres d'un Danois à son ami.* Paris, an IX/1801.

Nesci, Catherine. *La Femme mode d'emploi: Balzac, de la Physiologie du mariage à La Comédie humaine.* Lexington: French Forum, 1993.

———. *Le Flâneur et les flâneuses: Les Femmes et la ville à l'époque romantique*. Grenoble: ELLUG, 2007.
Newcomer, James. *Lady Morgan the Novelist*. Lewisburg: Bucknell University Press, 1990.
Newton, Joy. "The Atelier Novel: Painters as Fictions." In *Impressions of French Modernity*. Ed. Richard Hobbs. Manchester: Manchester University Press, 1998. 173–89.
Nochlin, Linda. *The Politics of Vision: Essays on Nineteenth-Century Art and Society*. New York: Harper & Row, 1989.
———. *Representing Women*. London: Thames and Hudson, 1999.
———. *Women, Art, and Power and Other Essays*. New York: Harper & Row, 1988.
——— and Ann Sutherland Harris. *Women Artists: 1550–1950*. Los Angeles: Los Angeles County Museum of Art, 1976.
Nodier, Charles. *Romans*. Paris: Charpentier, 1850.
Noon, Patrick, ed. *Crossing the Channel: British and French Painting in the Age of Romanticism*. London: Tate, 2003.
Nunn, Pamela Gerrish. *Canvassing*. London: Camden, 1986.
———. "A Pre-Raphaelite Sisterhood?" In Marsh and Nunn, *Pre-Raphaelite Women Artists*. 54–101.
———. "The 'Woman Question': Ruskin and the Female Artist." In *Ruskin's Artists: Studies in the Victorian Visual Economy*. Ed. Robert Hewison. Aldershot: Ashgate, 2000. 167–83.
Oberter, Rachel. "Spiritualism and the Visual Imagination in Victorian Britain." Diss. Yale University, 2007.
Ockman, Carol. *Ingres's Eroticized Bodies: Retracing the Serpentine Line*. New Haven: Yale University Press, 1995.
Ojalvo, David, et al. *Léon Cogniet, 1794–1880*. Orléans: Musée des Beaux-Arts, 1990.
Oppenheimer, Margaret. *The French Portrait: Revolution to Restoration*. Northampton: Smith College Museum of Art, 2005.
Orr, Clarissa Campbell. *Women in the Victorian Art World*. Machester: Manchester University Press, 1995.
Orr, Lyndon. "Famous Affinities of History: The Story of George Sand." *Munsey's Magazine* 43.4 (July 1910): 494–507.
Owen, Alex. *The Darkened Room: Women, Power and Spiritualism in Late Victorian England*. London: Virago, 1989.
Owenson, Sydney (Lady Morgan). *France*. 2 vols. London: Henry Colburn, 1817.
———. *France in 1829–30*. 2 vols. New York: Harper, 1830.
———. *Glorvina; ou la jeune Irlandaise, histoire nationale*. Paris: Gide, 1813.
———. *Italy*. 1821. 3 vols. London: Henry Colburn, 1824.
———. *Lady Morgan's Memoirs*. Ed. H. Hepworth Dixon. London: W. H. Allen, 1862.
———. *The Life and Times of Salvator Rosa*. 1824. London: Bryce, 1855.
———. *The Princess; or The Beguine*. 3 vols. London: Bentley, 1835.
———. *The Wild Irish Girl: A National Tale*. 1806. Oxford: Oxford University Press, 1999.
———. *Woman; or, Ida of Athens*. Philadelphia: Bradford and Inskeep, 1809.
Parkes, Bessie Raynor. "What Can Educated Women Do?" *English Woman's Journal* (December 1859). Reprinted in Lacey. 150–62.
Passez, Anne Marie. *Adélaïde Labille-Guiard, 1749–1803. Biographie et Catalogue Raisonné de son oeuvre*. Paris: Arts et Métiers Graphiques, 1971.
Peel, Ellen and Nanora Sweet. "*Corinne* and the Woman as Poet in England: Hemans, Jewsbury and Barrett Browning." In *The Novel's Seductions*. Ed. Szmurlo. 204–20.
Peintures pour un Château, cinquante tableaux (XVIe–XIXe siècle) des collections du Château de Fontainebleau. Paris: RMN, 1998.
Person, Leland. "Henry James, George Sand, and the Suspense of Masculinity." *PMLA* 106.3 (1991): 512–28.
Peterson, Linda. "Collaborative Life Writing as Ideology: The Auto/biographies of Mary Howitt

and Her Family." *Women's Life Writing and Imagined Communities.* Ed. Cynthia Huff. London: Routledge, 2005. 176–95.

———. "Mother-Daughter Productions: Mary Howitt and Anna Mary Howitt in *Howitt's Journal, Household Words* and Other Mid-Victorian Publications." *Victorian Periodicals Review* 31.1 (Spring 1998): 31–54.

Pilbeam, Pamela. *French Socialists before Marx: Workers, Women, and the Social Question in France.* Montreal: McGill-Queen's University Press, 2000.

Planté, Christine. *La Petite Soeur de Balzac: Essai sur la femme auteur.* Paris: Seuil, 1989.

Pliny. "Modelling." *The Elder Pliny's Chapters on the History of Art.* Ed. Raymond Schoder. Chicago: Ares, 1976. 175.

Pointon, Marcia. "Surrounded with Brilliants: Miniature Portraits in Eighteenth-Century England." *Art Bulletin* 83 (2001): 48–71.

Pollock, Griselda. *Differencing the Canon: Feminist Desire and the Writing of Art's Histories.* London: Routledge, 1999.

———. *Vision and Difference: Femininity, Feminism and the Histories of Art.* London: Routledge, 1988.

Poovey, Mary. *Uneven Developments: The Ideological Work of Gender in Mid-Victorian England.* Chicago: University of Chicago Press, 1988.

Powell, David, ed. *George Sand Today.* Lanham: University Press of America, 1992.

Pratt, Mary Louise. *Imperial Eyes: Travel Writing and Transculturation.* New York: Routledge, 1992.

Praz, Mario. *On Neoclassicism.* Evanston: Northwestern University Press, 1969.

Prettejohn, Elizabeth. *The Art of the Pre-Raphaelites.* London: Tate, 2007.

Quatremère de Quincy, Antoine. *Histoire de la vie et des ouvrages de Raphael.* Paris: Le Clere, 1833.

———. *Notice historique sur la vie et les ouvrages de M. Vincent.* Paris, 1817.

Rancière, Jacques. *The Future of the Image.* London: Verso, 2007.

———. *The Ignorant Schoolmaster: Five Lessons in Intellectual Emancipation.* Trans. Kristin Ross. Stanford: Stanford University Press, 1991.

———. *La Nuit des prolétaires.* Paris: Fayard, 1981.

———. *On the Shores of Politics.* London: Verso, 2007.

———. *The Politics of Aesthetics.* London: Continuum, 2004.

Reiset, Tony Henri Auguste, Vicomte de. *Marie-Caroline, Duchesse de Berry 1816–1830.* Paris: Calmann-Lévy, 1907.

Renan, Ernest. "What Is a Nation?" In *Becoming National: A Reader.* Ed. Eley and Suny. 42–55.

Rendall, Jane. *The Origins of Modern Feminism: Women in Britain, France and the United States, 1780–1860.* Chicago: Lyceum, 1985.

Reynolds, Joshua. *Discourses on Art.* London: Yale University Press, 1997.

Riccoboni, Marie Jeanne. *Histoire d'Ernestine.* New York: MLA, 1998.

Richardson, Alan. "Romanticism and the Colonization of the Feminine." In *Romanticism and Feminism.* Ed. Anne K. Mellor. Bloomington: Indiana University Press, 1988. 13–25.

Ridolfi, Carlo. *The Life of Tintoretto and of his Children Domenico and Marietta.* Trans. Catherine and Robert Enggass. University Park: Pennsylvania State University Press, 1984.

Ripa, Cesare. *Iconologia.* Garden City: Garland, 1976.

Riviere, Joan. "Womanliness as Masquerade." In *Formations of Fantasy.* Ed. Victor Burgin, James Donald, and Cora Kaplan. New York: Methuen, 1986. 35–44.

Roberts, Caroline. *The Woman and the Hour: Harriet Martineau and Victorian Ideologies.* Toronto: University of Toronto Press, 2002.

Robertson, Andrew. *Letters and Papers of Andrew Robertson.* Ed. E. Robertson. London, 1879.

Roget, John Lewis. *A History of the "Old Water-Colour" Society.* 2 vols. London: Longmans, Green and Co, 1891.

Rosenfeld, Jason. "Pre-Raphaelite 'Otherhood' and Group Identity in Victorian Britain." In *Artistic Brotherhoods.* Ed. Morowitz and Vaughan. 67–81.

Rosenthal, Angela. "Angelica Kauffman Ma(s)king Claims." *Art History* 15.1 (March 1992): 38–59.

———. "She's Got the Look! Eighteenth-Century Female Portrait Painters and the Psychology of a Potentially 'Dangerous Employment.'" In *Portraiture: Facing the Subject.* Ed. Woodall. 147–66.
Ross, Kristin. "On Jacques Rancière." *Artforum International* 45.7 (March 2007): 245.
Rossetti, William Michael. "Art News from London." *The Crayon* 1.16 (18 April 1855): 263.
———. *Ruskin, Rossetti, Preraphaelitism.* New York: Dodd Mead, 1899.
———. *Some Reminiscences.* London: Brown, Langham, 1906.
Rowlinson, Matthew. "Reading Capital with Little Nell." *Yale Journal of Criticism* 9 (1996): 347–48.
Roworth, Wendy Wassyng. *Angelica Kauffman: A Continental Artist in Georgian England.* London: Reaktion, 1992.
Ruskin, John. *The Works of John Ruskin.* Ed. E. T. Cook and Alexander Wedderburn. 39 vols. London: George Allen, 1903–12.
Ruth, Jennifer. *Novel Professions: Interested Disinterest and the Making of the Professional in the Victorian Novel.* Columbus: The Ohio State University Press, 2006.
Sahlins, Peter. *Boundaries: The Making of France and Spain in the Pyrenees.* Berkeley: University of California Press, 1989.
Sainte-Beuve, C. A. "Madame Desbordes-Valmore." In *Portraits contemporains.* 3 vols. Paris: Calmann Levy, 1889. 115–37.
———. *Memoirs of Madame Desbordes-Valmore.* Trans. Harriet Preston. Boston: Roberts Brothers, 1873.
"Salon de 1843." *L'Artiste* (1843): 209–10.
Sand, George. *Le Château de Pictordu.* In *Contes d'une grand-mère.* Meylan: Editions de l'Aurore, 1982. 32–112.
———. *Correspondance.* Ed. Lubin. 25 vols. Paris: Garnier, 1964–91.
———. *Elle et lui.* Meylan: Editions de l'Aurore, 1986.
———. *Horace.* In *George Sand: Vies d'artistes.* Paris: Omnibus, 1992. 311–562.
———. *Indiana.* 1832. Paris: Gallimard, 1984.
———. "Lettres familières de George Sand." *Revue encyclopédique* (1 septembre 1893): 853–64.
———. *Les Maîtres mosaïstes.* Paris: Chêne, 1993.
———. *Oeuvres autobiographiques.* Ed. Lubin. 2 vols. Paris: Gallimard-Pléiade, 1970–71.
———. *Story of My Life: The Autobiography of George Sand.* Ed. and trans. Thelma Jurgrau. Albany: SUNY Press, 1991.
———. *Valentine.* In *George Sand: Romans 1830.* Paris: Omnibus, 1991. 191–382.
Schehr, Lawrence. *Figures of Alterity: French Realism and Its Others.* Palo Alto: Stanford University Press, 2003.
Schor, Naomi. *Breaking the Chain: Women, Theory, and French Realist Fiction.* New York: Columbia University Press, 1985.
———. *George Sand and Idealism.* New York: Columbia University Press, 1993.
———. "The Portrait of a Gentleman: Representing Men in (French) Women's Writing." *Representations* 20 (1987): 113–33.
———. *Reading in Detail: Aesthetics and the Feminine.* London: Methuen, 1987.
Schultz, Gretchen. *The Gendered Lyric: Subjectivity and Difference in Nineteenth-Century French Poetry.* West Lafayette: Purdue University Press, 1999.
Scott, David. *Pictorialist Poetics: Poetry and the Visual Arts in Nineteenth-Century France.* Cambridge: Cambridge University Press, 1988.
Scott, Walter. *The Abbott.* 1820. Edinburgh: Adam and Charles Black, 1862.
Sedgwick, Eve Kosofsky. *Between Men: English Literature and Male Homosocial Desire.* New York: Columbia University Press, 1985.
Seigel, Jerrold. *Bohemian Paris: Culture, Politics, and the Boundaries of Bourgeois Life, 1830–1890.* Baltimore: Johns Hopkins University Press, 1999.
Shee, Martin. *Rhymes on Art; or, The Remonstrance of a Painter.* London: John Murray, 1805.
Sheriff, Mary. *The Exceptional Woman: Elizabeth Vigée-Lebrun and the Cultural Politics of Art.* Chicago: University of Chicago Press, 1996.

Shires, Linda. *Perspectives: Modes of Viewing and Knowing in Nineteenth-Century England.* Columbus: The Ohio State University Press, 2009.
Shortliffe, Glen. "Populism in the Novel before Naturalism." *PMLA* 54.2 (June 1939): 589–96.
Sidlauskas, Susan. *Body, Place, and Self in Nineteenth-Century Painting.* Cambridge: Cambridge University Press, 2000.
Siegfried, Susan. *The Art of Louis-Léopold Boilly: Modern Life in Napoleonic France.* New Haven: Yale University Press, 1995.
Simpson, David. *Romanticism, Nationalism and the Revolt against Theory.* Chicago: University of Chicago Press, 1993.
Sloan, Kim. *'A Noble Art': Amateur Artists and Drawing Masters, c. 1600–1800.* London: British Museum Press, 2000.
Smiles, Samuel. "Harriet Martineau." *Brief Biographies.* Chicago: Belford, Clarke, 1883.
Smith, Barbara Leigh. *Women and Work.* London: Bosworth and Harrison, 1857.
"The Society of Female Artists." *The Athenaeum* (April 3, 1858): 439.
Solomon-Godeau, Abigail. *Male Trouble: A Crisis in Representation.* New York: Thames and Hudson, 1997.
———. "Male Trouble: A Crisis in Representation." *Art History* 16.2 (June 1993): 286–312.
Soulié, Frédéric. *Physiologie du Bas-Bleu.* Paris: Aubert, 1840.
Souvestre, Emile. "Du Roman." *Revue de Paris,* 2e série, vol. 34 (1836): 116–28.
Sparrow, Walter Shaw. *Women Painters of the World.* London, 1905; New York: Hacker, 1976.
Spooner, S. *Anecdotes of Painters, Engravers, Sculptors, and Architects and Curiosities of Art.* 3 vols. New York: Worthington, 1853.
———. *De l'Allemagne.* 2 vols. Paris: Garnier-Flammarion, 1968.
Staël, Germaine de. *Corinne, or Italy.* Trans. Sylvia Raphael. Oxford: Oxford University Press, 1998.
———. *Corinne, ou l'Italie.* Paris: Gallimard, 1985.
———. *De la littérature.* Paris: Flammarion, 1991.
Steiner, Wendy. *The Colors of Rhetoric: Problems in the Relation between Modern Literature and Painting.* Chicago: University of Chicago Press, 1982.
Stendhal. *Le Rouge et le noir.* Ed. Henri Martineau. Paris: Garnier, 1950.
Stephens, Sonya, ed. *A History of Women's Writing in France.* Cambridge: Cambridge University Press, 2000.
Stevenson, Lionel. "*Vanity Fair* and Lady Morgan." *PMLA* 48.2 (1933): 547–51.
———. *The Wild Irish Girl. The Life of Sydney Owenson, Lady Morgan.* London: Chapman & Hall, 1936.
Stoichita, Victor. *The Self-Aware Image: An Insight into Early Modern Meta-Painting.* Cambridge: Cambridge University Press, 1997.
Stoneman, Patsy. "The Brontë Myth." In *The Cambridge Companion to the Brontës.* Ed. Glen. 214–41.
Suddaby, Elizabeth and P. J. Yarrow, eds. *Lady Morgan in France.* Newcastle: Oriel, 1971.
Sussman, Herbert. *Victorian Masculinities: Manhood and Masculine Poetics in Early Victorian Literature and Art.* Cambridge: Cambridge University Press, 1995.
Sydney, Philip. *The Poems of Sir Philip Sydney.* Oxford: Oxford University Press, 1962.
Szmurlo, Karyna, ed. *The Novel's Seductions: Staël's Corinne in Critical Inquiry.* Lewisburg: Bucknell University Press, 1999.
Tacitus. *The Annals.* Trans. John Jackson. Cambridge: Loeb Library/Harvard University Press, 1981.
Talley, Lee A. "Anne Brontë's Method of Social Protest in *The Tenant of Wildfell Hall.*" In *New Approaches to the Literary Art of Anne Brontë.* Ed. Nash and Suess. 127–51.
Temps des Passions: Collections romantiques des musées d'Orléans. Musée des Beaux-Arts d'Orléans, 1997.
Tenenbaum, Susan. "*Corinne:* Political Polemics and the Theory of the Novel." In *The Novel's Seductions.* Ed. Szmurlo. 154–62.

Tennyson, Alfred. "The Princess." In *Tennyson's Poetry*. Ed. Robert Hill. New York: Norton, 1999. 129–203.
Tennyson, Charles. *Alfred Tennyson*. New York: Macmillan, 1949.
Terdiman, Richard. *Discourse/Counter-Discourse: The Theory of Symbolic Resistance in Nineteenth-Century France*. Ithaca: Cornell University Press, 1985.
Tessone, Natasha. "Displaying Ireland: Sydney Owenson and the Politics of Specular Antiquarianism." *Éire-Ireland: A Journal of Irish Studies* 37.3–4 (2002): 169–86.
Thackeray, William. *The Paris Sketchbook*. 2 vols. London: John Macrone, 1840.
Thomas, Greg. "Instituting Genius: The Formation of Biographical Art History in France." In *Art History and its Institutions: Foundations of a Discipline*. Ed. Elizabeth Mansfield. London: Routledge, 2002. 260–70.
Thomson, Pamela. "*Wuthering Heights* and *Mauprat*." *Review of English Studies* 24, no. 93 (1973): 26–37.
Tombs, Robert and Isabelle. *That Sweet Enemy: French and the British from the Sun King to the Present*. New York: Knopf, 2007.
Tristan, Flora. *Méphis*. 1838. 2 vols. Paris: Indigo & Côté-femmes, 1996–97.
Tromp, Marlene. "Spirited Sexuality: Sex, Marriage, and Victorian Spiritualism." *Victorian Literature and Culture* (2003): 67–81.
Trumpener, Katie. *Bardic Nationalism: The Romantic Novel and the British Empire*. Princeton: Princeton University Press, 1997.
Tscherny, Nadia. "A Fascination with the Enemy: Subjects from British History." In *Romance and Chivalry*. Ed. Tscherny and Sainty. 106–23.
——— and Guy Stair Sainty, eds. *Romance and Chivalry: History and Literature Reflected in Early Nineteenth-Century French Painting*. New York: Stair Sainty Mattiesen, 1996.
Valabrègue, Antony. "Les Femmes Artistes du XIXe siècle: Madame Haudebourt-Lescot." In *Les Lettres et les Arts: Revue Illustrée*. Paris: Boussod, Valadon, 1887. 102–9.
Vallois, Marie-Claude. "Old Idols, New Subjects: Germaine de Staël and Romanticism." In *Germaine de Staël: Crossing the Borders*. Ed. Gutwirth, Goldberger, and Szmulro. 82–97.
Van Slyke, Gretchen. *Rosa Bonheur: The Artist's (Auto)Biography*. Ann Arbor: University of Michigan Press, 2001.
Vincent, Patrick. *The Romantic Poetess: European Culture, Politics and Gender 1820–1840*. Lebanon: University Press of New England, 2004.
Wahrman, Dror. *The Making of the Modern Self: Identity and Culture in Eighteenth-Century England*. New Haven: Yale University Press, 2004.
Walker, Lynne. "Women Patron-Builders in Britain: Identity, Difference and Memory in Spatial and Material Culture." *Local/Global: Women Artists in the Nineteenth Century*. Ed. Deborah Cherry and Janice Helland. Aldershot: Ashgate, 2006. 121–36.
Waller, Margaret. *The Male Malady: Fictions of Impotence in the French Romantic Novel*. New Brunswick: Rutgers University Press, 1993.
Ward, Ian. "The Case of Helen Huntingdon." *Criticism* 49.2 (2007): 151–82.
Weisberg, Gabriel and Jane Becker. *Overcoming All Obstacles: The Women of the Académie Julian*. New Brunswick: Rutgers University Press, 1999.
Wendorf, Richard. *The Elements of Life, Biography, and Portrait-Painting in Stuart and Georgian England*. London: Clarendon Press, 1990.
Wenk, Silke. "Gendered Representations of the Nation's Past and Future." In *Gendered Nations*. Ed. Blom, Hagemann, and Hall. 63–80.
West, Shearer. *Portraiture*. Oxford: Oxford University Press, 2004.
Westcott, Andrea. "A Matter of Strong Prejudice: Gilbert Markham's Self Portrait." In *New Approaches to the Literary Art of Anne Brontë*. Ed. Julie Nash and Barbara Suess. Aldershot: Ashgate, 2001. 213–25.
Wettlaufer, Alexandra. "Composing Romantic Identity: Berlioz and the Sister Arts." *Romance Studies* 25.1 (2007). 45–58.

———. "Dibutades and Her Daughters: The Female Artist in Postrevolutionary France." *Nineteenth-Century Studies* 18 (2004): 9–38.

———. "Girodet/Endymion/Balzac: Representation and Rivalry in Post-Revolutionary France." *Word & Image: A Journal of Verbal/Visual Inquiry* 17.4 (2001): 401–11.

———. *In the Mind's Eye: The Visual Impulse in Diderot, Baudelaire and Ruskin*. Amsterdam: Rodopi, 2003.

———. *Pen vs. Paintbrush: Girodet, Balzac and the Myth of Pygmalion in Postrevolutionary France*. New York: Palgrave, 2001.

White, Roberta. *A Studio of One's Own: Fictional Women Painters and the Art of Fiction*. Cranbury: Fairleigh Dickinson University Press, 2005.

Williams, Raymond. *Culture and Society, 1780–1950*. New York: Columbia University Press, 1983.

Wilson, Michael. *Rebels and Martyrs: The Image of the Artist in the Nineteenth Century*. London: National Gallery, 2006.

Wise, T. J. and J. A. Symington, eds. *The Brontës; Their Lives, Friendships and Correspondence*. 4 vols. Oxford: Blackwell, 1933.

Wittkower, Margot and Rudolf Wittkower. *Born Under Saturn: The Character and Conduct of Artists*. New York: New York Review of Books, 2007.

Wolff, Janet. *Feminine Sentences: Essays on Women and Culture*. Berkeley: University of California Press, 1990.

"Woman's Position in Art." *The Crayon* 8 (February 1861): 25–28.

Woodall, Joanna, ed. *Portraiture: Facing the Subject*. Manchester: Manchester University Press, 1997.

Woodring, Carl. *Victorian Samplers: William and Mary Howitt*. Lawrence: University of Kansas Press, 1952.

Woolf, Virginia. *A Room of One's Own*. London: Granada, 1981.

———. *Three Guineas*. New York: Harcourt Brace Jovanovich, 1966.

———. *To the Lighthouse*. New York: Harcourt, 2005.

Wordsworth, William. *Sonnets*. Ed. Hannaford Bennett. London: Lang, 1907.

Wright, Beth. "Walter Scott and French Art: Imagining the Past." In *Romance and Chivalry*. Ed. Tscherny and Sainty. 180–93.

Wrigley, Richard. "Genre Painting with Italy in Mind." In *French Genre Painting in the Eighteenth Century*. Ed. Philip Conisbee. New Haven: Yale University Press, 2003. 245–55.

Yeldham, Charlotte. *Margaret Gillies RWS, Unitarian Painter of Mind and Emotion*. Lewiston: Edwin Mellen, 1997.

———. *Women Artists in Nineteenth-Century France and England*. 2 vols. New York: Garland, 1984.

Zola, Emile. *L'Oeuvre*. 1886. Paris: Garnier-Flammarion, 1974.

Index

The Abbott (Scott), 150–51
Académie Julian, 263, 276n34
Académie Royale de peinture et de sculpture, 32, 39, 40, 42, 43, 81, 265, 275n5, 275n7. *See also* artistic education
Academy of Saint Luke, 135
L'Accordée du village (Greuze), 143
Ackermann's (London dealer), 65
Adams, William Bridges, 198
Adler, Laure, 175, 176
aesthetic ideologies: in *Château de Pictordu*, 262; discourse of Victorian, 14; in *Elle et lui*, 247, 248, 250, 252–53, 256, 258–59; of female subjectivity, 10–11; and folklore, 143–44; politics of, 11, 12; and professional women artists, 264; in *Tenant of Wildfell Hall*, 226, 242
Agen, Boyer d', 278n19
Agnes Grey (Brontë), 107, 222, 223, 230
Ainger, Canon, 289n21
Alaux, Jean, 43, 46
Albistur, Maïté, 172, 293n14
Alliston, April, 134
The Altpörtel, Speyer (Best), 69, *70*
amateur, women artists as: 31–33, 48, 50, 58, 60, 64, 103, 195, 230. *See also* professionalism
Amic, Mlle, 152
"Ancients" (brotherhood), 16
Andersen, Hans Christian, 101, 281n18
Angers, David d', 152

Ansiaux, Jean-Joseph, 43
"antipainting," 40
Apostolat des Femmes, 175
Appiah, Kwame Anthony, 126
Aristotle, 255, 289n7
Armogathe, Daniel, 172, 293n14
Armstrong, Nancy, 4
Arnaud, Angélique, 173–90; background of, 173; career of, 176–77, 287n15; on Code Civil, 179; on female subjectivity, 11; influences on, 27, 121; on nation, gender, and identity, 134; as Saint-Simonian, 176, 287n13
Arnaud, Angélique, works of: *Clémence*, 2, 11, 27, 171, 173, 177, 178–90, 267, 288n20; *La Comtesse de Servy*, 177; *Coralie*, 177; *Une Tendre dévôte*, 287n15
Arnaud, Laure, 287n15
art, definition of, 7–8
Artemisia Gentileschi (Garrard), 3
artisanal production: in artistic hierarchy, 35; Pre-Raphaelite Brotherhood on, 98; in Sand's troubadour novel, 251, 252; in *Sisters in Art*, 108, 109; validation of, 7–8. *See also* illustration and design
L'Artiste, 279n31
artistic education: in Britain, 56, 58, 64, 65, 97; of British and French women artists, 263–65; comparison of French and British, 55–56, 74; on European Continent, 64–65, 69–71, 97; for history painting,

117, 248; A. M. Howitt on women's exclusion from, 114–15; in A. M. Howitt's sisterhood, 101, 115; as means to financial self-sufficiency, 57, 100–101; in Paris, 16; in private collections, 65, 74; under Restoration, 46; in *Sisters in Art,* 108, 109, 112; in Tennyson's *Princess,* 113. See also *Académie Royale de peinture et de sculpture;* ateliers; British Royal Academy; education; studio culture

artistic identity: in *Château de Pictordu,* 261–62; construction in Britain, 97, 125–26, 269; construction in France, 39, 45–46, 50–53, 125–26, 269; Desbordes-Valmore on, 76, 79, 80, 84–87; discourse/counter-discourse on, 14–18; in *Elle et lui,* 246–50, 252–59; gender and nation in, 126–34; in Margaret Gillies's portraits, 201; of Haudebourt-Lescot, 90, 135; A. M. Howitt's construction of, 73–74, 101; influence of Old Masters on, 288n23; in *To the Lighthouse,* 266–68; Owenson on, 159–70; in public sphere, 33, 56; Sand's construction of, 243, 246; Rolinda Sharples's portrayal of, 62; in *Sisters in Art,* 109; Caroline Thévenin's portrayal of, 55; through clothing and accessories, 139; through paintings and novels, 265–69

"artist-monk," 18

artist myths, 13–19. See also Romanticism

artists, female: Balzac on, 80–84, 86; Mary Ellen Best's portrayal of, 67–69; Bonheur as model and mentor for, 264; Brontës' construction of, 223–25; Anne Brontë's portrayal of, 225–27, 229–42; comparison of French and British, 58, 74, 263–65; at David's studio, 38; decline of image, 20–22; Desbordes-Valmore on legitimacy of, 84–96; exhibitions of British, 56, 65, 74; in Germany, 65, 71–72; history of, 1, 6–8; A. M. Howitt's hopes for British, 117; A. M. Howitt's model of, 104–6; A. M. Howitt's portrayal of, 108; Leigh Hunt's satire of, 213–20; identity of French, 45–52; in narratives, 69–74; periodical articles by British, 71; portrayal in *Corinne,* 133; Ruskin on, 119–20; Sand's persona of, 243–44, 259; Rolinda Sharples's portrayal of, 58–62; in social structure, 17; as students in France, 38; Caroline Thévenin's portrayal of, 53–55; as threat to male artistic image, 9, 18, 95, 112, 217; underrepresentation at Broad Museum, 294n12. See also brotherhood/sisterhood of arts; femininity; gender ideology; painters, female; women

artists, male: in *Clémence,* 182; collective identity of, 16–18, 274n53; creation and destruction by, 83, 92–93, 116; denial of women's artistic traits, 85; Haudebourt-Lescot's comparison to female painters, 90; identity of French, 45–46; images in Capet's painting, 43–45; influence on Labille-Guiard, 40, 42; in social structure, 13, 17, 47; threat of women to, 9, 18, 95, 112, 217. See also brotherhood/sisterhood of arts; gender ideology; masculinity; painters, male

Artist's Studio (Leprince), 46

Art-Journal, 71, 100, 277n55

arts d'agrément, 31, 40, 81–82, 245. See also marriage

An Art Student in Munich (Howitt), 69–74; 277n55, 290n32; emotion in, 73, 277n58; A. M. Howitt's sisterhood in, 104, 106; W. M. Rossetti on, 277n56; Ruskin's epigraph in, 118. See also Howitt, Anna Mary, works of

Associated Homes, 106, 206–7, 282n34

"L'Atelier comme autoportrait" (Junod), 34

L'Atelier d'Abel de Pujol (Grandpierre-Deverzy), 47–50, *49,* 53, 82

L'Atelier de David (Cless), 35, *37*

Atelier des jeunes filles (Thévenin), 53–55, *54*

L'Atelier d'Ingres à Rome (Alaux), 46

L'Atelier d'un peintre (Desbordes-Valmore): biographical reading of, 79, 278n19; comparison to *Clémence,* 189; comparison to *Sisters in Art,* 107, 108, 112–13; description of, 79–80; female subjectivity in, 11; influence on, 27; portrayal of female artist in, 84–96; portrayal of studio life in, 81; publication of, 78; Pujol's story in, 93, 280n41; as self-portrait, 89. See also Desbordes-Valmore, works of

L'Atelier du peintre (Vernet), 46–47

ateliers: Balzac's portrayal of women in, 92; as battleground, 46–47; Desbordes-Valmore's image of, 80, 89, 94, 95; Germany as, 73; of Haudebourt-Lescot,

152; men and women sharing, 74; Owenson on, 286n9; portraits of artists in, 34–55; as private space, 84; and professionalism, 33–34; as setting for French fiction, 75; as space between domestic and public, 48–50; women admitted to, 263, 279n33. *See also* artistic education; studio culture; working space
Athanassoglou-Kallmyer, Nina, 46
Athenaeum, 71, 99, 100, 117–19, 277n55, 280n9
Aurevilly, Barbey d', 76
Auricchio, Laura, 39
Aurora: A Medley of Verse (Howitt and Watts), 100
Austen, Jane, 31–32
authors: competition among, 172; definition of, 5; in *Elle et lui,* 248; on female painters, 1. *See also* novelists; poets
authors, female: aesthetic in *Clémence,* 184–85; on artist's model, 116; Brontës as, 221–25; Desbordes-Valmore on, 92; in France, 80–81, 84, 172, 247; Leigh Hunt's satire of, 213–20; Martineau's identity as, 204–5; novels about male painters, 272n17; professionalism of, 103, 202; representation of, 24; rivalry with visual artists, 75, 83–84; Sand's parallel with painters, 244–46; sentimentalism of, 171–72; as socialists, 190. *See also* authors; women
authors, male: and childbirth metaphor, 93; and gender in labor, 103; on gender of painting, 6. *See also* authors
Autobiography (Howitt), 100, 277n56, 289n8
Autobiography (Martineau), 202
Auzou, Pauline, 38
Avenir des femmes, 177

Baillie, Joanna, 18, 101
Le Baisement des pieds de la statue de saint Pierre dans la basilique Saint-Pierre de Rome (Haudebourt-Lescot), 145–49, *146*
Balzac, Honoré: on color, light, and life, 94; comparison to Arnaud, 183–84; comparison to A. M. Howitt, 107, 108, 282n37; comparison to Owenson, 162; competition with other authors, 172; contrast with Sand, 251, 259; Desbordes-Valmore's dialogue with, 95; on gender in art, 15, 80–85, 92; influence on Arnaud, 181, 190; on painters, 75; portrayal of family relations, 86–87; Realist aesthetic, 80, 82, 171, 173, 178, 293n18; references to Girodet, 87–88; reference to Sand as man, 249, 293n15; Sand's relationship with, 243, 249; Souvestre on, 178; troubadour style of, 293n18
Balzac, Honoré, works of: *Le Chef-d'oeuvre inconnu,* 75, 80, 83, 92, 94, 251; *La Comédie humaine,* 80, 171; *Eugénie Grandet,* 178; *Histoire des Treize,*272n27; *La Maison du chat-qui-pelote,* 80, 83, 84; *Le Père Goriot,* 172, 177, 180, 183–84, 288n24; *Pierre Grassou,* 108; *Sarrasine,*80, 82, 83; *La Vendetta,* 81–87, 89, 90, 92, 93, 108
Bann, Stephen, 26, 278n19
Barbauld, Anna Letitia, 20
Barbus, 16
Barker, Emma, 143
bas bleu, 20, 22, 24, 274n62
Bateman, Edward, 281n19
Battersby, Christine, 15, 16
Baudelaire, Charles, 10, 76, 77, 272n23
Beckett, Samuel, 155
Behn, Aphra, 25, 216
Belgium, 69, 159–70, 173
Bell, Acton, 223–24, 230
Bell, Currer, 223–24, 230
Bell, Ellis, 223–24, 230
Bell, Vanessa, 266
Benham, Jane: articles by, 71, 277n55; in A. M. Howitt's sisterhood, 101, 104; and Pre-Raphaelite brotherhood/sisterhood, 99, 280n8; success of, 101–2; training in Germany, 65, 69–72; in "Ye Newe Generation," 104–6, *105*
Benjamin, Walter, 10, 272n28
Benoist, Marie-Guillemine Laville de, 38, 39
Bentham, Jeremy, 201, 202, 204
Béraud, Antony, 135
Bermingham, Ann, 31
Bernini, Gianlorenzo, 147
Berry, Duchesse Marie Caroline de, 148–50, 152, 181–82, 185–88
Berthe Morisot's Images of Women (Higonnet), 3
Bertrand-Jennings, Chantal, 94
Best, Mary Ellen, 64–69; *The Altpörtel,*

Speyer, 70; *Green Drawing Room at Castle Howard,* 66; *Painting Room in our House in York,* 68
Best, Rosamond, 64
Beyond the Frame: Feminism and Visual Culture, Britain 1850–1900 (Cherry), 3
"Biographical Notice of Ellis and Acton Bell" (Brontë), 223–24
Bildungsroman, 109, 129, 161, 179, 260. See also *Kunstlerroman*
Bird, Edward, 57, 60
Blanc, Charles, 135, 136, 285n27
Bleak House (Dickens), 219, 290n43
Bloom, Harold, 262
Bloomsbury Group, 266
"Blue-Stocking Revels: or, The Feast of the Violets" (Hunt), 24, 213–20
Blue-Stockings, 20–24
Boadicea Brooding over her Wrongs (Howitt), 117–21, 283n51
"Boadicea" (Cowper), 121
Boadicea (Thornycroft), 121
Bodichon, Barbara Leigh Smith. See Leigh Smith, Barbara
bohemians, 14, 16–18, 47, 55, 104, 273n47, 273n50
Bohrer, Susan, 205–6
Boilly, Louis-Léopold, 35, *36,* 45–46, 141
Bolster, Richard, 80
Bonaparte, Lucien, 136, 148
Bonheur, Rosa, 264
The Book of the Courtier (Castiglione), 90, 279n36
Borel, Petrus, 16
Borghese collection, 144, 145
Bouchot, Henri, 157
Boucoiran, Jules, 246
Bourbon monarchy, 82, 149, 150, 158, 179, 182
Bourdieu, Pierre, 4, 172. See also field of cultural production
Boyce, Joanna, 99, 280n8, 283n52
Breaking Up of the Blue Stocking Club (Rowlandson), 20–22, *23*
Bremer, Fredrika, 101
Brereton, Thomas, 62–64
A Brief Summary in Plain English of the Most Important Laws of England concerning Women (Leigh Smith), 102
Brilliant, Richard, 196
Briscoe, Lily, 266–69

Briséis pleurant Patrocle (Cogniet), 52
Bristol Riots of 1831, 62
Bristol School, 57
Britain: as anti-France, 24, 274n64; Blue-Stockings in, 24; brotherhood of artists in, 16; collective domesticity in, 207; connection between painting and literature in, 4–5; discourse/counter-discourse in, 14; female Realist authors in, 287n2; focus on cultural context of, 2; gender ideology in, 19–22, 197, 220; Haudebourt-Lescot's history scenes of, 149–53; hierarchies and exclusion in, 13, 98, 99; A. M. Howitt on past and future of art in, 116, 117; A. M. Howitt's legacy in, 121; images of women artists in, 269; marriage laws in, 226, 291n10; national and cultural identities in, 24–27, 125–27, 134, 150; Owenson's popularity in, 158; Owenson's portrayal in *Princess,* 160–70; portraiture in, 195, 196, 199, 201; radical Unitarians in, 198; Romanticism in, 18; Sand's popularity in, 243; social structure in, 11; studio culture in, 32–34, 55, 276n39; symbolized in "Ye New Generation," 104; tensions with France, 149–50; travel to and from France, 156–57; women's training and exhibition in, 33, 229, 263–65. See also England; Scotland; Victorian England
British Royal Academy: academic doctrine of, 55–56; Benham's work at, 101–2; Branwell Brontë at, 222; brotherhoods as opposition to, 98; George Haugh at, 64; A. M. Howitt on women's exclusion from, 114–15; A. M. Howitt's paintings at, 100; Leigh Hunt's portrait at, 217; miniature portraits at, 199–201, 208, 211; James Sharples at, 57; Rolinda Sharples's exhibition at, 62; women admitted to, 32, 263, 275n5, 294n1; women's productions at, 32, 264. See also artistic education
Broad Museum of Contemporary Art (Los Angeles), 294n12
Brontë, Anne: on artistic brotherhood/sisterhood, 17; background and career of, 221–25; counter-discourse in *Tenant of Wildfell Hall,* 14, 227, 233; critics of, 242; on female subjectivity, 10; influences on, 27; portrait of child and flower,

316

291n13; reference in *Sisters in Art,* 107; response to caricatures, 24; similarities to Helen Huntingdon, 222–23, 230, 242
Brontë, Anne, works of: *Agnes Grey,* 107, 222, 223, 230; *The Tenant of Wildfell Hall,* 2,10, 14, 107, 221, 222, 224, 225–42, 248, 249, 257, 291n6, 291n14
Brontë, Branwell, 221–22, 224
Brontë, Charlotte: background and career of, 221–25; criticism of *Tenant of Wildfell Hall,* 224, 225, 291n6
Brontë, Charlotte, works of: "Biographical Notice of Ellis and Acton Bell," 223–24; *Jane Eyre,* 222–23, 229, 230, 241
Brontë, Emily, 221–25, 226; *Wuthering Heights,* 223, 226, 229, 291n12
The Brontë Myth (Miller), 223
Brooke, Frances, 25
brotherhood/sisterhood of arts: among authors and visual artists, 75; in Britain, 97–98; end of A. M. Howitt's, 281n22; in France and Britain, 5, 6, 26; of French poets, 77; A. M. Howitt on, 97–116; Leigh Hunt on, 217; Musset's refusal of, 252; operas about, 17; in Owenson's *Princess,* 163–64; in Romanticism, 16–18; Sand's inclusion in, 243; in studio, 34–38. *See also* artists, female; artists, male; collective identity; Pre-Raphaelite Brotherhood
Brown, Emma, 280n8
Browning, Elizabeth Barrett, 102, 127, 158, 208, 215, 289n9
Browning, Robert, 101, 158, 197, 198
Brown, Lucy Madox, 265
Bryson, Norman, 5
Buffon, Comte de, 171
Burke, Peter, 139
Burne-Jones, Georgiana, 280n8
Butler, Judith, 9
Byron, Lord, 14, 98, 158, 213, 220

Caïn et Abel (Cogniet), 52
Calaresu, Melissa, 139
Cambridge University, 101, 103
Cameron, Julia Margaret, 265
Canova, Antonio, 50, 145, 285n44
Canvassing (Nunn), 3
Capet, Gabrielle, 2, 14, 27, 39, 40, 43–46, 44, 48, 58, 74, 89, 285n43

caricature, 10, 20–24, 204, 213–20, 257
Carlyle, Thomas, 18, 72, 273n52, 274n53
Carnell, Rachel, 225–26
Carter, Elizabeth, 20
Cary, Francis, 276n39
Cassatt, Mary, 265
Castiglione, Baldassare, 90, 279n36
Castle Howard collection, 65–66
Certeau, Michel de, 139
Chapeau de Paille (Rembrandt), 90
Chardin, Jean-Baptiste-Siméon, 141
Le Charivari, 190
Charles X, 148–50, 164
Charles X Distributing Prizes to Artists at the Salon of 1824 (Heim), 90
Charpentier, Constance, 38
Chateaubriand, François-René, 19
Chaucer, Geoffrey, 216
Chaudet, Jeanne-Elisabeth, 39
Le Château de Pictordu (Sand), 260–62. *See also* Sand, George, works of
Le Chef-d'oeuvre inconnu (Balzac), 75, 80, 83, 92, 94, 251, 282n37, 293n18. *See also* Balzac, works of
Cherry, Deborah, 3, 32, 97, 282n40
childbirth, 92–93, 255. *See also* motherhood
The Children's Year (Howitt and Howitt), 100
Chopin, Frédéric, 243
Chorley, Henry, 71
Christ, Carol, 18
class: in Arnaud's novels, 173, 180–90; and artists' collective identity, 16, 17; in Mary Ellen Best's portrait, 67, 69; and collective domesticity, 207; effect of women's education on, 103; *femmes nouvelles* on, 175; in fiction about visual arts, 75; in French novels, 80; in Haudebourt-Lescot's Italian paintings, 140–41; Howitts on, 100, 106; inequalities of, 13; in oil painting of Martineau, 204; in Owenson's *Princess,* 160, 161, 164–65, 167, 170; political resistance to hierarchies of, 126; and portraiture, 195, 199; and professionalism, 32; radical Unitarians on, 198; and representation of women, 19, 20; Saint-Simonian movement on, 173–75; in sentimental social novels, 172–73; in *Sisters in Art,* 109; in studio culture, 47; in *Tenant of Wildfell Hall,* 230; in *Valentine,* 245–46; and visuality/visibility in art, 10. *See also* social structure

317

Index

Clawson, Mary Ann, 98
Claxton, Adelaide, 276n39
Clayton, Ellen, 263
Clémence (Arnaud), 178–90; comparison to painting, 184–85; effect of, 188, 190; female subjectivity in, 11; and inequality of women authors, 173; plot, 179–80; prohibition of divorce in, 288n20; publication of, 177; references to *Le Père Goriot* in, 177; regeneration in, 184–85; sacrifice for collective good in, 184, 186. *See also* Angélique Arnaud, works of
Cless, Jean-Henri, 35, *37,* 38, 45, 48
The Clifton Racecourse (Sharples), 62
Cloakroom, the Clifton Assembly Rooms (Sharples), 62
clothing, 139, 145–47, 162, 170, 196, 203, 243, 286n16
Cogniet, Léon, 50–53, 55, 276n34, 276n36
Cogniet, Marie-Amélie, 2, 24, 27, 50–53; comparison to Mary Ellen Best, 69; comparison to Rolinda Sharples, 58; *Intérieur de l'atelier de Léon Cogniet,* 50, *51,* 276n34; portrayal of studio life, 50–53, 74, 108; training and reputation of, 50–53
Cohen, Margaret, 4, 25, 172, 173, 287n2
Colburn, Henry, 158
Coleridge, Samuel Taylor, 98
Colet, Louise, 247
collaboration: of Brontës, 221–24; Gillies sisters on, 197, 206–13; of William and Mary Howitt, 211; A. M. Howitt's commitment to, 99–106; A. M. Howitt's spiritual drawings as, 120; promotion of women and men's, 103, 251, 262; in *Sisters in Art,* 112, 116
collective identity: in *L'Atelier d'un peintre,* 94, 95; of British women artists, 72–74, 263; of Brontë sisters, 223, 225; in *Clémence,* 180, 181, 187, 189; Desbordes-Valmore on, 86–87; of *femmes nouvelles,* 175; of French Romantic poets, 76–80; and generations and gender, 7, 45, 60; Gillies sisters on, 206–7, 213; in A. M. Howitt's sisterhood, 99, 101–4, 114, 116; in *To the Lighthouse,* 266; and miniatures as engravings, 202; in minor literature, 156; in Owenson's *Princess,* 169; in the public sphere, 1; Sand on, 256, 262; in Rolinda Sharples portrait, 62;

and social utopian ideals, 143; in studio culture, 34, 35–38, 40–42, 55–56, 75. *See also* brotherhood/sisterhood of arts
colonized cultures, 126, 134, 135, 163
La Comédie humaine (Balzac), 80, 171. *See also* Balzac, works of
Comolli, Jean-Louis, 10
La Comtesse de Servy (Arnaud), 177
Condorcet, Nicolas, 174
La Confession d'un enfant du siècle (Musset), 250, 258
La Confirmation par un évêque grec dans la basilique de Sainte-Agnès (Haudebourt-Lescot), 148
Considérant, Victor, 174, 175
Constant, Benjamin, 157
Contes d'une Grand-mère (Sand), 259. *See also* Sand, works of
convents, 87, 279n32
Coralie (Arnaud), 177
Corbett, David Peters, 10
Corinne, ou l'Italie (Staël), 18, 27, 126–34, 139, 148, 152, 255, 284n9, 284n18; comparison to *Clémence,* 180, 181; comparison to *Elle et lui,* 249–50; comparison to *Mary Queen of Scots Fainting,* 152; comparison to Owenson's *Princess,* 159–62, 167, 170; comparison to *Tenant of Wildfell Hall,* 234; nation, gender, and difference in, 126–34; Owenson's admiration of, 127–28, 284n13; religion in, 148; as Romantic novel, 18. *See also* Staël, works of
Cornforth, Fannie, 280n8
Corn Laws, 101
Le Corsaire-Satan, 17
cosmopolitanism, 126, 134, 141
La Cousine Adèle (Arnaud), 287n15
Cowper, William, 121
The Crayon, 99, 100, 272n18, 277n56
creation: Anne Brontë on, 224; in *Château de Pictordu,* 261; in *Elle et lui,* 248, 249, 253, 258–60; in French novels, 81, 83; in *To the Lighthouse,* 267–68; metaphors and tropes of, 92–93, 116; Pre-Raphaelite Brotherhood on, 98; Sand on, 244, 251; in *Sisters in Art,* 108; studio as site of, 34; in *Tenant of Wildfell Hall,* 232, 235, 236, 239–41. *See also* cultural production
The Critic: London Literary Journal, 100

Critique sur le Salon de 1819 (Jal), 136
Croker, John Wilson, 158, 286n10
Crossing the Channel: British and French Painting in the Age of Romanticism (Noon), 26
Crow, Thomas, 34
Cruikshank, Frederick, 200
"le culte des images" (Baudelaire), 10
cultural identity: in France and Britain, 24–27; in Haudebourt-Lescot's Italian paintings, 141, 145, 147, 148; in national tales, 156; in Owenson's and Staël's novels, 126–34
cultural production: approach to British and French, 4; Arnaud's place in, 177; Balzac's position in, 83; Capet's place in, 43; Amélie Cogniet's portrayal of, 50–53; Desbordes-Valmore's position in, 79, 80, 116; by French and British women, 6, 74, 265, 269; and French-British cultural exchange, 26; genres of, 9; Margaret Gillies's place in, 201; A. M. Howitt's promotion of women's, 104; Leigh Hunt on women in, 213; Labille-Guiard's place in, 40; and professionalism, 33; promotion of women's place in, 202, 204; role of gender in, 5, 18; Sand on women's position in, 244, 253, 262; Staël's ideas of, 130, 284n18; in *Valentine*, 247; of women authors, 172. *See also* creation
Cushman, Charlotte, 201
Cuvier, Georges, 171

Danahy, Martin, 76
Danby, Francis, 57
Dante, 216
Daumier, Honoré, 17, 190, *191*
David, Jacques-Louis, 35, 37, 38, 45, 50, 55, 88, 140
Davies, Emily, 101
Davin, Césairine Mirvault, 38
Dead Pheasant (Turner), 119–20
death and destruction: association with women, 6; in *L'Atelier d'un peintre*, 79–80, 94, 95; in Balzac's novels, 80, 82–84, 92; in *Clémence*, 189, 190; in Desbordes-Valmore's poetry, 87; in *Elle et lui*, 257; A. M. Howitt on women artists', 120; in Musset's troubadour novel, 252; in *Tenant of Wildfell Hall*, 238

Declaration of the Rights of Woman (Gouges), 274n59
Degas, Edgar, 263
DeJean, Joan, 25
Delacroix, Eugène, 16, 50, 189, 243
De la littérature (Staël), 128
De l'Allemagne (Staël), 18, 128, 157
Delaroche, Paul, 278n19
De la santé des gens de lettres (Tissot), 255
Delécluze, E.-J., 38, 140, 275n14
Deleuze, Gilles, 155
Denon, Vivant, 157
Deraismes, Maria, 177
Derrida, Jacques, 8, 9, 22
Desbordes, Constant, 79–80, 279nn32–33
Desbordes-Valmore, Marceline: acting career of, 77, 278n12; on collective identity of artists, 86; comparison to A. M. Howitt, 107, 108, 112–13, 116, 282n37; dedication of poem, 78, 278n14; discourse/counter-discourse of, 14; on female subjectivity, 11, 18; influences on, 27; portrayal of female artist, 84–96; portrayal of studio life, 81; as Romantic poet, 76–80
Desbordes-Valmore, works of: *L'Atelier d'un peintre*, 2, 11, 27, 75, 78–80, 81, 84–96, 107, 108, 189, 278n19; *Domenica*, 94; *Elégies, Marie et romances*, 76; *Les Pleurs*, 78–79; *Poésies complètes*, 77–78; "To M Alphonse de Lamartine," 78–79
Desbordes-Valmore, Ondine, 93, 279n34
Desire and Domestic Fiction (Armstrong), 4
Dever, Carolyn, 25
Diana myth, 82, 279n28
Dibutades, 90, 93, 195, 279n35
Dickens, Charles: 10, 99, on bohemians, 273n47; and A. M. Howitt's "Sisters in Art," 107–9; on female miniature painters, 199–200; Gillies' association with, 197; and *Household Words*, 99; A. M. Howitt's connection to, 101; A. M. Howitt's letters in journal of, 277n55; and *The Old Curiosity Shop*, 107, 108, 282n38; portrait of Leigh Hunt, 219, 290n43; Gillies's portraits of, 200, 201, 220, 289n19
Dickens, Charles, works of: *Bleak House*, 219, 290n43; *Great Expectations*, 109, 272n27; *Master Humphrey's Clock*, 107; *Nicholas Nickleby*, 199–200; *The Old Curiosity Shop*, 107–8, 282n28

319

Diderot, Denis, 25
Dieudonné, Henri, 149, 150
difference: between authors and visual artists, 75; in *Clémence,* 186; Desbordes-Valmore on transcending, 85, 95; in *Elle et lui,* 254; and female artists, 14; in French Romantic poetry, 76–80; in gender, nation, and identity, 126, 129, 131–35; in Haudebourt-Lescot's Italian paintings, 140–41, 143, 148; A. M. Howitt's equality based on, 113; in national tales, 156; in Owenson's *Princess,* 161; Saint-Simonians on gender, 174; in Sand's model of artistic identity, 262
Directoire, 136, 148
Discophore, 144, 145
discourse/counter-discourse, 13–19, 92, 98, 126, 133, 155
Discourse/Counter-Discourse (Terdiman), 4
Discourses (Reynolds), 55
distribution of the sensible (Rancière), 11–13, 64, 128, 265
"dix-neuf Illustres," 81
Dixon, W. Hepworth, 284n10
Domenica (Desbordes-Valmore), 94
domestic life: Gillies on, 197, 206; in *To the Lighthouse,* 266, 267; and miniature painting, 199; and portraiture, 195; Saint-Simonian movement on, 174–75; in *Tenant of Wildfell Hall,* 226, 228, 236–37, 242. *See also* Associated Homes; family; marriage; motherhood
domestic space: of British women artists, 56, 64–69, 71–72; in Haudebourt-Lescot's Italian paintings, 141, 144; Howitts on, 100; Leigh Hunt on, 216–17; in national tales, 156; in Owenson's *Princess,* 167, 169; in *Sisters in Art,* 107; in studio culture, 84, 85; transition from, 48–50. *See also* family; marriage; motherhood
Doody, Margaret, 25
Douglas, Mary, 6
Drolling, Martin, 136, 152
Dubufe, Edouard, 264
Dudevant, Aurore. *See* Sand, George
Duguet, Charles, 176–77, 287n13
Du Maurier, George, 16, 17, 273n48, 273n50
Durdent, R. J., 39
"Du Roman" (Souvestre), 178
Dutch genre painting, 141

Duthilloeul, M., 278n18
Duvivier, Aimée, 38

Ecole des Beaux-Arts, 34–35, 263
Ecole Gratuite de dessin pour les jeunes filles, 32
École Polytechnique, 173
economic production: Arnaud's writing for, 176; of British women, 102, 281n25; in *Château de Pictordu,* 261; in *Elle et lui,* 254–55; of French women, 46, 50; A. M. Howitt's promotion of women's, 104; Owenson's writing for, 166; and portraiture, 195, 199; removal of Lizzie Siddal from, 119; in Saint-Simonian movement, 173, 174; in *Sisters in Art,* 107–8; in *Tenant of Wildfell Hall,* 222, 225, 234, 237–38, 241; in *Valentine,* 245, 246. *See also* labor and productivity; professionalism
Edgeworth, Maria, 155, 216
education for women: in *Château de Pictordu,* 260–62; A. M. Howitt's support of women's, 102–4, 106, 113–14; Martineau on, 202; in Owenson's and Staël's novels, 129; Owenson's support of, 167; radical Unitarians on, 198; role in Brontës' lives, 221–25; in *Valentine,* 245. *See also* artistic education
Ekphrasis (Kreiger), 5
Elégies, Marie et romances (Desbordes-Valmore), 76. *See also* Desbordes-Valmore, works of
Elgiva (Boyce), 283n52
Elgiva seized by order of Odo, Archbishop of Canterbury (Millais), 117
Eliot, George, 102, 196–97, 288n6. *See also* Evans, Mary Ann
Elizabeth I, Queen of England, 149, 150, 286n50
Elle et lui (Sand), 246–59; art metaphors in, 250–52, 257, 258; comparison to *Tenant of Wildfell Hall,* 239; comparison to troubadour novels, 252; copying in, 255; criticism of, 247; discourse/counter-discourse of, 14; ethical values in, 250; female subjectivity in, 11; model of representation in, 257; motherhood in, 253–54; as personal story, 247, 258–59; real vs. ideal in, 248–50, 253, 255–58;

and Sand's and Musset's Troubadour novels, 250–51. *See also* Sand, works of
Ellet, Elizabeth Fries Lummis, 1, 6–8
Elliott, Ebenezer, 198, 201
"Eloge de Richardson" (Diderot), 25
Endymion, 82, 279n28
Enfantin, Prosper, 173–76, 287n13
England, 117, 131–32, 152, 165–66. *See also* Britain; Victorian England
English Female Artists (Clayton), 263
The English Woman's Journal, 101, 102, 104
equality: Castiglione on, 279n36; in *Clémence*, 182, 185, 187–88; and collective domesticity, 207; in France, 80; of French women authors, 173; A. M. Howitt on, 73–74, 97, 113; Howitts' support of, 101, 114; in *To the Lighthouse*, 269; of nation and gender, 126; in Owenson's *Princess*, 165; in painting and fiction, 7; politics of, 12, 13; radical Unitarians on, 198; Rancière on, 13, 273n36; Saint-Simonian movement on, 173–74; in Sand's troubadour novel, 251. *See also* feminism
Erskine, Margaret, 150–52
Essays on Women's Work (Parkes), 101
ethnography, 135, 139, 141, 143
Eugénie, Empress, 264
Eugénie Grandet (Balzac), 178
Eux et Elles: Histoire d'un scandale (Lescure), 247
Evans, Mary Ann (George Eliot), 102, 196–97, 288n6
Evans, Richard, 204
Examiner, 213
The Exceptional Woman: Elizabeth Vigée-Lebrun and the Cultural Politics of Art (Sheriff), 3
"exceptional woman," 2, 3, 15, 33, 40, 76, 95, 152, 180
L'Expédition d'Egypte sous les orders de Bonaparte (Cogniet and Cogniet), 52

The Fair at Grottaferrata (Haudebourt-Lescot), 141
family: artistic brotherhoods as, 98; Desbordes-Valmore's use of metaphor, 86–87, 94; Gillies on, 211; Howitts on, 100; laws of, 125; loss as Romantic theme, 18; in Owenson's and Staël's novels, 131, 133, 134; "romance" in *Clémence*, 182; in Sand's and Musset's troubadour novels, 250–52; in *Sisters in Art*, 107; in *La Vendetta*, 83; in *Wild Irish Girl*, 129. *See also* domestic life; domestic space; motherhood
Faucit, Helen, 201
Faust (Goethe), 117, 283n51, 283n55
"Feast of the Poets" (Hunt), 213–20
Female Design Schools, 32
female Messiah, 174, 176, 187, 287n7, 287n13
femininity: in French art and literature, 76–80, 83; Leigh Hunt on, 216–17; of Martineau, 202, 204–6, 289n22; of miniature portraits, 199, 201; of painting, 6, 216; predicament of, 3; and professionalism, 32; in *Tenant of Wildfell Hall*, 228–29, 234, 237. *See also* artists, female; gender ideology
feminism: of Arnaud, 173, 176, 179; in *Boadicea Brooding over her Wrongs*, 117; of British women artists, 263; in *Clémence*, 181, 183, 187; and female artistic identity, 265; French and British attitudes toward, 7, 19–20; of French Second Republic, 190; of Gillies sisters, 197, 220; and William and Mary Howitt, 100, 114; A. M. Howitt's commitment to theological, 120–21; in A. M. Howitt's sisterhood, 102–4, 106, 116; and miniatures as engravings, 202; of Owenson, 158, 167–68; Pollack on, 2; publications, 175–76; use of term, 274n59; and visuality/visibility in art, 13. *See also* equality; *femmes nouvelles*; politics
La Femme de l'avenir, 175
La Femme libre, 175–76
La Femme nouvelle, 175
femmes nouvelles, 175, 181. *See also* feminism
Les Femmes socialistes (Daumier), 190, *191*
Fenwick, Isabella, 208
Ferris, Ina, 154, 156
Fiammingo, Paulo, 277n54
field of cultural production (Bourdieu), women artists and authors in, 1, 4–6, 18, 28, 33, 40, 50, 79, 80, 83, 112, 116, 172, 177, 201, 202, 213, 244, 247, 253, 262, 265, 269. *See also* professionalism
Le Fils du Titien (Musset), 250–53, 259
The First Steps (Haudebourt-Lescot), 141

Fisher, Judith, 204
Flaubert, Gustave, 243, 259, 294n28
flâneur, 272n28, 292n1
Flint, Kate, 272n24, 273n41
folklore, 143–44
Foucault, Michel, 2, 10, 272n27
Fourier, Charles, 174–75
Fourierist movement, 80, 121, 174–75
Fox, Eliza, 276n39, 280n13
Fox, William Johnson, 101, 197, 198, 201, 202, 204, 220
Fragonard, Jean-Honoré, 141, 279n28
France: Arnaud on women in politics of, 178–79; Arnaud's novels on condition in, 173, 185; as Britain's Other, 24, 274n64; connection between painting and literature in, 4–5; female authors in, 80–81, 84, 171, 172, 247, 287n2; female subjectivity in, 18; focus on cultural context of, 2; gender ideology in, 19–22, 253; Haudebourt-Lescot's history scenes of, 149, 152; Haudebourt-Lescot's popularity in, 134–36, 148–49; hierarchies and exclusion in, 13, 34–38, 80, 83, 95–96; in history painting, 140; images of women artists in, 269; national and cultural identities in, 24–27, 125–27, 134, 150; Owenson's popularity in, 157–58; Owenson's works on, 128; perception of German aesthetic in, 72; portraiture in, 195, 196; portrayal of culture in *Corinne,* 132–33; professionalization of female artists in, 3, 74; religion in, 148; Sand's popularity in, 243; Walter Scott's popularity in, 150; sentimental social novels' focus on, 172; social structure in, 11; studio culture in, 55–56; studio portraits in, 34–54; tensions with Britain, 149–50; travel to and from Britain, 156–57; women's training and exhibition in, 33, 263–65
France in 1829–30 (Owenson), 27, 157
France (Owenson), 157, 158, 286n9, 286n10
Frank, Robin Jaffe, 199
Fraser's Magazine, 204
French Academy (Rome), 136–37, 144
French Gallery, 102
Friedman, Susan Stanford, 92, 93
From a Window (Howitt), 283n54
Frow, John, 9
Fuchs, Jeanne, 293n17

Fuller, Margaret, 127
Full-Length Painting Representing a Woman Painting and Two Pupils Watching Her (Labille-Guiard), 40–42, *41,* 60
The Future of the Image (Rancière), 269

Gaelic language, 155
Gagnier, Regenia, 102–3
Gambart, Ernest, 264
Garb, Tamar, 3, 196, 263
Garrard, Mary, 3
Gaskell, Elizabeth, 71, 101, 102, 223, 224, 277n56
Gathering of Artists in Isabey's Studio (Boilly). See *Réunion d'artistes dans l'atelier d'Isabey* (Boilly)
Gautier, Théophile, 16, 26, 286n16
Gavarni, (Paul), 17
Gay, Delphine, See Girardin, Delphine Gay de
Gay, Sophie, 77
Gazette des Beaux-Arts, 1
gender ideology: in Arnaud's novels, 173, 183–84, 190; in art criticism, 118; and artistic identity, 6; in Balzac, 15, 80–85, 92; in Mary Ellen Best's portrait, 69; and boundaries in Romanticism, 18–19, 26, 112–13, 125–26; Brontës' negotiation of, 222–24; in *Château de Pictordu,* 260–62; and collective identity, 7, 207; Desbordes-Valmore on, 85–96; and difference in French Romantic poetry, 76–80; discourse/counter-discourse on, 14–16; in *Elle et lui,* 248–50, 252–59; in French Realist fiction, 171–72; in French studio portraits, 34–55; Gillies' attempts to reshape, 197, 211–13; in Margaret Gillies's portraits, 201–6; in Haudebourt-Lescot's Italian paintings, 141; hierarchies of, 8, 13; in historical novels, 155; in A. M. Howitt's narrative, 73–74, 107; and "law of genre," 9; in *To the Lighthouse,* 266–69; and Martineau's boundary crossing, 202–6; and national identity, 126–54, 156; of Leigh Hunt, 213–20; in portraiture, 195–96, 199–200; and representation of women, 19–24; role in cultural experience, 3–5, 265; of Saint-Simonians, 174, 175; Sand on, 244; in sentimental social novels, 172; in studio

culture, 84; in *Tenant of Wildfell Hall*, 226–42; and visuality/visibility in art, 10. *See also* artists, female; artists, male; femininity; masculinity
generations: collective identity between, 45, 60, 89; A. M. Howitt's dialogue with, 105; in *To the Lighthouse*, 266, 268; in Owenson's *Princess*, 160; rivalries between in Owenson's and Staël's novels, 131; Sand's influence on, 262; in *Scène de Déluge*, 88; in *Sisters in Art*, 107, 108, 116
Genette, Gérard, 84
genius: Charlotte Brontë on Romantic cult of, 222; definition of, 15–16; in *Elle et lui*, 248, 249, 253–56, 258–59; in Margaret Gillies's portraits, 204, 206, 208; Leigh Hunt on, 214; as male, 1, 92–93, 255; in Sand's and Musset's troubadour novels, 251–52; spirituality of in *Clémence*, 188. *See also* Romanticism
Genlis, Mme de, 157, 216
genre painting: by Mary Ellen Best, 65; comparison to Owenson's fiction, 157; femininity of, 32; French, 141–43, 285n39; by Grandpierre-Deverzy, 50; Haudebourt-Lescot's Italian, 134–48, 285n27; in Rolinda Sharples portrait, 58
genres: competition between, 6, 80–84; crossing borders between, 16, 26, 112–13, 125–26, 132, 156; Desbordes-Valmore on transcending differences in, 85, 86; differences in literary, 76, 77; Gillies' attempts to reshape, 197, 220; hierarchies of, 8, 80, 86, 248–49; Leigh Hunt on gender of, 216; laws of, 8–9, 22; and Martineau's boundary crossing, 202; metaphors in *Elle et lui*, 250, 259; women in "minor," 32. *See also* literature; painting
Gentileschi, Artemisia, 1
Geoffrin, Marie-Thérèse, 20
Gérard, François, 35, 39, 50, 127
Géricault, Théodore, 50
The Germ, 99, 280n7
Germany, 56, 64–65, 69–74, 104, 160–62
Gillies, Adam, Lord, 197, 288n7
Gillies, Margaret: in "Blue-Stocking Revels," 215; career of, 196–98; and collective domesticity, 207; comparison to A. M. Howitt, 69; crossing of artistic boundaries, 26; goals for women in society, 211–13; and Howitts, 101, 197, 282n34, 288n6, 289n8; male subjects of, 202, 204; as miniature portrait painter, 200–201, 289n21; portrait of Dickens, 200, 289n19; portrait of Leigh Hunt, 24, 217–20, *218,* 290n42; portraits of artistic couples, 207–13, *210, 212;* portrait of William and Mary Howitt, 211–13, *212;* portraits of Martineau, 201–6, *203,* 289n23; portraits of William and Mary Wordsworth, 208–11, *210;* and radical Unitarians, 197–99
Gillies, Mary: career of, 197; editorship of *Monthly Repository,* 213, 289n9; on family, 211; and Howitts, 101, 197, 282n34, 288n6, 289n8; social engagement of, 206, 220
Gillies, Mary Leman Grimstone, 198, 201, 215
Gillies, William, 288n7
Gillray, James, 17
Girardin, Delphine Gay de, 127, 272n17
Girodet, Anne-Louis, 35, 38, 39, 50, 53, 82, 87–89, 140, 148, 279n33
Girton College, 101, 263
Godwin, William, 197
Goethe, Johann Wolfgang, 93, 117–18, 161, 283n51, 283n55
Goncourt, Edmond and Jules, 75
Gonzalès, Eva, 265
Gotlieb, Marc, 50
Gouges, Olympe de, 174, 274n59
Govdiva's Ride (Mermin), 4
Grandpierre-Deverzy, Adrienne: *L'Atelier d'Abel de Pujol,* 47–50, *49,* 82, 93; comparison to Amélie Cogniet, 50, 52; comparison to Haudebourt-Lescot, 144; comparison to Caroline Thévenin, 53; training and reputation of, 47–50
Les Grands Artistes de l'école française du XIXe siècle, 264
Grand Tour, 139, 157
Green Drawing Room at Castle Howard (Best), 65–66, *66,* 277n54
Greer, Germaine, 276n23, 276n34
Grétry, André-Ernest, 89, 136
Greuze, Jean-Baptiste, 38, 141, 143, 285n39
Griffith, Elizabeth, 20, 25
grisettes, 17, 18
Gros, Antoine-Jean, 35, 148
Guattari, Félix, 155

Guérin, Pierre-Narcisse, 50
Guerrilla Girls, 294n12
Guiard, Nicolas, 276n27
Guillemard, Sophie, 38
Guindorf, Reine, 175
Guise, Marie de, 149

Habermas, Jurgen, 156, 206
Hagstrom, Jean, 5
Hall, Donald E., 282n45
Harrison, Anna, 100, 280n17
Haudebourt-Lescot, Hortense, 134–53;
    Le Baisement des pieds de la statue de saint Pierre, 146; and Antonio Canova, 145, 285n44; career of, 134–36, 152–53; comparison to Owenson, 157; Desbordes-Valmore on, 89–92; Desbordes-Valmore's daughter as student of, 279n34; on dominated culture, 144; influence of, 26–27; *Le Jeu de la main chaude, 142; Mary Queen of Scots Fainting on Being Forced to Abdicate, 151;* in Owenson's *France,* 286n9; Italian genre painting, 128, 134–48; as part of "petits peintres," 135, 285n27; portrait of, 137, *138,* 285n35; reference in *Clémence,* 181, 185; *Self-Portrait, 91;* on transnational boundary crossing, 126
Haudebourt, Louis, 148
Haugh, George, 64
Hawthorne, Nathaniel, 6
Hay, Jane Benham. *See* Benham, Jane
Haywood, Eliza, 25
Head of Lizzie Siddal (Howitt), *110*
Head of Lizzie Siddal (Leigh Smith), *111*
Heffernan, James, 5
Heim, François-Joseph, 90
Helen of Troy, 55
Hemans, Felicia, 18, 101, 127
Herford, Laura, 294n1
Higonnet, Anne, 3
Hill, Gertrude, 288n6
Hill, Octavia, 196, 288n6
Histoire de la vie et des ouvrages de Raphael (Quincy), 279n31
Histoire de ma vie (Sand), 243, 253
Histoire d'Ernestine (Riccoboni), 277n1
Histoire des Peintres (Blanc), 135
historical novel, 25, 154–55, 171, 178, 250. *See also* novel

history: of British women painters, 263; in *Château de Pictordu,* 262; in Owenson's *Princess,* 156; Sand's troubadour novel based on, 251; subjects of British, 117, 283nn51–52; women's role in, 129, 132, 149, 163
The History of Napoleon (Horne), 206
history painting: approaches to, 140; of Léon Cogniet, 50, 52; comparison to nature painting, 89; at David's studio, 35; by Grandpierre-Deverzy, 50; by Haudebourt-Lescot, 144, 149; prestige of, 117, 248; and professionalism, 32; in Rolinda Sharples portrait, 58
Homer, 216
Hoock, Holger, 56
Horace (Sand), 181
Horne, Richard Hengist: collaboration with Mary Gillies, 206; and collective domesticity, 207; Dickens's engraving in journal of, 200; editorship of *Monthly Repository,* 213, 289n9; Gillies' association with, 197, 198, 289n9; Margaret Gillies's letter to, 211–13; and Howitts, 101; miniature portraits of, 201, 219; in *Monthly Repository,* 198; on Wordsworth's portrait, 208
The Horse Fair (Bonheur), 264
Hosmer, Harriet, 8
Houdon, Jean-Antoine, 43
Household Words, 71, 99, 273n47, 277n55
Howard, Simon, 277n54
Howitt, Anna Mary: articles by, 71, 277n55; and artistic brotherhood/sisterhood, 17, 97–98; on art, labor, and collaboration, 99–106; Art-lectures of, 115; background, 99–100; *Boadicia,* 117–21; comparison to Mary Ellen Best, 69; comparison to Desbordes-Valmore, 85; crossing of artistic boundaries, 26; exhibit of *The Sensitive Plant,* 283n51; failure to create sisterhood, 116; on female subjectivity, 11; first use of term "the sisters," 106; Gillies' association with, 197; Margaret Gillies's influence on, 196; *Head of Lizzie Siddal, 110;* heroism of, 117–21; idea of sisterhood, 102, 106, 282n34; legacy of, 121; marriage of, 281n19; portrait of, 211; in Pre-Raphaelite Sisterhood, 280n8; on Ruskin's criticism, 119–20; shift to pastels, 120; on studio life,

69–74; training in Germany, 65; as translator, 100, 281n18; in "Ye Newe Generation," 104–6, *105*
Howitt, Anna Mary, works of: *An Art Student in Munich*, 69–74, 104, 106, 118, 272n32, 277nn55–58; *Aurora: A Medley in Verse* (with Alfred Watts), 100; *Pioneers of the Spiritual Reformation*, 120; *The Sisters in Art*, 2, 11, 27, 73, 97, 99, 101, 103, 106–16, 117, 239, 282n34
Howitt, Margaret, 100, 281n18
Howitt, Mary: in "Blue-Stocking Revels," 215; career of, 100–101; editing and promotion of daughter's letters, 277n56; and gender boundaries, 220; Gillies' association with, 101, 197, 282n34, 288n6, 289n8; letter to sister, 100, 280n17; miniature portraits of, 201, 211, 219; support of property bill, 102; on women's art production, 115; on women's education and social position, 113, 282n41
Howitt, Mary, works of: *Autobiography*, 100, 277n56, 289n8; "Margaret von Ehrenberg: The Artist Wife (with William Howitt), 272n17
Howitt's Journal, 100, 197, 201, 204, 206, 211, 281n18, 282n34
Howitt, William: to Australia, 289n9; "Biographical Sketches" of, 120; career of, 100–101; Gillies' association with, 101, 197, 282n34, 288n6, 289n8; on Martineau, 205; miniature portraits of, 211, 219, 220; relationship with Ruskin, 118; on Tennyson's *Princess*, 113–14; on women's art production, 115
Huet, Pierre Daniel, 25
Hugo, Victor, 16, 76, 94
Hunt, Leigh: on Blue-Stockings, 24, 213–20; Dickens's portrait of, 219, 290n43; on Margaret Gillies, 208; Gillies' association with, 197; and Howitts, 101; portraits of, 14, 201, 217–20, 290n42
Hunt, William Holman, 98
hybridity, 130, 132–33, 150, 169, 284n18

Idealism, 250, 259, 261, 262
The Illustrated Exhibitor and Magazine of Art, 106–7
Illustrated London News, 100

illustration and design, 112, 120, 221–22. See also artisanal production
Illustrations of Political Economy (Martineau), 201, 202
Impressionists, 232, 265
independence: Arnaud's assertion of, 176, 179–82; Anne Brontë on, 224; in *Elle et lui*, 254; in A. M. Howitt's sisterhood, 101–3, 107, 115; in Owenson's *Princess*, 159; Pre-Raphaelite Brotherhood on, 98, 119; spiritualism as, 120; in *Tenant of Wildfell Hall*, 222, 230, 233–39, 241, 242; in Tennyson's *Princess*, 113; in *Valentine*, 245–46
Indiana (Sand), 173, 179, 236, 237, 240, 244, 291n15, 292n9. See also Sand, works of
Ingelbien, Raphael, 157
Ingres, J.-A.-D., 136–39, *138*
Intérieur de l'atelier de Léon Cogniet (Amélie Cogniet), 50–53, *51*, 276n34
Ireland: authors from, 155, 156; national identity in Owenson's *Princess*, 162, 164; novel about culture of, 126–34; Owenson's defense of, 159; Owenson's plea for freedom in, 163, 173; personification of, 127, 130, 139; religion in, 148; union with England, 131–32
Isabey, Jean-Baptiste, 35, *36*, 43, 45–46
Isbell, John, 127
Italy: Benham in, 102; British artists' training in, 56; Corinne's personification of, 127; Greuze in, 285n39; Haudebourt-Lescot's genre paintings in, 134–48; Haudebourt-Lescot's success in, 90; novel about culture of, 126–34; Owenson's plea for freedom in, 163; Owenson's volume on, 128, 157, 158; publication of *The Liberal* in, 213; as a woman, 130
Italy (Owenson), 128, 157, 158

Jacobs, Naomi, 226
Jacques (Sand), 177
Jal, Auguste, 136
James, Henry, 247, 259
Jameson, Anna, 101, 102
Jameson, Fredric, 9
James VI of Scotland (James I of England), 149, 150
Jane Eyre (Brontë), 222–23, 229, 230, 241

Janin, Jules, 249, 293n15
Jaquet, Constance, 279n33
Jeffrey, Lord, 197
Le Jeu de la main chaude (Haudebourt-Lescot), 141–45, *142*
Les Jeunes France, 16, 104
La Jeunesse de Marceline (Desbordes-Valmore), 278n19
Jewsbury, Geraldine, 101, 102
Jewsbury, Maria, 101
Johnson, Barbara, 76
Johnstone, Christian Isobel, 170
Journal des femmes artistes, 263
Joyce, James, 155
July Monarchy: accounts of artists' lives published during, 85; changes at onset, 75; feminist journals under, 175–76; Haudebourt-Lescot's success during, 92, 152; literature of, 172, 173; masculine beauty during, 82; popularity of women writers during, 81; tensions of artistic identity under, 50.
Junod, Philippe, 34, 52

Kauffman, Angelica, 1, 20, 33, 55, 90, 116, 164, 216, 275n5
Kaulbach, Wilhelm von, 69–72
Keats, John, 19, 158
Kendrick, Walter, 25
Kerner, Justinus, 120
Keyser, Nicaise de, 264
Kirshenblatt-Gimblett, Barbara, 143
Klumpke, Anna, 264
Knox, Katharine McCook, 276n43
Korsmeyer, Carolyn, 255
Kreiger, Murray, 5
Kris, Ernst, 182
Kristeva, Julia, 2
Kunstlerroman, 16, 75, 80, 106–7
Kurz, Otto, 182

Labille, Claude-Edme, 42
Labille-Guiard, Adélaïde, 39–42; back of the painting trope, 40; Capet's portrait of, 43–45, 89; comparison to Rolinda Sharples, 58–60; on lack of institutions for women, 276n24; marriages, 43, 276n27; self-portrait of, 40–42, *41*; in studio, 39–42

labor and productivity: in Britain, 56, 102, 281n25; in *Clémence*, 179, 181; in *Elle et lui*, 256; *femmes nouvelles* on, 175; Mary Gillies on, 206, 207; Margaret Gillies on, 211–13; A. M. Howitt on, 98–107, 109, 114; masculine association with, 15, 103; radical Unitarians on, 198; Saint-Simonian movement on, 173, 174; in Sand's troubadour novel, 251; women's rights regarding, 13, 265. *See also* economic production
Lacan, Jacques, 2, 261
"Le Lac" (Lamartine), 78
Ladies' Companion, 71
"The Lady Clare" (Tennyson), 119
"The Lady of Shallott" (Tennyson), 119
Lafayette, Mme de, 50, 157, 247
Lagrange, Léon, 1, 6, 7, 9, 13, 272n18
Lamartine, Alphonse de, 19, 76, 78–79, 95, 278n14, 278n18
Lami, Eugène, 286n49
Landon, C. P., 135, 137, 275n19
Landon, Leticia, 18, 101, 127, 215
landscape painting, 32, 58, 67, 73, 264
Langham Place Group, 102, 104
Langland, Elizabeth, 291n14
Laville Leroulx, Madame. *See* Benoist, Marie-Guillemine Laville de
Lawrence, Sir Thomas, 222
Lebreton, Joachim, 276n24
Leerssen, J. Th., 130
legitimacy, 13, 84–96, 97, 114–15, 119, 125, 248, 254, 264
Leigh Hunt (Gillies), *218*
Leigh Hunt's London Journal, 213
Leigh Smith, Barbara: and artistic brotherhoods, 98; in *An Art Student in Munich*, 72, 73; and *Boadicea*, 117, 118, 120; clothing of, 104, 281n32; correspondence about British Royal Academy, 114–15; correspondence about marriage proposal, 281n19; establishment of Society of Female Artists, 263; *Head of Lizzie Siddal*, *111;* in A. M. Howitt's sisterhood, 101–4; and Lizzie Siddal, 109–10; on married women's rights, 101, 102, 281n25, 291n10; name, 281n22; and Pre-Raphaelite Brotherhood, 99; relationship with A. M. Howitt, 97; and Tennyson's *Princess*, 113; in "Ye Newe Generation," 104–6, *105*

326

Leila (Sand), 176–77
Lennox, Charlotte, 20
Leonardo, 75, 140, 251
Leprince, Auguste-Xavier, 46–47
Leroux-Veunevot, Gaston, 264
Le Sage, Alain-René, 25
Lescault, Catherine, 90–92
Lescure, Mathurin de, 247
Lespinasse, Julie de, 20
Lethière, Guillaume Guillon, 136–37, 145, 148
Letter to the Deaf (Martineau), 206
Lettres à David sur le Salon de 1819, 137
Lewes, Charles, 198, 288n6
Lewes, George Henry, 25, 198, 288n6
The Liberal, 213
Liberty Leading the People (Delacroix), 189
The Life and Times of Salvator Rosa (Owenson), 128, 158–59. See also Owenson, works of
life classes, 32, 38. See also models; history painting
Life in the Sickroom (Martineau), 206
The Life of Charlotte Brontë (Gaskell), 223
Liszt, Franz, 243
Literary Gazette, 71, 277n55
literature: Balzac on women in, 80; connection to painting, 4–5, 86; discourse/counter-discourse on, 16; as dominant genre, 9; female artists in, 75, 265; A. M. Howitt on women's portrayal in, 112–13; Howitts' friends in, 101; link to painting in *To the Lighthouse,* 266–69; minor, 154–59; promotion of women's rights through, 103; studio culture in, 50; style of A. M. Howitt's later, 120; Unitarian ideal of power in, 197, 202. See also genres; poetry
livret, 40, 43, 275n7
Lokke, Kari, 132
Longfellow, Henry Wadsworth, 102
Lord Byron and his Contemporaries (Hunt), 220
Losano, Antonia, 4, 112, 241, 265
Louis David: Son école et son temps (Delécluze), 275n14
Louis Napoleon (Emperor), 190
Louis-Philippe (King of France), 149, 152
Louis XVI, 95, 150
Louvre, 39, 52, 81–82, 286n9
love: in *L'Atelier d'un peintre,* 93–95; in *Château de Pictordu,* 262; in *Clémence,* 179, 182, 184, 187, 189, 190; in *Elle et lui,* 256–59; in Owenson's *Princess,* 165, 167, 168; in Sand's and Musset's Troubadour novels, 250–52; in *Tenant of Wildfell Hall,* 233–36, 241, 242
Lovenjoul, Spoelberch de, 247
Loy, Aimé de, 278n14
Lui (Colet), 247
Lui et elle (Musset), 247
Le Luxe français: La Restauration (Bouchot), 157
Luxembourg Palace, 148
Lynch, Deidre, 156
Lytton, Bulwer, 197

Macaulay, Catherine, 20
Les Maîtres mosaïstes (Sand), 250–51, 259. See also Sand, works of
Maclise, Daniel, 204, 282n38, 289n19
Macready, William, 197, 201
Madame Adélaïde Labille-Guiard peignant le portrait de Joseph-Marie Vien (Capet), 43–46, 44
Mademoiselle de Maupin (Gautier), 286n16
Le Magazin pittoresque, 279n31
Maginn, William, 204
La Maison du chat qui pelote (Balzac), 80, 83, 84
male gaze, 130, 165, 196, 214, 228–29, 257. See also visuality/visibility
The Male Malady: Fictions of Impotence in the French Romantic Novel (Waller), 4
Male Trouble: A Crisis in Representation (Solomon-Godeau), 3
Manet, Edouard, 265
Marble Faun (Hawthorne), 6
Marbouty, Caroline, 173
Margaret at the Well (Howitt), 117, 280n9, 283n51, 283n55
Marie-Antoinette, 150
A Market (Sharples), 62
marriage: British laws regarding, 226, 291n10; in *Clémence,* 180, 182, 185, 190; Margaret Gillies's portrayal of Wordsworths', 210–11; Margaret Gillies's refusal of, 197; A. M. Howitt on, 100, 281n19; in *To the Lighthouse,* 267; and national identity, 288n20; in Owenson's and Staël's novels, 131, 132; radical Uni-

tarians on, 198; rejection in Owenson's *Princess*, 169; resistance to, 107, 169–70; Saint-Simonian movement on, 174–75; in *Tenant of Wildfell Hall*, 224, 226, 228, 230, 233, 235–38, 240–42; in Tennyson's *Princess*, 113, 115; in *Valentine*, 244–45; and women's education, 103. See also *arts d'agrément;* domestic life; domestic space; Napoleonic Code

Married Women's Property Bill (1856), 101, 102, 281n25, 291n10

Marsh, Jan, 3, 280n8, 280n12

Martineau, Harriet: 201–6; in "Blue-Stocking Revels," 215; on Charlotte Brontë's novels, 224; comparison to Mary Gillies, 206; disability of, 204–6; and gender boundaries, 202, 204–6, 220, 289n22; in *Monthly Repository*, 198; portraits of, 201–6; support of property bill, 102

Mary Queen of Scots. See Stuart, Mary

Mary Queen of Scots Fainting on Being Forced to Abdicate (Haudebourt-Lescot), 150–52

masculinity: in *Clémence*, 190; discourse/counter-discourse on, 14, 15; of French novels, 172; of French Romantic poetry, 76–80, 86; of historical novels, 154; A. M. Howitt's challenge to, 109; of Martineau, 202, 204–6, 289n22; of studio culture, 34–39, 89; in *Tenant of Wildfell Hall*, 234, 242; in "Ye Newe Generation," 104. See also artists, male; gender ideology

Massardier-Kenney, Françoise, 254

Mayer, Constance, 38, 88, 93, 96

McMurran, Mary Helen, 25

McWilliam, Neil, 140

Méchoulan, Eric, 12

Méditations poétiques (Lamartine), 76

Mellor, Anne K., 4, 126, 156

Memoirs of a London Doll (Gillies), 206

Memoirs of Madame Desbordes-Valmore (Sainte-Beuve), 77

Méphis (Tristan), 173, 181

Merchant of Venice (Shakespeare), 190, 288n25

Mercoeur, Elisa, 77

Mérimée, Jean-François, 43

Mermin, Dorothy, 4, 274n58

Meynier, Charles, 43

Michallon, Achille-Etna, 137, 140

Michelet, Jules, 274n64

Millais, John Everett, 98, 110, 117, 280n7

Miller, Annie, 280n8

Miller, Lucasta, 223

Mill, John Stewart, 197, 198

miniature painting: 199–201; criticism of, 199, 289n16; description of, 199; Margaret Gillies career in, 198–201; as popular form of art, 199; portrait of Leigh Hunt in, 24, 217–20, 290n42; portrait of Martineau in, 201–6; portraits of artistic couples in, 206–13; by Sharples family, 57

Mitchell, W. J. T., 5, 125, 271n13

models, 35, 38, 48, 90, 92, 111–12, 116, 144. See also life classes

Modernist novel, 266, 269

Modern Painters (Ruskin), 118, 119

Mon Coeur mis à nu (Baudelaire), 272n23

Mongez, Angélique, 38

Montagu, Elizabeth, 20

The Monthly Repository: "Blue-Stocking Revels" in, 217, 220; Gillies' collaborations in, 197; Mary Gillies's co-editorship of, 206; Horne's editorship of, 213, 289n9; Leigh Hunt's editorship of, 213; Martineau's contributions to, 201; miniature portraits in, 201, 204; radical Unitarians' ideas in, 198

Moore, George, 225, 291n7

Moore, Lisa L., 127

morality: in *Clémence*, 179–81, 188, 190; of female authors, 223; in novels, 178–79, 288n19; in Owenson's *Princess*, 161, 163, 165–67, 173; in Saint-Simonian movement, 175; of Sand, 177; in sentimental social novels, 173. See also religion

Moreau, Véronique, 144

More, Hannah, 20

Morgan, Sir Charles, 157

Morisot, Berthe, 3, 265

Morowitz, Laura, 46, 97–98

Morris, Jane, 280n8

Moser, Mary, 275n5

Mossman, Mark, 154

motherhood: Desbordes-Valmore on, 87, 88, 93; in *Elle et lui*, 250, 253–54, 256–59; in *To the Lighthouse*, 267, 268; muse of, 259–62; and national identity, 133; as Romantic theme, 18; in *Sisters in Art*, 107, 109, 116; in *Tenant of Wildfell Hall,*

232, 237, 240–41; in Tennyson's *Princess,* 113; in *Valentine,* 245; in *La Vendetta,* 83, 84. *See also* childbirth; domestic life; domestic space; family
Mothers of the Nation (Mellor), 156
Mulvey, Laura, 10, 45, 272n30
Munich, 55, 69–74, 106, 115, 277nn55–56
Munsey's Magazine, 285n35
Murdoch, John, 199
Murger, Henry, 16, 17, 273n47
Musée de la Vie Romantique, 274n73
Museum of Words (Heffernan), 5
Musset, Alfred de: *La Confession d'un enfant du siècle,* 250; *Le Fils du Titien,* 250, 251–53; reference to Sand as man, 249, 293n15; Sand's relationship with, 243, 247, 249, 250, 252, 258–59, 293n12, 293n17, 294n28
Mutrie, Annie, 119
Mutrie, Martha, 119

Nabis, 16
Naginski, Isabelle, 250
Nameless and Friendless (Osborn), 230, *231*
Napoleon, 81, 82, 145, 147, 148, 156, 158, 179
Napoleonic Code, 19–20, 179, 288n20
Napoleonic Wars, 25
national identity: in Arnaud's novels, 173; boundaries of, 125–26, 284n2; of female artists, 3, 6, 7, 125–26; in France and Britain, 24–27, 149, 150; gender in, 126–34; Mary Gillies on women's role in, 206–7; in Haudebourt-Lescot's Italian paintings, 134–48; and marriage, 288n20; Mellor's work on, 4; in national tales, 156; in Owenson's and Staël's novels, 126–34; in Owenson's *Princess,* 159–70; Staël's ideas of, 130, 284n18. *See also* pluralistic nationalism
national tale, 154–59, 171. *See also* novel
Navarre, Marguerite de, 216
Nazarene brotherhood, 18, 104, 163–64, 274n53
Necker, Suzanne, 20
Neergaard, Bruun, 38–39
Neo-Classical style, 140
Newcomer, James, 170
A New Spirit of the Age, 197, 200, 201, 206, 208, 289n9

Nicholas Nickleby (Dickens), 199–200. *See also* Dickens, works of
The Nine Living Muses of Great Britain (Samuel), 20, *21*
Noailles, Mme de, 275n14
Nochlin, Linda, 2, 32, 271n5
Nodier, Charles, 75
Noon, Patrick, 26
The Notary Public (Haudebourt-Lescot), 141
novelists, female: Arnaud on job of, 178–79, 288n19; artistic identity of, 84; and Desbordes-Valmore, 84–86; influence in France, 80–81; sentimental, 171–73, 177; threat to male authors, 15
novelists, male, 75, 90, 95–96
novel: Arnaud's preference for writing, 177; on artistic brotherhood/sisterhood, 17–18, 106–7; construction of Brontës', 223; development in France and Britain, 25–26; expansion of genre, 129; female artistic identity through, 265–69; female subjectivity in, 1, 2, 7, 18, 19; and gender in France, 80–84; images of women in British and French in, 269; professional women artists in, 74; promotion of women's rights through, 103; Sand's pastoral, 244; Souvestre on genesis of, 178; study of in France, 4. *See also* historical novel; national tale; sentimental social novel
La Nuit des prolétaires (Rancière), 13, 273n35
Nunn, Pamela Gerrish, 3, 119, 280n8

Oberter, Rachel, 120
Ockman, Carol, 34
L'Oeuvre (Zola), 16, 75
The Old Curiosity Shop (Dickens), 107, 108, 282n38. *See also* Dickens, works of
Old Masters: accounts of lives of, 85, 182, 279n31, 288n23; in British women's art education, 58, 64–67, 72; female artists' references to, 90; and miniature painting, 200
Oliphant, Margaret, 120
Olivet, Fabre d', 152
"On the Rank of Women in the Arts" (Lagrange, "Du rang des femmes dans les arts"), 1, 6, 7, 9, 13, 272n18
Ophelia (Millais), 110
Oppenheimer, Margaret, 39

Orléans monarchy, 149
Orr, Lyndon, 285n35
Osborn, Emily, 230, *231*, 263
Otherness: of Balzac's painter, 80; of Britain and France, 24; in *Clémence*, 186; in construction of modern identities, 17; and Desbordes-Valmore, 77, 85; in *Elle et lui*, 257, 258; in foreign cultures, 128, 129, 131–34; in Haudebourt-Lescot's Italian paintings, 140, 141, 143–44; in national tales, 154; in Owenson's *Princess*, 164, 167; in paintings and novels by women, 28; of Pre-Raphaelite Brotherhood, 98; through *physiologies*, 22
Owen, Alex, 120
Owenism, 198
Owenson, Sydney (Lady Morgan): 126–34; 154–70; admiration of Staël, 128, 284n13; on artistic brotherhood/sisterhood, 17; background and career of, 127, 166, 284n18; comparison to Haudebourt-Lescot, 134–35, 139, 141; comparison to sentimental social novelists, 173; criticism of art, 158; on female subjectivity, 10; formulation of art in *Princess*, 161, 163–64; in France, 157, 286n9; as Glorvina, 284n10; influences on, 27; marriage of, 157; on national identity, gender, and difference, 126–34; national tale of, 154–59; on *St. Clair*, 286n14; on transnational boundary crossing, 126
Owenson, Sydney, works of: *France*, 128, 157–58, 286n10; *France in 1829–30*, 128, 157–58; *Italy*, 128, 157–58; *The Life and Times of Salvator Rosa*, 128, 158–59; *The Princess; or the Beguine*, 2, 10, 27, 154–56, 159–70, 284n13; *The Wild Irish Girl*, 27, 126–34, 154, 157

painters: cultural exchange of Romantic, 26; definition of, 5; focus of study on, 2; French fiction about, 75; of portraits, 195–96; social change by, 198; and visuality/visibility in art, 12. *See also* visual arts/artists
painters, female: Arnaud's portrayal of, 173, 178–90; as Balzac's rivals, 83, 84; Anne Brontë's portrayal of, 229–30; Capet's portrayal of, 43–46; critics of, 39, 275n14; Desbordes-Valmore on, 84–86, 92, 94–95; in *Elle et lui*, 246–59; Haudebourt-Lescot's comparison to male artist, 90; Haudebourt-Lescot's pursuit of career as, 136–37; A. M. Howitt's portrayal of, 103–4, 106–16; image of miniature, 199–200; images in Britain and France, 269; invisibility in Britain, 99; mother muse of, 259–62; Owenson's portrayal of, 159, 163–70, 173; professionalism of, 202, 264–65; representation of, 7, 24; Sand's parallel with authors, 244–46; studios operated by, 38; as subjects of novels, 6, 10, 272n17
painters, male: Balzac's portrayal of, 92; in *Elle et lui*, 246–50, 252–59; novels about, 272n17; rivalry with male authors, 75, 94
painting: act of in *To the Lighthouse*, 266–69; of Brontës, 221–23; connection to literature, 4–5, 86; discourse/counter-discourse on, 16; as dominant genre, 9; in *Elle et lui*, 252–53; female artistic identity through, 265–69; female subjectivity in Romantic, 19; femininity of, 6, 216; within painting, 58, 65–69; promotion of women's rights through, 103; in *Sisters in Art*, 109; in *Tenant of Wildfell Hall*, 232, 239. *See also* genres
Painting Room in our House in York (Best), 67, *68*
Painting Women: Victorian Women Artists (Cherry), 3
Pajou, Augustin, 42, 43
Pallière, Etienne, 43
Pallière, Léon, 43
Palmer, Samuel, 16
Palm, Etta, 174
Pankhurst, Emmeline, 121
paragone, 75, 80
paratext, 84, 131, 132
Paris: artistic culture in, 56; ateliers for women in, 263; British artists' training in, 55, 56; brotherhood of artists in, 16, 17; Desbordes-Valmore's acting career in, 278n12; *Discophore* shipped to, 145; Margaret Gillies's education in, 26; Haudebourt-Lescot's exhibitions in, 138, 141, 148; Haudebourt-Lescot's teaching career in, 135; Labille-Guiard in, 39; museum for Sand's belongings in, 274n73; Owenson in, 27, 157, 286n9;

Saint-Simonian movement in, 174; Sand in, 246; Sand's alternative to vision of, 244; schools in, 32; Sommariva's art collection in, 50; studio culture in, 34–35; Caroline Thévenin in, 53
Paris Sketch Book (Thackeray), 16
Parkes, Bessie Rayner: clothing of, 104, 281n32; in A. M. Howitt's sisterhood, 101–4; and Siddall, 109; and Tennyson's *Princess*, 113; on Victoria Press, 281n24; on women's rights, 103; in "Ye Newe Generation," 104–6, *105*
partage du sensible. *See* distribution of the sensible
patriarchal ideology: in *Château de Pictordu*, 260, 261; and creativity, 92; Desbordes-Valmore on, 88; *femmes nouvelles*' resistance to, 175; in Girodet, 88; Labille-Guiard on, 42; in *To the Lighthouse*, 266–68; in Owenson's and Staël's novels, 131–32; of Pre-Raphaelite Brotherhood, 98; and Romantic male gaze, 257; in *Tenant of Wildfell Hall*, 224, 227–28, 238; in *Valentine*, 245; Vernet on, 47. *See also* power
Pâris, Pierre-Adrien, 145
peasants, French, 157–58, 245
peasants, Italian, 128, 134–48, 185, 186
Le Peintre de Salzbourg (Nodier), 75
Pen vs. Paintbrush (Wettlaufer), 5
The People's Journal, 197, 201, 204, 206, 208
Le Père Goriot (Balzac), 172, 177, 180, 183–84, 288n24. *See also* Balzac, works of
performed identity: in 'Blue-Stocking Revels," 214, 217; of Brontës, 222, 223, 225; in *Clémence*, 185–87; of Leigh Hunt, 219; in Owenson's *Princess*, 159–70; in portraiture, 196, 200, 204; in *Tenant of Wildfell Hall*, 230. *See also* women's identities
Person, Leland, Jr., 259
Peterson, Linda, 100, 120
La Petite Soeur de Balzac: Essai sur la femme auteur (Planté), 4
Petrarch, 216
Physiologie du bas-bleu (Soulié), 22–24
physiologies, 22–24. *See also* caricature
Picot, François, 43
Pierre Grassou (Balzac), 108
The Piferari Playing before the Madonna (Haudebourt-Lescot), 141

Pilbeam, Pamela, 173
Pinelli, Bartolomeo, 139
Pioneers of the Spiritual Reformation (Howitt), 120
Planté, Christine, 4
Plato, 92
Les Pleurs (Desbordes-Valmore), 78–79
pluralistic nationalism, 128, 150, 165. *See also* national identity
Poems (Bell, Bell, and Bell), 224
Poems (Parkes), 101
Poésies complètes de Mme Desbordes-Valmore, 78
poètes maudits, 76
poetry: aesthetic of Romantic, 77; female subjectivity in Romantic, 18, 19; A. M. Howitt's later, 120; masculinity of, 76–80, 86; national identity through, 132; promotion of women's rights through, 103; themes of Desbordes-Valmore's, 87, 88
poets, 78, 101. *See also* authors
poets, female: as broken vessels, 79; Desbordes-Valmore's success as, 116; as gleaners, 79; Haudebourt-Lescot and Corinne as, 134; Leigh Hunt's beliefs about, 213–14; marginalization of French, 76–80, 89. *See also* authors; poets
poets, male: Desbordes-Valmore's dialogue with, 77–80, 90, 95–96; on gender differences, 77; Leigh Hunt's satire of, 213. *See also* authors; poets
Pointon, Marcia, 199
police order (Rancière), 11–13, 19, 125, 226
politics: and aesthetics, 4, 5, 11; of art criticism, 118; in Mary Ellen Best's work, 64; of British women artists, 56, 65; in *Château de Pictordu*, 262; in *Clémence*, 178, 181, 186–90; in *Elle et lui*, 247; of *femmes nouvelles*, 175; of French women artists, 263; of gender, nation, and identity, 2, 19, 125–26, 159–70; in genre scenes, 157–58; of Howitts, 98–101; and "law of genre," 8; in *To the Lighthouse*, 268; in Martineau's writings, 201–6; in national tales, 154–55; in novels, 127, 172, 173; in Owenson's and Staël's novels, 129–30; in Owenson's *Princess*, 156, 159–70; in painting and sculpture, 3; and portraiture, 196, 199; of radical

331

Unitarians, 198; in Rolinda Sharples portrait of Brereton, 64; in *Tenant of Wildfell Hall*, 224, 226, 242; in *Valentine,* 245; in *La Vendetta,* 81–82; in Vernet's studio scene, 46; and visuality/visibility in art, 10–13, 74; women's participation in, 6, 7, 126–34, 149–52, 163, 167–68, 173, 178, 188. *See also* feminism; public sphere
The Politics of Aesthetics (Rancière), 11–14, 19, 34, 75, 125, 128, 134, 226, 265, 273n36
Pollock, Griselda, 2, 93, 282n40
Poovey, Mary, 4
Portfolio Club, 99, 280n7
Portland Gallery, 100
Portrait of Edward Bird, RA (Rippingille), 60, *61*
Portrait of Harriet Martineau (Gillies), *203*
Portrait of Mlle Lescot (Ingres), 137, *138*
portraiture: of artists in French studios, 34–55; by Mary Ellen Best, 64, 65; of Bonheur, 264; by British women artists, 56; in *Château de Pictordu,* 261; children and flowers in, 232, 291n13; in *Elle et lui,* 248–50, 256–59; by French women artists, 39–43, 50, 56; gender and identity in, 195–96; in miniature, 198–201; in Musset's troubadour novel, 252; and Sand's artistic identity, 243; by Sharples family, 56–62; subjects of Margaret Gillies, 198–99; in *Tenant of Wildfell Hall,* 227, 232–33, 236, 239–40, 242; as women's genre, 32. *See also* self-portraits
Poussin, Nicolas, 140, 158, 251, 293n18
Powell, Thomas, 208
power: in *Elle et lui,* 248, 253, 254, 257; of mother muse, 262; in Owenson's *Princess,* 162, 164, 170; resistance to in Owenson's and Staël's novels, 130–31; in sentimental social novels, 172; in *Tenant of Wildfell Hall,* 233, 236, 237. *See also* patriarchal ideology
Pratt, Mary Louise, 145
Prédication dans l'église de St Laurent, hor des murs, à Rome (Haudebourt-Lescot), 135
Pre-Raphaelite Brotherhood: collective identity through, 16; A. M. Howitt's dialogue with, 117; individuality in, 116; as model for Howitt's sisterhood, 98–99, 280n8; Ruskin in, 118; and Siddal, 110, 282n40; women's painting in style of, 117–19, 265. *See also* brotherhood/sisterhood of arts
Pre-Raphaelite Women Artists (Nunn and Marsh), 3, 280n8
Prettejohn, Elizabeth, 98
Prévost, abbé, 25
Pride and Prejudice (Austen), 31–32
Primitifs, 104
La Princesse de Clèves (Mme de Lafayette), 50, 247–48
The Princess; or The Beguine (Owenson), 159–70; comparison to *Clémence,* 186; critics of, 170; cultural encounters in, 161–62; female subjectivity in, 10; language in, 155; Staël's reading of, 284n13
The Princess (Tennyson), 112–15, 119, 282n45
private sphere: and collective domesticity, 207; gender, nation, and identity in, 128–29, 135; in national tales, 156; and portraiture, 195; in Sand's troubadour novel, 251, 252; studio as, 84, 85; in *Tenant of Wildfell Hall,* 226, 238
Prix Décennie (1810), 88
Prix de Rome, 55, 137
professionalism/professional identity: 1, 3, 4, 7, 11–13, 19, 27, 38, 40, 45, 46, 99, 100; in British studio scenes, 55–74; of British women artists, 3, 56, 60, 64, 71–72, 74, 97, 264, 265; of Charlotte Brontë, 222; contributions to, 7; establishment of, 31–34; of French women artists, 264, 265; and Margaret Gillies portraits, 202, 204; of Hortense Haudebourt-Lescot, 90; in A. M. Howitt's sisterhood, 101–6; in *To the Lighthouse,* 267; Ruskin on women's, 119; in *Sisters in Art,* 109; in studio culture, 35, 48–50, 53–55, 74, 89; in *Tenant of Wildfell Hall,* 229, 233, 237–39
Proust, Antonin, 285n35
Prud'hon, Pierre-Paul, 50, 88, 96
public sphere: Arnaud on women's role in, 190; atelier as, 84; British women artists in, 97, 99, 101; and collective domesticity, 207; A. M. Howitt's sisterhood in, 103; Martineau in, 205, 206; miniature painting in, 199, 201; in national tales, 156; in Owenson's *Princess,* 168; Saint-Simonians in, 174; Sand's anxiety in,

246; in Sand's troubadour novel, 251, 252; in *Tenant of Wildfell Hall*, 226, 230; women's artistic identity in, 33, 56, 62, 64, 69, 74, 126, 127, 129, 133. See also politics; social sphere
Pujol, Abel de, 47–50, 82, 93, 280n41
Purity and Danger (Douglas), 6
Pyne, James Baker, 57

Quadrille de Mary Stuart, 149, 286n49
Quarterly Review, 158, 166
Quincy, Quatremère de, 279n31

race, 13, 161
Rancière, Jacques, 11–13; on artistic images, 269; on distribution of the sensible, 11, 13, 128, 265; on equality, 273n36; on invisibility of women artists, 75, 134; and *To the Lighthouse*, 267; on police order, 11–13, 19, 125, 226; on politics, 4, 14, 126; on visibility of female artist, 34, 248; on workers' claim of the night, 13, 273n35
Rape of the Sabine Women (David), 88
Raphael, 89, 90, 140, 251
Realism: Balzac's aesthetic of, 80, 82, 171, 173, 178, 293n18; contrast to Sand's Idealism, 250, 259; in cultural production, 9; discourse/counter-discourse of, 14; gender of French, 171–72, 287n2; and sentimental novels, 4, 173, 177, 179, 190; in *Tenant of Wildfell Hall*, 224, 225, 234, 242
The Red Shoes (Andersen), 281n18
Réflexions sur quelques-uns de mes contemporains (Baudelaire), 77
Regnault, Mme, 38
Reinagle, Philip, 57
The Relic Seller (Haudebourt-Lescot), 141
religion, 147, 148, 163–64, 172, 173. See also morality; spirituality
Rembrandt, 40, 90, 141
Renaudin, Rosalie, 279n33
Rendall, Jane, 103
Restoration, 46, 158, 179–80, 185
Réunion d'artistes dans l'atelier d'Isabey (Boilly), 35, *36,* 45–46
Revolutionary period, 174, 178, 181, 185–90
Revue de Paris, 177, 178

Reynolds, Joshua, 16, 55, 65
Riccoboni, Marie-Jeanne, 25, 216, 277n1
Richardson, Alan, 18, 77
Richardson, Samuel, 25
Rippingille, Edward, 57, 60, *61*
Robert, Fanny, 279n33
Robert, Léopold, 137, 140
Roberts, Caroline, 289n22
Robertson, Andrew, 200
Robinson, William, 222
Robusti, Marietta, 1, 251
Roe Head, 222
Roland, Pauline, 190
Romanticism: and accounts of Old Masters, 288n23; art as religion in, 87; artists' contributions to, 46; in *L'Atelier d'un peintre*, 85, 88–89, 95; British symbols of, 60; Charlotte Brontë and genius of, 222, 224, 225; in *Clémence*, 184, 185; Amélie Cogniet's representation of, 53; creation metaphors and tropes in, 92–93; in cultural production, 9; discourse/counter-discourse on, 14–19; in *Elle et lui*, 248–59; feminine version of, 250, 256; Romantic genius, 11, 15, 16, 60, 167, 204, 208, 224, 255, 256, 258; German, 72, 198; Margaret Gillies's work with genius of, 204, 208; Hugo's socially engaged, 94; of Leigh Hunt, 213, 214, 220; image of bohemian life in, 16–18; of Mary Stuart's story, 149; Mellor's work on, 4; Romantic myth of the artist, 13–19; Owenson's sensibility of, 158, 162; and relationship among arts, 6; and Saint-Simonian movement, 173; subjects of portraiture in, 198–99; in *Tenant of Wildfell Hall*, 227–30, 234–36, 238, 239, 241, 242; in Caroline Thévenin's studio scene, 55; in *Valentine*, 244; in *Wild Irish Girl*, 129; and women's domestic fiction, 156
Romany, Adèle, 38
Rome, 6, 55, 100–101, 134–38, 141, 144–45, 148
Rosa, Salvator, 158–59, 167
Rosemond, Mlle de, 40
Rosenfeld, Jason, 98
Rossetti, Christina, 99, 274n58
Rossetti, Dante Gabriel, 16, 98, 99, 109–10, 119, 280n7, 283n62
Rossetti, William Michael, 98, 120, 277n56

Index

Ross, Kristin, 12
Rowlandson, Thomas, 17, 20–22, *23*
Rowlinson, Matthew, 107
Rownham Ferry (Sharples), 62
Royal Northern Society for the Encouragement of Fine Arts, 221
Royal Scottish Academy, 201, 211
Rubens, Peter Paul, 90, 107
Rural Life (Howitt), 118
Ruskin, John, 72, 109, 118–20, 283n52, 283n62
Ruth, Jennifer, 103
Rydal Mount, 208–10

Sahlins, Peter, 284n2
Sainte-Beuve, C. A., 76–77, 278n14, 293n17
Saint-Hilaire, Geoffroy, 171
Saint-Simon, Comte de, 173, 174. See also Saint-Simonian movement
Saint-Simonian movement: Arnaud's commitment to, 176, 180, 183; on collective good, 173; description of, 173–75; equality in, 80; influence in *Clémence*, 181, 184, 187, 188; influence on radical Unitarians, 198; journals of, 175–76; socialist utopian thought of, 121; split of, 175, 287n13. See also socialist utopian thought
Salon: Capet's painting of female artist in, 43–46; Amélie Cogniet's portrait in, 50; definition of, 275n7; French women's self-portraits in, 56; Haudebourt-Lescot in, 89, 135, 138, 141, 148, 152; hierarchies in, 34; Labille-Guiard's large-scale oil painting in, 42; Caroline Thévenin's exhibition in, 53; women's productions in, 32, 38–40, 50, 264, 265, 275n19
Salon des femmes, 263
salonnières, 20
Salon des Refusés, 265
Samuel, Richard, 20, *21*
Sand, George: on artistic brotherhood/sisterhood, 17; career of, 262; on caricatures, 24; collective good in troubadour novel of, 251, 252; comparison to Arnaud, 185; comparison to Anne Brontë, 236, 237, 239, 240, 291n15; comparison to A. M. Howitt, 282n37; on female subjectivity, 11; Haudebourt-Lescot identified as, 285n35; Howitts' promotion of, 101; ideal in *Elle et lui*, 258; and inequality of women authors, 173; influence on Arnaud, 27, 176–77, 179, 190; masculine qualities of, 15, 249, 262, 293n15; on motherhood, 245, 254, 259–62, 292n6, 293n28; museum of belongings, 274n73; and persona of female artist, 243–46, 262; on prohibition of divorce, 288n20; on proletarian painters, 181; pseudonym of, 84; relationship with Musset, 243, 247, 249, 250, 252, 258–59, 293n17, 294n28; and sentimental social novels, 172; and social utopian thought, 121; Souvestre on, 178; as threat to male artistic image, 18; use of *vous*, 292n5

Sand, George, works of: *Contes d'une Grand-mère*, 259; *Histoire de ma vie*, 243, 253; *Horace*, 181; *Indiana*, 173, 179, 236, 237, 240, 244, 291n15, 292n9; *Jacques*, 177; *Leila*, 176–77; *Les Maîtres mosaïstes*, 250–53, 259; *Valentine*, 244–46, 247
Sandys, Emma, 265
Sappho, 216, 217
Sarrasine (Balzac), 80, 82, 83. See also Balzac, works of
Sass's Academy, 99, 276n39
Saturday Review, 100
Scalands, 109
Scène de Déluge (Girodet), 88
Scènes de la vie de Bohème (Murger), 16, 17, 273n47
Scènes de la vie privée (Balzac), 84, 86
Scheffer, Ary, 26, 274n73
Schnetz, Jean-Victor, 137, 140
Schor, Naomi, 4, 257
Scotland, 149–52, 264. See also Britain
Scott, David, 16
Scott, Walter, 26, 150–52, 154, 155, 171, 178, 197
sculpture, 144–45, 147, 184
Seigel, Jerrold, 17
Self-Portrait (Haudebourt-Lescot), 89, *91*
Self-Portrait in a Straw Hat (Vigée-Lebrun), 90
self-portraits: of Mary Ellen Best, 67; in Cless's painting of David's studio, 38; influences of women's, 90; number of French vs. British, 56; and Sand's artistic identity, 243, 258; in *Tenant of Wildfell Hall*, 226–27; by women, 33; women's

artistic identity through, 74. *See also* portraiture
Self-Portrait with her Mother (Sharples), 58–60, *59*
The Sensitive Plant (Howitt), 277n56, 283n51
sentimentalism, 4, 143, 171–72
sentimental social novel, 172, 183, 185, 190, 250, 287n2. *See also* novel
Sévigné, Madame de, 160
sexuality, 158, 175, 230
Shakespeare, William, 92, 93, 190, 288n25
Sharples, Ellen Wallace, 57, 58–62, *59,* 276n43, 277n48
Sharples, James, 56–57
Sharples, Rolinda: 56–64; as chronicler in public sphere, 62–64, 69; ease with portrait subjects, 277n48; exhibitions in Leeds, 221; *Self-Portrait with her Mother, 59*
Shee, Martin Archer, 16, 289n16
Shelley, Mary, 18
Shelley, Percy Bysshe, 98, 213, 283n51
Sheridan, Elizabeth, 20
Sheriff, Mary, 2, 3, 33, 39
Sherman, Cindy, 195
Siddal, Lizzie, 109–10, 119, 280n8, 282n40, 283n62
Sidlauskas, Susan, 52
Siegfried, Susan, 35
Simon, Caroline, 176, 177, 287n13
Simon, Léon, 287n13
The Sister Arts (Hagstrom), 5
The Sisters in Art (Howitt), 106–16; commodification of art in, 107, 108; comparison to *Tenant of Wildfell Hall,* 239; concept of, 73; and female artistic identity, 109; female subjectivity in, 11; on place of British women artists, 99; promotion of women's rights through, 103–4; significance of, 101; space in, 107, 111. *See also* Howitt, A. M., works of
Sisters of the Brush: Women's Artistic Culture in Late Nineteenth-Century Paris (Garb), 3
slave/slavery, 114, 175, 198, 237, 238, 291n15
Smiles, Samuel, 205
Smith, Adam, 201
Smith, Charlotte, 18
Smith, Gertrude, 198
Smollett, Tobias, 25
social engagement, 101–3, 109, 250–51

socialist utopian thought, 121, 126, 132, 133, 143, 172, 202. *See also* Saint-Simonian movement
social reform: Arnaud's concern with, 179; British women artists' promotion of, 65, 74; in *Clémence,* 184–85, 187–90; Gillies sisters on, 197, 198, 200–201, 206–7, 211; Leigh Hunt on, 213; Martineau on, 201–2, 205, 206; in Owenson's *Princess,* 168; in Saint-Simonian movement, 173–75. *See also* social structure
social sphere, 34, 62. *See also* public sphere
social structure: artistic identity within, 125–26; in Mary Ellen Best's portrait, 69; Anne Brontë's rebellion against, 225, 226, 235, 237; and collective domesticity, 207; Desbordes-Valmore on marginalized members in, 94, 95; discourse/counter-discourse in, 14; Labille-Guiard's place in, 40; and "law of genre," 9; in *To the Lighthouse,* 266; in Martineau's portrait, 203; and novels, 172–73, 178; Owenson on, 156–60, 165, 169–70; and portraiture, 196; Pre-Raphaelite Brotherhood in, 98; and professionalism, 33; in Realist fiction, 171; spiritualism in, 120; in *Valentine,* 245–46; in Victorian England, 114; and visuality/visibility in art, 11, 12; women's presence in French, 45–46, 80. *See also* class; social reform
Society for Promoting the Employment of Women, 102
Society of British Artists, 57, 201
Society of Female Artists, 102, 263, 283n54
Solomon-Godeau, Abigail, 3, 15, 34
Sommariva, Giovanni, 50
Le Sommeil d'Endymion (Girodet), 82
Soulié, Frédéric, 22–24
Southey, Kate, 208, 213
Southwood Smith, Thomas, 101, 197, 198, 201, 207, 208, 214, 219, 288n6
Souvestre, Emile, 178, 287n16
Sparrow, Walter, 136
Spartali, Marie, 265
The Spectator, 100
spirituality: in *Clémence,* 188–89; effect of women's education on, 103; in A. M. Howitt's sisterhood, 106, 109, 115; A. M. Howitt's turn to, 120; in miniature portraits, 202, 208, 209; of Pre-Raphaelite Brotherhood, 98; in

Saint-Simonian movement, 173–74. *See also* religion
Staël, Germaine de: 126–34; background of, 127; in "Blue-Stocking Revels," 216; comparison to Haudebourt-Lescot, 134–35, 139, 141; comparison to Owenson, 157, 158; on female subjectivity, 18; hybridity of, 130, 284n18; influence of, 27; on national identity, gender, and difference, 126–34; Owenson's admiration of, 128, 284n13; political activity of, 156; on transnational boundary crossing, 126
Staël, Germaine de, works of: *Corinne, ou l'Italie*, 18, 27, 126–34, 139, 148, 152, 159, 160, 162, 167, 170, 180, 181, 234, 249, 250, 255, 284n13; *De l'Allemagne*, 18, 128, 157, 274n55; *De la littérature*, 128
Station de piferari devant une madone (Haudebourt-Lescot), 148
St. Clair (Owenson), 286n14
Steiner, Wendy, 5
Stendhal, 80–81, 109, 171–73
Stephens, Frederic George, 98
still life painting, 32, 67, 119–20
St James Fair (Sharples), 62
Stoichita, Victor, 40
Stoneman, Patsy, 223
St Peter's Basilica, 88, 145–49
Stuart, Mary, 149–52, 286n50
studio culture: in *L'Atelier d'un peintre*, 84–96; in British literature, 69–74; in British painting, 55–74; French men's paintings of, 45–47; French women's paintings of, 33–38, 43–55; and professionalism, 33–34; in *Sisters in Art*, 108, 111–12; in *La Vendetta*, 81–84. *See also* artistic education; ateliers; working space
subjectivity: in Mary Ellen Best's portrait, 67, 69; contributions to female, 7; Desbordes-Valmore on female, 88; in French novels, 81; in Margaret Gillies's portraits, 202, 204; in A. M. Howitt's feminist fiction, 98, 282n37; of Labille-Guiard, 40; Musset's denial of female, 252; in national tales, 154, 156; in Owenson's *Princess*, 162; in portraiture, 195–96, 199–201; and professionalism, 33, 50, 265; Sand's on, 244, 254; in *Sisters in Art*, 108; in *Tenant of Wildfell Hall*, 10, 227, 232, 233, 239, 242; in Caroline Thévenin's studio scene, 55; and visuality/visibility in art, 10, 12, 13; of women in art and nation, 126; of women in fiction, 112–13; of women Romantic artists, 18, 19
Sussman, Herbert, 15, 18, 98, 274n53
Sydney, Philip, 92
Symposium (Plato), 92

Tait's Edinburgh Magazine, 170
Talma, 152
Tastu, Amable, 77
Taylor, Harriet, 197, 198
The Tenant of Wildfell Hall (Brontë), 225–42; addressing of male audience, 227; art as theme in, 226, 233–36, 240, 241; comparison to *Elle et lui*, 248, 249, 257; criticism of, 224–25, 242, 291n6; discourse/counter-discourse of, 14, 227, 233; female hero of, 222; female subjectivity in, 10, 227, 232, 233, 239, 242; as narrative exchange, 233, 291n14; as personal story, 224; reference in *Sisters in Art*, 107; social correction in, 240; structure of, 225–26, 232, 235, 239, 242. *See also* Brontë, Anne, works of
Une Tendre dévôte (Arnaud), 287n15
Tenenbaum, Susan, 128
Tennyson, Alfred, 101, 113–15, 119, 282n45
Tennyson, Charles, 113, 282n41
Terdiman, Richard, 4, 14
Terpsichore (Canova), 285n44
Thackeray, William, 16, 273n50
Thévenin, Caroline, 53–55, 276n37
Thévenin, Charles, 43
Thévenin, Rosalie, 53, 276n37
Thornycroft, Mary, 284n72
Thornycroft, Thomas, 121
Tintoretto, 65, 251, 277n54
Tissot, Samuel, 255
Titian, 90, 250–52
Todorov, Tzvetan, 9
"To Madame Desbordes-Valmore" (Lamartine), 78
"To M. Alphonse de Lamartine" (Desbordes-Valmore), 78–79
To the Lighthouse (Woolf), 266–69
transcultural relations, 155, 159–60

transnational boundary crossing, 126, 134, 156
travel, 128–30, 139, 145, 147, 156–57, 161, 162, 169
The Trial of Colonel Brereton, After the Bristol Riots (Sharples), 62–64, *63*
Tribune des femmes, 175, 176
Trilby (Du Maurier), 16, 273n48, 273n50
Tristan, Flora, 94, 173, 174, 181
Tromp, Marlene, 120
Troubadour style, 43, 148–49, 250–51, 293n18
Trumpener, Katie, 154–55
Turner, J. M. W., 16, 119–20, 221

Uneven Developments (Poovey), 4
Union des Femmes Peintres et Sculpteurs (Union of Women Painters and Sculptors), 3, 263
Unitarians, 197–99, 201, 202, 213

Valabrègue, Antony, 135–36, 137
Valentine (Sand), 244–46
Valmore, Prosper, 278n12
Vanderbilt, Cornelius, 264
Van Dyck, Sir Anthony, 65, 255
van Slyke, Gretchen, 264
Vasari, 40
Vaughan, William, 46, 97–98
Velázquez, Diego, 40
La Vendetta (Balzac), 81–87, 89, 90, 92, 93, 108. *See also* Balzac, works of
Venice, 250, 251, 258
Veret, Désirée, 175
La Véritable histoire de Elle et lui (Lovenjoul), 247
Verlaine, Paul, 76
Vernet, Carle, 47
Vernet, Horace, 46–47, *47,* 152
Vernet, Joseph, 47
Versailles, 152
Victorian England: conception of identity in, 102; critique in *Tenant of Wildfell Hall,* 226; female painters in literature of, 265; Margaret Gillies's cultural production in, 201; A. M. Howitt's questioning of artistic hierarchies in, 112; limitations on women in, 114; women novelists in, 4, 225. *See also* Britain; England

Victoria Press, 101, 281n24
Victoria, Queen of England, 121, 264
Viel, Hortense. *See* Haudebourt-Lescot, Hortense
Vien, Joseph-Marie, 38, 43–46
Vigée-Lebrun, Elizabeth, 3, 33, 39, 40, 90, 93, 127, 275n8
Vigny, Alfred, 76
Villa Médici, 136
Vincent, André, 43, 276n27
Vincent, Patrick, 127
Vindication of the Rights of Woman (Wollstonecraft), 274n59
Vision and Difference: Femininity, Feminism, and the Histories of Art (Pollock), 2
visual arts/artists, 32, 75, 83–84, 215–16, 221–25. *See also* painters
visuality/visibility: of art and politics, 10–13, 74; of artistic images, 269; of artists as Seers, 72; of British women artists, 58, 97, 265; in *Château de Pictordu,* 260; in *Clémence,* 182–83, 185, 188, 189; in *Elle et lui,* 249, 256–57; in gender, nation, and identity, 128; in Haudebourt-Lescot's paintings, 135; A. M. Howitt's promotion of women's, 104; in *To the Lighthouse,* 266–67, 269; in Musset's *Le Fils du Titien,* 252; in Owenson's and Staël's novels, 129, 130, 134; in Owenson's *Princess,* 160, 162, 169; in portraiture, 196; and professionalism, 33–34; in *Tenant of Wildfell Hall,* 226, 229, 232–33, 235, 239; in *Valentine,* 244; of women in France, 39, 50, 75; of women in Romantic art, 19, 125. *See also* male gaze
Voeu à la madone pendant un orage (Haudebourt-Lescot), 148
von Steinbach, Sabina, 8
Vuillard, Edouard, 67

Walker, Lynne, 65, 69
Waller, Margaret, 4, 19, 253
Ward, Henrietta, 276n39
Ward, Ian, 291n10
Washington, George, 57
watercolor, 65, 67, 139, 150, 197, 199, 200
Watts, Alfred, 100, 281n19
Waverley (Scott), 155
Weisberg, Gabriel, 263

Werther (Goethe), 93, 95, 286n14
Westall, William, 210
Westcott, Andrea, 227
"What Can Educated Women Do?" (Parkes), 103
White, Roberta, 247
"Why Have There Been No Great Women Artists?" (Nochlin), 2
The Wild Irish Girl (Owenson): 126–34; comparison to *Mary Queen of Scots Fainting*, 152; comparison to Owenson's *Princess*, 164; footnotes in, 131, 155; language in, 155; as national tale, 154; nation, gender, and difference in, 126–34; religion in, 148
Wilhelm Meister (Goethe), 161
William and Mary Howitt (Gillies), *212*
William and Mary Wordsworth (Gillies), *210*
Williams, Raymond, 2, 273n38
Williams, Samuel, 282n38
Wilson, Michael, 14
Wolff, Janet, 4, 265
Wollstonecraft, Mary, 156, 274n59
The Woman Painter in Victorian Literature (Losano), 4
women: commonalities with artists, 85; Margaret Gillies's goals for in society, 211–13; A. M. Howitt on social and artistic constructions of, 108; Leigh Hunt's attitude toward, 213–20; marginalization of, 94; radical Unitarians on emancipation of, 198; representation in art, 19–24. *See also* artists, female; authors, female
Women and Work (Leigh Smith), 102
Women Artists in All Ages and Countries (Ellet), 1, 6
Women Painters of the World (Sparrow), 136

women's identities: in *Château de Pictordu*, 262; in *Elle et lui*, 253–54; Mary Gillies on, 206; Labille-Guiard's response to socially constructed, 42–43; in *To the Lighthouse*, 266; and market society, 102, 281n27; and portraiture, 195–96, 201; professions in, 102; in social structure, 13, 45–46; threat of, 225, 230, 238; in *Valentine*, 245–46. *See also* performed identity
women's rights, 5, 101, 103, 104, 106, 121
Women's Social and Political Union, 121
Women's Suffrage Committee, 101
Woodring, Carl, 101
Woolf, Virginia, 266–69
Woolner, Thomas, 98
Word and Image (Bryson), 5
Wordsworth, Dora, 208
Wordsworth, Mary, 208–11
Wordsworth, William, 14, 19, 98, 101, 201, 208–11, 213, 219, 220
working class. *See* class; labor and productivity
working space, 34, 48–50, 65, 67–69, 108, 109. *See also* ateliers; studio culture
Wright, Beth, 150
Wrigley, Richard, 144
Wuthering Heights (Brontë), 223, 226, 229, 291n12

Yeldham, Charlotte, 56, 204–5
"Ye Newe Generation" (Leigh Smith), 104, *105*, 281n32

Zeuxis, 55
Zola, Emile, 16, 75

www.ingramcontent.com/pod-product-compliance
Lightning Source LLC
Chambersburg PA
CBHW021846300426
44115CB00005B/34